Czech Yearbook
of International Law®

Czech Yearbook
of International Law®

Volume XIII

2022

International Justice and International Enforcement

Editors

Alexander J. Bělohlávek
Professor
at the VŠB TU
in Ostrava
Czech Republic

Naděžda Rozehnalová
Professor
at the Masaryk University
in Brno
Czech Republic

Questions About This Publication

www.czechyearbook.org; www.lexlata.pro; editor@lexlata.pro

COPYRIGHT © 2022

By Lex Lata B.V.

Printed in the EU.
ISBN/EAN: 978-90-829824-6-6
ISSN: 2157-2976

Lex Lata B.V.
Mauritskade 45-B
2514 HG – THE HAGUE
The Netherlands

Typeset by Lex Lata B.V.

„We regret to announce the death of our most reputable colleague Professor Peter Mankowski from Germany. We are thankful for his efforts invested in our common project. His personality and wisdom will be deeply missed by the whole editorial team."

Address for communication & manuscripts

Czech Yearbook of International Law®

Jana Zajíce 32, Praha 7, 170 00, Czech Republic

editor@lexlata.pro

Editorial support:

Jan Šamlot, DrTF. Lenka Němečková,

Dipl. Ing. Karel Nohava, Anna Dušková

Impressum

Institutions Participating in the CYIL Project

Academic Institutions within Czech Republic

Masaryk University (Brno)
    Faculty of Law, Department of International and European Law
    [*Masarykova univerzita v Brně, Právnická fakulta,*
    Katedra mezinárodního a evropského práva]

University of West Bohemia in Pilsen
    Faculty of Law, Department of Constitutional Law & Department
    of International Law
    [*Západočeská univerzita v Plzni, Právnická fakulta,*
    Katedra ústavního práva & Katedra mezinárodního práva]

VŠB – TU Ostrava
    Faculty of Economics, Department of Law
    [*VŠB – TU Ostrava, Ekonomická fakulta, Katedra práva*]

Charles University in Prague
    Faculty of Law, Department of Commercial Law, Department of
    European Law & Centre for Comparative Law
    [*Univerzita Karlova v Praze, Právnická fakulta,*
    Katedra obchodního práva, katedra evropského práva & Centrum
    právní komparatistiky, PrF UK]

University College of International and Public Relations Prague
    [*Vysoká škola mezinárodních a veřejných vztahů Praha*]

Institute of State and Law of the Academy of Sciences of the Czech Republic, v.v.i.
    [*Ústav státu a práva Akademie věd ČR, v.v.i.*]

University of Finance and Administration, Czech Republic
    [*Vysoká škola finanční a správní, a.s., Praha, Česká republika*]

Non-academic Institutions in the Czech Republic

Office of the Government of the Czech Republic
    Department of Legislation, Prague
    [*Úřad vlády ČR, Legislativní odbor, Praha*]

Arbitration Court attached to the Economic Chamber of the Czech Republic and Agricultural Chamber of the Czech Republic, Prague
[*Rozhodčí soud při Hospodářské komoře České republiky a Agrární komoře České republiky*]

International Arbitration Court of the Czech Commodity Exchange, Prague
[*Mezinárodní rozhodčí soud při Českomoravské komoditní burze, Praha*]

ICC National Committee Czech Republic, Prague
[*ICC Národní výbor Česká republika, Praha*]

Institutions outside the Czech Republic Participating in the CYIL Project

Austria

University of Vienna [*Universität Wien*]
Department of European, International and Comparative Law, Section for International Law and International Relations

Poland

Jagiellonian University in Krakow [*Uniwersytet Jagielloński v Krakowie*]
Faculty of Law and Administration,
Department of Private International Law

Slovakia

Slovak Academy of Sciences, Institute of State and Law
[*Slovenská akadémia vied, Ústav štátu a práva*], Bratislava

University of Matej Bel in Banská Bystrica
[*Univerzita Mateja Bela v Banskej Bystrici*],
Faculty of Political Sciences and International Relations,
Department of International Affairs and Diplomacy

Trnava University in Trnava [*Trnavská Univerzita v Trnave*],
Faculty of Law, Department of Labour Law and Social Security Law

Proofreading and translation support provided by: SPĚVÁČEK překladatelská agentura s.r.o., Prague, Czech Republic and Pamela Lewis, USA.

Contents

CASE LAW

BIBLIOGRAPHY, CURRENT EVENTS, IMPORTANT WEB SITES

All contributions in this book are subject to academic review.

Neither the editorial board nor the publisher collects any fees or other performance for publishing contributions from the authors and distances itself from such practices. Authors do not receive any royalty or other remuneration for their contributions.

List of Abbreviations

AG	Aktiengesellschaft (joint stock company)
BBNJ	Biodiversity Beyond National Jurisdiction
BelCCI	The Belarusian Chamber of Commerce and Industry
BILOS	The Brazilian Institute for the Law of the Sea
BIT	Bilateral Investment Treaty
Brussels Convention	Convention on jurisdiction and the recognition and enforcement of judgments in civil and commercial matters[1]
Brussels I Regulation	Council Regulation (EC) No. 44/2001 of 22 December 2000 on jurisdiction and the recognition and enforcement of judgments in civil and commercial matters[2]
Brussels Ia Regulation	Council Regulation (EC) No 1215/2012 of 20 December 2012 on jurisdiction and the recognition and enforcement of judgments in civil and commercial matters[3]
CISG	UN Convention on Contracts for the International Sale of Goods of 11 April 1980
CJEU	Court of Justice of the European Union
CLOUT	Case Law on UNCITRAL Texts
CMR	Convention on the Contract for the

---

[1] OJ L 339/3, 21 December 2007, p. 3–41. [EUR-Lex: 22007A1221(03)].
[2] OJ L 12, 16 January 2001, p. 1–23. [EUR-Lex: 32001R0044].
[3] OJ L 338, 23 December 2003, p. 1–29. [EUR-Lex: 32003R2201].

	International Carriage of Goods by Road
ECB	European Central Bank
ECHR	European Convention on Human Rights
ECJ	European Court of Justice
ECT	Energy Charter Treaty
ECtHR	European Court of Human Rights
EEC	European Economic Community
EEZ	The Exclusive Economic Zone
ELI	European Law Institute
EMS	Express Mail Service
EU	The European Union
FCIArb	Fellow of the Chartered Institute of Arbitrators
GmbH	Gesellschaft mit beschränkter Haftung (company with limited liability)
HRAS	The Human Rights at Sea
ICJ	International Court of Justice
ICSID	International Centre for the Settlement of Investment Disputes
ICSID Convention	Convention on the Settlement of Investment Disputes between States and Nationals of Other States
ILA	The International Law Association
ILC	International Law Commission
ISA	The International Seabed Authority
ITLOS	The International Tribunal for the Law of the Sea
IUU fishing	Illegal, unreported and unregulated fishing
LCIA	The London Court of International Arbitration
LOSC / UNCLOS / UN Charter	The United Nations Convention on the Law of the Sea, 1982 (Signed 10 December 1982, Entered into force 16 November 1994)
Lugano Convention	Convention of 16 September 1988 on jurisdiction and the recognition and enforcement of judgments in civil and commercial matters,

	optionally Convention of 30 October 2007 on jurisdiction and the recognition and enforcement of judgments in civil and commercial matters (the later Lugano Convention II)
Macau CPC	Macau Civil Procedure Code (as approved by Decree-Law No. 55/99/M of October 8, 1999, and as amended up to Law No. 9/2004 of August 16, 2004, on Changes and Additions to the Law on Judicial Organization and Civil Procedure Code)
MIT	Multilateral Investment Treaty
MKAS	The International Commercial Arbitration Court at the Chamber of Commerce and Industry of the Russian Federation (The ICAC at the RF CCI)
NPC	National People's Congress
PRC	People's Republic of China
REJs	Recognition and enforcement of judgments
SARs	Special Administrative Regions
SCC	Arbitration Institute of the Stockholm Chamber of Commerce
SPC	Supreme People's Court
TEU	Treaty on European Union
TFEU	Treaty on the Functioning of the European Union
UK	The United Kingdom of Great Britain and Northern Ireland
UN	The United Nations
UNCITRAL	United Nations Commission On International Trade Law
UNGA	The United Nations General Assembly
UNIDROIT	International Institute for the Unification of Private Law
US	The United States of America
VIAC	Vienna International Arbitration

	Centre
VCCA	Vilnius Court of Commercial Arbitration
VCLT	Vienna Convention on the Law of Treaties
WTO	World Trade Organization

Articles

Czech Yearbook of International Law®

Martin Jarrett

Implicit Legality Requirements in Investment Treaty Arbitration: A Doctrinal Critique of Current Jurisprudence

Key words:
Cortec Mining v. Kenya | Investment treaties | Legality requirements | Article 31 VCLT

Abstract *| Various arbitral tribunals have made obiter statements that legality requirements relevant to their jurisdiction can be read into investment treaties, but only one such tribunal has gone a step beyond that by making such jurisprudence the ratio decidendi of its decision, namely the arbitral tribunal in Cortec Mining v. Kenya. The investor challenged the adverse decision on jurisdiction that came its way. The annulment committee has now issued its annulment decision – and it does not make for good reading for investors. Effectively, it green-lighted the practice of arbitral tribunals reading legality requirements into investment treaties.*

This contribution examines the doctrinal foundations of this jurisprudential practice. With specific regard to Article 31 of the Vienna Convention on the Law of Treaties, it argues that those doctrinal foundations are shaky, with the result that this jurisprudence on reading in legality requirements should be seen as bad law. But advocates for international investor accountability need not worry that investors will evade justice. There are other options for sanctioning investor misconduct, one of which could deliver better rule-of-law outcomes compared to subjecting an investor to an implicit legality requirement.

Dr. Martin Jarrett is a Senior Research Fellow at the Max Planck Institute for Comparative Public Law and International Law. He is qualified as a Solicitor and Barrister in New South Wales, Australia and holds the following academic degrees: Bachelor of Arts, Bachelor of Laws (with first class honours), Graduate Diploma of Legal Practice, and Doctor of Laws (*soma cum laude*). E–mail: jarrett@mpil.de

| | |

I. Background: Annulment Decision in *Cortec Mining* v. *Kenya*[*]

1.01. The confirmation is in: in investment treaty arbitration, reading in implicit requirements stipulating that an investment must be established in accordance with host state law is legitimate. This is the new jurisprudence from the ICSID annulment decision for *Cortec Mining* v. *Kenya*.[1]

1.02. In the preceding arbitration for this dispute, the arbitral tribunal declined to exercise jurisdiction.[2] The fundamental reason underpinning that decision was that the investment in question failed the legality requirement.[3] What made that legality requirement unique was that it was read into the applicable investment treaty; in other words, this treaty did not contain words to the effect that the investment had to be established in accordance with host state law, but the arbitral tribunal effectively inserted such wording in there.[4] That reasoning made the arbitral award a prime candidate to be challenged under Article 52 of the ICSID Convention, noting that this arbitration was conducted under the ICSID Convention Arbitration Rules. Now, the annulment decision has been rendered. It does not make for good reading for the investor. One of the grounds for the challenge was that the arbitral tribunal 'manifestly exceeded its power' by reading a legality requirement into the applicable investment treaty.[5] The annulment committee held that to prove this ground for challenge, the investor had to show that the arbitral tribunal 'failed to apply the applicable law', as opposed to merely misapplying it.[6] Additionally, that failure had to be 'manifest',[7] which is a standard that would be reached if the legal reasoning in support of the conclusion (that a legality requirement could be read in) was untenable.[8] The problem for the investors was that the legal reasoning was tenable, most specifically because the arbitral tribunal could rely on a body of case law to support its view of the law.[9]

---

[*] The author thanks August Reinisch and Stephan Schill for their comments and critique on an earlier draft of this contribution. All errors are my own.
[1] *Cortec Mining Kenya Limited, Cortec (Pty) Limited and Stirling Capital Limited* v. *Republic of Kenya*, ICSID Case No. ARB/15/29, Award of March 19, 2021.
[2] *Cortec Mining Kenya Limited, Cortec (Pty) Limited and Stirling Capital Limited* v. *Republic of Kenya*, ICSID Case No. ARB/15/29, Award of October 23, 2018.
[3] *Ibid.*, at 333.
[4] *Ibid.*, at 319-321.
[5] *Cortec Mining* v. *Kenya*, Annulment, *supra* note 1, at 108 – 116.
[6] *Ibid.*, at 125.
[7] *Ibid.*, at 124.
[8] *Ibid.*, at 129.
[9] *Ibid.*, at 138.

1.03. The practical result is that the annulment committee in *Cortec Mining* v. *Kenya* has green-lighted the reading in of legality requirements. But this decision does not serve as confirmation of the *correctness* of this jurisprudence. Indeed, the annulment committee emphasised that '[w]hether that ruling was right or wrong is not a matter within the competence of this Committee'.[10] It went on to further note that 'perhaps many arbitrators' would disagree with the jurisprudence that holds that legality requirements can be read into investment treaties,[11] but the fact that this jurisprudence might represent a minority view did not make its application a manifest excess of power.[12]

1.04. This reasoning cannot be objected to. Even if this jurisprudence represents a minority view, it is still 'law' of some sort, although not good law. The purpose of this contribution is to defend that thesis. That specifically means showing that the practice of reading legality requirements into investment treaties and declining to exercise jurisdiction when they are not satisfied,[13] is doctrinally incorrect. The process towards that thesis comprises three steps, the first of which is to explore the doctrinal foundations of this jurisprudence. That exploration is undertaken in Section 2, while Section 3 proceeds to critique these doctrinal foundations. The conclusion of that critique is that this jurisprudence should be discarded, the practical consequence of which is apparently that 'illegal investments' will be given protection under investment treaties, and investor misconduct, more generally, will go unsanctioned. That apparent outcome is refuted in Section 4. There, it is shown that there are still various mechanisms that can be activated to exclude illegal investments and punish investor misconduct. The conclusions of this contribution are summarised in Section 5.

I.1. Doctrinal Foundations of Implicit Legality Requirements

1.05. What is the genesis of reading legality requirements into investment treaties? As the annulment committee in *Cortec Mining* v. *Kenya* noted,[14] the arbitral tribunal could point to some other arbitral awards to support its view, the most prominent among them being *Phoenix Action* v. *Czechia*.[15] The

---

[10] *Ibid.*, at 133.
[11] *Cortec Mining* v. *Kenya*, Annulment, *supra* note 1, at 141.
[12] *Ibid.*, at 144.
[13] Note that the question of whether a legality requirement can be read into an investment treaty and applied when considering the merits of the case is a distinct issue that this contribution does not cover.
[14] *Ibid.*, at 140.
[15] *Ibid.*, at 138.

arbitral award in *Phoenix Action* v. *Czechia* provides that an investment must be made (both) 'bona fide' and 'in accordance with host state law',[16] even if words to that effect do not appear in the applicable investment treaty for the case.[17] The arbitral tribunal indicated that these were two separate jurisdictional requirements, although it failed to precisely define their scope.[18]

1.06. In any case, the arbitral tribunal in *Phoenix Action* v. *Czechia* pointed to the arbitral award in *Plama* v. *Bulgaria* to support the reading in of legality requirements,[19] while the arbitral award for *Inceysa* v. *El Salvador* provided support for the requirement of *bona fides*.[20] Interestingly, in its reasoning, the arbitral tribunal in *Plama* v. *Bulgaria* relied on the jurisprudence coming from *Inceysa* v. *El Salvador*,[21] with such reliance meaning that the genesis of reading in legality requirements is the arbitral award for *Inceysa* v. *El Salvador*. What this entails is that if an understanding of the doctrinal foundations of reading in legality requirements is sought, then a close examination of the legal reasoning in this arbitral award is required.[22]

1.07. In *Inceysa* v. *El Salvador*,[23] the investor won a bid for a government concession to provide car-inspection services on an exclusive basis. Subsequently, El Salvador engaged other companies to carry out these services. Additionally, it sought to invalidate the investor's concession in the El Salvadorian courts. The investor initiated ICSID arbitration under the El Salvador-Spain BIT. During the jurisdictional phase, it came to light that the investor acted fraudulently to secure its concession.

---

[16] *Phoenix Action, Ltd.* v. *The Czech Republic*, ICSID Case no. ARB/06/5, Award of April 15, 2009.

[17] *Ibid.,* at 101.

[18] It has to be said that these two requirements could be conceptually distinguished, particularly because the legality could be breached by conduct other than corruption and fraud, with *Cortec Mining* v. *Kenya* offering a prime example of this. But, generally speaking, there is a large degree of overlap between these jurisdictional requirements, because they should cover instances of both corruption and fraud.

[19] Although the arbitral tribunal erred in this respect. When the arbitral tribunal in *Plama* v. *Bulgaria* found that the Energy Charter Treaty contained a legality requirement, it held that this legality requirement was relevant to the merits of the case, as opposed to its jurisdictional competence, see *Plama Consortium Limited* v. *Republic of Bulgaria*, ICSID Case no. ARB/03/24, Award of February 08, 2005. Note that the arbitral tribunal in *Phoenix Action* v. *Czechia* held, after citing the arbitral award in *Plama* v. *Bulgaria*, that implicit legality requirements should ordinarily be relevant to an arbitral tribunal's jurisdiction, see *Phoenix Action* v. *Czechia, supra* note 16, at 101.

[20] *Phoenix Action* v. *Czechia, supra* note 16, at 111.

[21] *Plama Consortium Limited* v. *Republic of Bulgaria*, ICSID Case no. ARB/03/24, Award of August 27, 2008.

[22] *Inceysa Vallisoletana S.L.* v. *Republic of El Salvador*, ICSID Case no. ARB/03/26, Award of August 2, 2006.

[23] For a more comprehensive overview of the facts, see *Alejandro A. Escobar, Inceysa Vallisoletana, S.L.* v. *Republic of El Salvador*, ICSID Case no. ARB/03/26, Award of August 2, 2006, 23 ICSID Review 311, 312 – 314 (2008).

1.08. The arbitral tribunal went through the El Salvador-Spain BIT in search of a legality requirement, locating one in the article on protection of investments:[24]

> *Each Contracting Party shall protect in its territory the investments made in accordance with its legislation... The travaux préparatoires attaching to the El Salvador-Spain BIT were referenced in order to argue that these words created a legality requirement in respect of the states' consent to arbitration.[25] The arbitral tribunal then turned its focus to determining whether the investor had fallen foul of this requirement. In a curious piece of legal reasoning,[26] the arbitral tribunal concluded that 'legislation' only included the provisions of the El Salvador-Spain BIT.[27] This treaty did not contain provisions that imposed obligations on investors regarding the establishment of their investment.[28] Because of this absence, the arbitral tribunal concluded that it had to "analyse other legal instruments to decide this issue".[29] It then reverted to the governing law clause in the El Salvador-Spain BIT.[30] That clause specified that 'principles of international law' were an applicable source of law.[31] One of these principles was good faith. After concluding that the investor had breached the obligation to act in good faith towards El Salvador through its fraudulent acts,[32] it followed that the investor failed to satisfy the legality requirement and the arbitral tribunal declined jurisdiction.[33] For good measure, the arbitral tribunal then went*

---

[24] *Inceysa* v. *El Salvador*, n *supra* note 22, at 201. Note that in the El Salvador-Spain BIT, the clause containing the standard on protection of investments reads as follows: "Cada Parte Contratante protegerá en su territorio las inversiones efectuadas, conforme a su legislación, por inversores de la otra Parte Contratante y no obstaculizará, mediante medicas injustificadas o discriminatorias, la gestión. el mantenimiento, el desarrollo, la utilización, el disfrute, la extensión, la venta ni, en su caso. fa liquidación de tales invesiones." See *Acuerdo para la Promoción y Protección Reciproca de Inversiones entre el Reino de España y la República de El Salvador* (1995), Article 3(3), available at: https://investmentpolicy.unctad.org/international-investment-agreements/treaty-files/1136/download (accessed on 26 November 2021).

[25] *Inceysa* v. *El Salvador, supra* note 22, at 195.

[26] Other arbitral tribunals that have looked at this issue have determined that 'law' refers to the corpus of rules in the host state's domestic law, see Jean Kalicki, Mallory Silberman, and Bridie McAsey, *What Are Appropriate Remedies for Finding of Illegality in Investment Arbitration?*, in ANDREA MENAKER, INTERNATIONAL ARBITRATION AND RULE OF LAW: CONTRIBUTION AND CONFORMITY, Alphen aan den Rijn: Kluwer Law International (2017), et. 726.

[27] *Inceysa* v. *El Salvador, supra* note 22, at 220.

[28] *Ibid.,* at 223.

[29] *Ibid.,* at 223.

[30] *Ibid.,* at 224.

[31] El Salvador-Spain BIT, Article 11(3).

[32] *Inceysa* v. *El Salvador, supra* note 22, at 234 – 37.

[33] *Ibid.,* at 239.

on to hold that the investor had also breached other principles of international law through the illegality of its investment, including 'nemo auditur propiam turpitudinem allegans',[34] 'international public policy',[35] and 'unlawful enrichment'.[36]

1.09. The arbitral tribunal in *Inceysa* v. *El Salvador* laid down a technique for adding implicit legality requirements to investment treaties. That technique consists of referring to the governing law clause, noting that this clause designates 'principles of international law' as an applicable source of law, which it invariably will,[37] identifying good faith as one of those principles, and specifying that a manifestation of the principle of good faith is the obligation to establish investments in accordance with host state law. Since the pronouncement of this jurisprudence, numerous arbitral tribunals have held that implicit legality requirements can be read into investment treaties,[38] with most citing the arbitral award in *Inceysa* v. *El Salvador* as their authority.[39]

II. Critique of Doctrinal Foundations of Reading in Legality Requirements

II.1. Critique 1: Vagueness of Good Faith

1.10. Notwithstanding the arbitral authority that it now stands on, the technique of deriving an implicit legality requirement from the principle of good faith should be rejected. The first reason underpinning this rejection is the vagueness that afflicts good faith. Writing on the use of good faith in international investment law, Schill and Bray have noted that:[40]

> *Reliance on a vague principle may lead to legal uncertainty, create a risk of unpredictability for*

---

[34] *Inceysa* v. *El Salvador*, *supra* note 22, at 240.

[35] *Ibid.*, at 252.

[36] *Ibid.*, at 253.

[37] PATRICK DUMBERRY, A GUIDE TO GENERAL PRINCIPLES OF LAW IN INTERNATIONAL INVESTMENT ARBITRATION, Oxford: Oxford Univerzity Press (2020), et. 2.32.

[38] *Cortec Mining* v. *Kenya*, *supra* note 2, at 319; *David Minnotte and Robert Lewis* v. *Republic of Poland*, ICSID Case no. ARB(AF)/10/1, Award of May 16, 2014; *Khan Resources Inc., Khan Resources B.V., and CAUC Holding Company Ltd.* v. *The Government of Mongolia and MonAtom LLC*, PCA Case no. 2011-09, Award of July 25, 2012; *SAUR International SA* v. *Republic of Argentina*, ICSID Case no. ARB/04/4, Décision sur la Compétence et sur la Responsabilité (06 June 2012); *Liman Caspian Oil BV and NCL Dutch Investment BV* v. *Republic of Kazakhstan*, ICSID Case no. ARB/07/14, Award of June 22, 2010; and *Phoenix Action* v. *Czechia*, *supra* note 16, at 101.

[39] *Minnotte* v. *Poland*, *supra* note 38, at 131; *Khan Resources* v. *Mongolia*, *supra* note 38, at 382; *Liman* v. *Kazakhstan*, *supra* note 37, at 193; and *Phoenix Action* v. *Czechia*, *supra* note 16, at 111.

[40] Stephan Schill and Heather Bray, *Good Faith Limitations on Protected Investments and Corporate Structuring*, in ANDREW MITCHELL, GOOD FAITH AND INTERNATIONAL ECONOMIC LAW, Oxford: Oxford University Press (2015), et. 88.

> *foreign investors, and provide decision-makers with an abundance of discretion that is subject to personal valuation and biases, which may lead to arbitrary results.*

1.11. It is apparent that the risk of legal uncertainty has come to pass.[41] For while some arbitral tribunals have been prepared to add implicit legal requirements to investment treaties via the principle of good faith, other arbitral tribunals have dismissed this practice.[42] The arbitral tribunal in *Bear Creek* v. *Peru*, for example, reasoned that it was for the treaty parties to define their consent to arbitration, as opposed to the arbitrators.

1.12. Bearing in mind the *ad hoc* nature of investment treaty arbitration, it is unlikely that one line of jurisprudence will emerge as the correct line. The other factor that near guarantees this outcome is the fact that parties have the chance to choose their arbitrators.[43] In composing the arbitral tribunal, well-informed lawyers will seek to appoint arbitrators who subscribe to a view of legality requirements that suits their case. This inconsistency of jurisprudence is not a problem that states are prepared to live with. In the 'identification and consideration of concerns' phase of the UNCITRAL reform process for investor-state dispute resolution, the first concern that was identified was the 'inconsistency of arbitral decisions'.[44] And this is not a problem that states should tolerate. As Fuller famously explained with his story on the reforming-ruler King Rex, vague rules are one of the key ingredients for unpredictability in a legal order.[45] For this reason, one of Fuller's principles of legality is 'clarity'.[46] Every time that an arbitral tribunal relies on good faith to reach a decision, it does not pay due respect to this requirement for clarity, thereby putting it at odds with the formal rule of law.

---

[41] *Bear Creek Mining Corporation* v. *Republic of Peru*, ICSID Case No. ARB/14/21, Award of November 30, 2017. See also EMILY SIPIORSKI, GOOD FAITH IN INTERNATIONAL INVESTMENT ARBITRATION, Oxford: Oxford University Press (2018), et. 98.

[42] *Bear Creek* v. *Peru supra* note 41, at 320 (although the arbitral tribunal did indicate that there might be an exception in cases involving fraud, see et. 322); *Metal-Tech Ltd.* v. *Republic of Uzbekistan*, ICSID Case no. ARB/10/3, Award October 04, 2013; *Malicorp Limited* v. *The Arab Republic of Egypt*, ICSID Case no. ARB/08/18, Award of February 07, 2011; *Achmea B.V.* v. *The Slovak Republic*, PCA Case no. 2008-13, Award of December 07, 2012; *Saba Fakes* v. *Republic of Turkey*, ICSID Case no. ARB/07/20, Award of July 14, 2010; and *Plama* v. *Bulgaria*, Jurisdiction, *supra* note 19, at 130 & 229. The decision of the arbitral tribunal in *Lao Holdings* v. *Laos* also implicitly supports this view. There, the applicable investment treaty only contained an 'in accordance with host state law' clause in the article on the admission of investments. The arbitral tribunal analysed Laos' allegations of investor misconduct as relevant to the merits, see *Lao Holdings N.V.* v. *Lao People's Democratic Republic*, ICSID Case no. ARB(AF)/12/6, Award of August 06, 2019.

[43] See ICSID Convention Arbitration Rules, Rule 3(1)(a)(i); and UNCITRAL Arbitration Rules (as revised in 2010), Article 9(1).

[44] UNCITRAL Working Group III (Investor-State Dispute Settlement Reform), Working Paper 142 (A/CN.9/WG.III/WP.142, 18 September 2017), at 20.

[45] LON FULLER, THE MORALITY OF LAW, Yale: Yale University Press (1964), et. 36.

[46] *Ibid.*, at 63.

II.2. Critique 2: Using Governing Law Clause for Interpreting States' Consent to Investment Treaty Arbitration

1.13. Another, and the main, problem with the technique of reading legality requirements into investment treaties with the help of governing law clauses concerns its technical correctness. By reverting directly to governing law clauses to interpret states' consent to investment treaty arbitration, this technique defies the well-established rules on treaty interpretation. Those rules are authoritatively laid down in the Vienna Convention on the Law of Treaties.[47] The core rule[48] stipulates that interpreting treaty provisions involves giving the relevant words their ordinary meaning, as informed by the context in which those words appear and in light of the treaty's object and purpose.[49] The 'context' does include other provisions in the treaty,[50] meaning that governing law clauses can assist in the interpretation of words expressing states' consent to arbitration. But it is not the only factor having a bearing on the meaning thereof. When applying the core rule on treaty interpretation, what is required of the adjudicator is an 'encircling process', where each of the 'ordinary meaning', 'context', and 'object and purpose' are used to determine the meaning.[51] As detailed immediately below, if this encircling process is rigorously applied, it is doubtful whether legality requirements can be read into investment treaties.

1.14. Starting with the ordinary meaning, there is nothing in the ordinary meaning of the words expressing states' consent to investment treaty arbitration from which an implicit legality requirement could be inferred. These words most commonly provide that if an investor-state dispute cannot be amicably settled, then the states that are parties to the treaty consent to investment treaty arbitration. The clause providing for investment treaty arbitration from the Greece-Kuwait BIT provides a useful example:[52]

> *If such disputes cannot be settled within a period of six months...the dispute shall be submitted for*

---

[47] RICHARD GARDINER, TREATY INTERPRETATION, Oxford: Oxford University Press (2nd ed., 2015), et. 5.

[48] Jean-Marc Sorel and Valéric Boré Eveno, *Vienna Convention 1969, Article 31*, in OLIVER CORTEN, PIERRE KLEIN, THE VIENNA CONVENTINS ON THE LAW OF TREATIES: A COMMENTARY, Oxford: Oxford University Press (2011), et. 805.

[49] Vienna Convention on the Law of Treaties (1969), Article 31(1).

[50] *Ibid.*, at Article 31(2).

[51] Gardiner, *supra* note 47, at 162.

[52] Agreement between the Government of the Hellenic Republic and the Government of the State of Kuwait on the Promotion and Reciprocal Protection of Investments (2014), Article 9(2).

> *resolution, at the election of the investor party to the dispute, through one of the following means:*
>
> *...*
>
> *(c) to international arbitration*

1.15. In other investment treaties, the state's consent to arbitration is more explicitly spelled out, as is the case in the Austria-Kyrgyzstan BIT:[53]

> *Each Contracting Party hereby gives its unconditional consent to the submission of a dispute to international arbitration in accordance with this Part.*

1.16. The only way that an implicit legal requirement could be inferred from any of these clauses is to assert that states' consent is subject to some unexpressed condition regarding the lawful establishment of investments.[54] In usual human discourse, statements of consent always come with implied conditions of consent.[55] For example,[56] if the consent-giver consents to the consent-recipient to use his or her car, there will presumptively be an unspoken condition that the car cannot be used for any illegal purpose, such as being the get-away car in a bank robbery. But states' consent to investment treaty arbitration is not given in usual human discourse. It is usually expressed in treaties or, less often, another legal instrument, such as legislation relating to foreign investment.[57] Given the time and effort that goes into drafting them,[58] relative to the time and effort necessary to make a decision about lending a car to some person, arbitral tribunals should be slow to read in implicit conditions attaching to states' consent. And even if it could be proven that states' consent to arbitration should ordinarily be seen to be subject to conditions, then there is the challenge of proving that, in fact, one of the implicit conditions of the treaty parties was investment legality.

---

[53]   Agreement for the Promotion and Protection of Investment between the Government of the Republic of Austria and the Government of the Kyrgyzstan Republic (2016), Article 15.

[54]   See, for example, *Phoenix Action v. Czechia, supra* note 16, at 101 ("And it is the Tribunal's view that this condition – the conformity of the establishment of the investment with the national laws – is implicit even when not expressly stated in the relevant BIT"); and *Mamidoil Jetoil Greek Petroleum Products Societe S.A. v. Republic of Albania*, ICSID Case no. ARB/11/24, Award of March 30, 2015. ("In exchange for their acceptance to enter into investment treaties and giving their consent to the resolution of investment disputes by arbitral tribunals, States expect that such protection would extend only to investments that have been made lawfully") (emphasis added).

[55]   John Kleinig, *The Nature of Consent*, in FRANKLIN MILLER, ALAN WERTHEIMER, THE ETHICS OF CONSENT: THEORY AND PRACTICE, Oxford: Oxford University Press (2009), et. 18.

[56]   Example inspired by *ibid.*, at 8.

[57]   RUDOLF DOLZER, CHRISTOPH SCHREUER, PRINCIPLES OF INTERNATIONAL INVESTMENT LAW (2nd ed, 2012), et. 254.

[58]   Chester Brown, *Introduction: The Development and Importance of the Model Bilateral Investment Treaty*, in CHESTER BROWN, COMMENTARIES ON SELECTED MODEL INVESTMENT TREATIES, Oxford: Oxford University Press (2013), et. 10.

Czech Yearbook of International Law®

1.17. One place where some evidence for this purpose might be found is in the *travaux préparatoires*. As noted in Section 2.2. above, the arbitral tribunal in *Inceysa* v. *El Salvador* used this strategy.[59] In the *travaux préparatoires*, there was evidence that the treaty parties intended that only legally established investments could benefit from their offers of arbitration.[60] But this use of the *travaux préparatoires* is a paradigm case of how they should not be used. The use of the *travaux préparatoires* is regulated by Article 32 of the Vienna Convention on the Law of Treaties.[61] It stipulates that *travaux préparatoires* may be used to *confirm* a meaning generated by application of Article 31(1), which is the core rule on treaty interpretation.[62] In circumstances in which the application of Article 31(1) produces either an ambiguous or obscure meaning or a manifestly absurd or unreasonable result, then *travaux préparatoires* can be used to *determine* the meaning of treaty text,[63] but this rule is hardly applicable in respect of clauses through which states express their consent to arbitration. The simple reason for this conclusion is that these clauses are ordinarily very clear in their meaning, as demonstrated by the two clauses included above. This excludes the application of the second rule on the use of *travaux préparatoires*, thereby meaning that only the first rule will usually be applicable. This is the end of the road for the use of *travaux préparatoires* to derive a legality requirement from the words that are used to express consent to investment treaty arbitration. This is because such use adds meaning to these words, as opposed to merely confirming their meaning.[64] For this reason, even if there are words in the *travaux préparatoires* to the effect that the treaty parties' consent to investment treaty arbitration is limited by a legality requirement, that evidence cannot ordinarily be marshalled to create an implicit legality requirement.

1.18. Turning to the context method, governing law clauses form part of the context of the words expressing states' consent to investment treaty arbitration, thereby making them presumptively applicable when interpreting those words. But some caveats have to be registered against using governing law clauses to read in implicit legality requirements. First, this use might extend governing law clauses beyond their purpose.

---

[59] See generally *Inceysa* v. *El Salvador*, *supra* note 22, at 192 – 203.
[60] *Inceysa* v. *El Salvador*, *supra* note 22, at 193 (for El Salvador) & 196 (for Spain).
[61] ULF LINDERFALK, ON THE INTERPRETATION OF TREATIES: MODERN INTERNATIONAL LAW AS EXPRESSED IN THE 1969 VIENNA CONVENTION ON THE LAW OF TREATIES (2007), et. 238.
[62] Vienna Convention, Article 32.
[63] *Ibid.*, at Article 32(a) and (b).
[64] For a detailed exposition on the meaning of 'confirm', see Gardiner, *supra* note 47, at 355.

That purpose is to provide the law to determine the legal issues that arise out of the dispute between the parties. 'Dispute' undoubtedly refers to all substantive legal issues that the arbitral tribunal needs to address, but whether it extends to matters of procedure is more doubtful, noting that the question of arbitral tribunals' jurisdiction is a procedural issue.[65] The answer to this question will turn on the meaning of the word 'dispute' as it appears in the relevant governing law clause. It would be imprudent to lay down any hard-and-fast rule for this purpose, as the meaning of 'dispute' can differ between investment treaties.

1.19. A second caveat is that this technique does not conform to how the context method is usually used. Most typically, the meaning of the treaty text that is the 'context' is used to shine a light on the meaning of the treaty text being interpreted. As Gardiner explains, treaty text will usually have two or more ordinary meanings, and, because of this, the context can be used to decide which meaning should be given preference.[66] To illustrate this point, consider the following governing law clause:[67]

> An arbitration tribunal established under Articles 13 – 18 of this Agreement shall decide the dispute in accordance with this Agreement and applicable rules and principles of international law.

1.20. As previously noted, 'dispute' could cover all the substantive issues and procedural issues between the parties, or just the substantive issues. Imagine that the investor advocates for the second definition. To make its argument, it points to another piece of context, specifically the clause in which the state consents to investment treaty arbitration. That clause also uses the word 'dispute'. After showing that 'dispute' in this clause has a substantive import, it then argues that 'dispute' in the governing law clause should have the same meaning. Accordingly, the meaning of the word 'dispute' in one clause (the clause providing for investment treaty arbitration) informs the meaning of 'dispute' in another (the governing law clause). This is a traditional use of the context method of interpretation. The use that arbitral tribunals have made of the governing law clause is at odds with this tradition. More than looking at the words of this clause in order to give meaning to states' consent to investment treaty arbitration, arbitral tribunals have operationalised it by taking

---

[65] YUVAL SHANY, QUESTIONS OF JURISDICTION AND ADMISSIBILITY BEFORE INTERNATIONAL COURTS, Cambridge: Cambridge University Press (2015), et. 84.
[66] Gardiner, *supra* note 47, at 222.
[67] Agreement for the Promotion and Reciprocal Protection of Investment between the Government of the Republic of Austria and the Government of the Republic of Kazakhstan (2010), Article 17(1).

content out of it ('principles of international law') and adding that content to the words constituting states' consent to investment treaty arbitration. In effect, these words are made subject to all the rules making up the principles of international law, some of which, like good faith, are so vague that when arbitrators seek to define them, their personal values invariably inform the content of their definitions. Taking this into account, the fear is that when arbitral tribunals use the governing law clause as context to interpret states' consent to investment treaty arbitration, they engage in adjudicative law-making by adding content to those words. But the context method of interpretation is not usually used for that purpose. This is not surprising – the whole idea of the context method of interpretation is to let international adjudicative bodies have recourse to other parts *of the treaty* to shine a light on the meaning on some other particular treaty text, as opposed to having regard to extra-treaty sources.[68]

1.21. Moving on to 'object and purpose', it is not helpful in advancing the case for reading in implicit legality requirements. There are two theories on the object of purpose of investment treaties.[69] Traditionally, their object and purpose is viewed as economic,[70] particularly the fostering of economic development in the host states via foreign investment.[71] The other narrative is that investment treaties are fundamentally about promoting rule-of-law standards in host states.[72] As regards the clause providing for investment treaty arbitration, this second theory cannot be doubted. These clauses give investors access to international adjudication of their investment disputes with states because of concerns about the impartiality of states' domestic courts.[73] Noting that access to impartial adjudication is a key attribution of any theory of the rule of law,[74] this entails that clauses providing for investment treaty arbitration are fundamentally rule-of-law measures.

1.22. Accordingly, when clauses providing for investment treaty arbitration are interpreted with reference to their object and

---

[68] For a good illustration of this idea, see the context-based canons of interpretation in ANTONIN SCALIA, BRYAN GARNER, READING LAW: THE INTERPRETATION OF LEGAL TEXTS, Toronto: Thomson West (2012), et. 24-37.

[69] Jeswald Salacuse and Nicholas Sullivan, *Do BITs Really Work?: An Evaluation of Bilateral Investment Treaties and Their Grand Bargain*, 46 HARVARD INTERNATIONAL LAW JOURNAL (2005), 67, 75-76.

[70] KENNETH VANDEVELDE, BILATERAL INVESTMENT TREATIES: HISTORY, POLICY AND INTERPRETATION, Oxford: Oxford University Press (2010), et. 57-8.

[71] RUDOLF DOLZER, MARGARET STEVENS, BILATERAL INVESTMENT TREATIES, London: Martinus Nijhoff Publishers (1995), et. 12.

[72] Salacuse and Sullivan, *supra* note 69, at 75.

[73] Dolzer and Schreuer, *supra* note 57, at 235.

[74] Kenneth Keith, *The International Rule of Law*, 28 LEIDEN JOURNAL INTERNATIONAL LAW 403, 408 (2015).

purpose, the best interpretation is one that delivers outcomes for promoting the rule of law. Reading in implicit legality requirements fails on this count. While it promotes the domestic rule of law by bringing down legal consequences on investors for disrespecting domestic law, it simultaneously sacrifices the international rule of law by ensuring that states do not face any legal consequences for their wrongful actions. If arbitral tribunals refrain from reading in implicit legality requirements, then the international rule of law is maintained. But if no implicit legality requirement is read in, the objection will be that the domestic rule of law is sacrificed. For the reasons outlined immediately below, this objection is without foundation.

III. Lack of Requirement for Inherent Legality and Domestic Rule of Law

1.23. Putting together the analyses above, the conclusion is that deriving implicit legality requirements from the principle of good faith is doctrinally wrong. But that does not mean that arbitral tribunals should give a free hand to investors who have engaged in investment illegality.

1.24. As arbitral tribunals that have diverged from the jurisprudence originating in *Inceysa* v. *El Salvador* have frequently pointed out, if investment legality is not relevant to arbitral tribunals' jurisdiction, it might still be relevant to the merits.[75] For this purpose, there are various concepts in the substantive law of international investment law through which investment illegality could be made relevant. One such concept is contributory fault, although it could only apply if the investment illegality had some kind of causative role in the investor's ultimate loss.[76] Another concept is the defence of illegality. An example of its application can be seen in *Plama* v. *Bulgaria*. There, after finding that the investment illegality was irrelevant to its jurisdiction,[77] presumably because the applicable investment treaty did not contain an explicit legality requirement, the arbitral tribunal held that the investor's fraudulent actions in acquiring his investment served as a full defence to any breach of an investment protection standard by Bulgaria.[78]

---

[75] *Bear Creek* v. *Peru*, *supra* note 41, at 324; *Malicorp* v. *Egypt*, *supra* note 41, at 117 – 8; and *Plama* v. *Bulgaria*, Jurisdiction, *supra* note 19, at 229.

[76] For a proposal on dealing with instances of investment illegality through contributory fault, see Silja Vöneky, *Die Stellung von Unternehmen in der Investitionsschiedsgerichtsbarkeit unter besonderer Berücksichtigung von Korruptionsproblemen – Unternehmen als völkerrechtlich gleichberechtigte Verfahrensparteien?*, in AUGUST REINISCH AND OTHERS, UNTERNEHMENSVERANTWORTUNG UND INTERNATIONALES RECHT, Heidelberg: C. F. Müller (2020), et. 376, 378.

[77] *Plama* v. *Bulgaria*, Jurisdiction, *supra* note 19, at 130.

[78] *Plama* v. *Bulgaria*, Merits, *supra* note 21, at 146.

1.25. Another option for dealing with an investment's illegality is via the requirement of ownership. This is an omnipresent requirement for arbitral tribunals' jurisdiction in investment treaty arbitration.[79] As its name suggests, this requirement stipulates that the investor must own the thing that it designates as its investment. If the investment illegality was of such a nature that it meant that the investor was not the recognised owner of the investment under the host state's domestic law, then it would potentially follow that the investor failed to satisfy the ownership requirement. A good example of a case involving this kind of investment illegality is *Fraport v. The Philippines*. There,[80] the investor partially owned an airport terminal. Under Filipino law, foreign ownership of such an asset could not exceed 40 per cent. It was found that the investor's partial ownership exceeded this percentage because of a 'secret shareholder agreement',[81] which was the conclusion of both the arbitral tribunals in the two investment treaty arbitrations to which this dispute gave rise.[82] On the basis of this finding, its ownership was deemed illegal and the arbitral tribunals declined to exercise jurisdiction.[83] A key assumption of these conclusions is that the ownership requirement in the applicable investment treaty means ownership under the host state's domestic law, as opposed to an autonomous concept of ownership under international law that focuses on whether the investor factually controlled its investment. What kind of ownership is needed for the investor to own the investment under the applicable investment treaty will turn on its exact wording. Some investment treaties, for example, only specify that the investment must merely be 'of'[84] or 'controlled by'[85] the investor. If the investor buys the investment and exerts day-to-day factual control over its operations, then it could argue that the investment is 'of' or 'controlled by' it, notwithstanding that its ownership is illegal under domestic law.

---

[79] *Anglo-Adriatic Group Limited* v. *Republic of Albania*, ICSID Case no. ARB/17/6, Award of February 07, 2019.

[80] For a more in-depth overview, see Aurélia Antonietti, *Fraport AG Frankfurt Airport Services Worldwide* v. *Republic of the Philippines* (ICSID Case no. ARB/03/25) (Award of August 16, 2007), 22 ICSID REWIEW (2007), 438.

[81] *Fraport AG Frankfurt Airport Services Worldwide* v. *The Republic of the Philippines*, ICSID Case no. ARB/03/25, Award of August 16, 2007); and *Fraport AG Frankfurt Airport Services Worldwide* v. *Republic of the Philippines*, ICSID Case no. ARB/11/12, Award December 10, 2014.

[82] Because the arbitral award from the first arbitration was annulled, the investor initiated another arbitration.

[83] *Fraport* v. *Philippines (I)*, *supra* note 81, at 404; and *Fraport* v. *Philippines (II)*, *supra* note 81, at 468.

[84] See further *Standard Chartered Bank* v. *The United Republic of Tanzania*, ICSID Case no. ARB/10/12, Award of November 02, 2012.

[85] *Philip Morris Asia Limited* v. *The Commonwealth of Australia*, PCA Case no. 2012-12, Award of December 17, 2015.

1.26. The final option for dealing with an investment's illegality is to bring it before states' domestic courts. If an arbitral tribunal accepts jurisdiction over an investor's claim, even though the investor has acted illegally when establishing its investment, there is no legal impediment to the state bringing an action against the investor in its domestic courts. Indeed, the state might ask that the arbitral tribunal stay the arbitration while it prosecutes the investor or its officers. If the outcome of this prosecution could materially affect the outcome of the investment treaty arbitration, an arbitral tribunal should be predisposed to ordering such a stay. What makes this course of action particularly appealing is that it encourages domestic courts to act against illegal investments or investor misconduct. Not only is this a good outcome for the rule of law in the host state, but it also preserves the integrity of states' international obligations in investment treaties. When an investment treaty declines jurisdiction because an investor fails to satisfy a legality requirement, the result is that the state faces no examination of its conduct. In cases of egregious state-treatment of an investor's investment, this is particular unfair on the investor.

IV. Conclusions

1.27. The point is that if the arbitral tribunal does not read a legality requirement into the applicable investment treaty, there are still various options through which investor misconduct can be addressed. And as regards the option of addressing such misconduct domestically, it might prove to deliver better rule-of-law outcomes compared to declining jurisdiction in investment treaty arbitration. Moreover, the governing law clause–based technique that arbitral tribunals use to import implicit legality requirements into investment treaties is doctrinally suspect. In addition to the problem of the inherent vagueness of 'good faith', there is a bigger problem, specifically that if the rules from the Vienna Convention on the Law of Treaties on interpreting treaties are applied, it is difficult to see how a legality requirement can be derived from the words expressing states' consent to investment treaty arbitration. Such derivation cannot be made from the ordinary meaning of these words. Further, the use of the context method of interpretation to add a legality requirement, with the help of a governing law clause, is at odds with the usual manner in which this method of interpretation is used. Finally, if the object and purpose of these words is to give investors access to rule of law–compliant adjudication of their disputes with states, then the legality

Czech Yearbook of International Law ®

requirement does little to further this goal, because states avoid their international obligations.

| | |

Summaries

DEU   [*Implizite Legalitätsanforderungen im Schiedsverfahren gemäß Investitionsschutzabkommen: doktrinale Kritik an der aktuellen Rechtssprechung*]

Verschiedenste Schiedsgerichte haben bereits in Form von Obiter dicta die Rechtauffassung geäußert, es ließe sich aus dem Wortlaut diverser Investitionsschutzabkommen eine Legalitätsanforderung betreffend Kompetenz und Zuständigkeit herauslesen. Nur ein einziges der Schiedsgerichte – namentlich das ind er Rechtssache Cortec Mining v. Kenia – ging noch weiter und erhob dieses juristische Postulat zum eigentlichen Entscheidungsgrund. In dieser Rechtssache hatte der Investor eine für ihn nachteilig gelegene Entscheidung über die Gerichtsbarkeit/Zuständigkeit angefochten. Der Ausschuss zur Aufhebung von Schiedssprüchen veröffentlichte nunmehr seine Entscheidung über die Aufhebung – mit betrüblichem Ausgang für Investoren. Vielmehr gab der Ausschuss im Wesentlichen das grüne Licht für die Praxis derjenigen Schiedsgerichte, die behaupten, die Legalitätsanforderung sei fester Bestandteil der Investitionsschutzabkommen.

Der vorliegende Beitrag untersucht die doktrinalen Grundlagen dieser Anwendungspraxis. Unter ausdrücklichem Verweis auf Art. 31 der Wiener Vertragsrechtskonvention wird behauptet, dass diese doktrinalen Grundlagen recht wackelig sind, weswegen der Ansatz, wonach Legalitätsanforderungen Bestandteil von Investitionsschutzabkommen sind, als juristisch falsch zurückzuweisen wäre. Dennoch müssen die Befürworter der internationalen Haftung von Investoren nicht befürchten, dass sich Investoren der Gerechtigkeit entziehen: deren widerrechtliches Vorgehen lässt sich auch auf andere Arten ahnden. Zumindest eine davon dürfte aus Sicht der Rechtsstaatsanforderungen bessere Ergebnisse zeitigen als die Herleitung impliziter Legalitätsanforderungen in Bezug auf Investoren.

CZE *[Implicitní požadavky legality v rozhodčím řízení podle dohod o ochraně investic: doktrinální kritika aktuální judikatury]*
Nejrůznější rozhodčí soudy již konstatovaly formou obiter dicta, že ze znění dohod o ochraně investic lze vyčíst požadavky na legalitu ohledně pravomoci a příslušnosti. Pouze jediný takovýto rozhodčí soud, a sice rozhodčí soud ve věci Cortec Mining v. Keňa, však z tohoto rámce vykročil a tento právní postulát povýšil na ratio decidendi svého rozhodnutí. Investor v uvedené věci napadl rozhodnutí o pravomoci/příslušnosti, které pro něj vyznívalo nepříznivě. Výbor pro rušení rozhodčích nálezů nyní vydal své rozhodnutí o zrušení – a investory jím nepotěšil. V podstatě dal tento výbor zelenou praxi rozhodčích soudů, které tvrdí, že požadavek legality je součástí dohod o ochraně investic. Tento příspěvek zkoumá doktrinální základy této aplikační praxe. S výslovným odkazem na článek 31 Vídeňské úmluvy o smluvním právu tvrdí, že tyto doktrinální základy jsou poněkud vratké, v důsledku čehož by tento přístup, podle něhož jsou požadavky legality součástí znění dohod o ochraně investic, měl být považován za právně chybný. Nicméně obhájci mezinárodní odpovědnosti investorů se nemusí obávat, že se investoři spravedlnosti vyhnou. Existují i jiné možnosti sankcionování protiprávního jednání investorů. Jedna z nich by přitom mohla mít lepší výsledky z hlediska požadavků právního státu než dovozování implicitních požadavků legality ve vztahu k investorům.

| | |

POL *[Dorozumiany wymóg zgodności z prawem w postępowaniu arbitrażowym na gruncie umów o ochronie inwestycji: doktrynalna krytyka aktualnego orzecznictwa]*
W świetle ryzyka, które oznacza dla państw postępowanie arbitrażowe w sporach o ochronę inwestycji, państwa próbują ograniczać takie postępowania arbitrażowe, zwłaszcza przez wymóg dotyczący zgodności powstania inwestycji danych inwestorów z prawem. Wymóg ten często, choć nie zawsze, pojawia się w umowach o ochronie inwestycji. W przeciwnym razie dyskutuje się o tym, czy dany wymóg istnieje jako dorozumiany. Zgodnie z najnowszym orzecznictwem za najbardziej trafny należy uznać pogląd, iż najprawdopodobniej taki wymóg rzeczywiście powstaje. Artykuł podważa to, czy przedmiotowe orzecznictwo jest właściwe doktrynalnie.

FRA [*Les exigences implicites de légalité dans les arbitrages en vertu des traités d'investissement : une critique doctrinale de la jurisprudence actuelle*]

Au vu du risque que représente l'arbitrage dans les litiges relatifs à la protection des investissements, les États tendent à limiter ces procédures arbitrales, notamment à travers l'exigence d'une origine légale des investissements en question. Cette exigence figure habituellement, quoique non sans exception, dans les traités d'investissement. En son absence, on peut s'interroger sur l'existence d'une exigence implicite en ce sens. À la lumière de la jurisprudence récente, il convient de conclure qu'une telle exigence semble exister. Le présent article remet en question la solidité doctrinale de cette jurisprudence.

RUS [*Имплицитные требования законности в арбитраже в светесоглашенийозащитеинвестиций:доктринальная критика действующей судебной практики*]

С учетом риска, который представляет арбитраж в спорах о защите инвестиций, государства стремятся ограничить такой арбитраж, в частности, выдвигая требование законности возникновения инвестиции соответствующих инвесторов. Это требование обычно, но не всегда встречается в соглашениях о защите инвестиций. При его отсутствии же ведутся споры о том, возникает ли в данном случае имплицитное требование. В свете судебной практики последнего времени наиболее приемлемым следует считать мнение, что такое требование, очевидно, возникает. В данной статье ставится под сомнение доктринальная правильность этой судебной практики.

ESP [*Requisitos implícitos de legalidad en el arbitraje en el marco de los convenios de protección de inversiones: una crítica de la doctrina de la jurisprudencia actual*]

Dado el riesgo que supone para ellos el arbitraje en los litigios de protección de inversiones, los Estados han intentado restringirlo, en particular, exigiendo que las inversiones afectadas se hayan generado de forma legal. Este requisito suele aparecer, aunque no siempre, en los convenios de protección de inversiones. En caso contrario, se discute la posibilidad de que tal requisito esté presente implícitamente en dichos convenios. A la luz de las resoluciones actuales, parece que la opinión que más pertinencia ha ganado es que el requisito de legalidad de las inversiones se derive posiblemente de los convenios. Este trabajo cuestiona la solidez de la doctrina subyacente a las resoluciones recientes.

Bibliography:

Chester Brown, *Introduction: The Development and Importance of the Model Bilateral Investment Treaty*, in CHESTER BROWN, COMMENTARIES ON SELECTED MODEL INVESTMENT TREATIES, Oxford: Oxford University Press (2013).

RUDOLF DOLZER, MARGARET STEVENS, BILATERAL INVESTMENT TREATIES, London: Martinus Nijhoff Publishers (1995).

RUDOLF DOLZER, CHRISTOPH SCHREUER, PRINCIPLES OF INTERNATIONAL INVESTMENT LAW (2nd ed., 2012).

PATRICK DUMBERRY, A GUIDE TO GENERAL PRINCIPLES OF LAW IN INTERNATIONAL INVESTMENT ARBITRATION, Oxford: Oxford Univerzity Press (2020).

LON FULLER, THE MORALITY OF LAW, Yale: Yale University Press (1964).

RICHARD GARDINER, TREATY INTERPRETATION, Oxford: Oxford University Press (2nd ed., 2015).

Jean Kalicki, Mallory Silberman, and Bridie McAsey, *What Are Appropriate Remedies for Finding of Illegality in Investment Arbitration?*, in ANDREA MENAKER, INTERNATIONAL ARBITRATION AND RULE OF LAW: CONTRIBUTION AND CONFORMITY, Alphen aan den Rijn: Kluwer Law International (2017).

Kenneth Keith, *The International Rule of Law*, 28 LEIDEN JOURNAL INTERNATIONAL LAW 403 (2015).

John Kleinig, *The Nature of Consent*, in FRANKLIN MILLER, ALAN WERTHEIMER, THE ETHICS OF CONSENT: THEORY AND PRACTICE, Oxford: Oxford University Press (2009).

ULF LINDERFALK, ON THE INTERPRETATION OF TREATIES: MODERN INTERNATIONAL LAW AS EXPRESSED IN THE 1969 VIENNA CONVENTION ON THE LAW OF TREATIES (2007).

Jeswald Salacuse and Nicholas Sullivan, *Do BITs Really Work?: An Evaluation of Bilateral Investment Treaties and Their Grand Bargain*, 46 HARVARD INTERNATIONAL LAW JOURNAL 67 (2005).

ANTONIN SCALIA, BRYAN GARNER, READING LAW: THE INTERPRETATION OF LEGAL TEXTS, Toronto: Thomson West (2012).

YUVAL SHANY, QUESTIONS OF JURISDICTION AND ADMIS-

SIBILITY BEFORE INTERNATIONAL COURTS, Cambridge: Cambridge University Press (2015).

Stephan Schill and Heather Bray, *Good Faith Limitations on Protected Investments and Corporate Structuring*, in ANDREW MITCHELL, GOOD FAITH AND INTERNATIONAL ECONOMIC LAW, Oxford: Oxford University Press (2015).

EMILY SIPIORSKI, GOOD FAITH IN INTERNATIONAL INVESTMENT ARBITRATION, Oxford: Oxford University Press (2018).

Jean-Marc Sorel and Valéric Boré Eveno, *Vienna Convention 1969, Article 31*, in OLIVER CORTEN, PIERRE KLEIN, THE VIENNA CONVENTINS ON THE LAW OF TREATIES: A COMMENTARY, Oxford: Oxford University Press (2011).

KENNETH VANDEVELDE, BILATERAL INVESTMENT TREATIES: HISTORY, POLICY AND INTERPRETATION, Oxford: Oxford University Press (2010).

Silja Vöneky, *Die Stellung von Unternehmen in der Investitionsschiedsgerichtsbarkeit unter besonderer Berücksichtigung von Korruptionsproblemen – Unternehmen als völkerrechtlich gleichberechtigte Verfahrensparteien?*, in AUGUST REINISCH AND OTHERS, UNTERNEHMENSVERANTWORTUNG UND INTERNATIONALES RECHT, Heidelberg: C. F. Müller (2020).

Alexander J. Bělohlávek

ORCID iD 0000-0001-5310-5269
https://orcid.org/0000-0001-5310-5269

Scope of Jurisdiction of Tribunals and International Authorities in Interpretation of International Law

Key words:
autonomous interpretation | good faith | European Convention on Human Rights (ECHR) | European Court of Human Rights (ECtHR) | linguistic interpretation | comparative interpretation | interpretation methods | inconsistent interpretation | international tribunal | national court | source of law | precedent | relative precedent | case-law | stare decisis | temporality of interpretation | United Nations Convention on Contracts for the International Sale of Goods (CISG) | UNCITRAL | UNIDROIT | Vienna Convention on the Law of Treaties | national law | interpretation of an international treaty | interpretation rules

Czech Yearbook of International Law®

Abstract | *This paper focuses on the specific attributes of the interpretation of international law from the theoretical perspective and through the analysis of selected case-law at the international, European and national level. The key document that sets forth the basic interpretation rules is the Vienna Convention on the Law of Treaties (VCLT); deemed to be the codification of customary law, the VCLT is steadfastly respected in essentially all countries of the world. However, in the international environment, the interpretation procedures incorporated in the Convention, primarily Article 31 et seq. of the VCLT, must be applied autonomously, i.e. separately from national interpretation or interpretation supplied by other authorities; autonomous interpretation only permits the latter as a subsequent instrument used for some measure of inspiration. In view of its importance and recognition in case-law, the concept of autonomous interpretation is a pivotal topic of this paper. Apart from the description itself of the*

Alexander J. Bělohlávek,
Univ. Professor, Prof. zw., Dr. iur., Mgr., Dipl. Ing. oec (MB), prof. hon., Dr. h. c. Lawyer (Managing Partner of Law Offices Bělohlávek), Dept. of Law, Faculty of Economics, Ostrava, Czech Republic; Dept. of Int. law, Faculty of law, West Bohemia University, Pilsen, Czech Republic; Vice-President of the International Arbitration Court at the Czech Commodity Exchange, Arbitrator in Prague, Paris (ICC), Vienna (VIAC), Moscow, Vilnius, Warsaw, Minsk, Almaty, Kiev, Bucharest, Ljubljana, Sofia, Kuala Lumpur, Beijing – CIETAC (China), Shenzhen (China) etc., Arbitrator pursuant to UNCITRAL Rules. Member of ASA, DIS, ArbAut etc. Immediately past president of the WJA – the World Jurist Association, Washington D.C./USA.
E-mail: office@ablegal.cz

functioning of the autonomous interpretation, the author also analyses several associated issues and challenges.

| | |

I. Specific Features of Interpretation of International Law

2.01. The general purpose of international treaties[1] is to define rules applicable in various legal systems.[2] This purpose is manifested in the principles of customary international law, which stipulate that agreements must be kept[3] and that a party to an international treaty[4] cannot invoke its national law as grounds for non-performance of the treaty.[5] However, in order to reach an agreement on the formulation of the rules applicable in various legal systems, the parties to international treaties often choose terms and formulations that represent a compromise drawn from the wording proposed by the individual States, which are naturally developed on the basis of their own legal concepts, ideas and doctrines. Hence, the final wording of international treaties is often rather general, sometimes even *prima facie* unclear or ambiguous.[6] Naturally, this must not and does not jeopardise the importance of the rule and its binding force.

2.02. Consequently, the interpretation of international treaties attracts major attention. Principally, it is hard to imagine a general legal rule that could be applied to a particular case without the need for interpretation. Hence, interpretation is the key factor determining the result of the majority of international disputes. However, there is no generally accepted definition of

---

[1] Article 2(1)(a) VCLT stipulates (cit.): *'treaty' means an international agreement concluded between States in written form and governed by international law, whether embodied in a single instrument or in two or more related instruments and whatever its particular designation.*

[2] See also Roderic Munday, *The Uniform Interpretation of International Conventions*, 27(2) INTERNATIONAL AND COMPARATIVE LAW QUARTERLY 450 (1978); Martin Gebauer, *Uniform Law: General Principles and Autonomous Interpretation*, 5(4) UNIFORM LAW REVIEW 683-705 (2000).

[3] The *pacta sunt servanda* principle is incorporated, *inter alia*, in Article 2(2) UN Charter or in Article 26 VCLT.

[4] Article 2(1)(a) VCLT stipulates (cit.): *'party' means a State which has consented to be bound by the treaty and for which the treaty is in force.*

[5] This principle is incorporated in Article 27 VCLT. *Civil law* countries have this principle traditionally embedded in their Constitutions.

[6] For instance, Aust notes (cit.): *[F]or multilateral treaties, the greater the number of negotiating states, the greater is the need for imaginative and subtle drafting to satisfy competing interests and concerns. The process inevitably produces some wording that is unclear or ambiguous. Despite the care lavished on drafting, and accumulated experience, there is no treaty which cannot raise some questions of interpretation* (ANTHONY AUST, MODERN TREATY LAW AND PRACTICE, New York: Cambridge University Press (2nd ed. 2007), et. 230).

the term *interpretation of international treaties*. Each author usually endeavours to coin their own definition.[7] The general premise is, however, that the interpretation of international treaties means a procedure that aims to ascertain the meaning of a particular provision of the international treaty. This definition, in turn, complies with the oft-invoked brief definition of legal interpretation that refers to attributing meaning to a written text.[8] Consequently, the practice has greatly simplified the process and concluded that the person interpreting the normative text describes it in other words to make it more comprehensible with respect to a particular set of facts, and prepares arguments for justifying the application of this interpreted text to the set of facts. However, such attempts at a definition usually only reflect one side of the process. The other side consists in, at least, ascertaining whether the rule, according to the *interpreted contents*, can be applied to particular facts of the case or, as applicable, a legal issue.

2.03.   The absence of any codified rules of international contract law prompted the adoption of the Vienna Convention on the law of treaties (VCLT) on 23 May 1969; the desired objective was, *inter alia*, to at least stipulate several fundamental rules for the interpretation of international treaties.[9] Presently, it is generally accepted that the provisions on the interpretation of international treaties incorporated in Articles 31 and 32 VCLT codify the preceding consistent customary law, making the Articles applicable even to international treaties that had been entered into before the adoption of the VCLT.[10] Nevertheless, the codification of the customary rules of interpretation has not reduced the number of issues concerning interpretation, because the rules articulated in the VCLT, which represent a

---

[7]   For instance, Potočný argues (cit.): [*I*]*nterpretation of an international treaty is a mental process which, in accordance with cognitive rules – such as logical and linguistic rules –, ascertains the true meaning of the treaty provisions and their legal effects, as intended by the parties to the treaty.* (MIROSLAV POTOČNÝ, JAN ONDŘEJ, PUBLIC INTERNATIONAL LAW: SPECIAL PART, Prague: C.H.Beck (6th ed. 2011), et. 244); Jankuv argues (cit.): *Interpretation of an international treaty is perceived as a mental process which aims to ascertain the true meaning of a treaty provision corresponding to the intention of the parties.* (JURAJ JANKUV, DAGMAR LANTAJOVÁ, INTERNATIONAL LAW OF TREATIES AND ITS INTERACTIONS WITH THE SLOVAK LEGAL SYSTEM, Pilsen: Aleš Čeněk Publishing (2011), et. 82).
[8]   CHRISTIAN DJEFFAL, STATIC AND EVOLUTIVE TREATY INTERPRETATION: A FUNCTIONAL RECONSTRUCTION, Cambridge: Cambridge University Press (2016), et. 9.
[9]   Codification of the law of international treaties was declared in 1949 by the newly established UN International Law Commission to be one of its priorities. The preparatory works took almost two decades and resulted in the adoption of the VCLT on the law of treaties on 22 May 1969 at the UN Conference on the Law of Treaties in Vienna. The Convention has been signed by 116 States, source: United Nations Treaty Collection, Depositary, available at: https://treaties.un.org/Pages/ViewDetailsIII. aspx?src=TREATY&mtdsg_no=XXIII-1&chapter=23&Temp=mtdsg3&clang=_en (accessed on 12 January 2022).
[10]   RICHARD K. GARDINER, TREATY INTERPRETATION, New York: Oxford University Press (2008), et. 13; Arbitration regarding the Iron Rhine ("Ijzeren Rijn") Railway, *The Kingdom of Belgium* v. *The Kingdom of Netherlands*, Award of 24 May 2005, marg. 45, et. 62.

compromise achieved by the State delegations participating in the creation of the VCLT, are indeed very general. One may, however, safely say that the VCLT (sometimes also referred to as the *treaty on treaties*) is one of the most successful and respected international treaties, which has significantly, through the codification of customary rules, contributed to the formation of a relatively comprehensive methodology of interpretation of international treaties.

2.04. Moreover, the VCLT interpretation rules are almost universally recognised and applied by international tribunals interpreting international treaties.[11] That being said, it needs to be emphasized that the case-law of international tribunals plays a principal role in the formation of interpretation rules, because the tribunals subsequently invoke these decisions, and their persuasive reasoning in turn helps to develop and refine the VCLT interpretation rules. This is, indeed, the reason why the need for developing a platform registering international case-law used to be frequently mentioned, as it would provide a guide to the tribunals in the application of the VCLT interpretation rules, which are, not exceptionally, articulated in a very general fashion. Some authors argue that this objective has been attained and international case-law has become a reality,[12] being created by dozens of institutions with the power to resolve disputes – and at least 24 of those institutions can be defined as international tribunals.[13]

2.05. Article 31(1) VCLT stipulates a general rule according to which an international treaty shall be interpreted in good faith in accordance with the ordinary meaning to be given to the terms of the treaty in their context and in light of its object and purpose. The Article sets forth the circumstances and principles that must be considered and applied for the purpose of the interpretation of an international treaty. Conversely, the provision fails to describe or stipulate the precise steps to be taken in the process of interpretation. One may therefore invoke the observation of the European Court of Human Rights (ECtHR), which described

---

[11]   CHRISTIAN DJEFFAL, STATIC AND EVOLUTIVE TREATY INTERPRETATION: A FUNCTIONAL RECONSTRUCTION, Cambridge: Cambridge University Press (2016), et. 3.

[12]   INGO VENZKE, HOW INTERPRETATION MAKES INTERNATIONAL LAW: ON SEMANTIC CHANGE AND NORMATIVE TWISTS, Oxford: Oxford University Press (2012), et. 140; identically and with reference to the former of the above authors, see also in: CHRISTIAN DJEFFAL, STATIC AND EVOLUTIVE TREATY INTERPRETATION: A FUNCTIONAL RECONSTRUCTION, Cambridge: Cambridge University Press (2016), et. 6.

[13]   KAREN ALTER, THE NEW TERRAIN OF INTERNATIONAL LAW: COURTS, POLITICS, RIGHTS, New Jersey: Princeton University Press (2014), et. 70–6, quoted in CHRISTIAN DJEFFAL, STATIC AND EVOLUTIVE TREATY INTERPRETATION: A FUNCTIONAL RECONSTRUCTION, Cambridge: Cambridge University Press (2016), et. 6. As concerns specific tribunals designated as international tribunals, see: https://elaw.org/system/files/intl%20tribunals%20synoptic_chart2.pdf (accessed on 12 January 2022).

the interpretation under Article 31 VCLT as a unity, a single combined operation, which places on the same footing all of the principles of interpretation (such as interpretation in good faith, ordinary meaning of words, purpose of the treaty...).[14]

2.06. Hence, the interpretation rules set forth in the VCLT only provide the national courts with an interpretation guideline. The precise process of interpretation of any specific provisions of an international treaty applicable to individual cases is chosen by the courts themselves. It comes as no surprise, then, that the courts interpret international treaties by applying procedures and theoretical knowledge with which they are familiar from their national law – despite the fact that such procedure can generally not be embraced as appropriate. Consequently, the interpretation of the individual provisions of an international treaty may rather significantly vary depending on the court or arbitral tribunal interpreting the particular international treaty, while, ideally, the individual interpretations should exhibit no differences at all. Applying national law (law of national origin) in such interpretation is thus naturally undesirable and contrary to the purpose of international treaties.

II. Necessity to Prevent Inconsistent Interpretation in International Law

2.07. The above has the undesirable result of inconsistent interpretation of international treaties, which, according to legal theory, can be resolved by no fewer than three possible approaches.

2.08. First, the setting up of a specialised tribunal resolving disputes from a particular international treaty and thereby unifying the interpretation of the treaty, such as the ECtHR competent to resolve disputes from breaches of the European Convention on Human Rights (ECHR).[15]

2.09. The second possibility of preventing inconsistent interpretation of international treaties is the incorporation of special interpretation rules (provisions) directly in the text of a particular international treaty. Such special provisions are intended to ensure a consistent interpretation of the treaty by

---

[14] Judgment of the ECtHR in *Golder* v. *United Kingdom*, 21 February 1975, Application No. 4451/70, A/18, paragraph 30. However, compare also judgment of the ECtHR in *Witold Litwa* v. *Poland*, 04 April 2000, Application No. 26629/95, in which the ECtHR has held that Article 31 VCLT must also be perceived as an indication of the order (the sequence of the circumstances to be assessed) which the process of interpretation of the treaty should follow.

[15] The category of special tribunals also includes the Court of Justice of the EU (CJ EU) in relation to the Convention on jurisdiction and the recognition and enforcement of judgments in civil and commercial matters (Brussels Convention).

various national courts. One of the most famous interpretation rules is Article 7 UN Convention on Contracts for the International Sale of Goods of 11 April 1980 (CISG), which stipulates that in the interpretation of this Convention, regard is to be had to its international character and to the need to promote uniformity in its application and the observance of good faith in international trade.[16] A similar provision is incorporated in the Rome Convention on the Law Applicable to Contractual Obligations (Rome Convention)[17] (Article 18 Rome Convention), which stipulates that in the interpretation of this Convention, regard shall be had to the international character of the rules incorporated therein and to the desirability of achieving uniformity in its interpretation and application.[18] An analogous rule is also enshrined in Article 4 UNIDROIT Convention on International Factoring[19] (Article 4), in the UNIDROIT Convention on International Financial Leasing[20] (Article 6),[21] and in the UNIDROIT Principles of International Commercial Contracts (Article 1.6).[22] Furthermore, the UNCITRAL Model Law on International Commercial Arbitration stipulates that in the interpretation of this Law, regard is to be had to its international origin and to the need to promote uniformity in its application and the observance of good faith.[23]

---

[16] Article 7(2) CISG stipulates that, when filling gaps in a treaty, the legal system of a signatory State can be had regard to only unless the gap can be filled autonomously, i.e. in conformity with the general principles of the Convention. Hence, the interpretation of the CISG always requires that a solution be primarily looked for within the framework of the Convention itself, even if there is a *gap* in the Convention. This should ensure a uniform interpretation thereof. The CISG thus prohibits any interpretation which would primarily invoke the legal system of a State. A reference to the legal system of a State signatory when filling gaps in the Convention is an *ultima ratio* solution.

[17] Rome Convention on the Law Applicable to Contractual Obligations, OJ C 27, 26 January 1998, et. 34–53. [EUR-Lex: 41998A0126(02)].

[18] Article 18 Rome Convention on the Law Applicable to Contractual Obligations (cit.): *Uniform interpretation – In the interpretation and application of the preceding uniform rules, regard shall be had to their international character and to the desirability of achieving uniformity in their interpretation and application.*

[19] UNIDROIT convention on international factoring (Ottawa, Canada, 28 May 1988), available at: https://www.unidroit.org/instruments/factoring (accessed on 16 January 2022).

[20] UNIDROIT convention on international financial leasing (Ottawa, Canada, 28 May 1988), available at: https://www.unidroit.org/instruments/leasing/convention/ (accessed on 16 January 2022).

[21] Article 6 UNIDROIT Convention on International Financial Leasing (cit.): *(1) In the interpretation of this Convention, regard is to be had to its object and purpose as set forth in the preamble, to its international character and to the need to promote uniformity in its application and the observance of good faith in international trade. (2) Questions concerning matters governed by this Convention which are not expressly settled in it are to be settled in conformity with the general principles on which it is based or, in the absence of such principles, in conformity with the law applicable by virtue of the rules of private international law.*

[22] See Article 1.6 The UNIDROIT Principles of International Commercial Contracts (cit.): '(1) In the interpretation of these Principles, regard is to be had to their international character and to their purposes including the need to promote uniformity in their application. (2) Issues within the scope of these Principles but not expressly settled by them are as far as possible to be settled in accordance with their underlying general principles.'

[23] See Article 2A(1) The UNCITRAL Model Law on International Commercial Arbitration (cit.): '*In the interpretation of this Law, regard is to be had to its international origin and to the need to promote uniformity in its application and the observance of good faith.*'

2.10. If an international treaty determines the jurisdiction of a special or, as applicable, a particular tribunal to resolve disputes arising therefrom and, at the same time, contains no special interpretation rule regarding the unification of interpretation, then the desired uniform interpretation [independent of the laws of the State signatories] requires (as the third approach) the application of autonomous interpretation. In this regard, one may refer to the Convention on the Recognition and Enforcement of Foreign Arbitral Awards (New York Convention (1958)). It has been argued that the terms used in the New York Convention (1958) are principally endowed with autonomous interpretation. Hence, the tribunals should not interpret the provisions of the New York Convention (1958) with reference to national law, because the desired effect is the accomplishment of a uniform interpretation in all State signatories.[24]

III. Autonomous Interpretation

III.1. Concept and Objectives of Autonomous Interpretation

2.11. Autonomous interpretation is a common method of interpreting international treaties, but it is rather difficult to define. For instance, *Linhart, K.* describes autonomous interpretation as an aspiration to interpret international treaties as an independent law, i.e. refraining from such interpretation of international treaties that would refer to concepts incorporated in the law of the State signatories.[25] *Meyer-Sparenberg, W.* adds that autonomous interpretation is the consequence of teleological interpretation, because the purpose and objective of international law is to approximate and consolidate multiple national legal systems.[26] *Gebauer, M.* notes that the definition of autonomous interpretation has a negative and a positive branch. He argues that, from the negative perspective, autonomous interpretation is defined as an interpretation in which the interpreter does not refer to the concepts of any specific national (domestic) law. From the positive perspective, autonomous interpretation is defined as an interpretation in which the interpreter interprets

---

[24] International Council for Commercial Arbitration, *ICCA's Guide to the Interpretation of the 1958, New York Convention: A Handbook for Judges, with the Assistance of the Permanent Court of Arbitration Peace Palace*, Den Haag (2011), et. 13.

[25] KARIN LINHART, INTERNATIONALES EINHEITSRECHT UND EINHEITLICHE AUSLEGUNG, Tübingen: Mohr Siebeck (2005), et. 37.

[26] WOLFGANG MEYER-SPARENBERG, STAATSVERTRAGLICHE KOLLISIONSNORMEN, Berlin: Duncker & Humblot (1990), et. 110. Also referred to in: KARIN LINHART, INTERNATIONALES EINHEITSRECHT UND EINHEITLICHE AUSLEGUNG, Tübingen: Mohr Siebeck (2005), et. 37.

the terms and rules of an international treaty exclusively within the context of the respective treaty and its purpose.[27]

2.12. Autonomous interpretation is one of the fundamental principles of interpretation of international treaties. It aims to sever the international treaty from the national laws of the signatory countries. The need for an autonomous interpretation of international treaties stems from the purpose itself of international treaties, as well as from the generally acknowledged customary law that was incorporated in Articles 31 to 33 VCLT. The general interpretation rule in Article 31(1) VCLT emphasises that an international treaty shall be interpreted (cit.): *in good faith in accordance with the ordinary meaning to be given to the terms of the treaty in their context and in light of its object and purpose.* This wording clearly implies that the interpretation must not attribute to the terms used in the treaty the same meaning that such terms possess in the legal theory of the individual States, let alone any specific legal cultures. Indeed, one must realize that these terms were used in the text of the particular international treaty as a compromise reflecting its object and purpose. The VCLT thus emphasises interpretation in compliance with the ordinary meaning of the terms, with the object and purpose of the treaty, and in compliance with the assessment of the overall circumstances surrounding the treaty and the term used. But it would be a mistake to refer to 'ordinary meaning' in terms of a simple semantic interpretation; it is necessary to refer to the ordinary meaning attributed to the respective terms and concepts from the legal perspective. These levels must be strictly distinguished, because it is by no means exceptional in practice that it is indeed the semantic interpretation that is used to interpret certain terms; and it is by no means exceptional that legal documents even go so far as to refer to general explanatory (linguistic) dictionaries. Although legal terminology employs general terms coined by ordinary language, it often attributes its own, specific legal meaning to such terms. Hence, attempts to construe the terms using general interpretations may be inappropriate and should instead be avoided whenever possible. Indeed, one must never abandon the *niveau* of law that must only be corrected by an effort to accomplish a reasonable universality of these legal terms.[28] The VCLT stipulates that

---

[27] Martin Gebauer, *Uniform Law, General Principles and Autonomous Interpretation*, 5(4) UNIFORM LAW REVIEW 683–705 (2000). Autonomous interpretation according to *Martin Gebauer* is primarily founded on the method of systematic and teleological interpretation because the linguistic and historical interpretations do not, in his opinion, lead to the autonomous interpretation.

[28] For more details concerning the semantic interpretation, see also MARTA CHROMÁ, LEGAL TRANSLATION IN THEORY AND IN PRACTICE, Prague: Karolinum (2014), et. 45, although the author's analysis of the issue is more closely connected with translations and exemplified by a specific substance.

Scope of Jurisdiction of Tribunals and International Authorities in Interpretation...

Czech Yearbook of International Law®

the context for the purpose of interpretation of a treaty shall comprise especially, without limitation, any agreement that was made between all the parties in connection with the conclusion of the international treaty, as well as any subsequent practice in the application of the treaty.[29] The VCLT also stipulates that if the meaning of a provision remains ambiguous, recourse may be had to supplementary means of interpretation (supplementary interpretation), including the preparatory work of the treaty (*travail préparatoire*) and the circumstances of its conclusion.[30] The interpretation rules incorporated in the VCLT also clearly imply that the VCLT has no provision stating that recourse may be had to the legal system of any of the State signatories. Consequently, as a rule, the interpretation must be autonomous, independent of the legal systems of the signatories.[31]

2.13. The above general rule in Article 31 VCLT contains three separate interpretation principles combined in a single combined operation that places all of them on equal footing.[32] This single combined operation results in the autonomous interpretation of the terms used in the international treaty. As mentioned above, the general rule provides no description or statement as to the precise steps to be taken in the process of interpretation.

2.14. First of all, the interpreter should apply all principles of the general rule within the framework of the single combined operation. This rule was also articulated by the WTO Appellate Body in its decision in *EC-chicken cuts* (cit.): *[I]nterpretation pursuant to the customary rules codified in Article 31 of the Vienna Convention is ultimately a holistic exercise that should not be mechanically subdivided into rigid components.*[33]

2.15. The first principle of the VCLT general interpretation rule stipulates that international treaties should be interpreted in good faith. Apart from the wording itself of Article 31 VCLT,

---

[29] See Article 31(2) and Article 31(3) VCLT.

[30] Article 32 VCLT stipulates (cit.): *Recourse may be had to supplementary means of interpretation, including the preparatory work of the treaty and the circumstances of its conclusion, in order to confirm the meaning resulting from the application of article 31, or to determine the meaning when the interpretation according to article 31: (a) leaves the meaning ambiguous or obscure; or (b) leads to a result which is manifestly absurd or unreasonable.*

[31] A certain definition or description of an independent (autonomous) interpretation is also included in other international treaties, such as the above-mentioned Article 7 CISG.

[32] Compare also judgment of the ECtHR in *Golder* v. *United Kingdom*, 21 February 1975, Application No. 4451/70, A/18, [1975] ECHR 1, (1979) 1 EHRR 524, IHRL 9 (ECHR 1975), paragraph 30.; Yearbook of the International Law Commission (1966), Vol. II, UN Document No. A/CN.4/SER.A/1966/Add.l, et. 219–220; OLIVER DÖRR, KIRSTEN SCHMALENBACH, VIENNA CONVENTION ON THE LAW OF TREATIES: A COMMENTARY, New York: Springer (2012), section 3, et. 39.

[33] Compare decision of the WTO Appellate Body in *European Communities — Customs Classification of Frozen Boneless Chicken Cuts*, No. AB-2005-5, Document No. WT/DS269/AB/R and WT/DS286/AB/R, 12 September 2005, paragraph 176.

this requirement directly follows from the rule prescribing the performance of contracts in good faith, as enshrined in Article 26 VCLT.[34] However, 'good faith' is not defined in the VCLT and, consequently, the principle of interpretation in good faith raises a number of further questions as to the precise meaning of 'interpretation in good faith' in practice. For instance, *Lo* supports the existence of specific criteria to test whether the given interpretation complies with the principle of good faith. Specifically, *Lo* proposes the following criteria to assess interpretation in good faith:[35]

a. fairness / unfairness of the interpretation – the interpreter should review whether the interpretation results in a manifest unfairness or inequality in the rights of one of the parties;

b. malicious intent – the tribunal should ascertain whether any objective circumstances exist that indicate bad faith / malice on the part of the entity submitting the interpretation;

c. rationality / irrationality – the interpreter should review whether the interpretation is reasonable or, as applicable, whether it is deemed reasonable by the relevant international community and the parties involved;

d. consistency / inconsistency – the interpreter should review whether the given interpretation significantly and groundlessly differs from an interpretation of the same provision that was performed in the past; and

e. compliance with the purpose of the international treaty – the interpreter should also review whether the interpretation complies with the general purpose of the international treaty.

2.16. Other authors in turn primarily emphasise the reasonableness of the interpretation. Hence, an interpretation in good faith should not be unreasonable. Quite the opposite, it should eliminate any strictly formally linguistic, or overly teleological, interpretation that could result in unreasonable conclusions.[36]

2.17. International courts and tribunals often fail to explicitly mention the principle of interpretation in good faith in their decisions. This may also be due to the fact that 'good faith' itself is very

---

[34] Article 26 VCLT (cit.): *Every treaty in force is binding upon the parties to it and must be performed by them in good faith.*

[35] Compare CHANG-FA LO, TREATY INTERPRETATION UNDER THE VIENNA CONVENTION ON THE LAW OF TREATIES, New York: Springer (2017), et. 294.

[36] See also OLIVER DÖRR, KIRSTEN SCHMALENBACH, VIENNA CONVENTION ON THE LAW OF TREATIES: A COMMENTARY, New York: Springer (2012), section 3, et. 61, or RICHARD K. GARDINER, TREATY INTERPRETATION, New York: Oxford University Press (2008), et. 151.

Scope of Jurisdiction of Tribunals and International Authorities in Interpretation...

Czech Yearbook of International Law®

difficult to define and that, for many interpreters, the term only represents an abstract principle the application of which is rather complicated. This approach is further corroborated by the cautious use of the principle – for instance, the NAFTA arbitral tribunal in *Terminal Forest Products* described this principle in very ambiguous words as a general rule applicable to the interpretation and application of international treaties.[37] A similarly ambiguous commentary was provided by the International Court of Justice (ICJ) in its decision in *Border and Transborder Armed Actions*, in which the ICJ ruled as follows (cit.):

> [*T*]*he principle of good faith is, as the Court has observed, 'one of the basic principles governing the creation and performance of legal obligations' (Nuclear Tests, Z.C.J. Reports 1974, p. 268, para. 46; p. 473, para. 49); it is not in itself a source of obligation where none would otherwise exist...*[38]

2.18. However, the extensive case-law of international courts and tribunals has also produced decisions in which these institutions describe the principle of good faith in greater detail. For instance, the WTO Appellate Body in its decision in *US – Import Prohibition of Certain Shrimp* ruled that the principle of good faith comprises, *inter alia*, the prohibition of abusing the law (*abus de droit*). In other words, the WTO Appellate Body confirmed the general rule that the interpretation of an international treaty provision should not result in an unreasonable detriment to the rights of the other party.[39]

2.19. The second principle requires that the interpretation of the individual terms always comply with the ordinary meaning of the terms used in the treaty. However, as noted by *Prof. Schwarzenberger*, almost every term has multiple meanings,

---

[37]   Decision of the NAFTA Arbitral Tribunal in the decision of 06 June 2006 in *Canfor Corporation* v. *United States of America; Terminal Forest Products Ltd.* v. *United States of America*, paragraph 182 (cit.): [G] *ood faith is a basic principle for interpretation of a treaty. It is stated in so many words in Article 31(1) of the Vienna Convention ('A treaty shall be interpreted in good faith . . .'). Good faith is also a basic principle in the performance of a treaty by States.*

[38]   Judgment of the ICJ in Border and Transborder Armed Actions (*Nicaragua* v. *Honduras*) of 20 December 1988, paragraph 94.

[39]   Decision of the WTO Appellate Body in *United States – Import Prohibition of Certain Shrimp and Shrimp Products*, 12 October 1998, paragraph 158 (cit.): [*T*]*he chapeau of Article XX is, in fact, but one expression of the principle of good faith. This principle, at once a general principle of law and a general principle of international law, controls the exercise of rights by states. One application of this general principle, the application widely known as the doctrine of abus de droit, prohibits the abusive exercise of a state's rights and enjoins that whenever the assertion of a right 'impinges on the field covered by [a] treaty obligation, it must be exercised bona fide, that is to say, reasonably.' 156 An abusive exercise by a Member of its own treaty right thus results in a breach of the treaty rights of the other Members and, as well, a violation of the treaty obligation of the Member so acting. Having said this, our task here is to interpret the language of the chapeau, seeking additional interpretative guidance, as appropriate, from the general principles of international law.*

including the word 'meaning' itself.[40] Hence, the determination of the ordinary meaning of a used term requires at least a substantiated consideration, i.e. an analysis of the term by the interpreter. In this connection, the ordinary meaning of a term used in an international treaty must be determined by a non-isolated consideration of the term that has due regard for the context, i.e. primarily a consideration of the nature and purpose of the treaty and of the provision in which the term being interpreted is used – in compliance with the third principle. *Dörr* notes that the ordinary meaning ought to be assessed from the perspective of a person reasonably familiar with the subject matter of the international treaty, and points out that international tribunals frequently assess such meaning with the help of specialised or general dictionaries.[41] However, the use of dictionary definitions can only be perceived as the potential first step towards the interpretation of the term, which needs to be refined in accordance with the remaining two principles of the general interpretation rule. The reason is that the dictionary definitions totally ignore the circumstances attending the formation and purpose of the individual international treaties, which could have a fundamental impact on the ordinary meaning of the term used in the treaty. Hence, they cannot be the sole resources relied on in the interpretation of concepts in international treaties.

2.20.　The third principle follows the preceding two and stipulates that the ordinary meaning should be assessed in the comprehensive context of the treaty and in compliance with the object and purpose thereof. This principle is primarily the manifestation of the fact that no treaty provision was created in a contextual vacuum. Quite the opposite. Each treaty provision has its purpose, justification and systematic connections in the general scheme of the treaty. This fact itself requires that the treaty be interpreted with due regard for these circumstances in order to prevent a literal isolated interpretation that could even contradict the purpose itself of the provision and, by extension, the entire international treaty. The primary goal of searching for the context of the provision or expression is then especially the confirmation of the ordinary meaning (second principle).

---

[40]　See also Georg Schwarzenberger, *Myth and realities of Treaty Interpretation: Articles 27–29 of the Vienna draft Convention on the law of treaties*, 9(1) VIRGINIA JOURNAL OF INTERNATIONAL LAW 13 (1968). Adopted from RICHARD K. GARDINER, TREATY INTERPRETATION, New York: Oxford University Press (2008), et. 161.

[41]　See also OLIVER DÖRR, KIRSTEN SCHMALENBACH, VIENNA CONVENTION ON THE LAW OF TREATIES: A COMMENTARY, New York: Springer (2012), section 3, margin 41.

2.21. As the above-mentioned individual principles of the general interpretation rule clearly indicate, the most important factor in the interpretation of an international treaty is naturally the wording itself of the treaty provisions.[42] The terms used must be interpreted in their ordinary meaning, which essentially means that the tribunal should identify the meaning that would be attributed to the term by an informed expert in the field, in view of the type of the international treaty in which the term is used. When considering the meaning of the terms used, international tribunals often refer in their decisions to definitions of terms in specialised dictionaries and other publications.[43] But gleaning the actual meaning of a particular term only from the wording itself is rather exceptional. The second principle of the general rule thus stipulates that one must also review the general context of the term used. The interpreting tribunal should therefore primarily apply systematic interpretation and consider the meaning of the term in the context of the remaining provisions of the treaty, the general scheme of the treaty and other factors, such as the recitals (preamble), location of the expression in the text, use of the same expression elsewhere in the text, use of the same expression in another associated treaty,[44] or even the name itself of the treaty.[45] Moreover, the tribunal should review the meaning of the terms used with due regard for the object and purpose of the treaty. Hence, the tribunal should apply the teleological interpretation method and interpret the terms in such manner that their meaning is consistent with the objective and purpose of the treaty. Conversely, it is imperative to reject any interpretation conflicting with the objective and purpose of the international treaty. Similarly, it is necessary to reject any interpretation that would render the provision inapplicable, or otherwise purposeless or meaningless in any manner. The purpose of the treaty can most frequently be ascertained from its

---

[42] See also judgment of the ICJ in *Territorial Dispute (Libyun Aruh Jamuhiriyu/Chad)*, 03 February 1994, I. C. J. Reports 1994, et. 41; judgment of the ICJ in *Legality of Use of Force (Serbia and Montenegro v. Belgium)*, 15 December 2004, I.C.J. Reports 2004, et. 279, paragraph 100.

[43] See also: judgment of the ECtHR in *Golder* v. *United Kingdom*, 21 February 1975, Application No. 4451/70, A/18, [1975], (1979) 1 EHRR 524, IHRL 9 (ECHR 1975), paragraph 32; judgment of the ICJ in *Kasikili/Sedudu Island (Botswana/Namihia)*, 13 December 1999, I. C. J. Reports 1999, et. 1045, paragraph 30.

[44] See also judgment of the ICJ in *Land, Island and Maritime Frontier Dispute (El Salvador/Honduras: Nicaragua intervening)* of 11 September 1992, paragraph 374.

[45] See also judgment of the ICJ in *Oil Platforms (Islamic Republic of Iran* v. *United States of America)*, 12 December 1996, I.C.J. Reports 1996, et. 803, paragraph 47, in which the Court interpreted the individual terms of the Treaty with reference to, *inter alia*, the name of the Treaty and, in connection therewith, applied an extensive interpretation of the term 'commerce'.

opening provisions,[46] recitals (preamble),[47] name,[48] or the treaty provisions themselves, using a general rational interpretation in compliance with general social and legal well-known facts, which the decision-making bodies (tribunals, arbitrators and other institutions) are essentially presumed to have broad knowledge of and extensive experience with. Considering the nature and duration of the individual international treaties, the interpreting tribunal should have regard to the temporal perspective and consider the meaning of the respective term at the time at which it was used by the parties.

2.22. Last, but not least, the tribunal should implement the entire process of interpreting the treaty provision in compliance with the principle of good faith. This principle also corresponds to the basic rule of the international law of treaties, i.e. that treaties should be performed in good faith.[49] The *principle of good faith* is a rather ambiguous concept; nonetheless, in view of the above doctrinal premises of interpretation in good faith, it is at least reasonable to assume that one of its integral components is the imperative of reasonableness and judiciousness.[50] In other words, the resulting interpretation of a treaty term must lead to the fulfilment of the purpose of the treaty and shall not result in unfair or unreasonable, let alone absurd conclusions in any individual case. This must always be assessed on an individual basis, and it is the liability of the interpreter (tribunal) to consider whether the preferred interpretation results in any undesirable outcomes contrary to the principle of interpreting an international treaty in good faith. The core of the assessment is a consideration as to whether or not the implemented interpretation is fair, rational and consistent, and complies with the purpose of the interpreted provision / the international treaty itself.[51] In view of the general nature of VCLT provisions and the diversity of the interpretation practice, there are no fixed rules governing the assessment. Similarly, there is no generally recognised definition of good faith. Hence, the tribunals are endowed with a relatively broad discretion. However, such

---

[46] See also Article 1 Charter of the United Nations.
[47] See also the Charter of the United Nations, CISG, UN Convention relating to the Status of Refugees of 1951, VCLT et al.
[48] See also judgment of the ICJ in Oil Platforms (*Islamic Republic of Iran v. United States of America*), 12 December 1996, I.C.J. Reports 1996, et. 803, paragraph 47. For more details, see RICHARD K. GARDINER, TREATY INTERPRETATION, New York: Oxford University Press (2008), et. 180.
[49] See Article 26 VCLT (cit.): '*Every treaty in force is binding upon the parties to it and must be performed by them in good faith.*'
[50] RICHARD K. GARDINER, TREATY INTERPRETATION, New York: Oxford University Press (2008), et. 157, 148.
[51] See CHANG-FA LO, TREATY INTERPRETATION UNDER THE VIENNA CONVENTION ON THE LAW OF TREATIES, New York: Springer (2017), et. 294.

Scope of Jurisdiction of Tribunals and International Authorities in Interpretation...

Czech Yearbook of International Law®

approach in turn places a heavier burden on the tribunal, which is obliged to substantiate its decisions and any conclusions made therein in great detail.

2.23. Article 31(2)(a) VCLT supplements or refines the general interpretation rule by stipulating that the context shall also comprise (cit.): '*... any agreement relating to the treaty which was made between all the parties in connection with the conclusion of the treaty;*'

2.24. This means that the interpretation of the treaty by the tribunal should also involve an assessment of the parties' agreements, which are connected to the treaty without being an integral part thereof. However, such materials must be the result of a consensus reached by all parties to the international treaty and must relate to the object thereof. Such agreements may, for instance, provide an authentic interpretation of certain concepts or particularise the actual functioning of the mechanisms anticipated in the treaty. This applies, for instance, to the *Harmonized Commodity Description and Coding System*, considered by the WTO Appellate Body to be a part of the WTO Agreement.[52]

2.25. The important requirement is that the agreements be made *in connection with the conclusion of the treaty*, i.e. approximately in the period during which the treaty was being negotiated and concluded. The words '*in connection with the conclusion of the treaty*' suggest that the agreements should be made within the scope of a particular interval in order to be deemed made, in view of Article 31(2) VCLT, in the context of that provision. However, no precise definition of this interval has been stipulated in international law so far.[53] The main reason for the lack of such definition is the fact that international law has no precisely delimited meaning for the 'conclusion of the treaty'. This is neither the case in the VCLT, in which the 'conclusion of the treaty' must be interpreted in the context of the individual provisions, and the contents of the term may include any of the two different intervals[54] analysed below.

2.26. The first interval is the period between the opening of negotiations and the moment at which the parties approve the

---

[52] See decision of the WTO Appellate Body in *European Communities — Customs Classification of Frozen Boneless Chicken Cuts*, No. AB-2005-5, Document No. WT/DS269/AB/R and WT/DS286/AB/R, 12 September 2005, paragraph 195.
[53] BERT VIERDAG, THE CONCEPT OF DISCRIMINATION IN INTERNATIONAL LAW, The Netherlands: Springer (1973), et. 79. See also ULF LINDERFALK, ON THE INTERPRETATION OF TREATIES, The Netherlands: Springer (2007).
[54] Bert Vierdag, *The time of the Conclusion of a multilateral treaty: Article 30 of the Vienna convention on the law of treaties and related provisions*, 59(1) THE BRITISH YEARBOOK OF INTERNATIONAL LAW 80 (1988).

text of the treaty, without yet agreeing to be bound by it.[55] Such a delimitation, however, cannot be applied for the purpose of Article 31(2) VCLT, because the parties to an international treaty may still agree, in the period between the signing and the ratification of the treaty, that the meaning of any particular provisions will be interpreted in a particular manner. For the purpose of interpreting an international treaty using the context in terms of Article 31(1) VCLT, the 'conclusion of the treaty' must be interpreted as the interval between the opening of the negotiations and the day on which the treaty takes effect with respect to the last party, as this definition is analysed in detail by *Vierdag*.[56]

2.27.   The author of this paper agrees with *Vierdag* that the 'conclusion of the treaty' should contain the interval from the opening of the negotiations to the moment at which the treaty becomes binding on the last of the parties.

2.28.   But the important factor is that the agreement on the method of interpreting the international treaty provisions actually be agreed to by all parties, whether or not the agreement was also entered into by any authority superior to the parties. An agreement entered into by an international body of which all parties are members does not meet the requirements under Article 31(2)(a) VCLT unless the agreement is unanimously accepted by all parties.

2.29.   Article 31(3) VCLT then stipulates that the context of the treaty also includes:

> *(a) any subsequent agreement between the parties regarding the interpretation of the treaty or the application of its provisions;*
> *(b) any subsequent practice in the application of the treaty which establishes the agreement of the parties regarding its interpretation; and*
> *(c) any relevant rules of international law applicable in the relations between the parties.*

2.30.   These 'contextual' aspects of Article 31(3) VCLT are generally linked by the fact that, as opposed to the circumstances listed in Article 31(2) VCLT, they have no relation to the conclusion

---

[55]   Bert Vierdag, *The time of the Conclusion of a multilateral treaty: Article 30 of the Vienna convention on the law of treaties and related provisions*, 59(1) THE BRITISH YEARBOOK OF INTERNATIONAL LAW 80 (1988).

[56]   BERT VIERDAG, THE CONCEPT OF DISCRIMINATION IN INTERNATIONAL LAW, The Netherlands: Springer (1st ed. 1973), et. 86. *Ex multis*, see also ULF LINDERFALK, ON THE INTERPRETATION OF TREATIES, The Netherlands: Springer (2007), et. 148–151; Linderfalk ponders the existence of 3 time intervals, [...] *to my knowledge no support for either alternative can be drawn from the preparatory work of the convention. Nor does it appear that the expression at issue has yet been seriously brought into focus by international courts and tribunals. My conclusion is that at this moment the prevailing legal state of affairs cannot be convincingly determined.*

of the treaty and are only developed later, independently of the process of negotiation and conclusion of the treaty. They comprise subsequent agreements on treaty interpretation, later practice of the parties, or generally recognised rules of international law applicable in relations between the parties.[57] Paragraph 3 (just like Paragraph 2) prescribes no particular form, which means that all of the above-enumerated acts can be performed in any identifiable form. The application of the treaty by the parties ought to be repeated, consistent and applied, or at least recognised and accepted by all parties to the treaty. There is no temporal test. The temporal aspect may attest to the general nature and consistency of a particular practice. However, international law requires no particular minimal duration of such practice. The practice must be repeated and consistent, but there is no mandatory limit for reporting such practice. By identifying international law as the applicable interpretation instrument, the VCLT emphasises the fact that international treaties are a concept and source of international law, and it is therefore appropriate to interpret the treaties with due regard for international law.[58]

2.31. Article 31(3)(c) VCLT has regard to the fact that the purpose of international treaties does not consist in the codification of any and all existing rules of international law applicable between the parties. The subject matter of international treaties, however broad, is always limited. This is why it is supplemented by legal principles and customary international law, which are both on an equal footing with international treaties. Essentially, unless the international treaty excludes the application of any general principle or of customary international law, the rule continues to apply between the parties. Indeed, the international treaty need not specify any and all rules relating to a particular subject matter; it must only identify the rules the application of which ought to be excluded. As the hitherto published opinions imply, the VCLT can be used in the interpretation of an international treaty even if it is not attached to it.

2.32. Similarly, general principles of law remain applicable even if they are not explicitly or otherwise mentioned in the international

---

[57] For instance, (1) Paragraph 5.2 Doha Ministerial Decision on Implementation related concerns 14 November 2001 to CISG; (2) The 'understandings and additional agreements' adopted by the Biological Weapons Convention of 1975 Review Conference; (3) Resolutions adopted by the Conference of States Parties under the London (Dumping) Convention from 1975; (4) Recommendations adopted by the International Whaling Commission (IWC) under the International Convention for the Regulation of Whaling from 1948.
[58] This rule was also emphasised in the ICJ Advisory Opinion in *Legal Consequences for States of the Continued Presence of South Africa in Namibia (South West Africa)* of 21 June 1971, I.C.J. Reports 1971, paragraph 53 (cit.): '(...) *Moreover, an international instrument has to be interpreted and applied within the framework of the entire legal system prevailing at the time of the interpretation.* (...).'

treaty, as corroborated by the case-law of international tribunals. For instance, in the *Chorzów Factory* case, the Permanent Court of International Justice (PCIJ) has held that an obligation exists to pay compensation for a breach of an international treaty even if it does not directly and explicitly follow from the treaty.[59] The Appellate Body has also held that customary international law covers WTO agreements to the extent that it does not conflict with the WTO agreements, or is not directly incorporated therein.[60]

2.33. One must also mention that Article 31(4) VCLT sets forth an exception to the rule of interpretation of the ordinary meaning in that it stipulates that a special meaning shall be given to a term if it is established that the parties so intended. For instance, the main reason why the International Law Commission (ILC) decided to explicitly incorporate this provision in its proposal was its emphasis on the fact that the burden of proof lies with the party that invokes the special meaning of any particular concept. In its commentary to the VCLT, the Commission (ILC) also pointed out that this exception had been mentioned on several occasions by the PCIJ.[61] The ILC has invoked the PCIJ opinion in *Legal Status of Eastern Greenland*, in which the PCIJ held (cit.): '*The geographical meaning of the word "Greenland", i.e. the name which is habitually used in the maps to denominate the whole island, must be regarded as the ordinary meaning of the word. If it is alleged by one of the Parties that some unusual or exceptional meaning is to be attributed to it, it lies on that Party to establish its contention.*'[62] Regardless of the obvious meaning of a term, the parties may, pursuant to Article 31(4)

---

[59] Chorzów Factory (*Germany* v. *Poland*), Merits, 1928 PCIJ (ser. A) paragraph 73, available at: http://www.worldcourts.com/pcij/eng/decisions/1928.09.13_chorzow1.htm (accessed on 19 January 2022).

[60] World Trade Organization, *Korea – Measures Affecting Government Procurement*, Report of the Panel, WT/DS163/R, 01 May 2000, paragraph 7.9.

[61] Draft Articles on the Law of Treaties with commentaries 1966, International Law Commission, 18th session, Commentary to Article 27, et. 222, paragraph 17, available at: http://legal.un.org/ilc/texts/instruments/english/commentaries/1_1_1966.pdf (accessed on 19 January 2022).

[62] PCIJ Judgment No. 20 (General List No. 43), 05 September 1933, *Denmark* v. *Norway* – Legal Status of Eastern Greenland, published in: 1933 P.C.I.J. (ser. A/B) No. 53 (April 05), paragraph 111, available at: http://www.worldcourts.com/pcij/eng/decisions/1933.04.05_greenland.htm (accessed on 19 January 2022). See also ICJ Advisory Opinion of 28 May 1948 in *Admission of a State to the United Nations* (Charter, Article 4), published in: ICJ Reports, 1948, et. 57 et seq. or Arbitral Award of the Permanent Court of Arbitration (PCA) set up in connection with a dispute relying on the Additional Protocol of 25 September 1991 to the Convention on the Protection of the Rhine Against Pollution by Chlorides of 03 December 1976 – Annex B to the Convention, on Arbitration – Annex III to the Additional Protocol, on 'Financial Arrangements' (Case Concerning the Auditing of Accounts Between the Kingdom of the Netherlands and the French Republic pursuant to the Additional Protocol of 25 September 1991 to the Convention on the Protection of the Rhine Against Pollution by Chlorides of 03 December 1976), of 12 March 2004, in a dispute between the Netherlands and France, published in: ICGJ 374 (PCA 2004), available in the original French version at: https://pcacases.com/web/sendAttach/76 (accessed on 19 January 2022), in an English translation available at: http://www.worldcourts.com/pca/eng/decisions/2004.03.12_Netherlands_v_France.pdf (accessed on 19 January 2022).

VCLT, invoke any special meaning thereof, but the burden of proof regarding the special meaning of the term lies with the party invoking such special meaning.

2.34.   Article 32 VCLT contains supplementary means of interpretation. These include primarily preparatory work of the treaty (*travaux préparatoires*) and the circumstances of its conclusion. However, these supplementary means can only be used in the final phase of interpretation, only **(i)** to confirm the meaning resulting from the tribunal's application of the interpretation rules in Article 31 VCLT, or **(ii)** to determine the meaning when the interpretation according to Article 31 VCLT leaves the meaning ambiguous or obscure; or leads to a result that is manifestly absurd or unreasonable.[63]

2.35.   **Re (i)** The application of the supplementary means of interpretation in order to confirm any meaning is entirely unlimited. The interpreter may always decide whether or not they apply the supplementary means to support or enhance their interpretation on the basis of Article 31 VCLT. But if the interpretation based on the text and context is clear, these means of interpretation are not necessary. Hence, the interpreter has the discretion to decide whether or not the means shall be used. This situation has been addressed, for instance, by the WTO Appellate Body, which has held that if the interpretation based on the text itself and on the context is clear, the supplementary means shall not be used.[64]

2.36.   **Re (ii)** It is at the interpreter's sole subjective discretion to decide whether, following an attempt at interpretation pursuant to Article 31 VCLT, the interpreter considers the meaning of the term or provision being interpreted as ambiguous or obscure. If this situation actually occurs, it will be resolved using the mechanism enshrined in Article 32 VCLT. This means that recourse to the supplementary means of interpretation under Article 32 VCLT is available if the meaning remains ambiguous or obscure after the interpretation rules incorporated in Article 31 VCLT are applied. The discretion in such cases has been well illustrated in *Chile Price Band System*,[65] in which the arbitral tribunal held as follows (cit.): '*[T]he text and context of "variable import levy" and "minimum import price" alone do not enable*

---

[63]   See also Article 32 VCLT.
[64]   Report of the WTO Appellate Body in DS397 European Communities – Definitive Anti-Dumping Measures on Certain Iron or Steel Fasteners from China – AB-2011-2- (Report of the Appellate Body) of 15 July 2011, in *China* v. *European Communities*, third parties: Brazil; Canada; Chile; Colombia; India; Japan; Norway; Taiwan; Thailand; Turkey and United States, paragraphs 352 and 353.
[65]   Chile – Price Band System and Safeguard Measures Relating to Certain Agricultural Products, WT/DS207/R, 03 May 2002.

us to determine the meaning of those terms without ambiguity.'[66] The arbitral tribunal subsequently refrained from an analysis of such interpretations that allow for multiple meanings, and directly explained further procedure as it held as follows (cit.): *'[T]he determination of their meaning should therefore include an analysis which goes beyond a purely grammatical or linguistic interpretation. Pursuant to Article 32 of the Vienna Convention, we will take recourse to supplementary means of interpretation'.*[67]

2.37. The second branch of Article 32 VCLT plays a far less significant role in practice, as it is activated only where the application of the general rule leads to a manifestly absurd or unreasonable result. Hence, the application of such procedure in practice must be rather exceptional, because the application of such a mechanism would result in an unacceptable weakening of the rule incorporated in Article 31 VCLT. Consequently, the situations requiring the use of the supplementary means of interpretation pursuant to the second branch of Article 32 VCLT should be exceptional, and recourse to this method should only be allowed in extreme cases, especially because the absurdity or unreasonableness of the term interpreted pursuant to Article 31 VCLT must be manifest.

2.38. However, the author of this paper is of the opinion that the VCLT thereby does not prevent the use of the supplementary means of interpretation, but only endeavours to prevent the use of such means as the main interpretation procedure. Hence, the first step is to attempt an interpretation pursuant to Article 31 VCLT and reach a conclusion. If the attempt at interpretation using the general rules pursuant to Article 31 VCLT fails, the use of the supplementary means of interpretation is essentially unlimited. Consequently, the interpreter of the international treaty enjoys discretion as to whether or not they use these supplementary means. This is clear from another function performed by these methods and means, namely their use as *confirmation*. Indeed, these methods and means not only provide an instrument to perform the interpretation itself when the general means fail, they also provide an instrument to confirm the accuracy of the interpretation performed using the general and basic means of interpretation.

2.39. Article 33 VCLT then contains interpretation rules to be applied in cases in which the treaty is authenticated in two or more languages. The fundamental rule is that the language versions

---

[66] Chile – Price Band System and Safeguard Measures Relating to Certain Agricultural Products, WT/DS207/R, 03 May 2002, paragraph 7.35.
[67] Chile – Price Band System and Safeguard Measures Relating to Certain Agricultural Products, WT/DS207/R, 03 May 2002, paragraph 7.35.

Scope of Jurisdiction of Tribunals and International Authorities in Interpretation...

Czech Yearbook of International Law®

are equally binding, unless the parties agree otherwise. Hence, when interpreting the terms used, the courts must, as a rule, examine any and all binding language versions of the treaty. At the same time, it is presumed that the terms used in the treaty have the same meaning in each of the original texts. However, if the terms used have a different meaning in the individual language versions of the treaty with the same binding force, the tribunal should adopt as decisive the meaning that best reconciles the texts, having regard to the object and purpose of the treaty.[68]

2.40.   Applying the above-mentioned interpretation rules, the tribunal should arrive at a fully autonomous interpretation of the treaty, i.e. an interpretation that is by no means tied to the legal systems and traditions of the individual State parties.

2.41.   However, the VCLT fails to mention another supplementary component of autonomous interpretation, namely **comparative interpretation.**[69] This method, however, follows from the hierarchy itself of the sources of international law that lists judicial decisions as a subsidiary source.[70] The tribunal interpreting international treaty provisions ought to look up and analyse the interpretation of the particular treaty provision provided in the decisions made by the tribunals of other State parties. The persuasive force of those decisions might assist the tribunal in clarifying the concepts or mechanisms of the international treaty, especially if the tribunal has to choose between two or more alternative interpretations that all comply with the rules of interpretation set forth in the VCLT. Following such procedure, tribunals contribute to the desirable unification of the application practice. Nevertheless, it is necessary to have regard to the fact that the tribunal should primarily consider the persuasiveness of the reasoning and its applicability to the given case, and not merely apply the resulting solution of the foreign tribunal. Indeed, decisions of foreign tribunals are not binding on other tribunals and have effects only in terms of the persuasiveness of the applied reasoning.

2.42.   It is not inconceivable, though, that by using autonomous interpretation in compliance with the above-mentioned rules,

---

[68]   See Article 33 VCLT. However, the procedure in practice is frequently different and the individual language versions with an identical validity and binding force are attributed different authority. For more details, see also OLIVER DÖRR, VIENNA CONVENTION ON THE LAW OF TREATIES-A COMMENTARY, Berlin: Springer (2012), et. 594; ANTHONY AUST, MODERN TREATY LAW AND PRACTISE, Cambridge: Cambridge University Press (2007), et. 254; PHILIPP WENDEL, STATE RESPONSIBILITY FOR INTERFERENCES WITH THE FREEDOM OF NAVIGATION IN PUBLIC INTERNATINAL LAW, Berlin: Springer (2007), et. 61.

[69]   Martin Gebauer, *Uniform Law: General Principles and Autonomous Interpretation*, 5(4) UNIFORM LAW REVIEW 683-705 (2000).

[70]   See also Article 38(1)(d) of the Statute of the International Court of Justice.

the tribunal arrives at the same interpretation or solution that would be applied to an identical situation under national law. It is undisputable that two tribunals may arrive at the same interpretation using fundamentally different interpretation methods. Such a situation is certainly not problematic in any respect. But the important thing is that the tribunal interpreting an international treaty must always proceed in compliance with the rules stipulated in the VCLT in order to make sure that its interpretation of the treaty is indeed autonomous, i.e. completely independent of national law.

III.2. Issues Relating to Autonomous Interpretation

III.2.1. Temporality of Interpretation

2.43.   Autonomous interpretation of an international treaty naturally gives rise to a number of challenges, the solutions to which are being extensively discussed. One of the most frequently discussed issues is the temporality of interpretation, i.e. the determination of the time period to which the interpretation of the treaty should relate. Generally, the approach to this issue can be **twofold, i.e. the approach can be static or dynamic** (the latter also being referred to as the *evolutive interpretation*). The static approach requires an analysis of the meaning of the terms in the context of the time during which the treaty was concluded. The dynamic approach requires an analysis of the meaning of the terms at the time at which the treaty is being interpreted. These two approaches answer the question of whether the meaning of the terms used in the treaty may vary in time. This problem used to be discussed in connection with the drafting of the VCLT, but no preference for one or the other of the solutions was incorporated in the final version due to varying opinions of the delegates.[71] Similarly, no clear conclusion was reached by the Study Group of the UN International Law Commission in its 2006 Report.[72] Hence, the issue has remained unresolved ever since.[73]

---

[71]   See also 2 Yearbook of the International Law Commission 222 (1966), A/CN.4/SER.A/1966/Add.l, margin 16.
[72]   See also Martti Koskenniemi, *Fragmentation of International Law: Difficulties Arising From the Diversification and Expansion of International Law. Report of the Study Group on the Fragmentation of International Law*, UNITED NATIONS – GENERAL ASSEMBLY, Fifty-eighth session, Geneva, 01 May – 09 June and 03 July – 11 August 2006 (2006), et. 476–478, available at: https://undocs.org/en/A/CN.4/L.682 (accessed on 10 December 2021).
[73]   For more details, see also Zdeněk Nový, *Evolutionary Interpretation of International Treaties*, in ALEXANDER BĚLOHLÁVEK, NADĚŽDA ROZEHNALOVÁ, VIII CYIL – CZECH YEARBOOK OF INTERNATIONAL LAW, Den Haag: Lex Lata (2017), et. 205–240; CHRISTIAN DJEFFAL, STATIC

2.44. The *temporality* issue has been tackled by the arbitral tribunal of the Permanent Court of Arbitration (PCA) in the Hague in its 1932 award in *Las Palmas*. The arbitral tribunal held that a treaty ought to be interpreted in light of the international law that was in force at the time of its formation. The application of the treaty provision, however, should be governed by the rules of international law in force at the time of its application.[74] The same solution was also proposed during the drafting of the VCLT.[75] To this day, however, no rule defining the precise procedure for applying the dynamic interpretation has been formulated, let alone codified. Nonetheless, the ICJ came up with a relatively extensive explanation in this regard in *Costa Rica* v. *Nicaragua*, in which the ICJ held that where the parties have used generic terms in a treaty, the parties necessarily having been aware that the meaning of the terms was likely to evolve over time, and where the treaty has been entered into for a very long period or is 'of continuing duration', the parties must be presumed, as a general rule, to have intended those terms to have an evolving meaning.[76] The ICJ has thus clarified that there are certain requirements that must be fulfilled in order for the dynamic interpretation to be applicable.

2.45. Firstly, the term that is to be the subject of the dynamic interpretation should be of a general nature and should comprise a general and broad set of several classes of things. If the term used in the international treaty is very specific, the room for a dynamic interpretation is rather limited, or such interpretation is even entirely excluded.

2.46. Secondly, the treaty must be entered into for a very long period of time or be 'of continuing duration' in order to justify the application of the dynamic interpretation. If the international

---

AND EVOLUTIVE TREATY INTERPRETATION: A FUNCTIONAL RECONSTRUCTION, Cambridge: Cambridge University Press (2016); Taslim Elias, *The Doctrine of Intertemporal Law*, 74 AMERICAN JOURNAL OF INTERNATIONAL LAW 285 (1980); Malgosia Fitzmaurice, *Dynamic (Evolutive) Interpretation of Treaties Part I*, 21 HAGUE YEARBOOK OF INTERNATIONAL LAW 101 (2008); DW GREIG, INTERTEMPORALITY AND THE LAW OF TREATIES, London: British Institute of International and Comparative Law (2003).

[74] Arbitral award in *ad hoc* arbitration in *Island of Palmas*, U.N. Reports of International Arbitral Awards (23 January 1923), et. 845.

[75] See also 2 YEARBOOK OF THE INTERNATIONAL LAW COMMISSION 8-9 (1964), A/CN.4/ SER.A/1964/ADD.1, proposal for Article 56 (cit.): '*1. A treaty is to be interpreted in the light of the law in force at the time when the treaty was drawn up. 2. Subject to paragraph 1, the application of a treaty shall be governed by the rules of international law in force at the time when the treaty is applied.*'

[76] Judgment of the ICJ in Dispute Regarding Navigational and Related Rights (*Costa Rica* v. *Nicaragua*), of 13 July 2009, paragraph 66 (cit.): '[w]*here the parties have used generic terms in a treaty, the parties necessarily having been aware that the meaning of the terms was likely to evolve over time, and where the treaty has been entered into for a very long period or is "of continuing duration", the parties must be presumed, as a general rule, to have intended those terms to have an evolving meaning.*' Available at: https://www.icj-cij. org/public/files/case-related/133/133-20090713-JUD-01-00-EN.pdf (accessed on 19 January 2022).

treaty was entered into for a short period of time or for a specific event, the dynamic interpretation is inapplicable.

2.47. Thirdly, if the above-mentioned requirements are fulfilled, one may assume that the parties intended the application of the dynamic interpretation. But it is a rebuttable presumption that could be opposed by arguing that the parties, conversely, had a clear desire not to apply the dynamic interpretation to a particular term. In the said case, the ICJ focused on the issue of whether 'commercio' has an evolving meaning suitable for the use of the dynamic interpretation. The ICJ found that to be the case, because 'commercio' is a general term that refers to a class of activities. The international treaty of 1858,[77] which was the subject of the proceedings, had been entered into for an indefinite period of time and, consequently, the idea from the very beginning had been to set up a long-term legal regime between the parties.[78]

2.48. The author of this paper believes that a tribunal should always start with an analysis of whether or not the parties made any provisions in the treaty for the issue of temporality of interpretation and application, or at least laid the basis for construction of the issue. If this is not the case, the tribunal should attribute the meaning to the terms used in the treaty that the respective terms had when the treaty was concluded.[79] At the same time, the tribunal should consider in good faith the parties' intention when using the term. Concepts with general contents, which even the parties must presume to evolve over time, form an exception to this rule. These concepts should be interpreted by the tribunal in light of the circumstances attending their application.[80] The tribunal must also consider

---

[77] The Treaty of Territorial Limits between Costa Rica and Nicaragua of 15 April 1858, available at: https://jusmundi.com/en/document/treaty/en-treaty-of-limits-between-costa-rica-and-nicaragua-1858-canas-jerez-treaty-1858-thursday-15th-april-1858 (access on 19 January 2022).

[78] Dispute Regarding Navigational and Related Rights (*Costa Rica* v. *Nicaragua*), Judgment,ICJ, 13 July 2009, paragraph 67.

[79] Similarly, see also decision of the *ad hoc* Commission in *Delimitation of the border between Eritrea and Ethiopia* of 13 April 2002, Reports of international arbitral awards, 2006, Vol. XXV, et. 83–195, here et. 110 (cit.): *It has been argued before the Commission that in interpreting the Treaties it should apply the doctrine of 'contemporaneity.' By this the Commission understands that a treaty should be interpreted by reference to the circumstances prevailing when the treaty was concluded. This involves giving expressions (including names) used in the treaty the meaning that they would have possessed at that time. The Commission agrees with this approach and has borne it in mind in construing the Treaties.*

[80] Such as, for instance the terms used in the *Namibia* case, namely 'the strenuous conditions of the modern world' or 'the well-being and development'. See also the ICJ Advisory Opinion in *Legal Consequences for States of the Continued Presence of South Africa in Namibia (South West Africa)* of 21 June 1971, I.C.J. Reports 1971, paragraph 53 (cit.): *Mindful as it is of the primary necessity of interpreting an instrument in accordance with the intentions of the parties at the time of its conclusion, the Court is bound to take into account the fact that the concepts embodied in Article 22 of the Covenant–'the strenuous conditions of the modern world' and 'the well-being and development' of the peoples concerned-were not static, but were by definition evolutionary, as also, therefore, was the concept of the 'sacred trust'. The parties to the Covenant must consequently be deemed to have accepted them as such. That is why, viewing the institutions of 1919,*

the nature of the international treaty being interpreted. For instance, the ECtHR has consistently held that the ECHR is a living instrument of law that must be interpreted in light of present-day conditions, primarily in order to make sure that the protection of fundamental rights afforded by this Convention is real, not merely illusory.[81] In doing so, the tribunal should always make sure that the resulting interpretation is not contrary to the purpose of the treaty and ensures its functional application.

III.2.2. Uniformity of Interpretation

2.49.   The uniformity of interpretation of an international treaty is a fundamental objective that should also be accomplished, ideally, by using autonomous interpretation. However, if the interpretation of the treaty is not subject to the jurisdiction of a single tribunal, one may frequently encounter the problem of divergent interpretations of the same provision by different tribunals, leading to inconsistencies in the application of the treaty. This problem fundamentally jeopardises the purpose and the functioning of the international treaty. In theory, no such differences should exist, because tribunals are obliged to interpret treaty provisions independently of the national law and in compliance with the VCLT interpretation rules or, as applicable, the interpretation rules incorporated in the particular international treaty. Theoretically, two foreign tribunals should, when applying the same interpretation rules, arrive at an identical interpretation of the respective treaty provision.

2.50.   But the practice is traditionally more complex, and differences arise in the interpretation of treaties. The reasons vary, but the most common cause is probably the complexity and intricacy of the entire process of interpretation, which the tribunals implement according to very generally formulated rules.

2.51.   The solution to this problem is not straightforward. First and foremost, it is necessary to make sure that all tribunals interpreting the treaty proceed completely independently of the national legal systems and let the interpretation be governed

---

the Court must take into consideration the changes which have occurred in the supervening half-century, and its interpretation cannot remain unaffected by the subsequent development of law, through the Charter of the United Nations and by way of customary law. Moreover, an international instrument has to be interpreted and applied within the framework of the entire legal system prevailing at the time of the interpretation.;

[81]   See also judgment of the ECtHR in *Demir and Baykara* v. *Turkey*, 12 November 2008, Application No. 34503/97, paragraph 68 (cit.): *'[T]he Court further observes that it has always referred to the "living" nature of the Convention, which must be interpreted in the light of present-day conditions, and that it has taken account of evolving norms of national and international law in its interpretation of Convention provisions (see Soering v. the United Kingdom, 7 July 1989, § 102, Series A no. 161; Vo v. France [GC], no. 53924/00, § 82, ECHR 2004-VIII; and Mamatkulov and Askarov v. Turkey [GC], nos. 46827/99 and 46951/99, § 121, ECHR 2005-I).'*

only by sources of international law. If there are two or more available alternative interpretations, it is also desirable that the tribunals execute a comparative study and review the interpretation of the same provision by foreign tribunals. In the interest of the unification of treaty interpretation, a persuasive reasoning of foreign tribunals could serve as an authority on interpretation that the tribunal reflects in its interpretation.

IV. Case-law

2.52. Generally, the procedure adopted by both national and international courts and tribunals in the autonomous interpretation of treaties ought to be identical. Hence, they should apply: (i) special interpretation rules set forth in the international treaty being interpreted, (ii) the interpretation rules provided for in Articles 31 to 33 VCLT, which are binding on the signatories of the treaty, as well as all others, because they represent customary international law that must always be applied due to the nature of international treaties as an instrument of international law.

2.53. If the resulting interpretation is ambiguous, the interpreting tribunals may supplement their considerations by a comparison of the case-law of foreign tribunals (authorities) that were called upon to interpret the same provision in the past that is the subject matter of interpretation in the respective case at hand. Autonomous interpretation can essentially be deemed a method of reasoning. In this connection, *Gebauer* emphasises the role of comparative law, arguing that regard must be had to the decisions of foreign tribunals in order to serve as sources of reasoning, i.e. ensure that their consideration could, despite the non-binding force of such foreign decisions, facilitate uniform autonomous interpretation. Hence, the importance of such decisions consists in their quality.[82] To this end, it is thus necessary to make sure that the tribunal analyses any relevant cases in great detail, disregards immaterial differences or similarities and, conversely, applies connections and differences of significant importance.

2.54. The need for a uniform autonomous interpretation lies at the very heart of the legal principles of legitimate expectations and legal certainty. By making similar decisions in similar cases and by duly considering the context, the tribunal ascertains whether the case submitted to the tribunal is identical or analogous to a previously interpreted case. After all, States and their tribunals

---

[82] Martin Gebauer, *Uniform Law, General Principles and Autonomous Interpretation*, 5(4) UNIFORM LAW REVIEW 683-705 (2000).

Scope of Jurisdiction of Tribunals and International Authorities in Interpretation...

Czech Yearbook of International Law®

are often bound to proceed in such manner, for instance, under Article 7 CISG or similar provisions of other international treaties. Tearing out of context means severing the causal nexus between the acts being assessed and the decision itself. Hence, national courts must have regard to specific factual and legal circumstances – otherwise, the reference to other decisions would be empty and hollow. A laconic *ratio decidendi* will not do justice to justice and it is not a desirable situation, despite the fact that it is presently considered as common practice. Hence, as pertinently argued by *Pelikánová*, a legal norm, whether described in any particular convention or arising from an agreement, obviously never exists only for the sake of existence itself, and its being has a purpose and it will always be embedded in a particular context in order to influence the behaviour of its addressees.[83]

2.55. Consistent case-law of State parties can also be considered as subsequent practice for the purposes of interpretation, because the case-law of tribunals of foreign countries bound by the treaty may also establish an understanding regarding interpretation, or at least an indication of such an understanding. This does not, however, give rise to *stare decisis*, and it is more likely a *relative precedent*. Interpretation of an international treaty naturally also requires the use of the rules of international customary law codified in the VCLT on the law of treaties.[84] National courts have engaged in such comparisons for some time already. When interpreting a source of law that is based on an international treaty, it is necessary to start with an interpretation of each *ratio decidendi*, with special importance being attributed to legal comparison (comparison with the law of other State parties). However, the requirement for, if possible, a uniform interpretation in all State parties must not preclude the possibility of having regard to the principles of other similar sources of law and thus departing from the interpretation principles, should such means of interpretation fail.[85,86]

---

[83] Irena Pelikánová, *Reason, Law and Interpretation*, 12 BULLETIN ADVOKACIE 23-31 (2010), (cit.): 'A *legal rule can never be perceived as self-serving, it always applies in a specific context and aims at a specific resultant behaviour of the addressees of the rule.*'
[84] Richard Happ, *Anwendbarkeit völkerrechtlicher Auslegungsmethoden auf das UN-Kaufrecht*, 5 RECHT DER INTERNATIONALEN WIRTSCHAFT 376, 376 (1997).
[85] Decision of the Supreme Court of Austria (*Oberstes Gerichtshof*), Case 4Ob594/78, 30 January 1979, available at the website of the Federal Chancellery of Austria at: https://www.ris.bka.gv.at/Dokument. wxe?ResultFunctionToken=876c8b08-ceea-4a3b-8778-55c377125bd2(accessed on 19 January 2022).
[86] A similar approach has also been adopted by the Czech Supreme Court. See judgment of the Supreme Court of the Czech Republic of 19 October 2016, Case 31 Cdo 1570/2015, paragraphs 16, 17. Similarly, see also judgment of the Supreme Court of the Czech Republic – chamber, of 17 December 2014, Case 23 Cdo 2702/2012.

2.56. Such approach may consequently mean the hybridisation and mutual approximation of the Anglo-Saxon system of 'precedents' and the continental 'legislative' system. However, this will not result in any transformation, only in the monitoring of changes in the interpretation climate. No new international doctrine is to be expected yet in terms of *stare decisis*; on the other hand, it is legitimate to require the tribunals to be versed in the contextual *realia* in analogous decisions rendered by other tribunals.[87]

2.57. Consequently, one may conclude, in connection with the above, that if a tribunal considers the reasoning and conclusions articulated by foreign tribunals as persuasive in terms of their applicability to the given case, and in compliance with the interpretation rules set forth in the international treaty being interpreted and in the VCLT, the tribunal may have regard to and reflect them in its decision in the interest of the uniform interpretation and application of the international treaty.

2.58. In other words, the manner in which other tribunals (international tribunals or national courts) apply autonomous interpretation is irrelevant for the interpreting tribunal, because all institutions and individuals interpreting the international treaty provisions should proceed according to the same rules of autonomous interpretation.

2.59. The only aspect potentially relevant for the tribunal called upon to provide an interpretation is the determination of how other tribunals construed the same provision of the international treaty that is submitted to the respective tribunal for interpretation. When applying this comparative method, however, the tribunal should primarily consider the case-law of the tribunals that have interpreted the same provision of the relevant international treaty. Indeed, each international treaty is encased in a different context, which has to be considered by the tribunals in their autonomous interpretation in compliance with Articles 31 to 33 VCLT. Similarly, no difference should theoretically exist between the autonomous interpretation performed by international courts and tribunals and the autonomous interpretation provided by national courts and tribunals. Indeed, all interpreters should apply the same procedure.

---

[87] John Felemegas, *The United Nations Convention on Contracts for the International Sale of Goods: Article 7 and Uniform Interpretation*, REVIEW OF THE CONVENTION ON CONTRACTS FOR THE INTERNATIONAL SALE OF GOODS 115–265 (2000–2001) (under the citation no. 525). See also James E. Bailey, *Facing the Truth: Seeing the Convention on Contracts for the International Sale of Goods as an Obstacle to a Uniform Law of International Sales*, 32 CORNELL INTERNATIONAL LAW JOURNAL 273– 317 (1999) (under the citation no. 125).

2.60. In any case, decisions of foreign tribunals (national courts or international tribunals) are not, as a rule, binding on the interpreting tribunal throughout the process of the autonomous interpretation. The interpreting tribunal should have regard to their decisions only after the tribunal performs the autonomous interpretation of the given provision in compliance with the procedure specified above. These decisions should be relevant for the conclusions of the tribunal only if the tribunal is faced with two or more alternative interpretations as a result of its own autonomous interpretation. In such case, the tribunal should undertake a meticulous comparative analysis and ponder which foreign tribunal's solution is the most suitable due to the persuasiveness of the foreign tribunal's reasoning from the perspective of the autonomous meaning and uniform application of the provision being interpreted.

2.61. The application of the interpretation rules codified in the VCLT has become an unquestionable standard for the interpretation of all international treaties. In other words, it has been generally accepted that the interpretation of an international treaty requires that the interpreter proceed in compliance with the rules set forth in Articles 31 to 33 VCLT, which represent consistent customary law. For instance, the ICJ has applied the said interpretation rules ever since the VCLT was adopted and in essentially all cases submitted to it.[88] A similar approach has also been adopted by other international courts and tribunals, such as the ECtHR, the International Tribunal for the Law of the Sea, WTO dispute resolution bodies, as well as a number of arbitral tribunals.[89]

IV.1.   Case-law of International Tribunals

IV.1.1.   *European Court of Human Rights*

2.62. Autonomous interpretation has been regularly addressed by the ECtHR. The history of the ECtHR requires a few words about Protocol No. 16 to the European Convention on Human Rights (ECHR), which entered into force in 2018 and enables

---

[88]   OLIVER DÖRR, KIRSTEN SCHMALENBACH, VIENNA CONVENTION ON THE LAW OF TREATIES: A COMMENTARY, New York: Springer (2012), section 3 – Interpretation of treaties, margin 6 (cit.): '*It is by now generally recognized that the provisions on treaty interpretation contained in Arts 31 and 32 reflect pre-existing customary international law. For many years now, the ICJ has applied the rules of interpretation laid down in the Convention as codified custom to virtually every treaty that came before it.*'
[89]   See also ANTHONY AUST, MODERN TREATY LAW AND PRACTICE, New York: Cambridge University Press (2nd ed. 2000), et. 230; OLIVER DÖRR, KIRSTEN SCHMALENBACH, VIENNA CONVENTION ON THE LAW OF TREATIES: A COMMENTARY, New York: Springer (2012), section 3 – Interpretation of treaties, margin 6, in which the authors quote a number of specific decisions in connection with each of the dispute resolution authorities.

Czech Yearbook of International Law®

the highest tribunals and States to request that the ECtHR give advisory opinions on questions of principle relating to the interpretation or application of the ECHR. From the perspective of the ECtHR case-law and the contribution to international practice, it is important that the ECtHR office searches for decisions (i) considered significant for specific periods, because, *inter alia*, they represent a major benefit for the evolution of case-law and address issues of broader importance, or (ii) contributing to the interpretation and clarification of principles underlying the ECHR or the protection of human rights as such. Such cases then frequently provide guidance with respect to the autonomous interpretation of various terms and concepts, both from the perspective of the interpretation and application of the ECHR itself, and from a broader perspective, i.e. with respect to the international interpretation of concepts in the area of fundamental and human rights. The qualified and organised basis of the ECtHR thus ensures that the ECHR essentially has at its disposal its own mechanism for the creation and dissemination of a uniform interpretation basis. Hence, if a particular international treaty, such as the ECHR, has such a potential at its disposal, the significance of the case-law is even more enhanced; on the other hand, the importance of the individualisation of each individual case is not to be diminished. Admittedly, autonomous interpretation must always be implemented from the perspective of each individual international act (international treaty); nevertheless, the interpretation mechanisms of international treaties, such as the ECHR, also represent an important guidance for broader international practice from the perspective of the general interpretation of sources and instruments of international law. See, for instance, the recent clarification provided by the ECtHR in respect of the interpretation of the fundamental principles of *ne bis in idem*,[90] etc.

2.63. In *Engel* v. *The Netherlands*,[91] the ECtHR performed an autonomous interpretation of '*criminal charge*' pursuant to Article 6 ECHR. In order to assess whether a particular sanction has a criminal nature, the ECtHR stipulated three criteria;[92] the

---

[90] *Aurelian-Erik Mihalache* v. *Romania*, Judgment of the ECtHR, Application No. 54012/10, 08 July 2019.
[91] *Engel, van der Wiel, de Wit, Dona and Schul* v. *The Netherlands*, Judgment of the ECtHR, Application No. 5100/71, 5101/71, 5102/71, 5354/72 and 5372, 08 June 1976, The ECtHR has held that the concept of *criminal charge* has an autonomous meaning in terms of Article 6 ECHR regardless of the classification used by the national legal systems (paragraph 81).
[92] In this regard, see also the following decisions (selection from recent years): judgment of the ECtHR, Application No. 24130/11 and 29758/11, *A and B* v. *Norway*, 15 November 2016, judgment of the ECtHR, Application No. 55391/13, 06 November 2018, *Ramos Nunes de Carvalho e Sá* v. *Portugal*, paragraph 107; judgment of the ECtHR, Application No. 54012/10, 08 July 2019, *Aurelian-Erik Mihalache* v. *Romania*, paragraph 54.

Czech Yearbook of International Law®

assessment according to national law has been considered by the ECtHR merely as an *informative circumstance* or, in this particular case, as one of the evaluation criteria. The ECtHR held that the most important factor is the assessment of the seriousness of the act and the harshness of the stipulated penalty. Conversely, classification of a particular act according to the governing law, according to the ECtHR, plays no major role. The author is of the opinion that using classification according to national law as one of the evaluation parameters can be considered as rather exceptional in criminal matters, because criminal offences (acts that could be sanctioned by criminal penalties) could be highly contingent on the location, i.e. dependant, *inter alia*, on local circumstances, which may potentially significantly differ from one country or region to another. However, a comparison of the classifications adopted by various State signatories may also serve as a guidance; such procedure could, depending on the facts of the case, eliminate potential extremes from the perspective of an autonomous assessment. Hence, the ECtHR endeavoured to discover the common denominator of all parties to the treaty. The ECtHR thereby stipulated entirely independent criteria that the tribunals must have regard to in their interpretation of the term 'criminal' as incorporated in Article 6 ECHR. The ECtHR also stipulated that the interpretation of terms contained in the ECHR cannot be governed by national law. The ECtHR considered the individual evaluation criteria as alternative, not cumulative.[93] The cumulative application of the evaluation criteria is only conceivable if no clear interpretation can be arrived at using a single criterion,[94] or if the use of a single criterion is impossible.[95] But the conclusion regarding the alternative use of the individual criteria, as articulated by

---

[93] Judgment of the ECtHR, Application No. 61821/00, 01 February 2005, *Cristian Ziliberberg* v. *Modova*, paragraph 31 et seq.

[94] See also Handbook on European law relating to access to justice, Luxembourg: Publications Office of the European Union (2016), et. 26–26, available at: https://www.echr.coe.int/Documents/Handbook_access_justice_ENG.PDF (accessed on 19 January 2022).

[95] See also judgment of the ECtHR, Applications No. 39665/98 and No. 40086/98, 09 October 2003, *Ezeh and Connors* v. *United Kingdom*, paragraph 86; see also MARIA BERGSTRÖM, ANNA JONSSON CORNELL, EUROPEAN POLICE AND CRIMINAL LAW CO-OPERATION, London: Bloomsbury Publishing (2014), et. 117; DENIS ABELS, PRISONERS OF THE INTERNATIONAL COMMUNITY: THE LEGAL POSITION OF PERSONS DETAINED AT INTERNATIONAL CRIMINAL TRIBUNALS, Berlin: Springer Science & Business Media (2012), et. 399; SUSAN EASTON, CHRISTINE PIPER, SENTENCING AND PUNISHMENT: THE QUEST FOR JUSTICE, Oxford: Oxford University Press (2012), et. 292 et al. See also judgment of the ECtHR, Application No. 14939/03, 10 February 2009, *Sergey Zolotukhin* v. *Russia*, paragraph 53, judgment of the ECtHR, Applications Nos. 24130/11 and 29758/11, 15 November 2016, *A and B* v. *Norway*, paragraph 105, judgment of the ECtHR, Application No. 26780/95, 28 October 1999, *Escoubet* v. *Belgium*, paragraph 32; see also JOHAN BOUCHT, THE LIMITS OF ASSET CONFISCATION: ON THE LEGITIMACY OF EXTENDED APPROPRIATION OF CRIMINAL PROCEEDS, London: Bloomsbury Publishing (2017), et. 123; WILLIAM A. SCHABAS, THE EUROPEAN CONVENTION ON HUMAN RIGHTS: A COMMENTARY, Oxford: Oxford University Press (2015), et. 283 et al.

the ECtHR, is rather debatable. Such a categorical conclusion could, conversely, result in prioritising interpretation based on a single criterion and eliminating a completely or significantly different interpretation based on another criterion. Hence, the assessment should principally be performed according to all conceivable criteria or, as applicable, according to all criteria that could be deemed primary; only then may it become necessary to look for potential intersections or use substitute criteria.

2.64. The decision in *Engel* was immediately followed by ECtHR's decision in *König* v. *Germany*[96] in which the ECtHR also subsumed the phrase *civil rights and obligations* under autonomous interpretation. However, the criterion according to national law becomes more important with respect to civil rights or obligations, as opposed to criminal offences (criminal charges), because it is necessary for the classification to be made by national law; the qualification under the ECHR, from the perspective of ECtHR jurisdiction, may only follow afterwards.[97]

2.65. Another judgment in which the ECtHR applied autonomous interpretation is *Chassagnou and Others*,[98] in which the ECtHR, inter alia, addressed the issue of whether or not a local hunters' association is an *association* in terms of Article 11 ECHR. France, as the respondent, argued that hunters' associations are public-law corporations entrusted with the exercise of State power by the law and, consequently, do not fall within the scope of Article 11 ECHR. The ECtHR rejected such reasoning and held that if the State signatories were allowed to formally determine whether an association or a corporation was a public-law body, and thereby remove the entity from the scope of Article 11 ECHR, the purpose and object of the ECHR would be jeopardised. Hence, the ECtHR was of the opinion that the term *association* must possess an autonomous meaning. Its classification according to French law only has relative value for the interpretation, and constitutes no more than a *starting-point*. The ECtHR subsequently reviewed the valid and

---

[96] Judgment of the ECtHR, Application No. 6232/73, 28 June 1978, *Dr. Eberhard König* v. *Germany*, paragraphs 88 and 89.

[97] Judgment of the ECtHR, Application No. 37575/04, 03 April 2012, *Boulois* v. *Luxembourg*, paragraph 90. Such rights in terms of the ECHR include, according to the case-law of the ECtHR, the following rights: tax matters except those falling within the scope of criminal sanctions (judgment of the ECtHR, Application No. 44759/98, 12 July 2001, *Ferrazzini* v. *Italy*, paragraph 29), matters relating to the entry, stay and deportation of aliens (judgment of the ECtHR, Application No. 399652/98, 5 October 2000 *Maaouia* v. *France*, paragraph 40), or matters relating to passive voting right (judgment of the ECtHR, Application No. 24194/94, 21 October 1997, *Pierre-Bloch* v. *France*, paragraphs 49–52). See also Handbook on European law relating to access to justice, Luxembourg: Publications Office of the European Unio (2016), et. 27–28, available at: https://www.echr.coe.int/Documents/Handbook_access_justice_ENG.PDF (accessed on 19 January 2022).

[98] Judgment of the ECtHR, Applications Nos. 25088/94, 28331/95 and 28443/95, 29 April 1999, *Chassagnou and Others* v. *France*.

54 |

Scope of Jurisdiction of Tribunals and International Authorities in Interpretation...

Czech Yearbook of International Law®

applicable French law on hunters' associations[99] and concluded that it is an *association* in terms of the ECHR, primarily in view of the purpose and object of Articles 9 to 11 ECHR, which ought to guarantee freedom of thought and opinion, freedom of expression, and freedom of association to individuals.[100]

IV.1.2. Inter-American Court of Human Rights

2.66. The Inter-American Court of Human Rights[101] also applied autonomous interpretation of the law. In *Mayagna (Sumo) Awas Tingni Community* v. *Nicaragua*, the Court held as follows:

> *[T]he terms of an international human rights treaty have an autonomous meaning, for which reason they cannot be made equivalent to the meaning given to them in domestic law. Furthermore, such human rights treaties are live instruments whose interpretation must adapt to the evolution of the times and, specifically, to current living conditions.*[102]

---

[99] The ECtHR reviewed, *inter alia*, the process of formation of the association, conditions of membership, election of the chairman, powers of the association, etc.

[100] Judgment of the ECtHR, Applications Nos. 25088/94, 28331/95 and 28443/95, 29 April 1999, *Chassagnou and Others* v. *France*, paragraphs 100–102.

[101] The Inter-American Court of Human Rights has jurisdiction to interpret and to resolve disputes arising from the American Convention on Human Rights adopted under the auspices of the Organization of American States (OAS) on 22 November 1969 (O.A.S.T.S. No. 36, 1144 et seq.), which entered into force on 18 July 1978.

[102] Judgment of the Inter-American Court of Human Rights of 31 August 2001 in *Mayagna (Sumo) Awas Tingni Community* v. *Nicaragua*, see the judgment on *Merits, Reparations and Costs*, paragraph 146 (specific application of this approach in relation to the discussed issue in the merits was incorporated primarily in paragraph 148 of the decision). In this regard, the judgment invokes the Advisory Opinion OC-16/99 of 01 October 1999, in *The Right to Information on Consular Assistance in the Framework of Guarantees for Due Legal Process*). A Series No. 16, paragraph 114. The above-mentioned judgment of the Inter-American Court of Human Rights is also available at: http://www.corteidh.or.cr/docs/casos/articulos/seriec_79_ing.pdf (accessed on 19 January 2022). The decision is cited as IACtHR, 06 September 2002, in academic literature. See also Jonathan P. Vuotto, *Awas Tingni v. Nicaragua: International Precedent for Indigenous Land Rights?*, 22 BOSTON UNIVERSITY INTERNATIONAL LAW JOURNAL 232 (2004); Leonardo J. Alvarado, *Prospects and Challenges in the Implementation of Indigenous People's Human Rights in International Law: Lessons From the Case of Awas Tingni v. Nicaragua*, 24(3) ARIZONA JOURNAL OF INTERNATIONAL & COMPARATIVE LAW 612 (2007); MARTIN FORREST, STEPHEN SCHNABLY, RICHARD WILSON, JONATHAN SIMON, MARK TUSHNET, INTERNATIONAL HUMAN RIGHTS & HUMANITARIAN LAW: TREATIES, CASES & ANALYSIS, Cambridge: Cambridge University Press (2006), et. 913 et seq.; Alexandra Xanthaki, *Indigenous Rights in International law Over the Last 10 Years and Future Developments*, 10 MELBOURNE JOURNAL OF INTERNATIONAL LAW (2009), available at: https://law.unimelb.edu.au/__data/assets/pdf_file/0009/1686060/Xanthaki.pdf (accessed on 19 January 2022); Jo M. Pasqualucci, *International Indigenous Land Rights: A Critique of the Jurisprudence of the Inter-American Court of Human Rights in Light of the United Nationals Declaration on the Rights of Indigenous Peoples*, 27(1) WISCONSIN INTERNATIONAL LAW JOURNAL 65 (2009); GEORG NOLTE, TREATIES AND SUBSEQUENT PRACTICE, Oxford: Oxford University Press (2013), et. 270; Valerio De Oliveira Mazzuoli, Dilton Ribeiro, *Indigenous Rights Before the Inter-American Court of Human Rights: A Call for a Pro Individual Interpretation*, 2 THE TRANSNATIONAL HUMAN RIGHTS REVIEW 32-62 (2015), available at: https://digitalcommons.osgoode.yorku.ca/cgi/viewcontent.cgi?referer=https://www.google.cz/&httpsredir=1&article=1013&context=thr (accessed od 19 January 2022); Diana Contreras-Garduño, Sebastiaan Rombouts, *Collective Reparations for Indigenous Communities Before the Inter-American Court of Human Rights*, 27(72) MERKOURIOUS – UTRECHT JOURNAL OF INTERNATIONAL AND EUROPEAN LAW 4-17 (2010); EIRIK BJORGE, THE EVOLUTIONARY INTERPRETATION OF TREATIES, Oxford:

2.67. This approach also complies with the conclusions made in the referenced decisions mentioned above. It is noteworthy that the conclusion reached by the Court in the said case and articulated on the merits was indeed revolutionary in terms of adjudicating the ownership title belonging to members of a community through the collective ownership title of the original people.[103] Evolutive interpretation of international treaties and international standards as such is especially prominent in the area of human rights, as outlined above in connection with the case-law of the ECtHR. An interesting aspect transpires in this particular connection, important for the interpretation of international treaties, namely the interaction between international legal instruments.[104] Hence, a comparison with the interpretations of similar concepts contained in other international treaties undoubtedly constitutes one of the auxiliary approaches in the interpretation of concepts and terms in international treaties. In such case, however, it is imperative to make a thorough assessment of the contents, object and purpose, as well as the circumstances attending the conclusion of such *other* international treaties, and especially the issue of whether any qualified connection exists to the interpreted international treaty. Thus, in *Mayagna (Sumo) Awas Tingni Community* v. *Nicaragua*, the Court emphasised the need for reflecting objective criteria. At the same time, however, the Court highlighted that the interpretation of certain concepts and

---

Oxford University Press (2014); Bryan Neihart, *Awas Tingni v. Nicaragua Reconsidered: Grounding Indigenous Peoples' Land Rights in Religious Freedom*, 42(1) DENVER JOURNAL OF INTERNATIONAL LAW AND POLICY (2013); Núria Reguart-Segarra, *Business, Indigenous Peoples' Rights and Security in the Case Law of the Inter-American Court of Human Rights*, 4(1) BUSINESS AND HUMAN RIGHTS JOURNAL 109–130 (2019); Francisco Pascual-Vives, *Consensus-Based Interpretation of Regional Human Rights Treaties*, 129 INTERNATIONAL STUDIES IN HUMAN RIGHTS 114–115 (2019); Tara Ward, *The Right to Free, Prior, and Informed Consent: Indigenous Peoples' Participation Rights within International Law*, 10(2) NORTHWESTERN JOURNAL OF INTERNATIONAL HUMAN RIGHTS 56 (2011), available at: https://scholarlycommons.law.northwestern.edu/cgi/viewcontent.cgi?article=1125&context=njihr (accessed on 19 January 2022); Siegrried Wiessner, *The Cultural Rights of Indigenous Peoples: Achievements and Continuing Challenges*, 22(1) EUROPEAN JOURNAL OF INTERNATIONAL LAW 121-140 (2011), available at: https://academic.oup.com/ejil/article/22/1/121/436597 (accessed od 19 January 2022); Lucas Lixinski, *Treaty Interpretation by the Inter-American Court of Human Rights: Expansionism at the Service of the Unity of International Law*, 21(3) THE EUROPEAN JOURNAL OF INTERNATIONAL LAW 597 (2010), available at: https://academic.oup.com/ejil/article/21/3/585/508638 (accessed od 19 January 2022).
[103] See also Leonardo J. Alvarado, *Prospects and Challenges in the Implementation of Indigenous Peoples' Human Rights in International Law: Lessons From the Case of Awas Tingni v. Nicaragua*, 24(3) ARIZONA JOURNAL OF INTERNATIONAL & COMPARATIVE LAW 612 (2007).
[104] See also Alan Boyle, *Soft Law in International Law-Making* in MALCOLM EVANS, INTERNATIONAL LAWS, Oxford: Oxford University Press (2nd ed. 2006), et. 148, as well as Alexandra Xanthaki, *Indigenous Rights in International law Over the Last 10 Years and Future Developments*, 10 MELBOURNE JOURNAL OF INTERNATIONAL LAW (2009), available at: https://law.unimelb.edu.au/__data/assets/pdf_file/0009/1686060/Xanthaki.pdf (accessed on 19 January 2022), invoking the previously mentioned author in footnote 58.

Scope of Jurisdiction of Tribunals and International Authorities in Interpretation...

Czech Yearbook of International Law®

terms must be perceived as a whole,[105] i.e. as an interpretation of a particular international treaty as a whole.

IV.1.3. Decision-making of WTO (World Trade Organization)

2.68.   Decisions rendered under the auspices of the WTO represent another example of the institutionalised decision-making practice of an international forum. This applies, for instance, to the WTO decision in *Arguments made by the European Communities in Korea – Definitive Safeguard Measure on Imports of Certain Dairy Products*. In this case, the decision-making authority found as follows in its Report (cit.):

> *'[T]he interpretation of Article 5.1 of the Agreement on Safeguards, in the light of its wording, context and purpose and in accordance with the principle of effective treaty interpretation, mandates this conclusion: each provision was drafted with its own meaning and must be given its autonomous meaning when being interpreted. On the contrary, by denying the binding character of the necessity requirement except within very strict limits, Korea is trying to unduly reduce the scope of its obligations under the WTO Agreements, and thus the rights arising thereunder to the European Communities. Reduction or modification of rights and obligations is emphatically not allowed under the WTO.'[106]*

---

[105]   See also GEORG NOLTE, TREATIES AND SUBSEQUENT PRACTICE, Oxford: Oxford University Press (2013), et. 270.

[106]   WTO Panel Report in WT/DS98: *Korea – Definitive Safeguard Measure on Imports of Certain Dairy Products (Korea – Dairy), European Communities* v. *Korea*, third party: USA, 21 June 1999, paragraph 4.649. As concerns this case, it should also be noted that the Appellate Body departed from the opinion of the first-instance authority in certain aspects concerning the interpretation of the international treaty, albeit not in the quoted part. See also: YANG GUOHUA, BRYAN MERCUIO, LI YONGJIE, WTO DISPUTE SETTLEMENT UNDERSTANDING: A DETAILED INTERPRETATION, The Hague: Kluwer Law International (2005), et. 224; AUGUST REINISCH, MARY FOOTER, CHRISTINA BINDER, INTERNATIONAL LAW AND ... SELECT PROCEEDINGS OF THE EUROPEAN SOCIETY OF INTERNATIONAL LAW, Oxford: Bloomsbury Publishing (2016), et. 124; Daniel Pickard, Tina Potuto Kimble, *Can U.S. Safeguard Actions Survive WTO Review: Section 201 Investigations in International Trade Law*, 29 LOYOLA OF LOS ANGELES INTERNATIONAL AND COMPARATIVE LAW REVIEW 43-45 (2007); Lee Yongshik, *Test of Multilateralism in International Trade: U.S. Steel Safeguards*, 25(1) NORTHWESTERN JOURNAL OF INTERNATIONAL LAW & BUSINESS (2004); Terrence Stewart, Patrick McDonough, Marta Prado, *Opportunities in the WTO for Increased Liberalization of Goods: Making Sure the Rules Work for All and That Special Needs are Addressed*, 24(1) FORDHAM INTERNATIONAL LAW JOURNAL 652–725 (2000); Cherie O. Taylor, *Impossible Cases: Lessons from the First Decade of WTO Dispute Settlement*, 28(2) UNIVERSITY OF PENNSYLVANIA JOURNAL OF INTERNATIONAL ECONOMIC LAW 325-326 (2007); Henry Gao, *Taming the Dragon: China's Experience in the WTO Dispute Settlement System*, 34(4) RESEARCH COLLECTION SCHOOL OF LAW, SINGAPORE MANAGEMENT UNIVERSITY 369-392 (2007), available at: https://ink.library.smu.edu.sg/cgi/viewcontent.cgi?article=1800&context=sol_research (accessed on 19 January 2022); Ho Cheol Kim, *Burden of Proof and the Prima Facie Case: The Evolving History and its Applications in the WTO Jurisprudence*, 6(3) RICHMOND JOURNAL OF GLOBAL LAW &

IV.1.4. Decision-making Practice of ICSID and Other Decisions in Investment Protection Disputes

2.69. Autonomous interpretation of investment protection treaties has been repeatedly addressed by arbitral tribunals established for resolving disputes within the framework of the ICSID.[107] The ICSID case-law is mostly a typical example of 'searching and finding' an autonomous interpretation. The domain of economic transactions has indeed revealed that a consistent international interpretation of specific terms and concepts is very hard to find.[108] The reason is that this area is typical for the overlapping of multiple laws and regulations with varying purposes and different origins. Apart from special national regimes reflecting territorial specifics, including the peculiarities of various investment interests of the individual States, mostly depending on the particular level of their economic development, the area represents a platform upon which safety, currency, climatic and other interests combine. The use of an interpretation developed in the case-law of other fora or international interpretation practice in relation to a different international treaty could be very problematic, because one and the same State participates in certain international initiatives, while abstains from others that are contrary to the State's idea of a particular type of international cooperation, and consequently reflect the specifics of the particular country. The use of the

---

BUSINESS 254 (2007).

[107] See also: Alberto Álvarez Jiménez, *The interpretation of necessity clauses in bilateral investment treaties after the recent ICSID annulment decision*, 94 REVISTA ACADÉMICA E INSTITUTIONES DE LA UCPR (2014); Annamaria Viterbo, *Dispute Settlement Over Exchange Measures Affecting Trade and Investments: The Overlapping Jurisdictions of the IMF, WTO, and the ICSID* (13 July 2008), Society of International Economic Law (SIEL) Inaugural Conference (2008), available: https://papers.ssrn.com/sol3/papers.cfm?abstract_id=1154673 (accessed on 19 January 2022); William Burke-White, Anndreas von Staden, *Investment Protection in Extraordinary Times: The Interpretation and Application of Non-Precluded Measures Provisions in Bilateral Investment Treaties*, 48(2) VIRGINIA JOURNAL OF INTERNATIONAL LAW 307-410 (2008); Todd Henderson, James C. Spindler, *Corporate Heroin: A Defense of Perks, Executive Loans, and Conspicuous Consumption*, 93 GEORGETOWN LAW JOURNAL 1835 (2004–2005); Martin Paparinskis, *Franck Charles Arif v. Republic of Moldova: Courts Behaving Nicely and What to Do About It*, 31(1) ICSID REVIEW – FOREIGN INVESTMENT LAW JOURNAL 122-128 (2016); Hussein Haeri, *A Tale of Two Standards: 'Fair and Equitable Treatment' and the Minimum Standard in International Law: The Gillis Wetter Prize*, 27(1) ARBITRATION INTERNATIONAL 27-46 (2011); Steffen Hindelang, *The Autonomy of the European Legal Order* in MARC BUNGENBERG, CHRISTOPH HERRMANN, COMMON COMMERCIAL POLICY AFTER LISBON (EUROPEAN YEARBOOK OF INTERNATIONAL ECONOMIC LAW, Berlin: Springer (2013); Flavien Jadeau, Fabien Gelinas, *CETA's Definition of the Fair and Equitable Treatment Standard: Toward a Guided and Constrained Interpretation* in BJORKLUND, A. ET AL. (eds.) THE COMPREHENSIVE ECONOMIC AND TRADE AGREEMENT BETWEEN THE EUROPEAN UNION AND CANADA (CETA). Transnational Dispute Management, special edition (2016), available at: https://ssrn.com/abstract=2931503 (accessed on 19 January 2022).

[108] See also Annamaria Viterbo, *Dispute Settlement Over Exchange Measures Affecting Trade and Investments: The Overlapping Jurisdictions of the IMF, WTO, and the ICSID* (July 13, 2008), Society of International Economic Law (SIEL) Inaugural Conference (2008), available at: https://papers.ssrn.com/sol3/papers.cfm?abstract_id=1154673 (accessed on 19 January 2022).

case-law developed in relation to other international treaties, or other States, could thus be debatable. Moreover, the protection of investments is typically regulated by bilateral agreements, whether in the form of BITs or in the form of investment protection clauses incorporated in agreements on commercial cooperation, etc; there are presently approximately 6,000 such treaties concluded since 1958 worldwide. Nevertheless, the case-law in investment protection disputes clearly illustrates how the endeavour to develop an autonomous interpretation intertwines with attempts to balance the global interpretation relating to certain concepts and terms, on the one hand, and the interpretation from the perspective of a particular international treaty, on the other. The factor that tips the balance is the use of case-law from the perspective of treaties for the reciprocal promotion and protection of investments (BITs), each of which constitutes a special source of law, yet they all express a certain globalised practice. Consequently, the parties and investors to whom the treaties apply may also reasonably rely on the fact that the international practice attributes a uniform meaning to the individual concepts, as long as the particular BIT contains no special provisions.[109]

2.70. While the ICSID platform is not the only venue for the resolution of investment disputes, its case-law is rather important, primarily because it is published and therefore easily accessible and widely known. This aspect is significant especially due to the creation of an expectation regarding a particular qualified interpretation. Besides, although the ICSID decisions are decisions rendered by particular arbitral tribunals, the ICSID – to some extent – also guarantees the uniformity of the interpretation. In this connection, however, it is necessary to bear in mind that investment disputes are specific for the fact that one of the parties is always the investor, as the person deriving and applying their rights directly from the international treaty, whereas the decisions made by the WTO or the International Monetary Fund[110] are decisions rendered in disputes between States as parties to a particular international treaty.[111]

---

[109] From the perspective of overlapping regulations, see also Brian Havel, John Mulligan, *The Cape Town Convention and The Risk of Renationalization: A Comment in Reply to Jeffrey Wool and Andrej Jonovic*, 3(1) CAPE TOWN CONVENTION JOURNAL 81-94 (2014); Martin Gebauer, *Uniform Law, General Principles and Autonomous Interpretation*, 5(4) UNIFORM LAW REVIEW 683 (2000).

[110] See also RICHARD EDWARDS, INERNATIONAL MONETARY COLLABORATION, New York: Translation (1985).

[111] As concerns the intersection of the case-law of the WTO and of the International Monetary Fund, see also JOOST PAUWELYN, CONFLICT OF NORMS IN PUBLIC INTERNATIONAL LAW: HOW WTO LAW RELATES TO OTHER RULES OF INTERNATIONAL LAW, New York: Cambridge University Press (2003); Deborah E. Siegel, *Legal Aspects of the IMF/WTO Relationship: the Fund's Articles of Agreement and the WTO Agreements*, 96(3) AMERICAN JOURNAL OF INTERNATIONAL LAW 620 (2002).

2.71. However, the ICSID case-law also constitutes a prominent benchmark and standard because of its position between purely public-law disputes, on the one hand, and private-law disputes, on the other. From the private-law perspective, one ought to mention the interpretation practice regarding the New York Convention (1958),[112] which, conversely (as opposed to the case-law of the WTO and the International Monetary Fund), represents an interpretation of the said international treaty (New York Convention (1958)) in private-law disputes, despite the fact that the parties to the arbitration are also, and not exceptionally, States. After all, even the decisions rendered in proceedings conducted at the ICSID are arbitral awards covered by the New York Convention (1958).

2.72. For instance, in *Orascom TMT Investments,*[113] the arbitral tribunal interpreted the term *siége social* (*registered office*) referred to in the Agreement between the Belgo-Luxembourg Economic Union and the People's Democratic Republic of Algeria on the Reciprocal Promotion and Protection of Investments signed in 1991 (BIT). First of all, the arbitral tribunal held that *siége social* clearly did not refer to the national law of any State party. Then the arbitral tribunal explained that the grammatical and syntactic structure of the provision and the context in which the term was employed in the respective BIT made it clear that the term had an autonomous meaning. The arbitral tribunal added that if the parties to the BIT had wanted to include a reference to national law, they could have done so explicitly.[114] The arbitral tribunal thus correctly considered the autonomous interpretation of the BIT as the *starting point,* and, conversely, the interpretation of the terms according to national law as an undesirable interpretation that the parties would have to have explicitly agreed on if they had intended such interpretation. Such perception of the interpretation of international treaties is fully consistent with the above-described premises of autonomous interpretation. The arbitral tribunal in the said case generally held, in compliance with the above, that it is by no means exceptional if the terms used in a BIT have a different (autonomous) meaning when compared to the same terms in the context of national legal systems. The purpose of autonomous interpretation is indeed to ensure a uniform

---

[112] See also Jan van den Berg, *Appeal Mechanism for ISDS Awards: Interaction with the New York and ICSID Conventions,* 34(1) ICSID REVIEW-FOREIGN INVESTMENT LAW JOURNAL 156-189 (2019).

[113] ICSID Arbitral Award in *Orascom TMT Investments S.à r.l. v. People's Democratic Republic of Algeria,* ICSID No. ARB/12/35, 31 May 2017.

[114] ICSID Arbitral Award in *Orascom TMT Investments S.à r.l. v. People's Democratic Republic of Algeria,* ICSID No. ARB/12/35, 31 May 2017, paragraphs 278 and 279.

application of the international treaty of the State signatories.[115] The arbitral tribunal concluded, in the said case, that *'siège social'* had an autonomous meaning specifically in the context of the respective (individual) BIT.

2.73.   Then the arbitral tribunal proceeded to the determination of the contents of the term. The arbitral tribunal first examined the meaning of the said term in all three official language versions. Then the tribunal analysed the meaning of the term from the perspective of its purpose and efficiency of interpretation, as well as from the perspective of interpretation in good faith and the purpose and objectives of the BIT. Having completed this extensive analysis, the ICSID arbitral tribunal held that *siège social* in the context of the BIT meant the registered office of a company.[116]

2.74.   A similar approach was adopted by another ICSID arbitral tribunal in *Tecmed,*[117] which construed *'fair and equitable treatment'* (used in Article 4 of the BIT between Spain and Mexico) as autonomous, applying the criteria set forth in Article 31 VCLT.[118]

2.75.   Although the ICSID case-law is more important for painting a cross-border picture of the autonomous interpretation of specific agreements on the reciprocal promotion and protection of investments due to its publicity, one should not ignore other decisions whose contents are frequently known only from annotations or partial references. In this connection, see for instance the decision of the *ad hoc* arbitral tribunal (arbitration governed by the UNCITRAL Rules) in *Jürgen Wirtgen, Stefan Wirtgen, Gisela Wirtgen and JSW Solar (zwei) GmbH & Co. KG* v. *Czech Republic,*[119] in which the arbitrators performed an autonomous interpretation of the term 'juridical person' using the VCLT interpretation rules. The tribunal held that a juridical person must exhibit, *inter alia*, the following features: capacity to invest, enter into contracts, acquire property, and sue and be sued in its own name. The arbitrators then emphasised that the interpretation must always be congruent with the object and purpose of the particular international treaty (in this particular case, in order to interpret the *'investor'* according

---

[115]   ICSID Arbitral Award in *Orascom TMT Investments S.à r.l.* v. *People's Democratic Republic of Algeria*, ICSID No. ARB/12/35, 31 May 2017, paragraphs 280 and 281.

[116]   ICSID Arbitral Award in *Orascom TMT Investments S.à r.l.* v. *People's Democratic Republic of Algeria*, ICSID No. ARB/12/35, 31 May 2017, paragraphs 282–298.

[117]   ICSID Arbitral Award in *Técnicas Medioambientales Tecmed* v. *Mexico*, ICSID No. ARB(AF)/00/2.

[118]   ICSID Arbitral Award in *Técnicas Medioambientales Tecmed* v. *Mexico*, ICSID No. ARB(AF)/00/2, paragraph 155.

[119]   Arbitral award rendered in *ad hoc* arbitration, 11 October 2017, *Jürgen Wirtgen, Stefan Wirtgen, Gisela Wirtgen and JSW Solar (zwei) GmbH & Co. KG* v. *Czech Republic* (solar energy).

to the particular international treaty). In this connection, the arbitral tribunal, *inter alia*, made a comparison with a preceding decision in investment matters, specifically the ICSID decision in *Abaclat and Others* v. *Argentina*.[120]

IV.2.   Case-law of CJ EU

2.76.   The issue of autonomous interpretation has also been regularly addressed in the case-law of the EU courts. Among others, the need for an autonomous interpretation has been repeatedly dealt with by the ECJ in decisions concerning the interpretation of provisions of the Brussels Convention. For instance, in C-189/87 (*Athanasios Kalfekis*),[121] the German Federal Court of Justice made a reference for a preliminary ruling to the ECJ as to whether the phrase 'matters relating to tort, delict or quasi delict' must be given an independent meaning, or whether it can be construed in accordance with the applicable German law. The Court of Justice (ECJ) held that in order to ensure the equality and uniformity of the rights and obligations arising out of the Brussels Convention, the concepts incorporated in the Convention should not be interpreted simply as referring to the national law. Accordingly, the concept of 'matters relating to tort, delict or quasi-delict' must be regarded as an autonomous concept that is to be interpreted, for the application of the Convention, principally by reference to the scheme and objectives of the Convention in order to ensure that the latter is given full effect.[122] The ECJ arrived at similar conclusions in C-26/91 (*Jakob Handte*),[123] where the French Cour de Cassation made a reference to the ECJ in respect of the interpretation of the phrase '*matters relating to a contract*'. According to the Court of Justice (ECJ), the Court has consistently held that the phrase is to be interpreted independently, primarily having regard to the objectives and general scheme of the Brussels Convention, in order to ensure that it is applied uniformly in all the Contracting States. The phrase should therefore not be taken as referring to how the legal relationship in question before the

---

[120]   ICSID decision on jurisdiction and admissibility, case no. ARB/07/5. See also Ridhi Kabra, *Has Abaclat v. Argentina left the ICSID with a massive problem?*, 31(3) ARBITRATION INTERNATIONAL 425-453 (2015).

[121]   Judgment of the ECJ, Case C-189/87, 27 September 1988, *Athanasios Kalfelis* v. *Bankhaus Schröder, Münchmeyer, Hengst and Co. and Others*, European Court Reports 1988 -05565 et seq. [ECLI:EU:C:1988:459] [EUR-Lex: 61987CJ0189].

[122]   Judgment of the ECJ, Case C-189/87, 27 September 1988, *Athanasios Kalfelis* v. *Bankhaus Schröder, Münchmeyer, Hengst and Co. and Others*, European Court Reports 1988 -05565 et seq. [ECLI:EU:C:1988:459], paragraphss 14 through 16.

[123]   Judgment of the ECJ, Case C-26/91, 17 June 1992, *Jakob Handte & Co. GmbH* v. *Traitements Mécano-chimiques des Surfaces SA.*, European Court Reports 1992 I-03967 et seq. [ECLI:EU:C:1992:268]. [EUR-Lex: 61991CJ0026].

national court is classified by the relevant national law.[124] The ECJ specifically held in this case that it is immaterial how the particular relationship is classified by the national law of the Member State or, as applicable, the law of the forum.[125] The ECJ has ruled similarly in other matters relating to the interpretation of the Brussels Convention.[126]

IV.3.   Comparison with Case-law of Czech Courts

2.77.   The autonomous interpretation of international treaties is naturally applied not only by international tribunals, whether operating on a specific institutionalised platform or as *ad hoc* tribunals, but also by national courts.

2.78.   For instance, in a dispute arising from a contract of carriage entered into pursuant to the Convention on the Contract for the International Carriage of Goods by Road (CMR), the Supreme Court of the Czech Republic construed the requirement of the written form prescribed for a claim in terms of Article 32(2) CMR.[127,128] First, the Supreme Court held that the CMR did not provide any detailed specification of the concept of the written form. Then the Supreme Court added that the interpretation of the requirement of the written form could not be directly based on national law as the sole source of law. National law can only be applied to the resolution of issues that are not covered by the CMR on the contract of carriage, or with respect to which the Convention directly refers to national law. Hence, the Czech Supreme Court correctly explained that the CMR is a unification international treaty whose purpose is to unify the law regulating the terms of a contract of carriage in the international carriage

---

[124]   Judgment of the ECJ, Case C-26/91, 17 June 1992, *Jakob Handte & Co. GmbH* v. *Traitements Mécano-chimiques des Surfaces SA.*, European Court Reports 1992 I-03967 et seq. [ECLI:EU:C:1992:268]. [EUR-Lex: 61991CJ0026]. In English (cit.): *[I]n replying to the question from the national court, it should first be observed that the Court has consistently held that the phrase 'matters relating to a contract' in Article 5(1) of the Convention is to be interpreted independently, having regard primarily to the objectives and general scheme of the Convention, in order to ensure that it is applied uniformly in all the Contracting States. The phrase should not therefore be taken as referring to how the legal relationship in question before the national court is classified by the relevant national law.* The case concerned the interpretation of the word *contract*.

[125]   See also ULRICH MAGNUS, PETER MANKOWSKI, BRUSSELS I. REGULATION, Nex York: Walter de Gruyter (2011), et. 123; ANDREJ SAVIN, JAN TRZASKOWSKI, RESEARCH HANDBOOK ON EU INTERNET LAW, Denmark: Edward Elgar Publishing (2014), et. 232.

[126]   See also judgment of the ECJ, Case C-34/82, 22 March 1983, *Martin Peters Bauunternehmung GmbH* v. *Zuid Nederlandse Aannemers Vereiniging*, paragraphs 9 and 10. European Court Reports 1983 -00987. [ECLI:EU:C:1983:87]. [EUR-Lex: 61982CJ0034]; judgment of the ECJ, Case C-9/87, 08 March 1988, *SPRL Arcado* v. *SA Haviland*, paragraphs 10 and 11. European Court Reports 1988 -01539. [ECLI:EU:C:1988:127]. [EUR-Lex: 61987CJ0009].

[127]   Convention of 19 May 1956 which entered into force on 02 July 1961. Published in the Czech Republic as Decree of the (Czech) Minister of Foreign Affairs on Convention on the Contract for the International Carriage of Goods by Road (CMR) No. 11/1975 Coll. Entered into force for the Czech Republic on 03 December 1974.

[128]   Judgment of the Supreme Court of the Czech Republic – Grand Chamber, 19 October 2016, Case 31 Cdo 1570/2015.

of goods by road and, as such, the interpretation must be based on the same foundation in all State parties, regardless of the State in which the claim is made. The Supreme Court has ruled as follows (cit.):

> [*t*]*he terms of the Convention must be interpreted independently of their meaning in the national law (unless the convention makes a direct reference to the latter). In order to make sure that the Convention has analogous effects in all State signatories, it is necessary to implement autonomous interpretation, with due regard for the purpose, objectives and general scheme of the Convention.*[129]

2.79.   The Czech Supreme Court finally concluded its general introduction to the method of interpretation by stating that autonomous interpretation in the case of the CMR meant such interpretation that honoured the best observance of the purpose and objectives of the respective international treaty and complied with the general decision-making practice across the State signatories.[130] This conclusion is to be fully embraced. Moreover, the quoted judgment of the Czech Supreme Court is also highly commendable from the perspective of a comparative supplementation of the interpretation, as the Court based its autonomous interpretation of the term *written form* on extensive research into judicial decisions rendered in other State signatories and invoked the interpretation of the term provided by German, Dutch, Hungarian and Austrian courts. The Court thus endeavoured to develop an interpretation that would be acceptable in all State signatories in good faith.

V.   Conclusion

2.80.   Interpretation employed in the international environment, specifically the interpretation used by international tribunals, exhibits a number of specifics that distinguish this interpretation from interpretation at the national level. Apart from the individual interpretation methods and nuances, for instance, the need for a comparative analysis of the various language versions of one and the same international treaty, the absolutely fundamental basis for interpretation of an international source of law is the necessity of an autonomous interpretation. Autonomous interpretation represents an interpretation

---

[129]   Judgment of the Supreme Court of the Czech Republic – Grand Chamber, 19 October 2016, Case 31 Cdo 1570/2015, paragraph 15.
[130]   Judgment of the Supreme Court of the Czech Republic – Grand Chamber, 19 October 2016, Case 31 Cdo 1570/2015, paragraph 16.

independent of the national legal systems and the applicable case-law bases. At the same time, the analysis provided in this paper suggests that the doctrine and legal theory, as well as the case-law (international and national), agree on the principal requirement that the autonomous interpretation must first and foremost observe the purpose and meaning of the interpreted source of law. Autonomous interpretation in the international environment remains a very topical issue, and it is reasonable to expect that future case-law will continue to use and develop the concept.

| | |

Summaries

FRA [*L'étendue de la compétence des juridictions et des autorités internationales en matière d'interprétation du droit international*]

Le présent article examine les spécificités de l'interprétation du droit international d'abord dans une perspective théorique, puis en analysant plusieurs décisions de justice rendues aux niveaux international, européen et national. Le texte fondamental énonçant les principales règles d'interprétation est la Convention de Vienne sur le droit des traités (CVDT), qui est considérée comme une codification du droit coutumier, et qui jouit à ce titre d'un grand respect dans la quasi-totalité des États du monde. Les procédés d'interprétation prévus par la Convention, notamment par son article 31 et ss., lorsqu'ils sont appliqués dans un contexte international, doivent cependant l'être de manière autonome, c'est-à-dire en faisant abstraction de l'interprétation nationale ou de celle utilisée par d'autres autorités. Ces dernières peuvent être utilisées à titre subsidiaire, comme source d'inspiration. Étant donné l'importance de l'interprétation autonome et de son respect dans la jurisprudence, cette notion est le thème central de l'article. Outre les caractéristiques de l'interprétation autonome, l'auteur se penche également sur les problèmes qui y sont associés.

CZE [*Rozsah pravomoci soudů a mezinárodních orgánů při výkladu mezinárodního práva*]

Tento článek se zaměřuje na specifika výkladu mezinárodního práva, a to jednak z teoretického hlediska, jednak rovněž analýzou vybrané judikatury na úrovni mezinárodní, evropské i vnitrostátní. Základním dokumentem poskytující výchozí výkladová pravidla je Vídeňská úmluva o smluvním právu

(VCLT), která se považuje za kodifikaci obyčejového práva, tudíž požívá silného respektu napříč v podstatě všemi státy světa. Úmluvou poskytnuté interpretační postupy, obsažené zejména v jejím čl. 31 a násl., je však zapotřebí v mezinárodním prostředí činit autonomně, tj. s oproštěním se od interpretace vnitrostátní či poskytnuté jinými orgány, přičemž tato může při autonomním výkladu sloužit pouze následně a v mezích jakési inspirace. Vzhledem k důležitosti autonomního výkladu a jeho dodržování v rozhodovací praxi je tak tento pojem stěžejním tématem tohoto článku, přičemž autor se zabývá kromě popisu samotného fungování autonomního výkladu rovněž problémy s ním spojenými.

| | |

POL [*Zakres kompetencji sądów i organów międzynarodowych w interpretacji prawa międzynarodowego*]
Praktyka wykładnicza międzynarodowych źródeł prawa ma swoją specyfikę, czego najbardziej wyrazistym przykładem jest konieczność przeprowadzania autonomicznej interpretacji. Dlatego niniejszy artykuł nie tylko wskazuje inne odmienności, ale również omawia sens i cel autonomicznej wykładni, sposób jej przeprowadzania oraz związane z tym problemy. Perspektywy doktrynalne w końcowej części artykułu są analizowane w oparciu o praktykę orzeczniczą wybranych instytucji sądowniczych jak na poziomie międzynarodowym, tak europejskim i krajowym.

DEU [*Reichweite der Kompetenzen von Gerichten und internationalen Stellen bei der Auslegung des internationalen Rechts*]
Die Auslegungsprinzipien der internationalen Rechtsquellen bergen zahlreiche Besonderheiten – eine der markantesten von ihnen ist die Notwendigkeit der autonomen Auslegung. Deshalb konzentriert sich der Artikel neben der Definition weiterer Unterschiede v.a. auf den Sinn und Zweck der autonomen Auslegung, die Art und Weise, in der sie erfolgt, und die mit ihr verbundenen Probleme. Die doktrinalen Ausgangspunkte werden vom Artikel in einer abschließenden Passage ebenfalls analysiert, und zwar anhand der Entscheidungspraxis ausgewählter Gerichte sowohl auf internationaler und europäischer als auch auf nationaler Ebene.

Scope of Jurisdiction of Tribunals and International Authorities in Interpretation...

Czech Yearbook of International Law®

RUS [*Объем компетенции судов и международных органов при толковании международного права*]

В процедурах толкования международных источников права можно обнаружить целый ряд особенностей, наиболее существенной из которых является необходимость осуществления автономного толкования. В данной связи, помимо перечисления других отличительных черт, настоящая статья главным образом посвящена смыслу и цели автономного толкования, способу его осуществления и связанным с ним проблемам. В заключительной части статьи также анализируются доктринальные основы в свете практики принятия решений некоторыми судебными организациями как на международном и европейском уровне, так и на национальном уровне.

ESP [*Alcance de la competencia de los tribunales y organismos internacionales en la interpretación del derecho internacional*]

Los métodos de interpretación de las fuentes de derecho internacionales presentan numerosas particularidades, de las cuales la más significativa es la necesidad de una interpretación autónoma. Por lo tanto, este artículo, además de delimitar las otras diferencias, se centra, en particular, en el sentido y el objetivo de la interpretación autónoma, su aplicación y los problemas relacionados. El artículo concluye con el análisis de los fundamentos doctrinales dando cuenta de las resoluciones de varios organismos judiciales tanto en el ámbito internacional y europeo como en el nacional.

| | |

Bibliography:

DENIS ABELS, PRISONERS OF THE INTERNATIONAL COMMUNITY: THE LEGAL POSITION OF PERSONS DETAINED AT INTERNATIONAL CRIMINAL TRIBUNALS, Berlin: Springer Science & Business Media (2012).

KAREN ALTER, THE NEW TERRAIN OF INTERNATIONAL LAW: COURTS, POLITICS, RIGHTS, New Jersey: Princeton University Press (2014).

Leonardo J. Alvarado, *Prospects and Challenges in the Implementation of Indigenous People's Human Rights in International Law: Lessons From the Case of Awas Tingni v. Nicaragua*, 24(3) ARIZONA JOURNAL OF

INTERNATIONAL & COMPARATIVE LAW 612 (2007).

ANTHONY AUST, MODERN TREATY LAW AND PRACTICE, New York: Cambridge University Press (2nd ed. 2007).

James E. Bailey, *Facing the Truth: Seeing the Convention on Contracts for the International Sale of Goods as an Obstacle to a Uniform Law of International Sales*, 32 CORNELL INTERNATIONAL LAW JOURNAL 273–317 (1999).

Jan van den Berg, *Appeal Mechanism for ISDS Awards: Interaction with the New York and ICSID Conventions*, 34(1) ICSID REVIEW-FOREIGN INVESTMENT LAW JOURNAL 156-189 (2019).

MARIA BERGSTRÖM, ANNA JONSSON CORNELL, EUROPEAN POLICE AND CRIMINAL LAW CO-OPERATION, London: Bloomsbury Publishing (2014).

EIRIK BJORGE, THE EVOLUTIONARY INTERPRETATION OF TREATIES, Oxford: Oxford University Press (2014).

JOHAN BOUCHT, THE LIMITS OF ASSET CONFISCATION: ON THE LEGITIMACY OF EXTENDED APPROPRIATION OF CRIMINAL PROCEEDS, London: Bloomsbury Publishing (2017).

Alan Boyle, Soft Law in International Law-Making in MALCOLM EVANS, INTERNATIONAL LAWS, Oxford: Oxford University Press (2nd ed. 2006).

William Burke-White, Anndreas von Staden, *Investment Protection in Extraordinary Times: The Interpretation and Application of Non-Precluded Measures Provisions in Bilateral Investment Treaties*, 48(2) VIRGINIA JOURNAL OF INTERNATIONAL LAW 307-410 (2008).

Diana Contreras-Garduño, Sebastiaan Rombouts, *Collective Reparations for Indigenous Communities Before the Inter-American Court of Human Rights*, 27(72) MERKOURIOUS – UTRECHT JOURNAL OF INTERNATIONAL AND EUROPEAN LAW 4-17 (2010).

CHRISTIAN DJEFFAL, STATIC AND EVOLUTIVE TREATY INTERPRETATION: A FUNCTIONAL RECONSTRUCTION, Cambridge: Cambridge University Press (2016).

OLIVER DÖRR, KIRSTEN SCHMALENBACH, VIENNA CONVENTION ON THE LAW OF TREATIES: A COMMENTARY, New York: Springer (2012).

SUSAN EASTON, CHRISTINE PIPER, SENTENCING AND PUNISHMENT: THE QUEST FOR JUSTICE, Oxford: Oxford University Press (2012).

RICHARD EDWARDS, INERNATIONAL MONETARY COLLABORATION, New York: Translation (1985).

Taslim Elias, *The Doctrine of Intertemporal Law*, 74 AMERICAN JOUR-

NAL OF INTERNATIONAL LAW 285 (1980).

John Felemegas, *The United Nations Convention on Contracts for the International Sale of Goods: Article 7 and Uniform Interpretation*, REVIEW OF THE CONVENTION ON CONTRACTS FOR THE INTERNATIONAL SALE OF GOODS 115–265 (2000–2001).

Malgosia Fitzmaurice, *Dynamic (Evolutive) Interpretation of Treaties Part I*, 21 HAGUE YEARBOOK OF INTERNATIONAL LAW 101 (2008).

MARTIN FORREST, STEPHEN SCHNABLY, RICHARD WILSON, JONATHAN SIMON, MARK TUSHNET, INTERNATIONAL HUMAN RIGHTS & HUMANITARIAN LAW: TREATIES, CASES & ANALYSIS, Cambridge: Cambridge University Press (2006).

Henry Gao, *Taming the Dragon: China's Experience in the WTO Dispute Settlement System*, 34(4) RESEARCH COLLECTION SCHOOL OF LAW, SINGAPORE MANAGEMENT UNIVERSITY 369-392 (2007).

RICHARD K. GARDINER, TREATY INTERPRETATION, New York: Oxford University Press (2008).

Martin Gebauer, *Uniform Law: General Principles and Autonomous Interpretation*, 5(4) UNIFORM LAW REVIEW 683-705 (2000).

DW GREIG, INTERTEMPORALITY AND THE LAW OF TREATIES, London: British Institute of International and Comparative Law (2003).

YANG GUOHUA, BRYAN MERCUIO, LI YONGJIE, WTO DISPUTE SETTLEMENT UNDERSTANDING: A DETAILED INTERPRETATION, The Hague: Kluwer Law International (2005).

Hussein Haeri, *A Tale of Two Standards: 'Fair and Equitable Treatment' and the Minimum Standard in International Law: The Gillis Wetter Prize*, 27(1) ARBITRATION INTERNATIONAL 27-46 (2011).

Richard Happ, *Anwendbarkeit völkerrechtlicher Auslegungsmethoden auf das UN-Kaufrecht*, 5 RECHT DER INTERNATIONALEN WIRTSCHAFT 376, 376 (1997).

Brian Havel, John Mulligan, *The Cape Town Convention and The Risk of Renationalization: A Comment in Reply to Jeffrey Wool and Andrej Jonovic*, 3(1) CAPE TOWN CONVENTION JOURNAL 81-94 (2014).

Todd Henderson, James C. Spindler, *Corporate Heroin: A Defense of Perks, Executive Loans, and Conspicuous Consumption*, 93 GEORGETOWN LAW JOURNAL 1835 (2004–2005).

Steffen Hindelang, *The Autonomy of the European Legal Order* in MARC BUNGENBERG, CHRISTOPH HERRMANN, COMMON COMMERCIAL POLICY AFTER LISBON (EUROPEAN YEARBOOK OF INTERNATIONAL ECONOMIC LAW, Berlin: Springer (2013).

MARTA CHROMÁ, LEGAL TRANSLATION IN THEORY AND IN

PRACTICE, Prague: Karolinum (2014).

Flavien Jadeau, Fabien Gelinas, *CETA's Definition of the Fair and Equitable Treatment Standard: Toward a Guided and Constrained Interpretation* in BJORKLUND, A. ET AL. (eds.) THE COMPREHENSIVE ECONOMIC AND TRADE AGREEMENT BETWEEN THE EUROPEAN UNION AND CANADA (CETA), Transnational Dispute Management, special edition (2016).

JURAJ JANKUV, DAGMAR LANTAJOVÁ, INTERNATIONAL LAW OF TREATIES AND ITS INTERACTIONS WITH THE SLOVAK LEGAL SYSTEM, Pilsen: Aleš Čeněk Publishing (2011).

Alberto Álvarez Jiménez, *The interpretation of necessity clauses in bilateral investment treaties after the recent ICSID annulment decision*, 94 REVISTA ACADÉMICA E INSTITUTIONES DE LA UCPR (2014).

Ridhi Kabra, *Has Abaclat v. Argentina left the ICSID with a massive problem?*, 31(3) ARBITRATION INTERNATIONAL 425-453 (2015).

Ho Cheol Kim, *Burden of Proof and the Prima Facie Case: The Evolving History and its Applications in the WTO Jurisprudence*, 6(3) RICHMOND JOURNAL OF GLOBAL LAW & BUSINESS 254 (2007).

Martti Koskenniemi, *Fragmentation of International Law: Difficulties Arising From the Diversification and Expansion of International Law. Report of the Study Group on the Fragmentation of International Law*, UNITED NATIONS – GENERAL ASSEMBLY, Fifty-eighth session, Geneva, 01 May – 09 June and 03 July – 11 August 2006 (2006).

ULF LINDERFALK, ON THE INTERPRETATION OF TREATIES, The Netherlands: Springer (2007).

KARIN LINHART, INTERNATIONALES EINHEITSRECHT UND EINHEITLICHE AUSLEGUNG, Tübingen: Mohr Siebeck (2005).

Lucas Lixinski, *Treaty Interpretation by the Inter-American Court of Human Rights: Expansionism at the Service of the Unity of International Law*, 21(3) THE EUROPEAN JOURNAL OF INTERNATIONAL LAW 597 (2010).

CHANG-FA LO, TREATY INTERPRETATION UNDER THE VIENNA CONVENTION ON THE LAW OF TREATIES, New York: Springer (2017).

ULRICH MAGNUS, PETER MANKOWSKI, BRUSSELS I. REGULATION, Nex York: Walter de Gruyter (2011).

Valerio De Oliveira Mazzuoli, Dilton Ribeiro, *Indigenous Rights Before the Inter-American Court of Human Rights: A Call for a Pro Individual Interpretation*, 2 THE TRANSNATIONAL HUMAN RIGHTS REVIEW 32-62 (2015).

Roderic Munday, *The Uniform Interpretation of International Conven-*

tions, 27(2) INTERNATIONAL AND COMPARATIVE LAW QUARTERLY 450 (1978).

Bryan Neihart, *Awas Tingni v. Nicaragua Reconsidered: Grounding Indigenous Peoples' Land Rights in Religious Freedom*, 42(1) DENVER JOURNAL OF INTERNATIONAL LAW AND POLICY (2013).

GEORG NOLTE, TREATIES AND SUBSEQUENT PRACTICE, Oxford: Oxford University Press (2013).

Zdeněk Nový, *Evolutionary Interpretation of International Treaties*, in ALEXANDER BĚLOHLÁVEK, NADĚŽDA ROZEHNALOVÁ, VIII CYIL – CZECH YEARBOOK OF INTERNATIONAL LAW, Den Haag: Lex Lata (2017).

Martin Paparinskis, *Franck Charles Arif v. Republic of Moldova: Courts Behaving Nicely and What to Do About It*, 31(1) ICSID REVIEW – FOREIGN INVESTMENT LAW JOURNAL 122-128 (2016).

Francisco Pascual-Vives, *Consensus-Based Interpretation of Regional Human Rights Treaties*, 129 INTERNATIONAL STUDIES IN HUMAN RIGHTS 114–115 (2019).

Jo M. Pasqualucci, *International Indigenous Land Rights: A Critique of the Jurisprudence of the Inter-American Court of Human Rights in Light of the United Nationals Declaration on the Rights of Indigenous Peoples*, 27(1) WISCONSIN INTERNATIONAL LAW JOURNAL 65 (2009).

JOOST PAUWELYN, CONFLICT OF NORMS IN PUBLIC INTERNATIONAL LAW: HOW WTO LAW RELATES TO OTHER RULES OF INTERNATIONAL LAW, New York: Cambridge University Press (2003).

Irena Pelikánová, *Reason, Law and Interpretation*, 12 BULLETIN ADVOKACIE 23-31 (2010).

Daniel Pickard, Tina Potuto Kimble, *Can U.S. Safeguard Actions Survive WTO Review: Section 201 Investigations in International Trade Law*, 29 LOYOLA OF LOS ANGELES INTERNATIONAL AND COMPARATIVE LAW REVIEW 43-45 (2007).

MIROSLAV POTOČNÝ, JAN ONDŘEJ, PUBLIC INTERNATIONAL LAW: SPECIAL PART, Prague: C.H.Beck (6th ed. 2011).

Núria Reguart-Segarra, *Business, Indigenous Peoples' Rights and Security in the Case Law of the Inter-American Court of Human Rights*, 4(1) BUSINESS AND HUMAN RIGHTS JOURNAL 109–130 (2019).

AUGUST REINISCH, MARY FOOTER, CHRISTINA BINDER, INTERNATIONAL LAW AND ... SELECT PROCEEDINGS OF THE EUROPEAN SOCIETY OF INTERNATIONAL LAW, Oxford: Bloomsbury Publishing (2016).

ANDREJ SAVIN, JAN TRZASKOWSKI, RESEARCH HANDBOOK

ON EU INTERNET LAW, Denmark: Edward Elgar Publishing (2014).

WILLIAM A. SCHABAS, THE EUROPEAN CONVENTION ON HUMAN RIGHTS: A COMMENTARY, Oxford: Oxford University Press (2015).

Georg Schwarzenberger, *Myth and realities of Treaty Interpretation: Articles 27–29 of the Vienna draft Convention on the law of treaties*, 9(1) VIRGINIA JOURNAL OF INTERNATIONAL LAW 13 (1968).

Deborah E. Siegel, *Legal Aspects of the IMF/WTO Relationship: the Fund's Articles of Agreement and the WTO Agreements*, 96(3) AMERICAN JOURNAL OF INTERNATIONAL LAW 620 (2002).

Terrence Stewart, Patrick McDonough, Marta Prado, *Opportunities in the WTO for Increased Liberalization of Goods: Making Sure the Rules Work for All and That Special Needs are Addressed*, 24(1) FORDHAM INTERNATIONAL LAW JOURNAL 652–725 (2000).

WOLFGANG MEYER-SPARENBERG, STAATSVERTRAGLICHE KOLLISIONSNORMEN, Berlin: Duncker & Humblot (1990).

Cherie O. Taylor, *Impossible Cases: Lessons from the First Decade of WTO Dispute Settlement*, 28(2) UNIVERSITY OF PENNSYLVANIA JOURNAL OF INTERNATIONAL ECONOMIC LAW 325-326 (2007).

INGO VENZKE, HOW INTERPRETATION MAKES INTERNATIONAL LAW: ON SEMANTIC CHANGE AND NORMATIVE TWISTS, Oxford: Oxford University Press (2012).

BERT VIERDAG, THE CONCEPT OF DISCRIMINATION IN INTERNATIONAL LAW, The Netherlands: Springer (1973).

Bert Vierdag, *The time of the Conclusion of a multilateral treaty: Article 30 of the Vienna convention on the law of treaties and related provisions*, 59(1) THE BRITISH YEARBOOK OF INTERNATIONAL LAW 80 (1988).

Annamaria Viterbo, *Dispute Settlement Over Exchange Measures Affecting Trade and Investments: The Overlapping Jurisdictions of the IMF, WTO, and the ICSID (13 July 2008)*, Society of International Economic Law (SIEL) Inaugural Conference (2008).

Jonathan P. Vuotto, *Awas Tingni v. Nicaragua: International Precedent for Indigenous Land Rights?*, 22 BOSTON UNIVERSITY INTERNATIONAL LAW JOURNAL 232 (2004).

Tara Ward, *The Right to Free, Prior, and Informed Consent: Indigenous Peoples' Participation Rights within International Law*, 10(2) NORTHWESTERN JOURNAL OF INTERNATIONAL HUMAN RIGHTS 56 (2011).

PHILIPP WENDEL, STATE RESPONSIBILITY FOR INTERFERENCES WITH THE FREEDOM OF NAVIGATION IN PUBLIC INTERNA-

TINAL LAW, Berlin: Springer (2007).

Siegrried Wiessner, *The Cultural Rights of Indigenous Peoples: Achievements and Continuing Challenges*, 22(1) EUROPEAN JOURNAL OF INTERNATIONAL LAW 121-140 (2011).

Alexandra Xanthaki, *Indigenous Rights in International law Over the Last 10 Years and Future Developments*, 10 MELBOURNE JOURNAL OF INTERNATIONAL LAW (2009).

Lee Yongshik, *Test of Multilateralism in International Trade: U.S. Steel Safeguards*, 25(1) NORTHWESTERN JOURNAL OF INTERNATIONAL LAW & BUSINESS (2004).

Maria Elvira Méndez-Pinedo

Principle of Effectiveness in EU Law: Case-law of European Court of Justice over the Course of Decade 2010-2020

Key words:
European Union law | Court of Justice of the EU | General principles | Effectiveness | Case-law

Abstract | *The principle of effectiveness is an unwritten principle of European Union law (EU). This study explores how this concept/doctrine has been applied in practice by the Court of Justice of the European Union (ECJ) during the decade of 2010-2020. This European Court has consolidated the principle as inherent in the EU legal order and mostly refers to effectiveness in three different strands of jurisprudence (where effectiveness takes different meanings and is linked to other seminal European constitutional principles). The findings of the study show that, while the Court has rightly used the doctrine to guarantee the judicial protection and justiciability of individual rights on a case-to-case basis; it has not defined, clarified or elaborated on the meaning, content and scope of this important constitutional principle. The Court has also not created a comprehensive theory on it. The article is followed by a table of the most important case-law of the Court on effectiveness and its different meanings.*

Dr. Maria Elvira Méndez-Pinedo is a fully tenured Professor of European Law at the University of Iceland, an institution that she joined in 2007. She has general supervision over and responsibility for teaching and research in the areas of European Union and European Economic Area Law, as well as International Economic Law. She has directed doctoral theses in the field in Iceland, Italy and Denmark, obtained competitive grants and prizes for her European research. She is the author of several monographies and two important publications on the authority and effect of European/international/constitutional law by Oxford Constitutional Law and the *Max Planck Encyclopedia of Comparative Constitutional Law* (MPECCoL), available online at: https://oxcon. ouplaw.com/home/ MPECCOL. E-mail: mep@hi.is

| | |

I. Introduction

3.01. The term "effectiveness" originated in classic public international law (*effet utile* and the principle of *pacta sunt servanda*) and can be understood in comparative constitutional law as the old concept of the rule of law and its enforcement through to judicial review.[1] However, this dynamic principle has gained a seminal importance in the field of EU law due to the unique supranational nature and sui generis character of this legal order. In spite of being a non-written general legal principle, it is often used by the ECJ and widely accepted by most national courts.[2]

3.02. Effectiveness has become a legal principle and a doctrine created by the judicial interpretation of the Court of Justice of the European Union (CJEU or most simply ECJ)[3] that mostly deals with the effects of EU law in national law and before domestic courts. The two most common meanings refer either to the full effect of the EU Treaties or to the constraints and limits that EU law brings upon national procedural autonomy. However, the jurisprudence of the ECJ over the course of the last decade shows that the Court has articulated a complex framework (without theoretical explanations) using the term "effectiveness" in combination with other constitutional principles, such as the primacy of EU law over national law, its direct effect for private individuals/economic operators with certain conditions (limited in the case of Directives and horizontal situations), its indirect effect or the obligation of consistent interpretation and, most importantly, the Member State's liability for breaches of this supranational law and the EU Charter of Fundamental Rights.[4]

3.03. The references to the principle are often closely interrelated and sometimes even overlapping in a sequence of waves slowly but firmly constructed by the Court without much in the way of clarification or explanation. Due mostly to this lack of coherence and consistency, EU academia has had difficulty in dealing with

---

[1] Maria Elvira Méndez-Pinedo, Antoni Abat I Ninet, *Effectiveness*, THE MAX PLANCK ENCYCLOPEDIA OF COMPARATIVE CONSTITUTIONAL LAW (December 2017), available at: http://oxcon.ouplaw.com/page/mpeccol-articles (accessed on 23 January 2022).

[2] PAUL CRAIG, GRAINNE DE BURCA, EU LAW: TEXTS, CASES AND MATERIALS, Oxford: Oxford University Press (6th ed. 2015), et. 250-251. See also PAUL CRAIG, GRAINNE DE BURCA, EU LAW: TEXTS, CASES AND MATERIALS, Oxford: Oxford University Press (7th ed. 2020), et. 262-263, 266, 276, 288, 298 and 311-314. On the authority of EU law and current challenges to it, see DAMIAN CHALMERS, GARETH DAVIES, GEORGIO MONTI, EUROPEAN UNION LAW, Cambridge: Cambridge University Press (4th ed. 2019), et. 202-248.

[3] Reference is primarily made to the Court of Justice of the EU dealing with requests for preliminary rulings from national courts, the General Court. Therefore, the use in the article of the acronym ECJ is preferred, and not CJEU.

[4] Maria Elvira Méndez-Pinedo, *Principle of Effectiveness of EU Law: A Difficult Concept in Legal Academia*, 11(1) JURIDICAL TRIBUNE 5-29 (2021).

the conceptualization of the principle.[5] Since the Court uses the term in different ways, what the principle/doctrine means and its consequences can vary from case to case, leading to different strands of jurisprudence classically categorized as follows:[6]

1) effectiveness *strictu senso* (as *effet utile* or effective practical application of treaties);

2) effectiveness as a way to uphold the primacy and authority of EU law vis-à-vis formal and constraining national procedural laws, used alone or in combination with the principle of equivalence (a requirement of 'homogeneity' of remedies justified on Article 4(3) TEU);[7]

3) effectiveness as the centre of gravity of judicial protection and access to justice (courts) (Article 47 of the EU Charter of Fundamental Rights[8] and Article 19(1) TFEU).[9]

3.04.   This classical construction leaves aside the important interactions between effectiveness and other constitutional principles of EU law. Furthermore, academia has already pointed out how the current theory and typology of effectiveness is imprecise both in the doctrine and in the case-law of the ECJ, and should be open to accommodate new categories and subcategories.[10]

3.05.   In this context, the research question of the study is the following: What does effectiveness mean as a principle in the field of EU

---

[5]   The doctrine has tried to conceptualise the use of the principle by the ECJ trying to construct a more general theory over the course of the last decade. See, in this regard, the most important study on effectiveness as *effet utile* by Urska Sadl, *The role of Effet Utile in Preserving the Continuity and Authority of European Union Law: Evidence From the Citation Web of the Pre-accession Case-Law of the Court Of Justice of the European Union*, 8 EUROPEAN JOURNAL OF LEGAL STUDIES 18, 23 (2015). *Sadl* studies the principle of effectiveness on the basis of the 2004 EU pre-accession empirical data (most important cases of the so-called "acquis Communautaire" selected for translation by the European Commission Legal Service). In her view, this selection shows that the principle of effectiveness has a triple dimension: as a legal principle, as a facade for creative jurisprudence, and finally, as a rhetorical instrument used by the Court.

[6]   Koen Lenaerts, *What role for Justice in the European Union?*, lecture at the Assisses de la Justice, Brussels (21-22 November 2013). See also Koen Lenaerts, José A. Gutiérrez-Fons, *To Say What the Law of the EU Is*, EUI AEL, 2013/09, Distinguished Lecture delivered on the occasion of the XXIV Law of the European Union course of the Academy of European Law (6 July 2013), et. 25; and Sacha Prechal, Rob Widdershoven, *Redefining the relationship between "Rewe-effectiveness" and effective judicial protection*, 4(2) REVIEW OF EUROPEAN ADMINISTRATIVE LAW 31-50 (2011).

[7]   Former Article 10 of the EC Treaty, new Article 4(3) TEU reads: "Pursuant to the principle of sincere cooperation, the Union and the Member States shall, in full mutual respect, assist each other in carrying out tasks which flow from the Treaties. The Member States shall take any appropriate measure, general or particular, to ensure fulfilment of the obligations arising out of the Treaties or resulting from the acts of the institutions of the Union. The Member States shall facilitate the achievement of the Union's tasks and refrain from any measure which could jeopardise the attainment of the Union's objectives."

[8]   Article 47 of the EU's Charter of Fundamental rights specifies that anyone whose rights under EU law are violated has the right to an effective remedy before an independent tribunal and a fair trial.

[9]   Article 19(1) TFEU, brought by the Treaty of Lisbon, reads: "Member States shall provide remedies sufficient to ensure effective legal protection in the fields covered by Union Law".

[10]   Urska Sadl, Henrik Olsen Palmer, *Can Quantitative Methods Complement Doctrinal Legal Studies? Using Citation Network and Corpus Linguistic Analysis to Understand International Courts*, 30(2) LEIDEN JOURNAL OF INTERNATIONAL LAW 327-349, 327, 335-344 (2017).

law according to the ECJ´s case-law over the course of the last decade? The research is important, since it leads to the finding and conclusion that, at least for this Court, there is really no one single concept of effectiveness in EU law. The structure of the study is the following. First, we refer to the difficulties that arise when we try to define and conceptualize what we understand by "effectiveness" in our field. Second, the study lists and classifies the different cases in which the ECJ has used the concept in EU law, showing the different meanings of effectiveness. Special focus will be placed on the use of the term in order to secure the effective judicial protection of individual rights. The study posits how the concept, both in the case-law of the ECJ and in legal academia, reflects a variety of principles, doctrines and rules all connected under a generic multi-faceted or "umbrella" term. Third, the study will argue that there is no general theory on the topic. At least for the time being, the effectiveness of EU law and the relationship between Union law and national (constitutional) law is a question that the Court still has under construction, approached with ambivalence, which is always left open for interpretation.

II. Effectiveness of EU Law: Definition, Design, Scope and Limitations of Study

3.06. As stated above, it is clear that the definition and conceptualization of the principle presents some difficulties. The Court uses the concept of effectiveness in a variety of ways, and judicial outcomes are linked to the context of each singular case. On one hand, and on limited occasions, we find effectiveness as a stand-alone principle or as an expression of a general "*effet utile*" of EU Treaties. On the other hand, and on most occasions, the Court just refers to effectiveness as a twin principle to that of equivalence as a limit to national procedural autonomy (an assessment of domestic procedures, rules and remedies at the national level with respect to EU rights).

3.07. We also witness, however, how the term is strongly linked to the requirements of the effective judicial protection of individual rights in EU law. Most importantly, the empirical data collected shows that the concept is furthermore embedded in a complex matrix of various other seminal (constitutional) principles of EU law, namely primacy, direct effect, indirect effect or the obligation of consistent interpretation, Member State liability for breaches of EU law, and the protection of fundamental rights.

3.08. Since there is really not a single concept of effectiveness in EU law, nor a general theory on effectiveness, the study will define its scope and limits in the following way. The focus will be on the doctrine/principle of effectiveness in a broad sense, that is to say, the meanings of *effet utile* and effective judicial protection of individual rights, leaving aside the more frequent ECJ rulings dealing with the procedural autonomy of national law and the test that the twin principles of effectiveness and equivalence impose on national systems (although a selection of cases from 2018-2020 is offered). The study is limited to the field of EU law, and relies on the compilation and analysis of empirical data, that is to say, the most important rulings of the ECJ that deal with the "principle of effectiveness" (as a title) in the decade of 2020-2020.[11] The survey and commentary from EU legal academia on the topic is to be found in another connected study.[12] However, it is also important to remember that this principle has also been studied in the areas of public international law,[13] the European Economic Area (EEA) legal order,[14] the European Convention on Human Rights,[15] and in the discipline of comparative constitutional law in Europe.[16]

---

[11] Search of case-law of CJEU in EUR-lex database with keyword "effectiveness" in the titles of the rulings from 01 January 2010 until the end of 2020. The author assumes that the titles and keywords used by the Court reflect well the content of the judgements regarding the relevance of the principle, though that might not always be the case.

[12] Maria Elvira Méndez-Pinedo, *Principle of Effectiveness of EU Law: A Difficult Concept in Legal Academia*, 11(1) JURIDICAL TRIBUNE 5-29 (2021).

[13] Some important studies have already covered effectiveness in international law, focusing on international courts and international agreements. See, in chronological order: CEDRIC RYNGAERT, THE EFFECTIVENESS OF INTERNATIONAL CRIMINAL JUSTICE, Antwerp: Intersentia (2009); YUBAL SHANY, ASSESSING THE EFFECTIVENESS OF INTERNATIONAL COURTS, Oxford: Oxford University Press (2014); CESARE P.R. ROMANO, KAREN J. ALTER, YUVAL SHANY, THE OXFORD HANDBOOK OF INTERNATIONAL ADJUDICATION, Oxford: Oxford University Press (2014); CLIFFORD J. CARRUBBA, MATTHEW GABEL, INTERNATIONAL COURTS AND THE PERFORMANCE OF INTERNATIONAL AGREEMENTS: A GENERAL THEORY WITH EVIDENCE FROM THE EUROPEAN UNION, Cambridge: Cambridge University Press (2014); PHILIPPE COUVREUR, THE INTERNATIONAL COURTS OF JUSTICE AND THE EFFECTIVENESS OF INTERNATIONAL LAW, Leiden: Brill (2016).

[14] MARIA ELVIRA MÉNDEZ-PINEDO, EC AND EEA LAW: A COMPARATIVE STUDY OF THE EFFECTIVENESS OF EUROPEAN LAW, Groningen: Europa Law Publishing (2009); Maria Elvira Méndez-Pinedo, *The Effectiveness of EEA Law and the EFTA Court*, 1(2) INTERNATIONAL INVESTMENT LAW JOURNAL 124-150 (2021). See also Maria Elvira Méndez-Pinedo, Elizabeth Corrigan, *Effectiveness of EEA Law and Other General Principles: Some Thoughts after Literature Review*, 1 EUROPARÄTTSLIG TIDSKRIFT (ERT) 53-79 (2021); FRANKLIN CHRISTIAN, THE EFFECTIVENESS AND APPLICTION OF EU AND EEA LAW IN NATIONAL COURTS – PRINCIPLES OF CONSISTENT INTERPRETATION, Cambridge: Intersentia (2018).

[15] The concept of effectiveness has also been studied in the field of European Human Rights Law and the European Convention on Human Rights (ECHR, Rome 1950). See Daniel Rietiker, *The Principle of "Effectiveness" in the Recent Jurisprudence of the European Court of Human Rights: Its Different Dimensions and Its Consistency with Public International Law - No Need for the Concept of Treaty Sui Generis*, NORDIC JOURNAL OF INTERNATIONAL LAW 79 (2010), 245-277.

[16] See Juliane Kokott, Martin Kaspar, *Ensuring Constitutional Efficacy*, in MICHEL ROSENFELD, ANDRÁS SAJÓ, THE OXFORD HANDBOOK OF COMPARATIVE CONSTITUTIONAL LAW, Oxford: Oxford University Press (2012), et. 795–815.

III. Doctrine of Effectiveness as Constitutional Principle of EU Law

III.1. Two Most Common Different Meanings of Effectiveness: *"Effet Utile"* and Limit to National Procedural Autonomy

III.1.1. *Effectiveness as General "Effet Utile" of EU Treaties*

3.09. Effectiveness has traditionally been covered by the European doctrine as a legal principle in connection with the judicial interpretation of EU Treaties.[17] In general, academia agrees that the aim of the Court is to provide the maximum efficacy to EU Treaties and EU secondary law. Relying on this general meaning of *effet utile* as the practical effect of EU Treaties and rules of interpretation to secure justiciability, we find very interesting literature.[18] The Court, however, has not referred to this broad meaning of effectiveness as *effet utile* in the last decade. We find only an elliptical reference to it in the Opinion of AG Sharpston in the *Cargill* 2019 case.[19] Here an interesting distinction is made between a (procedural) principle of effectiveness and the so-called *effet utile* of a Directive (EU Secondary law). It is in a later case, in *Commission v. UK* 2018,[20] that *effet utile* is defined as a notion that is substantially equivalent to the 'purpose' and 'objective' of a legal provision. However, it is unclear whether this short definition can summarize and anchor the whole approach of the Court to the key concept of *effet utile*, which was first used by this Court in 1961.[21]

---

[17] TAKIS TRIDIMAS, THE GENERAL PRINCIPLES OF EU LAW, Oxford: Oxford University Press (2nd ed. 2007), et. 419.

[18] Urska Sadl, *The role of Effet Utile in Preserving the Continuity and Authority of European Union Law: Evidence From the Citation Web of the Pre-accession Case-Law of the Court Of Justice of the European Union*, 8(1) EUROPEAN JOURNAL OF LEGAL STUDIES 18-45 (2015). Most classic and recent literature focuses on "effectiveness" in its first meaning, as a legal principle and/or a tool of interpretation of EU treaties in order to provide *effet utile* to norms. The most critical study done by *Sadl* in 2015 focuses exclusively on *effet utile* and approaches the concept from a different framework in a triple dimension: as a legal principle, as a facade for creative jurisprudence, and finally, as a rhetorical instrument.

[19] ECJ Judgment of 19 December 2019, C-360/18, *Cargill Deutschland GmbH v. Hauptzollamt Krefeld*, Judgment of the Court (Third Chamber), EU:C:2019:1124, paragraphs 63 and 64.

[20] ECJ Judgment of 17 October 2018, C-503/17, *European Commission v. United Kingdom of Great Britain and Northern Ireland*, Judgment of the Court (Eighth Chamber), EU:C:2018:831, paragraph 43.

[21] ECJ Judgment, 30/59, *De Gezamenlijke S teenkolenmijnen in Limburg v. High Authority* [1961] ECR I. In this case, the Court stressed that the Community could affect questions of national sovereignty only in order to ensure that the *effet utile* of the Treaty was not considerably weakened and its aims and purposes were not seriously compromised.

III.1.2. Twin Principles of Effectiveness and Equivalence Framing and Limiting National Procedural Autonomy in EU Law

3.10. The most common use of the principle of effectiveness by the ECJ is in combination with the twin principle of equivalence as a limit to the general autonomy of procedural law that EU Member States enjoy under the EU Treaties (expressed in the phrase "European rights, national remedies"). For *Tridimas*,[22] "the starting point of the Courts´ approach to effectiveness remains the universality of remedies. Effective judicial protection, based on the maxim: where there is a right, there must be a remedy *(ubi jus ibi remedium)*". Effectiveness for *Tridimas* is above all a legal principle that means, at the end, that substantive rights must be complemented by procedural rights, or otherwise they do not become real or effective. The exercise of European rights in the daily life of citizens is closely linked to the proper existence of judicial redress mechanisms at the national level. National courts must provide a remedy for the protection of European rights, and what's more, offer individuals the opportunity to vindicate or assert these rights. Since the case-law is abundant on this meaning of effectiveness, here only some recent relevant ECJ rulings are provided. The most important case has probably been the *Vueling* 2020 case,[23] which provides a good summary of the most important case-law from the ECJ on this concept of effectiveness. Other cases can be referenced from recent years, such as the *Kantarev* 2018 case,[24] the *Eesti Pagar AS* 2019 case,[25] the *Cogeco* 2019 case,[26] the *PI* v. *Landespolizeidirektion Tirol* 2019 case,[27] the *Călin* 2019 case,[28] the *Cargill Deutschland* 2019

---

[22]   TAKIS TRIDIMAS, *Supra* note 466.

[23]   ECJ Judgement of 09 July 2020, C-86/19, *SL* v. *Vueling Airlines SA*, Judgment of the Court (Fourth Chamber), ECLI:EU:C:2020:538, paragraphs 39 and 40.

[24]   ECJ Judgement of 04 October 2018, C-571/16, *Nikolay Kantarev* v. *Balgarska Narodna Banka*, Judgment of the Court (Fifth Chamber), EU:C:2018:807, paragraphs 121-125 and 139-147 on procedural autonomy for Member States, principles of effectiveness and equivalence, liability for breaches of EU law and national deposit guarantee schemes.

[25]   ECJ Judgement of 05 March 2019, C-349/17, *Eesti Pagar AS* v. *Ettevõtluse Arendamise Sihtasutus and Majandus- ja Kommunikatsiooniministeerium*, Judgment of the Court (Grand Chamber), EU:C:2019:172, paragraphs 137-140 on effectiveness, State aid and national procedural laws.

[26]   ECJ Judgement of 28 March 2019, C-637/17, *Cogeco Communications Inc* v. *Sport TV Portugal SA and Others*, Judgment of the Court (Second Chamber), EU:C:2019:263, paragraphs 39-44, 55 and 62.2. on effectiveness, Article 102 TFEU, actions for damages under national law, infringements of competition law and limitation periods.

[27]   ECJ Judgement of 08 May 2019, C-230/18, *PI* v. *Landespolizeidirektion Tirol*, Judgment of the Court (Sixth Chamber), EU:C:2019:383, paragraph 78 on effectiveness of judicial review, prostitution and Article 47 EU Charter Fundamental Rights.

[28]   ECJ Judgement of 11 September 2019, C-676/17, *Oana Mădălina* v. *Direcția Regională a Finanțelor Publice Ploiești*, Judgment of the Court (Fourth Chamber), EU:C:2019:700, paragraphs 23-33, 42-43 and 57 on Article 47 of the EU Charter of Fundamental Rights, principles of sincere cooperation, equivalence, effectiveness and legal certainty (res iudicata and validity of limitation period).

case,[29] the *Nikolay Boykov Kolev and Others* 2020 case,[30] the *TK and others* 2020 case,[31] and last, but not least, the *Valoris* 2020 case.[32]

III.2. Effectiveness and Access-to-Justice-Effective Judicial Protection of Individual Rights

III.2.1. *Effectiveness: Primacy and Direct Effect of EU Law over National Law*

3.11. As stated above, effectiveness is usually grounded and anchored by other general principles of EU law, both substantive and formal, such as the general primacy of supranational law over conflicting national laws (also over national constitutions), as well as the direct effect of some EU law. The most important ruling in this regard in the last decade is in *Melloni* 2013,[33] which deals with the effectiveness, fundamental rights, primacy and direct effect of EU law over national (constitutional) law and fundamental rights, later clarified by the *Aranyosi and C* 2016 case.[34] Another seminal ruling is the *Taricco I* 2015 case,[35] where the Court rules on the consequences of the "full effect of EU law" (no reference to effectiveness) for national procedural laws and effective penalties, later clarified by the *Taricco II* 2017 case.[36]

---

[29] ECJ Judgement of 19 December 2019, C-360/18, *Cargill Deutschland GmbH* v. *Hauptzollamt Krefeld*, Judgment of the Court (Third Chamber), EU:C:2019:1124, paragraphs 46-47 and 51-52 on effectiveness and limitation periods.

[30] ECJ Judgement of 12 February 2020, C-704/18, *Criminal proceedings against Nikolay Boykov Kolev and Others*, Judgment of the Court (Fifth Chamber), ECLI:EU:C:2020:92, paragraphs 49 and 52-53 on effectiveness and observance of rights of defence.

[31] ECJ Judgement of 27 February 2020, C-773/18 to C-775/18, *TK and Others* v. *Land Sachsen-Anhalt*, Judgment of the Court (Seventh Chamber), EU:C:2020:125, paragraph 60-61, 68-69 on effectiveness and time limits for compensation.

[32] ECJ Judgement of 14 October 2020, C-677/19, *SC Valoris SRL* v. *Direcția Generală Regională a Finanțelor Publice Craiova*, Judgment of the Court (Sixth Chamber) EU:C:2020:825. Effectiveness is also linked to the principle of sincere cooperation in paragraphs 21-22, 28 and 38.

[33] ECJ Judgement of 02 October 2012, C-399/11, *Stefano Melloni* v. *Ministerio Fiscal*, EU:C:2012:600. See also Opinion of Advocate General Bot delivered on 02 October 2012 in paragraphs 59-60 reference is made to the primacy of EU law even over constitutional provisions.

[34] ECJ Judgements *PPU Pál Aranyosi* (C404/15) and *Robert Căldăraru* (C659/15). The Court does not follow the Opinion given by Advocate General Bot on 03 March 2016. ECLI:EU:C:2016:140. In the *Aranyosi and Căldăraru* case from 2016, the Court somehow backed up from the precedent from the *Melloni* case in 2013, stating that the risk of violation of fundamental rights served as valid grounds for postponing the execution of a European Arrest Warrant. So, while Member States cannot refuse to execute this European arrest order on the basis of their constitutional higher level of protection of some fundamental rights, they at least retain some fundamental power to assess the situation case-by-case and postpone any decision when the fundamental rights at stake are protected by the EU Charter of Fundamental Rights.

[35] ECJ Judgement of 08 September 2015, C105/14, *Taricco and Others*, EU:C:2015:555, paragraphs 49 and 58 on "full effect EU law", paragraphs 80 and 121 on procedural autonomy of Member States and paragraphs 82, 88 and 102 on effective penalties. See also Opinion of Advocate General Kokott delivered on 30 April 2015, ECLI:EU:C:2015:293.

[36] ECJ Judgement C42/17 *Criminal proceedings against M.A.S., M.B. (Taricco II)*, EU:C:2017:564. A similar

Last, but not least, referring to the effectiveness and direct effect of EU law, we find the seminal *Ajos* 2016 case,[37] which has led to extensive commentary from academia, as it became a case of judicial resistance from the Supreme Court of Denmark.[38]

III.2.2. Effectiveness: Obligations of National Judges (Indirect Effect or Duty of Consistent Interpretation and Simmenthal Mandate (set aside conflicting national legislation)

3.12.   Other EU constitutional principles that interplay with the principle of effectiveness in the case-law of the ECJ are the obligation to interpret national law in light of EU law (sometimes referred to as "indirect effect"), and the so called - *Simmenthal*[39] mandate to set aside all conflicting national law in cases disputed before domestic courts. This duty of consistent interpretation with practical consequences - rather than direct effect - is probably the main instrument through which the effective application of EU law is enforced in the pluralistic legal orders of the Member States within the judicial routine. Here we can refer to some seminal cases: the *Melki and Abdeli* 2010 case,[40] and most importantly, the *Dominguez* 2012 case.[41] Later on, we find the *A v. B. And others* 2014 case,[42] the *PFE* 2016 case,[43] and the important *Ajos* 2016 case.[44]

---

story can be said of the *Taricco I* 2015 and *Taricco II* 2017 cases on the primacy, direct effect and effectiveness of EU law, where the ECJ takes a step back and recognises the authority of a constitutional national legal order due to the concrete circumstances of the case. See also Opinion of Advocate General Bot on *Taricco II* on the limits to the principle of effectiveness in criminal law delivered on 18 July 2017, ECLI: EU:C:2017:564

[37]   ECJ Judgement of 19 April 2016, 441/14, *Dansk Industri v. Rasmussen or Ajos*, ECLI:EU:C:2016:278. See paragraph 29 on effectiveness and direct effect EU law. See also Opinion of Advocate General Bot 25 November 2015, ECLI:EU:C:2015:776.

[38]   For a commentary on this case, see also Rud Holdgaard Knudsen, Daniella Elkan, Gustav K. Schaldemose, *From Cooperation to Collision: The ECJ's Ajos ruling and the Danish supreme court's refusal to comply*, 55(1) COMMON MARKET LAW REVIEW 17–53 (2018); Urska Sadl, Sad Mair, *Mutual Disempowerment: Case C-441/14 Dansk Industri, acting on behalf of Ajos A/S v. Estate of Karsten Eigil Rasmussen and Case 15/2014 Dansk Industri (DI) acting for Ajos A/S v. The estate left by A.*, 13(2) EUROPEAN CONSTITUTIONAL LAW REVIEW 347–368 (2017); and the book from ULADZISLAU BELAVUSAU, KRISTIN HENRARD, EU ANTI-DISCRIMINATION LAW BEYOND GENDER, London: Bloomsbury Publishing (2018), on age discrimination and background to the substance of the dispute.

[39]   ECJ Judgement of 09 March 1978, 106/77, *Amministrazione delle Finanze dello Stato v. Simmenthal SpA*, ECLI:EU:C:1978:49 on the obligation to discard a law contrary to Community law by a national court.

[40]   ECJ Judgements C188/10 and C189/10 *Melki and Abdeli*, paragraphs 43-44, ECLI:EU:C:2010:363.

[41]   ECJ Judgements of 24 January 2021, C-282/10, *Maribel Dominguez* v. *Centre informatique du Centre Ouest Atlantique and Préfet de la région Centre*, Judgment of the Court (Grand Chamber), ECLI:EU:C:2012:33. See paragraph 24 on effectiveness and 44 on further reference and connection with case Ä *Fransson* 2013 (paragraph 46). ECJ Judgement of 26 February 2013, C617/10, *Åkerberg Fransson*, EU:C:2013:105. In the Dominguez ruling, the Court clarifies that the order of assessment for national courts regarding the authority and effects of EU law vis-à-vis national laws are as follows: 1) consistent interpretation, 2) direct effect of EU law, and 3) State liability for breaches of EU law.

[42]   ECJ Judgement of 11 September 2014, C-112/13, *A v. B and Others*, ECLI:EU:C:2014:2195, paragraphs 37 and 58.

[43]   ECJ Judgement of 05 April 2016, C-689/13, *Puligienica Facility Esco SpA (PFE)*, paragraphs 39-41.

[44]   ECJ Judgement of 19 April 2016, 441/14, *Dansk Industri v. Rasmussen or Ajos*, ECLI:EU:C:2016:278,

III.2.3. Effectiveness: State Liability for Breaches of EU Law (including judicial breaches)

3.13. The most powerful use of the principle of effectiveness by the ECJ leads us to the once revolutionary principle of State liability for all national breaches of EU law, inclusive of judicial breaches. Here the most important cases connecting effectiveness and EU liability are *Köbler* 2003[45] (where liability is extended to national judicial breaches), *Tomasova* 2016[46] and *Hochtief Solutions* 2019.[47] In the last ruling, the Court offers a very important summary in Paragraphs 34-48 of how the system of effective judicial protection is constructed in EU law, referring to the European review of judicial decisions in breach of EU law, the necessary conditions for State liability for judicial breaches, and the subsequent assessment by national courts of all these elements.[48] Conclusions follow in Paragraph 66 of the *Hochtief Solutions* 2019 ruling, where the Court states that the new State liability remedy is anchored in EU law, but is strongly dependent on national procedures and respecting Member States' general autonomy in the field. Other ECJ cases reflect these important constitutional dimensions of effectiveness and State liability, clarifying some other connected issues, such as the *Tarsia* 2015 case,[49] the *Ajos* 2016 case,[50] and more incidentally, the *Kantarev* 2018 case.[51]

IV. Scope and Limits of Effectiveness: Fundamental Rights and Criminal Law

3.14. The scope and limits of the principle of effectiveness and effective judicial review of individual rights have been defined by extensive jurisprudence of the ECJ on the difficult balance of European/national fundamental rights and the natural

---

paragraphs 31 and 35.

[45] ECJ Judgement C–224/01 *Köbler* [2003] ECR I-10239, ECLI:EU:C:2003:513.

[46] ECJ Judgement 168/15, *Milena Tomášová* v. *Slovenská republika - Ministerstvo spravodlivosti SR and Pohotovosť s.r.o.*, ECLI: EU:C:2016:602.

[47] ECJ Judgement 620/17, *Hochtief Solutions*, ECLI:EU:C:2019:630, paragraphs 34-48 and 66.

[48] According to the Court in paragraph 39, the classic principle of *res iudicata* is not a limit for State liability for breaches of EU law.

[49] ECJ Judgement C69/14, *Tărşia* [2015] ECR I-662, paragraphs 39-40 on the limits of effectiveness vis-à-vis *res iudicata*.

[50] ECJ Judgement of 19 April 2016, 441/14, *Dansk Industri* v. *Rasmussen or Ajos*, ECLI:EU:C:2016:278, paragraph 43 on the obligation for national judges of consistent interpretation not being a substitute for other important principles of EU law.

[51] ECJ Judgement of 04 October 2018, C-571/16, *Nikolay Kantarev* v. *Balgarska Narodna Banka*, Judgment of the Court (Fifth Chamber), EU:C:2018:807, paragraphs 121-125 and 139-147 on the procedural autonomy of Member States, principles of effectiveness and equivalence, liability for breaches of EU law and deposit guarantee schemes.

Principle of Effectiveness in EU Law: Case-law of European Court of Justice...

Czech Yearbook of International Law®

constraints that domestic and even European criminal law bring along.

3.15. First, the Court has established the strong connection between the primacy and effectiveness of EU law, the role of fundamental rights in general, as well as the necessity of secure effective judicial remedies for citizens in the European legal order (Article 47 EU Charter of Fundamental Rights). Here reference can be made to the *PPU* 2020 case[52] and the État *luxembourgeois* v. *B and Others* 2020 case,[53] where all these fundamental principles are established with a general character.

3.16. Second, we find a series of rulings where the effectiveness of EU law is not limited so much by other fundamental rights in criminal law, both at the national and European levels. Here we can refer to this series of cases: Opinion of AG Bot in the *Melloni* 2013 case[54] (European Arrest Warrant or EAW), the Ä *Fransson* 2013 case,[55] the *Radu* 2013 case,[56] the *A* v. *B. And others* 2014 case,[57] and the important *Taricco I* 2015 case.[58]

3.17. And third, somehow re-considering its previous case-law and setting limits to the principle (not a U-turn) after strong criticism, we find the *Aranyosi and C* 2016 case[59] (as a reply to the *Melloni I* 2013 case), the *Taricco II* 2017 case[60] (as a clarification to *Taricco I* case, with an elliptical or indirect reference to the *Melloni* case through the Ä *Fransson* 2013 case),[61] and last, but not least, the *XC and Others* v. *Generalprokuratur* 2018 case.[62] In all these important cases, the final scope of the principle of effectiveness is limited by other principles of criminal law, tax

---

[52] ECJ Judgements C-924/19 *PPU* and C-925 *PPU*. Judgment of the Court (Grand Chamber) of 14 May 2020, EU:C:2020:367, paragraphs 145 and 297.

[53] ECJ Judgements C-245/19 and C-246/19. Judgment of the Court (Grand Chamber) of 06 October 2020, EU:C:2020:795.

[54] ECJ Judgement C-399/11, *Stefano Melloni* v. *Ministerio Fiscal*, Opinion of Advocate General Bot delivered on 02 October 2012, ECLI:EU:C:2012:600, paragraphs 60 and 63 of the Opinion of Advocate General Bot not followed by the Court on this point.

[55] ECJ Judgement of 26 February 2013, C617/10, *Åkerberg Fransson*, EU:C:2013:105. On effectiveness and VAT/Tax fraud, see paragraph 29.

[56] ECJ Judgement of 29 January 2013, C-396/11, *Ciprian Vasile Radu*, ECLI:EU:C:2013:39, paragraph 41.

[57] ECJ Judgement of 11 September 2014, C-112/13, *A* v. *B and Others*, ECLI:EU:C:2014:2195, paragraph 44.

[58] ECJ Judgement of 08 September 2015, C105/14, *Taricco and Others*, EU:C:2015:555, paragraph 58 (VAT/Tax fraud). See also ECJ Judgement, C-105/14, *Ivo Taricco and others*, Opinion of Advocate General Kokott delivered on 30 April 2015, ECLI:EU:C:2015:293.

[59] ECJ Judgements C404/15 and C659/15 PPU *Pál Aranyosi* (C404/15) and *Robert Căldăraru* (C659/15 PPU). The Court does not follow the Opinion given by Advocate General Bot on 03 March 2016, ECLI:EU:C:2016:140.

[60] ECJ Judgement C42/17 *Criminal proceedings against M.A.S., M.B.* (*Taricco II*), EU:C:2017:564, paragraph 47, where the Court follows the Opinion of Advocate General Bot on the case delivered on 18 July 2017, EU:C:2017:564.

[61] ECJ Judgement of 26 February 2013, C617/10, *Åkerberg Fransson*, EU:C:2013:105.

[62] ECJ Judgement of 24 October 2018, C-234/17, *XC and Others* v. *Generalprokuratur*, Judgment of the Court (Grand Chamber), EU:C:2018:853, paragraphs 38-39 and 42.

law and fundamental rights, also important in the context of the European Convention on Human Rights (ECHR).

V.   Limits to Doctrine of Effectiveness Set by Other Principles of EU Law

3.18.   It is not only criminal law and fundamental rights that impose limits on the application of the principle of effectiveness in EU law in practice. Other general principles of European law have been recognized by the Court as formal and substantive constraints in this interplay and balance of European and national constitutional requirements. These are the well-established principles of legality, legal certainty, *res iudicata*, legal security, legitimate expectations and lack of retroactivity. Here we can refer to the *Tarsia* 2015 case,[63] the *Klausner* 2015 case,[64] the *Taricco II* 2017 case[65] (following the *Taricco I* 2015 case),[66] the *Ajos* 2016 case,[67] the *Hochtief Solutions* 2019 case,[68] and the *Călin* 2019 case.[69] In all these cases, the principle of effectiveness is found to be limited in its application by other general principles common to all national legal orders.

V.1.   Effectiveness: Advisory Opinions CJEU (Art. 267 TFEU) and National Constitutional Review

3.19.   Last, but not least, we must refer to the case-law of the Court regarding the principle of effectiveness and rights and obligations of (highest) national courts under Article 267.3 of the Treaty on the Functioning of the European Union (TFEU). Judicial

---

[63]   ECJ Judgement C69/14, *Târșia* [2015] ECR I-662, paragraphs 39-40 on *res iudicata*.

[64]   ECJ Judgement of 11 November 2015, C505/14, *Klausner,* ECLI:EU:C:2015:742, paragraphs 40-41.

[65]   ECJ Judgment C42/17, *Criminal proceedings against M.A.S., M.B.* (*Taricco II*), EU:C:2017:564. See in this connection, the following Order No. 24 of the Constitutional Court of Italy from 23 November 2016, available at: https://www.cortecostituzionale.it/documenti/download/doc/recent_judgments/O_24_2017. pdf (accessed on 26 January 2022).

[66]   ECJ Judgment of 08 September 2015, C105/14, *Taricco and Others,* EU:C:2015:555, paragraphs 103, 113, 115, 119.

[67]   ECJ Judgment of 19 April 2016, 441/14, *Dansk Industri v. Rasmussen or Ajos,* ECLI:EU:C:2016:278, paragraphs 38-43 and the following judgement from the Supreme Court of Denmark. Case No. 15/2014 *Dansk Industri acting for Ajos A/S v. The estate left by A.* Judgment of 06 December 2016, available at: https:// europeanlawblog.eu/wp-content/uploads/2020/05/Judgment-15-2014-Danish-Constitutional-Court-DI-Final-Judgment.pdf (accessed on 26 January 2022).

[68]   ECJ Judgment of 29 July 2019, C-620/17, *Hochtief Solutions AG Magyarországi Fióktelepe v. Fővárosi Törvényszék,* Judgment of the Court (Fourth Chamber), EU:C:2019:630, paragraphs 49, 54, 55, 56, 60 and 65 (*res iudicata* and revision of firm cases), paragraph 64 on State liability for breaches of EU law and paragraph 66 for final conclusions. See also Opinion of Advocate General Bobek delivered on 30 April 2019, EU:C:2019:340.

[69]   ECJ Judgment of 11 September 2019, C-676/17, *Oana Mădălina Călin v. Direcția Regională a Finanțelor Publice Ploiești,* Judgment of the Court (Fourth Chamber), EU:C:2019:700. See also Opinion of Advocate General Bobek delivered on 05 February 2019, EU:C:2019:94 where paragraphs 80-84 establish a theoretical duty to reopen final national judicial decisions based on the principle of effectiveness of EU law.

dialogue becomes obligatory when a breach of the obligation to refer a preliminary question to the ECJ on the interpretation of EU law by the highest national court qualifies as a violation of EU law and may lead the initiation of an infringement case by the Commission.[70] The most important ruling in this regard is the *Commission* v. *France* 2018 case,[71] preceded by the *Melki and Abdeli* 2010 case,[72] the *Križan and Others* 2013 case,[73] and the *A and B. and others* 2014 case.[74] In the *Križan and Others* case, an important conclusion is affirmed by the Court: "It follows from well-established case-law that rules of national law, even of a constitutional order, cannot be allowed to undermine the unity and effectiveness of European Union law ... Moreover, the Court of Justice has already established that those principles apply to relations between a constitutional court and all other national courts".[75]

VI. Lack of Theory on Effectiveness of EU Law

3.20. This compilation of case-law shows that, during the last decade, the ECJ has used the principle of effectiveness quite often, either alone or in combination with other important constitutional principles. Although the meanings of effectiveness depend on the line of cases at hand, it has found that this principle is inherent in the EU legal order. The findings of the study also

---

[70] The CILFIT doctrine on *acte clair* is very important in this regard. In the historical judgment of 06 October 1982, Case C-283/81 CILFIT [1982] ECR I-03415, the Court ruled that a final court of appeal can rely on an earlier ruling of the ECJ, provided that the point of law would be clear to all courts in the EU and to the Court. It also laid down three exceptions to the duty to refer of courts of last instance. These exceptions are: 1) the question is not relevant in the specific case; 2) a precedent has already been established by the Court ("acte éclairé"); 3) EU law is so clear that there is no reasonable doubt as to the manner in which the question raised is to be resolved ("acte clair"). According to the Opinion of Advocate General Bobek in the *Hochtief Solutions* 2019 case (Opinion delivered on 30 April 2019, C-620/17, *Hochtief Solutions AG Magyarországi Fióktelepe* v. *Fővárosi Törvényszék*, EU:C:2019:340, paragraphs 128-135 and 136), it is essential now to integrate the so-called *Köbler* standard in State liability for breaches of EU law ("sufficiently serious infringement" with the CILFIT standard (for the courts of last instance to be allowed to dispense with making a request for a preliminary ruling under Article 267.3) in the framework of infringement procedures for judicial breaches of EU law that may lead to State liability.

[71] ECJ Judgment of 04 October 2018, C-416/17, *European Commission* v. *French Republic*, Judgment of the Court (Fifth Chamber), EU:C:2018:811, paragraphs 105-114 and 115.2.

[72] ECJ Judgments C188/10 and C189/10 *Melki and Abdeli*, ECLI:EU:C:2010:363, paragraph 45.

[73] ECJ Judgment C-416/10, *Križan and Others*, ECLI: EU:C:2013:8, at paragraph 70 and the case-law cited.

[74] ECJ Judgment of 11 September 2014, C-112/13, *A* v. *B and Others*, ECLI:EU:C:2014:2195. See paragraph 38.

[75] This case does not mention the principle of effectiveness as a keyword in the title, but it has been included in the selection due to the importance of its content. ECJ Judgment, C-416/10, *Križan and Others*, ECLI:EU:C:2013:8, paragraph 70 says:"[...] it follows from well-established case-law that rules of national law, even of a constitutional order, cannot be allowed to undermine the unity and effectiveness of European Union law (Case 11/70 *Internationale Handelsgesellschaft* [1970] ECR 1125, paragraph 3, and Case C-409/06 *Winner Wetten* [2010] ECR I-8015, paragraph 61). Moreover, the Court of Justice has already established that those principles apply to relations between a constitutional court and all other national courts (Joined Cases C-188/10 and C-189/10 *Melki and Abdeli* [2010] ECR I-5667, paragraphs 41 to 45).

show that, while the Court has rightly used the doctrine to guarantee the judicial protection and justiciability of individual rights on a case-by-case basis, it has not defined, clarified or elaborated on the meaning, content and general scope of this important constitutional principle, elaborating a comprehensive theory on it. The constraints on the principle imposed by other general principles, criminal law or fundamental rights have been recognized by the Court on a series of rulings, without further theoretical explanation.

3.21.   The lack of a general theory on the effectiveness of EU law (as well as in EEA law) has been studied by this author in other recent studies.[76] After an extensive scholarly review, conclusions show that the effectiveness of EU law and the relationship between Union law and national (constitutional) law is a question that has been explored since the beginning of European integration, but that is still under construction and left always open for judicial and scholarly interpretation. "The main reasons are two: 1) the lack of a proper definition of the concept (neutral and fluid, but 'empty' in terms of substantive (value laden) content); and 2) a judicial technique of self-referential justification and partial legal clarification/reasoning/argumentation in the case-law of the Court of Justice."[77]

3.22.   As stated above, the case-law of the ECJ shows that the principle of effectiveness is used in different contexts and with different meanings (as *effet utile*/practical effect, as a twin claim to the primacy of EU law, leading to State liability for breaches of EU law, or as a limit on the national procedural autonomy, to name just a few). The Court has also not responded to the different petitions expressed by three different Advocate Generals to formulate a clearer conceptualization of the principle of effectiveness as a seminal principle of EU law (as it is the case with the primacy of EU law over national (constitutional) law). In this regard, reference must be made to the Opinion of AG Villalón in the *Elchinov* 2010 case[78] (effectiveness and supremacy of EU law and the role of national constitutional courts), the Opinion of AG Jaaskinen in the *Donau* 2013 case[79]

---

[76]   Maria Elvira Mendez Pinedo, *Principle of Effectiveness of EU Law: A Difficult Concept in Legal Academia*, 11(1) JURIDICAL TRIBUNE 5-29 (2021); Maria Elvira Mendez Pinedo, Elizabeth Corrigan, *Effectiveness of EEA Law and Other General Principles: Some Thoughts after Literature Review*, 1 EUROPARÄTTSLIG TIDSKRIFT (ERT) 53-79 (2021).

[77]   Maria Elvira Mendez Pinedo, *Principle of Effectiveness of EU Law: A Difficult Concept in Legal Academia*, 11(1) JURIDICAL TRIBUNE 26 (2021).

[78]   ECJ Judgment C-173/09, *Georgi Ivanov Elchinov* v. *Natsionalna zdravnoosiguritelna kasa*. Opinion of Advocate Generall Villalón delivered on 10 June 2010, ECLI:EU:C:2010:336, paragraph 27.

[79]   ECJ Judgment of 07 February 2013, C-536/11, *Bundeswettbewerbsbehörde* v. *Donau Chemie AG and Others*. Opinion of Advocate Generall Jääskinen delivered on 07 February 2013, ECLI:EU:C:2013:67, paragraphs 3, 5 and 47, where effectiveness is defined as "effective judicial protection", and paragraphs 49-51

Principle of Effectiveness in EU Law: Case-law of European Court of Justice...

Czech Yearbook of International Law®

(effectiveness in connection with the EU Lisbon Treaty, the ECHR and national constitutions), and more importantly, the Opinion of AG Spuznar in the *Santoro* 2017 case[80] (elaborating on two different uses of the principle of effectiveness). None of these calls for a clear judicial interpretation and formulation of a theory has led to a definitive answer from the ECJ in the period studied (2010-2020).

VII. Conclusions

3.23. The Court has consolidated effectiveness as a constitutional legal principle and fundamental doctrine in EU law over the course of the decade 2010-2020. While sometimes it appears to be playing a "solo" role, effectiveness is usually grounded and anchored by other general principles of EU law, both substantive and formal, such as the general primacy of supranational law over conflicting national laws (also over national constitutions), the direct effect of some EU law, the obligation to interpret national law in light of EU law and the European mandate to set aside all conflicting national law, and the State liability for all national breaches of EU law, inclusive of judicial breaches. At the same time, this construction of effectiveness as a constitutional doctrine finds several constraints. Important limits are set by other general principles of European law (legal certainty and security, *res iudicata*, etc.), as well as fundamental rights both at the national and European level (i.e., the interaction with the ECHR and constitutional rights in European criminal law). The leading cases in this regard are the *Melloni* 2013 case, the *Taricco I* 2015 and *Taricco II* 2017 cases, the *XC and Others* 2018 case, the *Hochtief Solutions* 2019 case, and the *Calin* 2019 case.

3.24. All in all, the sophistication and complexity of the general principle/doctrine of effectiveness transcend the limits of each individual case mentioned above, leading to a framework of wider legal consequences, both at the European and national level. From a citizen's perspective, we see a new matrix where European rights and remedies (i.e., State liability for all

---

on general principles concerning *effet utile*.

[80] ECJ Judgment C494/16, *Giuseppa Santoro* v. *Comune di Valderice*, Opinion of Advocate Generall Spuznar delivered on 26 October 2017, ECLI:EU:C:2017:822, paragraph 52 on two different uses of the principle of effectiveness, which reads: "It could be argued that the concept of 'effectiveness' is used by the Court in two different contexts: first in relation to the effectiveness of EU law in the broad sense of the term (*effet utile*) and, secondly, in relation to the principle of effectiveness, conveying the limits imposed by EU law on the procedural autonomy of the Member States. It would appear that it is primarily the effectiveness of EU law (*effet utile*) which requires Member States to adopt measures that are sufficiently effective and a sufficient deterrent to ensure that the provisions adopted pursuant to the Framework Agreement are fully effective, whilst the principle of effectiveness is limited to ensuring that the rules implementing rights conferred by EU law do not make it in practice impossible or excessively difficult to exercise those rights."

breaches of EU law of three powers) and European and national procedures are finally connected (i.e., infringement action against a Member State for judicial breaches, the *Köbler* 2003 case up to the *Hochtief* 2019 case, or because the High Court fails to send a case to the ECJ, as in the *Commission* v. *France* 2018 case). In this sense, it must be noted that the Court sometimes refers to the unity and effectiveness of EU law that together bind national constitutional courts (*Križan and Others* 2013 case).

3.25. However, at least for the decade studied, and according to the method followed, we witness an important gap and finding. There is not yet a general EU theory on the effectiveness of EU law created by the Court. Another secondary finding is that there seems to be a need to create a framework to deal with infringement procedures for judicial breaches of EU law and State liability in a holistic way (integrating the so-called *Köbler* standard ("sufficiently serious infringement") and the *CILFIT* standard (*acte clair* doctrine)). That would allow the national courts of last instance to have clear guidelines on whether or not making a request for a preliminary ruling under Article 267.3 is a breach of EU law, as the Opinion of Advocate General Bobek called for in the *Hochtief* 2019 case.

ANNEX. PRINCIPLE OF EFFECTIVENESS OF EU LAW MOST RELEVANT CASE-LAW CJEU 2010-2020

1.General effectiveness and other written and unwritten principles of EU law	
A. Primacy of EU law	*Melloni* 2013 case *Taricco I* 2015 case *Aranyosi and C* case *Taricco II* 2017 case
B. Direct effect of EU law	*Ajos* 2016 case
C. Indirect effect of EU law (consistent interpretation national law)	*Melki and Abdeli* 2010 case *Dominguez* 2012 case Ä *Fransson* 2013 case *A v. B. And others* 2014 case *PFE* 2016 case *Ajos* 2016 case
D. State liability for breaches of EU law, including judicial breaches	*Tarsia* 2015 case *Ajos* 2016 case *Hochtief Solutions* 2019 case *Kantarev 2018* case
2. Effectiveness as general *"effet utile"* (efficacy of EU Treaties)	*Commission* v. *UK* 2018?
3. Effectiveness as application, enforcement and judicial review of EU individual rights	
A. Effectiveness and Fundamental Rights (FR) in general- Effective judicial remedies	*PPU* 2020 case *État luxembourgeois* v. *B and Others* 2020 case
B. Effectiveness limited by FR and criminal law in EU law	*Melloni* 2013 case Ä *Fransson* 2013 case *Radu* 2013 case *A v. B. And others* 2014 case *Taricco I* 2015 case *Aranyosi and C* 2016 case *Taricco II* 2017 case *XC and Others* v. *Generalprokuratur* 2018 case

C. Limits to doctrine of effectiveness set by other general principles of law	*Tarsia* 2015 case *Klausner* 2015 case *Taricco I* 2015 case *Ajos* 2016 case *Taricco II* 2017 case *Hochtief Solutions* 2019 case *Călin* 2019 case
4. Effectiveness and equivalence (twin principles and tests for national procedural laws and autonomy)	Only selection of some recent cases from 2018-2020 *Kantarev* 2018 case *Eesti Pagar AS* 2019 case *Cogeco* 2019 case *PI* v. *Landespolizeidirektion Tirol* 2019 case *Călin* 2019 case *Cargill Deutschland* 2019 case *Nikolay Boykov Kolev and Others* 2020 case *TK and others* 2020 case *Vueling* 2020 case *Valoris* 2020 case (also link to principle sincere cooperation)
5. Advisory opinions CJEU (Art. 267 TFEU) and national constitutional review	*Melki and Abdeli* 2010 case *A and B. and others* 2014 case *Commission* v. *France* 2018 case
6. Opinions of AG so far not followed by CJEU: lack of EU theory on effectiveness	*Elchinov* 2010 case - Opinion of AG Villalón *Donau* 2013 case - Opinion of AG Jaaskinen. *Santoro* 2017 case – Opinion of AG Spuznar.

| | |

Czech Yearbook of International Law®

Summaries

DEU   [*Der Effektivitätsgrundsatz im Gemeinschaftsrecht: zur Rechtsprechung des Europäischen Gerichtshofs aus den Jahren 2010–2020*]
Beim Effektivitätsgrundsatz handelt es sich um einen ungeschriebenen Rechtsgrundsatz der Europäischen Union (EU). Der vorliegende Aufsatz untersucht, auf welche Art und Weise dieses Konzept bzw. diese Doktrin vom Gerichtshof der Europäischen Union (EuGH) in den Jahren 2010–2020 in der Praxis angewandt wurde. Der EuGH konsolidierte den genannten Grundsatz als einen dem EU-Recht inhärenten Grundsatz; von der Effektivität spricht er im Regelfall entlang dreier Linien, die sich durch seine Rechtssprechung ziehen (in Fällen, in denen das Institut der Effektivität verschiedene Bedeutung annimmt und mit weiteren verfassungsrechtlichen Schlüsselprinzipien des EU-Rechts verknüpft wird). Die im Rahmen dieses Artikels gemachten Befunde zeigen, dass der EuGH diese Doktrin folgerichtig umsetzt, um den gerichtlichen Schutz und die Beitreibbarkeit individueller Rechte vor Gericht in individuellen Fällen zu gewährleisten. Soweit es aber um die Bedeutung, die Inhalte und den Umfang dieses wichtigen verfassungsrechtlichen Prinzips geht, hat der Gerichtshof diese Aspekte bisher weder definiert noch geklärt oder im Einzelnen analysiert. Auch hat der EuGH zu diesem Problemkreis keine in sich geschlossene Theorie geschaffen. Der Kern des Artikels ist um eine Tabelle ergänzt, in der die wichtigsten Entscheidungen des EuGH zur Effektivität und deren jeweilige Bedeutung übersichtlich *aufgelistet sind.*

CZE   [*Zásada efektivity v unijním právu: judikatura Evropského soudního dvora z let 2010–2020*]
Zásada efektivity je nepsanou zásadou práva Evropské unie (EU). Toto pojednání zkoumá, jakým způsobem byla tato koncepce/doktrína v praxi aplikována Soudním dvorem Evropské unie (ESD) v průběhu let 2010–2020. Evropský soudní dvůr konsolidoval uvedenou zásadu jako zásadu inherentní právu EU a o efektivitě povětšinou hovoří ve třech různých liniích své judikatury (v případech, kde institut efektivity nabývá různých významů a je spojen s dalšími klíčovými ústavněprávními zásadami evropského práva). Ze zjištění učiněných v rámci tohoto pojednání vyplývá, že Soudní dvůr tuto doktrínu správně uplatňuje za účelem zajištění soudní ochrany a uplatnitelnosti individuálních práv u soudu v jednotlivých případech. Pokud však jde o význam, obsah a rozsah tohoto významného ústavněprávního principu, nijak tyto aspekty

nedefinoval, neobjasnil, ani je podrobně nerozebral. Soudní dvůr k této problematice rovněž nevytvořil žádnou ucelenou teorii. Po samotné kmenové části článku následuje tabulka s přehledem nejdůležitější judikatury Soudního dvora týkající se efektivity a jejích různých významů.

| | |

POL [***Zasada efektywności w prawie unijnym: orzecznictwo Trybunału Sprawiedliwości UE w latach 2010–2020***]
Artykuł poświęcony ogólnej zasadzie efektywności prawa unijnego i jej praktycznemu zastosowaniu przez Trybunał Sprawiedliwości w Luksemburgu (TSUE) w latach 2010–2020. Trybunał Sprawiedliwości skonsolidował istnienie oraz znaczenie konstytucyjno-prawne tej zasady w kilku liniach orzecznictwa, tam, gdzie koncepcja „efektywności" przyjmuje różne znaczenia w interakcji z innymi ogólnymi zasadami prawa europejskiego. Jednak Trybunał Sprawiedliwości, dążąc do zapewnienia ochrony indywidualnych praw obywateli, nie opracował żadnej ogólnej teorii, która dotyczyłaby owej zasady efektywności.

FRA [***Le principe d'effectivité dans le droit de l'Union : la jurisprudence de la Cour de justice de l'UE des années 2010 à 2020***]
Le présent article a pour objet le principe général d'effectivité du droit de l'Union et son application pratique par la Cour de justice de Luxembourg (CJUE) de 2010 à 2020. La Cour a consolidé l'existence et la pertinence constitutionnelle de ce principe dans plusieurs lignes de jurisprudence, où la notion d'effectivité prend des significations variées en interaction avec d'autres principes généraux du droit européen. Cependant, guidée par la volonté d'assurer la protection judiciaire des droits individuels des citoyens, la Cour n'a pas proposé de théorie générale du principe d'effectivité.

RUS [***Принцип эффективности в законодательстве ЕС: судебная практика Европейского суда в 2010–2020 годах***]
В статье основное внимание уделяется общему принципу эффективности законодательства ЕС и его практическому применению Европейским судом в Люксембурге (ЕСJ) в 2010-2020 годах. Суд консолидировал принцип как таковой и его конституционное значение по нескольким направлениям судебной практики, в частности, там,

где понятие «эффективность» приобретает различные значения при взаимодействии с другими общими принципами европейского права. Суд, руководствуясь желанием обеспечить судебную защиту индивидуальных прав граждан, однако, не разработал общую теорию применительно к принципу эффективности.

ESP [*El principio de efectividad en el Derecho europeo: jurisprudencia del Tribunal de Justicia de la Unión Europea durante la década 2010-2020*]
El estudio se centra en el principio general de efectividad del Derecho de la Unión Europea y su aplicación práctica por el Tribunal de Justicia de Luxemburgo (TJUE) durante la década 2010-2020. Este tribunal ha consolidado la existencia e importancia constitucional del principio en diversas líneas de jurisprudencia donde el concepto de "efectividad" adquiere diversos significados interactuando con otros principios generales del ordenamiento europeo. Guiado por el fin de asegurar la protección judicial de los derechos individuales de los ciudadanos, el TJUE no ha elaborado, sin embargo, una teoría general con respecto al principio de efectividad.

| | |

Bibliography:

ULADZISLAU BELAVUSAU, KRISTIN HENRARD, EU ANTI-DIS-CRIMINATION LAW BEYOND GENDER, London: Bloomsbury Publishing (2018).

CLIFFORD J. CARRUBBA, MATTHEW GABEL, INTERNATION-AL COURTS AND THE PERFORMANCE OF INTERNATIONAL AGREEMENTS: A GENERAL THEORY WITH EVIDENCE FROM THE EUROPEAN UNION, Cambridge: Cambridge University Press (2014).

PHILIPPE COUVREUR, THE INTERNATIONAL COURTS OF JUS-TICE AND THE EFFECTIVENESS OF INTERNATIONAL LAW, Leiden: Brill (2016).

PAUL CRAIG, GRAINNE DE BURCA, EU LAW: TEXTS, CASES AND MATERIALS, Oxford: Oxford University Press (6th ed. 2015).

PAUL CRAIG, GRAINNE DE BURCA, EU LAW: TEXTS, CASES AND MATERIALS, Oxford: Oxford University Press (7th ed. 2020).

DAMIAN CHALMERS, GARETH DAVIES, GEORGIO MONTI, EU-ROPEAN UNION LAW, Cambridge: Cambridge University Press (4th ed. 2019).

FRANKLIN CHRISTIAN, THE EFFECTIVENESS AND APPLICTION OF EU AND EEA LAW IN NATIONAL COURTS – PRINCIPLES OF CONSISTENT INTERPRETATION, Cambridge: Intersentia (2018).

Rud Holdgaard Knudsen, Daniella Elkan, Gustav K. Schaldemose, *From Cooperation to Collision: The ECJ's Ajos ruling and the Danish supreme court's refusal to comply*, 55(1) COMMON MARKET LAW REVIEW 17–53 (2018).

Juliane Kokott, Martin Kaspar, *Ensuring Constitutional Efficacy*, in MICHEL ROSENFELD, ANDRÁS SAJÓ, THE OXFORD HANDBOOK OF COMPARATIVE CONSTITUTIONAL LAW, Oxford: Oxford University Press (2012).

Koen Lenaerts, José A. Gutiérrez-Fons, *To Say What the Law of the EU Is*, EUI AEL, 2013/09, Distinguished Lecture delivered on the occasion of the XXIV Law of the European Union course of the Academy of European Law (6 July 2013).

MARIA ELVIRA MÉNDEZ-PINEDO, EC AND EEA LAW: A COMPARATIVE STUDY OF THE EFFECTIVENESS OF EUROPEAN LAW, Groningen: Europa Law Publishing (2009).

Maria Elvira Méndez-Pinedo, *Principle of Effectiveness of EU Law: A Difficult Concept in Legal Academia*, 11(1) JURIDICAL TRIBUNE – TRIBUNA JURIDICA 5-29 (2021).

Maria Elvira Méndez-Pinedo, *The Effectiveness of EEA Law and the EFTA Court*, 1(2) INTERNATIONAL INVESTMENT LAW JOURNAL 124-150 (2021).

Maria Elvira Méndez-Pinedo, Antoni Abat I Ninet, *Effectiveness*, THE MAX PLANCK ENCYCLOPEDIA OF COMPARATIVE CONSTITUTIONAL LAW (December 2017).

Maria Elvira Méndez-Pinedo, Elizabeth Corrigan, *Effectiveness of EEA Law and Other General Principles: Some Thoughts after Literature Review*, 1 EUROPARÄTTSLIG TIDSKRIFT (ERT) 53-79 (2021).

Sacha Prechal, Rob Widdershoven, *Redefining the relationship between "Rewe-effectiveness" and effective judicial protection*, 4(2) REVIEW OF EUROPEAN ADMINISTRATIVE LAW 31-50 (2011).

Daniel Rietiker, *The Principle of "Effectiveness" in the Recent Jurisprudence of the European Court of Human Rights: Its Different Dimensions and Its Consistency with Public International Law - No Need for the Concept of Treaty Sui Generis*, NORDIC JOURNAL OF INTERNATIONAL LAW 79 (2010).

CESARE P.R. ROMANO, KAREN J. ALTER, YUVAL SHANY, THE OXFORD HANDBOOK OF INTERNATIONAL ADJUDICATION, Oxford: Oxford University Press (2014).

CEDRIC RYNGAERT, THE EFFECTIVENESS OF INTERNATIONAL CRIMINAL JUSTICE, Antwerp: Intersentia (2009).

Urska Sadl, *The role of Effet Utile in Preserving the Continuity and Authority of European Union Law: Evidence From the Citation Web of the Pre-accession Case-Law of the Court Of Justice of the European Union*, 8 EUROPEAN JOURNAL OF LEGAL STUDIES 18-45 (2015)

Urska Sadl, Sad Mair, *Mutual Disempowerment: Case C-441/14 Dansk Industri, acting on behalf of Ajos A/S v. Estate of Karsten Eigil Rasmussen and Case 15/2014 Dansk Industri (DI) acting for Ajos A/S v. The estate left by A.*, 13(2) EUROPEAN CONSTITUTIONAL LAW REVIEW 347–368 (2017).

Urska Sadl, Henrik Olsen Palmer, *Can Quantitative Methods Complement Doctrinal Legal Studies? Using Citation Network and Corpus Linguistic Analysis to Understand International Courts*, 30(2) LEIDEN JOURNAL OF INTERNATIONAL LAW 327-349 (2017).

YUBAL SHANY, ASSESSING THE EFFECTIVENESS OF INTERNATIONAL COURTS, Oxford: Oxford University Press (2014).

TAKIS TRIDIMAS, THE GENERAL PRINCIPLES OF EU LAW, Oxford: Oxford University Press (2nd ed. 2007).

Massimiliano Pastore

Res Judicata and the Brussels Regulation (Recast)

Key words:
parliamentary immunity in the European Union | European arrest warrant | Catalonia | non-accountability | inviolability | mutual trust

Abstract | *This paper elaborates on the doctrine of res judicata in the context of judgments recognised (or enforced) under the Brussels Regulation (Recast), with a focus on issues arising from the possibility to re-litigate claims in different Member States in the European Union.*

It analyses the relevant case law of the European Court of Justice from the standpoint of a practitioner without ignoring the dense theoretical issues to which the topic remands.

It is suggested that many of the difficulties brought about by these cases could be avoided by introducing an EU-wide doctrine of res judicata, the exact contents of which remain to be discussed.

Dr. Massimiliano Pastore, MA, attorney at law is a practicing attorney and Adjunct Lecturer with the John Carey School of Law at the Anglo-American University in Prague, Czech Republic. He lectures also on International Business Law at the University of New York in Prague (Empire State College – SUNY). In his practice, he specializes in commercial and corporate law, with a focus on cross-border litigation. He is listed as an arbitrator with the Vienna International Arbitration Centre and the Arbitration Court attached to the Economic Chamber and the Agricultural Chamber of the Czech Republic. E-mail: massimiliano. pastore@aauni.edu

| | |

I.   Introduction

4.01.   The question that prompted this contribution was experiential. How does a defendant (B) prevent a plaintiff (A), whose claims against B have been rejected by a court of a European Union Member State (C), from abusively re-litigating the same claims in another Member State (D)?

4.02.   If A were to bring again the claims in Member State C's courts, they would be promptly rejected as *res judicata*.

4.03.   The Brussels Regulation (Recast), however, does not provide for a defense of *res judicata*. In theory, the courts in Member State D are not estopped from making a new decision, even if the dispute involves the very same cause of action between the same litigants.

4.04.   The gap in the Regulation does not result in leaving B defenseless, since they can rely upon the recognition of the judgment that was handed down by the court in Member State C. This is set forth in Article 36(1) of the Brussels Regulation (Recast), by which any 'judgment given in a Member State shall be recognised in the other Member States without any special procedure being required.'

4.05.   Hence the defendant (B) need not even show that the decision was a final one. The automatic recognition set forth by the Regulation does not mandate that a decision ought to be *res judicata* in the country where it was issued.[1] Instead, any judicial decision meeting the broad criteria of Article 2(a) of the Regulation, stands to be recognised, no matter if final or not, namely 'any judgment given by a court or tribunal of a Member State, whatever the judgment may be called, including a decree, order, decision or writ of execution [...] provisional, [...] protective measures ordered by a court or tribunal.'

4.06.   As explained in the report by Professor Paul Jenard on the 1968 Convention of Jurisdiction and the Enforcement of Judgments in Civil and Commercial Matters, the expression *res judicata* was 'expressly [...] omitted' for the reasons that decisions made *ex parte* or in interlocutory proceedings are capable of being recognized.[2] Professor Peter Schlosser in his report on the Convention of 09 October 1978 lucidly admitted that the 'effects of court decisions are not altogether uniform under the legal systems ... in the Member States of the Community.'[3]

---

[1]   Article 39 of the Regulation presupposes the existence of an enforceable judgment for the purposes of recognition. Strictly speaking, enforceability and *res judicata* are not synonyms.

[2]   Paul Jenard, *Report by Professor Paul Jenard on the Convention of Jurisdiction and the Enforcement of Judgments in Civil and Commercial Matters*, C 59 OFFICIAL JOURNAL OF THE EUROPEAN COMMUNITIES (1979).

[3]   Peter Schlosser, *Report by Professor Peter Schlosser on the Convention of 09 October 1978 on the Accession*

Czech Yearbook of International Law®

4.07. In the Brussels regime, the practical effect of recognition is enabling B to invoke the decision in the same way as a judgment given by the court that is being asked to recognize it. In the words of Professor Droz, recognition 'gives the foreign judgment the force of *res judicata*'.[4] In a manner of speaking, the plea of *res judicata* is brought back through the window after the framers of the Convention threw it out of the door.

4.08. Despite this, several issues remain open.

4.09. Firstly, is the court in Member State D to use its own rules of *res judicata* or, instead, adopt those of Member State C, where the decision was made?

4.10. Little is gained by saying that the foreign decision is 'incorporated' into the legal system of recognition, since the effects generated in C might be incompatible with those of a similar decision in D.

4.11. The conundrum is known in academic circles as the issue of whether the effects of a foreign judgment should be 'equalized' to those of a domestic decision or, instead, 'extended' as such, no matter if they are greater or less than a domestic judgment.

4.12. Back to our initial example, the question for the judge in Member State D would be if, in order to determine whether the decision is *res judicata* or not, they should look at it from the perspective of the laws of Member State C laws rather than those of Member State D.

4.13. In some situations, the question would be entirely academic; in others, it is decisive for the outcome of the dispute.

4.14. Suppose A believes that B owes € 10.000, € 5.000 and € 1.000, each on a separate basis under the same contract. Suppose then A acts in court only for € 10.000 and that court in Member State C rejects the claim. May A now pursue the remaining claims (€ 5.000, € 1.000 or both) in Member State D?

4.15. Also, does the *res judicata* extend to the *ratio decidendi* of that judgment or merely to the part of the decision that has rejected the claim for € 10.000? This problem was faced – and decided – by the European Court of Justice in 2011 (*Gothaer*).[5]

4.16. According to the Jenard Report on the Convention of Jurisdiction and the Enforcement of Judgments in Civil and Commercial Matters, recognition must 'have the result of conferring on judgments the authority and effectiveness accorded to them in

---

of the Kingdom of Denmark, Ireland and the United Kingdom of Great Britain and Northern Ireland to the Convention on jurisdiction and the enforcement of judgments in civil and commercial matters and to the Protocol on its interpretation by the Court of Justice, C 59 OFFICIAL JOURNAL OF THE EUROPEAN COMMUNITIES (1979), paragraph 191.

[4] Opinion of Advocate General Mayars delivered on 09 November 1976, European Court Reports 1977-00029.

[5] Judgment of the Court (Third Chamber) of 15 November 2012, C-456/11, *Gothaer Allgemeine Versicherung and Others*.

the State in which they were given.'[6] Indubitably, this is a clear authority for the 'extension of effects' approach.

4.17. In some situations, however, the other approach is more desirable. In 2009, the European Court of Justice ruled that, where *enforcement* of a foreign judgment is being sought, in no case the judgment should be granted effects that a similar, but domestic, judgment would not have: 'there is no reason for granting to a judgment given in one Member State, when it is enforced in another Member State, rights which it does not have in the Member State of origin.'[7] This case had an important bearing for a later decision in *Al Bosco* v. Gunter *Hober*.[8]

4.18. While usually a litigant looks for both recognition and enforcement of a favourable decision, there could be cases in which *recognition* will amply suffice. This happens when one – such as B in our example – looks to invoke the preclusive effects of a *res judicata* in the country where the case was already litigated. There, the plea of *res judicata* is used as a shield, not a sword.

4.19. Given the lack of precedents, in all those cases where the laws of the *res judicata* in two Member States differ even slightly, it will be disputable which of the two systems a defendant can successfully rely upon. The most recent judgment in *Gothaer* suggests that an EU-law, self-standing concept of *res judicata* is about to emerge. This would be a desirable development.

4.20. The other cases explored in the next paragraphs of this article will only confirm that the issue is clad as a procedural dichotomy between applying the *lex loci juditii* (the law of the Member State of origin – in our example, State C) or the *lex loci legitimationi* (the law of the Member State where recognition and enforcement is sought – State D).

II.   J. De Wolf v. Harry Cox BV[9]

4.21. This is a somewhat unusual case of re-litigation that exemplifies one of the difficulties generated by the absence of *res judicata* in the Brussels regime.

4.22. By an injunction issued in a Belgian court, a Dutch defendant was ordered to pay sums to the claimant. Having recovered nothing in Belgium, the claimant turned to the courts in the

---

[6]   Paul Jenard, *Report by Professor Paul Jenard on the Convention of Jurisdiction and the Enforcement of Judgments in Civil and Commercial Matters*, C 59 OFFICIAL JOURNAL OF THE EUROPEAN COMMUNITIES (1979), 42, 43.

[7]   ECJ Judgment of 28 April 2009, C-420/07, *Apostolides*, paragraph 66.

[8]   Judgment of the Court (Second Chamber) of 04 October 2018, C-379/17, *Società Immobiliare Al Bosco Srl*.

[9]   Judgment of the Court of 30 November 1976, C-42/76, *De Wolf* v. *Cox*.

Netherlands. Under the 1968 Brussels Convention it was open to the claimant to seek recognition of the Belgian court order in Dutch courts. However, because under Dutch procedural law this was costlier than lodging a fresh petition for the same subject-matter, he opted for the latter. Thence, the court in Boxmeer, Netherlands, granted the claimant an order for the same claim anew.[10]

4.23.   The Attorney General for the Supreme Court of the Netherlands filed an appeal against the decision, claiming that the order conflicted with the Brussels Convention (chiefly with Article 31).[11] The following question was then submitted to the Court of Justice of the European Communities:

> Does Article 31 of the Convention [...], prevent a plaintiff who has obtained a judgment in his favour in a Contracting State, being a judgment for which an order for enforcement within the meaning of Article 31 of the Convention may issue in another Contracting State, from making an application to a court in that other State, in accordance with Article 26 of the Convention, for a judgment against the other party on the same terms as the judgment delivered in the first State, instead of applying for the issue of such an order for enforcement in that other State, [...]?

4.24.   The Court of Justice answered in the negative, effectually inhibiting re-litigation even where it would be economically expedient for the claimant. Because the claimant had obtained a decision capable of being "automatically" recognised under the Convention, they were barred from applying for a new judgment in respect of the same cause of action.

4.25.   In his opinion delivered on 09 November 1976, Advocate General Henri Mayras argued that all judgments given in the then six Member States 'automatically have the force of *res judicata*', unless challenged on any of the grounds provided by the Convention.

4.26.   It has been commented that the decision appears 'implicitly to favour the extension of effects approach over the equalisation of effects approach'.[12] Once issued and final in accordance with

---

[10]   Confusingly, the order also recognized the Belgian judgment in pursuance of Article 26 of the Convention ('A judgment given in a Contracting State shall be recognized in the other Contracting States without any special procedure being required'), giving the claimant more than asked for.

[11]   'A judgment given in a Contracting State and enforceable in that State shall be enforced in another Contracting State when, on the application of any interested party, it has been declare enforceable there.'

[12]   Peter Barnett, *The Prevention of Abusive Cross-border Re-Litigation*, 51(4) THE INTERNATIONAL AND COMPARATIVE LAW QUARTERLY (2002), 943-957.

Belgian law, the injunction formed *res judicata* also for the Dutch court, extending its effects into the legal system there. Unlike the *Hoffmann* case, which is discussed next, there was no substantial tension between the effects of the decision across the two systems.

III.   Hoffmann[13]

4.27.   The claimant, a German national, had left his wife to live in the Netherlands. The wife, Ms Krieg, obtained an order for payment of maintenance from a court in Heidelberg, Germany. Parallelly, the husband had petitioned a Dutch court (Maastricht) for divorce; the petition was successful, and the marriage was dissolved there as of May 1980.

4.28.   The woman applied in the Netherlands to enforce the order against the husband. Enforcement was granted (under the Brussels Convention) as of July 1981; by April 1982, a notice of enforcement was served to Mr Hoffmann. He sought to terminate the maintenance order by issuing proceedings in Germany but failed, because the divorce had not been recognised there. The wife went on to serve an attachment of earnings order against the (ex) husband's employer in the Netherlands; Mr Hoffmann tried to set it aside, once again without success.

4.29.   In the subsequent appeal proceedings, the Supreme Court of the Netherlands asked the Court of Justice of the European Communities to clarify if the Convention meant that a foreign judgment whose enforcement has been ordered pursuant to Article 31 of the Convention 'must continue to be enforced in all cases in which it would still be enforceable in the State in which it was given even when, under the law of the State in which enforcement is sought, the judgment ceases to be enforceable for reasons which lie outside of the scope of the Convention.'[14]

4.30.   Advocate General Darmon adopted the view expressed by Profesor Droz that a judgment 'cannot have greater effects in the State in which enforcement is sought than it would have in the State in which it was delivered, nor can it produce greater effects than similar local judgments would.'[15] The Court of Justice concluded in terms slightly qualified (emphasis added), suggesting a partial non-alignment with the opinion of the Advocate General:

> It follows that [...] a foreign judgment which has been recognised by virtue of Article 27 of the Convention

---

[13]   Judgment of the Court of 04 February 1988, 145/86, *Horst Ludwig Martin Hoffmann* v. *Adelheid Krieg.*
[14]   Judgment of the Court of 04 February 1988, 145/86, *Horst Ludwig Martin Hoffmann* v. *Adelheid Krieg.*
[15]   Opinion of Advocate General Darmon delivered on 09 July 1987, European Court Reports 1988-00645.

must *in principle* have the same effects in the State in which enforcement is sought as it does in the State in which judgment was given.

4.31. To remedy injustice, the Court added that the Convention would not preclude the court of the Member State in which enforcement is sought from 'drawing the necessary inferences from a national decree of divorce'.

4.32. Despite these uncertainties, the decision is considered authority for the 'extension of effect' approach.[16]

4.33. This is a difficult case revealing part of the multi-faceted conundrum outlined at the beginning of this paper. The effects of the German maintenance order – as determined by German law (extension of effect approach) – could have not been destroyed by the subsequent divorce decree issued in the Netherlands, because the decree had not been recognised in Germany and the Convention did not apply to questions of status. On the other hand, the Dutch court could not by its own laws allow the enforcement to continue after the divorce had been granted (equalization approach). Past that moment, the enforcement had no longer *raison d'être*.

4.34. In giving the court of the Member State where enforcement is sought a degree of liberty in 'drawing the necessary inferences', the decision tries to strike a difficult balance between impassable, highly abstract legal logic and the necessity to do substantial justice between two disputants.

IV.   Gothaer[17]

4.35. This decision was given in the context of an apparently abusive re-litigation. It seems to support the broad proposition that in each case where national procedural doctrines or rules stand in the way of a full recognition of judgments as envisaged by the Regulation, the courts of the Member State can invoke a self-contained, EU-wide doctrine of *res judicata* to disapply such procedures.

4.36. Gothaer Allgemeine Versicherung AG and three other insurers had a claim against Samskip GmbH, the German subsidiary of a logistics firm established in the Netherlands, for damages caused to brewing equipment that had been shipped from Belgium to Mexico under a bill of lading containing a dispute resolution clause that conferred jurisdiction to the courts of Iceland. These

---

[16]   Konstantinos Voulgarakis, *Reflections on the scope of "EU res judicata" in the context of Regulation 1215/2012*, 3(16) JOURNAL OF PRIVATE INTERNATIONAL LAW (2020), 451-464.
[17]   Judgment of the Court (Third Chamber) of 15 November 2012, C-456/11, *Gothaer Allgemeine Versicherung and Others*.

German insurers initiated proceedings in Belgium but the Court of Appeal in Antwerp dismissed those for lack of jurisdiction.

4.37. In the so-called 'operative part' of its decision the Court limited itself to ruling that it had 'no authority to hear and decide the case'. It had arrived at that conclusion after finding that the term of the bill of lading giving jurisdiction to the Icelandic courts was a valid one. However, this finding was not included in the 'operative part' of the decision; instead, it was set out in the section of the judgment where the reasons for the decision were explained.

4.38. Gothaer and the other insures made a fresh application in Germany (Bremen), giving rise to the issues referred for the preliminary ruling of the European Court of Justice – namely, if the Belgian decision generated effects also with respect to the finding that jurisdiction lies with Icelandic courts, so that other courts within the European Union Member States would be bound. The defendant company Samskip, the Commission and the Belgian government argued for the affirmative.

4.39. Conversely, the German insurers submitted that the effects of the decision were limited to the finding of lack of jurisdiction; the parties would be bound only by the narrow 'operative part', not the *ratio decidendi*.

4.40. Following the 'extension of effects' approach, this issue would fall to be determined solely by Belgian law. Instead, under German procedural law a decision of the type issued by the Court in Antwerp would be incapable of being recognised, it being a mere 'judgment on a procedural matter'.

4.41. The European Court of Justice found that a '"judgment' in Regulation 44/2001 covers also a decision by which a court declines jurisdiction. Between the two possible outcomes, the Court took the view which was favourable for the defendant company and the Commission. Pointing to the 'high degree of mutual trust' that should subsist among courts applying common rules of jurisdiction, the Court cited Article 36 of the Regulation, which prohibits reviews of judgments delivered by courts of another Member State. Uniform application of the European Union law mandates – the Court continued – that this restriction cannot operate differently across the Member States, since each of them might follow different rules of *res judicata*.

4.42. Instead, the Court went on to state that a 'concept of *res judicata* under European Union law' exists as such. It attaches not only to the operative part of a judgment, but also to its *ratio decidendi*. Hence, where a court of a Member State has declined its jurisdiction on the basis of a forum selection clause which that very court has found valid, the courts of other Member States are bound by both parts of the decision.

4.43. The working of such as EU-law of *res judicata* remains presently unknown, except that it is an autonomous EU-law concept which does not vary according to the domestic rules of *res judicata*.

V.   Al Bosco v. Gunter Hober[18]

4.44. Although this decision does not deal with *res judicata* as such, the case shows the European Court of Justice opting for the 'equalization approach', hence breaking the chain of cases where the 'extension of effects' approach had been adopted.

4.45. An Italian company – the claimant – had obtained a preventative attachment order against a German national, who had real estate property there. The company did not look for charging the property by way of registration of the order issued by the Italian court.

4.46. After 8 years *Al Bosco* moved to register the order, but it was too late because German procedural law sets a preclusive time bar (1 year) past which the registration is rejected. As a result, enforcement of the Italian order was no longer possible for *Al Bosco* in Germany, although the type of order and its effects were substantially the same in both countries.

4.47. One can see the dichotomy here again at play: by German law (*lex loci legitimationi*) the order, although recognized, was not enforceable, while by Italian law (*lex loci juditii*) it would because no such limit time exists in the statutes there. Which of the two laws is to be applied?

4.48. The European Court of Justice was asked if the time limit was compatible with Article 38(1) of the Regulation No 44/2001. In their submissions, the German Government argued that the Regulation did not provide for the enforcement of the order in the strict sense, a matter which is left to the national law of the Member State where enforcement is sought; instead, the purpose and provisions of the Regulation only mean that no *exequatur* is required. The German Government turned to the conclusion reached in *Apostolides* that 'there is no reason to attribute to a judgment, at the time of its enforcement, effects which a judgment of the same type, given directly in the Member State addressed, would not produce.'[19] The Commission argued that a 'blind' application of the *lex loci legitimationi* could hamper

---

[18]   Judgment of the Court (Second Chamber) of 04 October 2018, C-379/17, *Società Immobiliare Al Bosco Srl.*

[19]   *Supra* note 6.

the 'free movement of judgments', a fundamental principle of on which the entire Regulation rests.

4.49. The decision reached by the European Court of Justice rests on the premise that the Regulation does not deal with enforcement 'in the strict sense'; instead, it only regulates 'the procedure' for obtaining 'an order for the enforcement'. The enforcement *per se* is a non-harmonised matter controlled by the national law of the Member State where the proceedings are being run, except where the application of that law could 'impair the effectiveness of the scheme laid down' by the Regulation. On this premise, the Court found that the German law procedural device at issue (i.e., registration of the order within a time bar) forms part of the procedural rules prescribed for the enforcement; as such, it does not strike at the *validity* of the preventative measure.

4.50. Formalistic as this approach might sound, it offers a limited guidance to solve the dichotomy – in this case, in favour of the *lex loci legitimationi*. Furthermore, the judgment appears to 'equalise' the effect of the Italian decision, rather than extending the effects of the latter as such into the German jurisdiction. The outcome is defensible from the standpoint of legal certainty, an important principle to all German jurists.

VI.   Conclusions

4.51. The cases discussed in the paragraphs above are a sub-set of a larger group of disputes that will prove difficult to decide absent a 'Brusselensis' doctrine of *res judicata.*

4.52. Defendants should be able to rely on a plea of *res judicata* in order to prevent abusive re-litigation of a claim that was already rejected in another Member State.

4.53. Until that time comes, many cases will continue to be adjudicated along binary lines: *lex loci juditii* versus *lex loci legitimationi*. Debating for an 'extension of effects' rather than 'equalization' of foreign decisions is unlikely to be resolutive.

4.54. Instead, it is desirable to expand the harmonisation process so as to plug the dangerous gap exposed in this paper. The decision in *Gothaer* should be taken as a first step into this direction.

Czech Yearbook of International Law®

Summaries

FRA [*La res iudicata et le règlement Bruxelles I bis*]
Le présent article se propose d'analyser la doctrine de la res iudicata dans le contexte des jugements reconnus (ou exécutés) selon le règlement Bruxelles I bis, en se concentrant sur les questions liées à la possibilité de réexamen judiciaire des demandes dans les pays membres de l'Union européenne.
L'article examine la jurisprudence pertinente de la Cour de justice de l'UE du point de vue de la pratique juridique, sans négliger les problèmes théoriques complexes que ce domaine soulève.
L'auteur est d'avis que bon nombre de difficultés causées par ces affaires pourraient être évitées en introduisant la doctrine de la res iudicata dans toute l'Union européenne ; le contenu exact de cette doctrine reste toutefois à être discuté.

CZE [*Res iudicata a nařízení Brusel I bis*]
Tento příspěvek rozebírá doktrínu rei iudicatae v kontextu rozsudků uznaných (nebo vykonaných) dle nařízení Brusel I bis, a to se zaměřením na otázky vyplývající z možnosti opětovného soudního projednávání nároků v různých členských státech Evropské unie.
Příspěvek rozebírá relevantní judikaturu Evropského soudního dvora z hlediska právní praxe, aniž by opomíjel složité teoretické problémy, s nimiž toto téma souvisí.
Autor uvádí, že řadě obtíží způsobených těmito případy by se dalo předejít zavedením doktríny rei iudicatae platné v rámci celé Evropské unie, o jejímž přesném obsahu by ještě bylo nutno jednat.

| | |

POL [*Res iudicata i rozporządzenie Bruksela I bis*]
Artykuł omawia problematykę res iudicata w kontekście rozporządzenia Bruksela I bis. Skupia się na problemach związanych z nadużywaną praktyką ponownego rozpatrywania przez sądy pozwów w kilku krajach członkowskich i wskazuje, że części z tych problemów nie da się wyeliminować bez nowelizacji wspomnianego rozporządzenia.

DEU [*Res iudicata und die EuGVVO*]
Dieser Artikel handelt den Problemkreis der rei iudicatae im Kontext der Brüssel-Ia-Verordnung (EuGVVO) ab. Er konzentriert sich dabei auf die Probleme, die sich aus der

missbräuchlichen Praxis einer gerichtlichen Neuverhandlung von Ansprüchen in mehreren Mitgliedsstaaten ergeben, und führt aus, dass einige dieser Schwierigkeiten ohne eine Neufassung der Verordnung nicht zu überwinden sind.

RUS [***Res iudicata и Регламент Брюссель I bis***]

В данной статье рассматривается вопрос res iudicata в контексте Регламента Брюссель I bis. В ней основное внимание уделяется проблемам, возникающим в результате неправомерной практики повторного судебного рассмотрения исков в некоторых государствах-членах, и отмечается, что некоторые из этих трудностей невозможно преодолеть без внесения поправок в данный Регламент.

ESP [***Res iudicata y el Reglamento Bruselas I bis***]

Este artículo aborda la cuestión de las res iudicata en el contexto del Reglamento Bruselas I bis. Se centra en los problemas derivados de la práctica abusiva de la tramitación reiterada de los derechos en varios Estados miembros, argumentando que algunas de estas dificultades no pueden superarse sin modificar el Reglamento.

| | |

Bibliography:

Peter Barnett, *The Prevention of Abusive Cross-border Re-Litigation*, 51(4) THE INTERNATIONAL AND COMPARATIVE LAW QUARTERLY (2002).

Paul Jenard, *Report by Professor Paul Jenard on the Convention of Jurisdiction and the Enforcement of Judgments in Civil and Commercial Matters*, C 59 OFFICIAL JOURNAL OF THE EUROPEAN COMMUNITIES (1979).

Peter Schlosser, *Report by Professor Peter Schlosser on the Convention of 09 October 1978 on the Accession of the Kingdom of Denmark, Ireland and the United Kingdom of Great Britain and Northern Ireland to the Convention on jurisdiction and the enforcement of judgments in civil and commercial matters and to the Protocol on its interpretation by the Court of Justice*, C 59 OFFICIAL JOURNAL OF THE EUROPEAN COMMUNITIES (1979).

Konstantinos Voulgarakis, *Reflections on the scope of "EU res judicata" in the context of Regulation 1215/2012*, 3(16) JOURNAL OF PRIVATE INTERNATIONAL LAW (2020).

Tereza Profeldová

Relationship between the EU Law and Constitutional System of Member States - Did EU Cross the Line?

Key words:
EU Law | Primacy of the EU Law | Constitution | Constitutional Systems of Member States | Court of Justice of the European Union | Treaty on the Functioning of the European Union | Treaty on European Union | Preliminary ruling | Competences of the EU | Supremacy of National Constitutional Law | Sovereignty

Abstract | *EU law is based on the principle of its primacy. It is argued that by voluntarily acceding to the EU, the Member States agreed to limit their sovereignty and to transfer certain powers to the EU. Such principles were undisputed as long as they concerned the interpretation and application of EU secondary law concerning specific rights and obligations that should take their full effect in every Member State. From this perspective, the autonomous and uniform interpretation of EU law seems to be fully accepted.*

Over the years, the EU took the stance that not only does EU law takes precedence over the national laws of the Member States, but cannot be repealed even by the constitutional systems of the Member States. The CJEU ruled that where the constitutional systems of the Member States collide with EU law, the national courts should not rely on the respective provisions of constitutional law.

This stance prompted a reaction from national constitutional courts. Examples can be found of decisions that clearly refuse the interference of EU law with elementary principles and values that form the core of their constitutional system. It is to be noted that they did so without generally refusing the primacy of EU law, and reserved the right to review the interpretation provided by the CJEU in exceptional circumstances where fundamental constitutional principles are at stake.

The debate became more heated when it moved from a strictly legal (jurisdictional) perspective. Recently, by relying on the primacy of EU law, EU

Mgr. Tereza Profeldová, attorney-at-Law, successfully completed the Law and Legal Science master´s programme at the Faculty of Law of the Charles University in Prague. Currently a Ph.D. student at the Faculty of Law, University of West Bohemia in Pilsen.
E-mail: tereza.profeldova@ablegal.cz

institutions have begun to interfere with decisions taken by the Member States (especially Poland and Hungary) that clearly fall outside the scope of EU competences. They did so by relying on Articles 1, 2 and 19 TEU. Should such interpretation of the powers of the EU be confirmed, it would lead to the ability of the EU to control any political decision of its Member States.

| | |

I.   Introduction

5.01.   The relationship between the EU and its Member States has never been an easy one. The entire system of EU law is based on the principle of primacy of EU law over national legal systems. The principle is not so much of a problem when it comes to the interpretation of Regulations1 (as a legal instrument that is binding and directly applicable throughout the EU) and Directives.2

5.02.   That is not to say that the decisions rendered by the Court of Justice of the European Union (CJEU) within its authority and concerning the interpretation and application of the aforementioned legal acts are universally accepted and do not create controversy. However, preliminary rulings with regard to such questions raised before the court of a Member State[3] are, as a general rule, not challenged as to their binding effect and the CJEU's authority to give them.

5.03.   Where disputes between the EU and its Member States begin is when the CJEU exercises its authority with regard to the interpretation of the Treaties stipulated in Article 267 TFEU. The Member States increasingly see the CJEU´s rulings as interference in their constitutional order and as an attack on their sovereignty. This is mainly caused by the impression that, apart from using the undisputed powers vested in the CJEU, the EU tries to control policies and fundamental principles on which the society of the Member States is built. By using general and, up to a certain extent, declamatory provisions of

---

[1]   Article 288 of the Treaty on the Functioning of the European Union (TFEU), available at: https://eur-lex.europa.eu/legal-content/EN/TXT/HTML/?uri=CELEX:12016E/TXT&from=CS (accessed on 24 March 2022).

[2]   Also Article 288 TFEU, which describes Directives as legal acts that are binding upon the respective Member States as to the result to be achieved, but that leave to the national authorities the choice with respect to the form and methods for how to achieve said result.

[3]   Article 267 TFEU.

Relationship between the EU Law and Constitutional System of Member States...

Czech Yearbook of International Law®

the Treaties,[4] the CJEU establishes its jurisdiction with regard to the examination of the compliance of national law (including constitutional law) with the values based on which the EU is based.[5]

5.04. The possibility to rely on these fundamental principles opens the door for the review of basically any legislation, and even the political decision that results in the enactment of such legislation, regardless of whether or not it falls within the scope of the Treaties. While it is undisputed that the Member States are not in a position to override or repeal EU law, to apply EU law inconsistently or to apply provisions of national law that are incompatible with EU law, it is questionable whether the primacy of EU law should exceed the adherence to substantive provisions that stipulate specific rights and obligations and that include the interpretation of and compliance with general democratic values.

5.05. The stance taken by the EU is often based on the argument that EU law amounts to more than just a body of legal regulations that is to be interpreted and applied by the national courts. One speaks of the creation of a completely new legal system, which the Member States voluntarily (by accessing the EU) accepted and thereby themselves limited the scope of their sovereignty.[6]

5.06. Examples can be found of Member States that fully accepted the primacy of EU law and the consequences thereof.[7] The majority of Member States, on the other hand, defend the supremacy of their constitutional norms over the entire (national) legal system, including EU law. As will be demonstrated below, while the problematics may be presented as a purely legal (jurisdictional) one, this is hardly the case. In fact, there is probably no universal answer. Apart from the clear political dimension and the fact

---

[4] See also the TFEU and the Treaty on European Union (TEU), available at: https://eur-lex.europa.eu/legal-content/EN/TXT/HTML/?uri=CELEX:12016M/TXT&from=CS (accessed on 24 March 2022). See Article 1 TEU.

[5] See Article 2 TEU, which refers to the values of respect for human dignity, freedom, democracy, equality, the rule of law and respect for human rights, including the rights of persons belonging to minorities. It is stressed that those values are common to the Member States, which should strive for a society in which pluralism, non-discrimination, tolerance, justice, solidarity and equality between women and men prevail.

[6] While statements like this would be rejected by many without further consideration, it is not so much the fact that EU law cannot be regarded and treated as a set of international (founding) treaties independent of the national legal systems of the Member State that is the core of the dispute. Nor is there a dispute as to the fact that EU law is an autonomous legal system with its own concepts and their interpretation. The real question concerns the scope and borders of EU competences. The need to draw a line between the competences of the EU and its Member States stems from Article 4(1) TEU, according to which competences not conferred upon the EU in the Treaties remain with the Member States. Moreover, the use of the competences conferred upon the EU is governed by the principles of subsidiarity and proportionality (Article 5 TEU). Where the opinions of the EU (CJEU) and the Member States differ is the scope of the competences transferred to the EU.

[7] Such as Estonia or Netherlands. See Michał Jerzy Dębowski, *EU and National Law: Which Is 'superior'?*, NEW EASTERN EUROPE (2021), available at: https://neweasterneurope.eu/2021/08/10/eu-national-law-which-is-superior/ (accessed on 24 March 2022).

that the CJEU seems to take on the role of defining the values referred to in Article 2 TEU, the case law usually referred to when discussing the conflict between EU law and the constitutional systems of the Member States concerns individual and at times incomparable situations. Thus, the question arises as to whether generally valid conclusions can really be drawn from it.

II.   Relationship between EU Law and Constitutional Order of Member States

II.1.   Position Taken by EU

5.07. The fact that the EU can only act within the scope of the competences conferred upon it seems to be implicitly confirmed by the wording of Article 4(2) TEU, which stipulates respect for the equality of Member States, as well as their national identities, inherent in their fundamental structures, political and constitutional, inclusive of regional and local self-government.

5.08. In other words, the Treaties seem to aim at a balance between the need for the primacy of EU law and its autonomous and universal interpretation in line with the common values and aims that the EU is striving to achieve, and the sovereignty of the individual Member States.[8]

5.09. However, from the very beginning, the EU and its institutions reiterated the notion that the founding treaties create a completely new legal system, and that a national law as a subsequent legislative act of the treaties´ signatories (Member States) cannot call into question the rights and obligations established under the treaties.[9] While the conclusions drawn

---

[8]   The reference to the right of the Member States to have their national identity respected as stipulated in Article 4(2) TEU is reaffirmed in the CJEU judgment of 22 December 2010, C-208/09. The CJEU further stated in this decision (paragraph 91) that it is not indispensable for the restrictive measure issued by the authorities of a Member State to correspond to a conception shared by all Member States as regards the precise way in which the fundamental right or legitimate interest in question is to be protected, and that, on the contrary, the need for, and proportionality of, the provisions adopted are not excluded merely because one Member State has chosen a system of protection different from that adopted by another Member State. See also the case law mentioned therein, as well as the CJEU judgment in joined cases C-58/13 and C-59/13 of 17 July 2014 (paragraph 54).

[9]   See also the judgment of the European Court of Justice (ECJ, which is the former designation of the CJEU) of 15 July 1964 in case C-6/64, where the following was held (quote): *By contrast with ordinary international treaties, the EEC Treaty has created its own legal system which, on the entry into force of the Treaty, became an integral part of the legal systems of the Member States and which their courts are bound to apply. By creating a Community of unlimited duration, having its own institutions, its own personality, its own legal capacity and capacity of representation on the international plane and, more particularly, real powers stemming from a limitation of sovereignty or a transfer of powers from the States to the Community, the Member States have limited their sovereign rights, albeit within limited fields, and have thus created a body of law which binds both their nationals and themselves. The integration into the laws of each Member State of provisions which derive from the Community, and more generally the terms and the spirit of the Treaty, make it impossible for the States, as a corollary, to accord precedence to a unilateral and subsequent measure over a legal system accepted by them on a basis of reciprocity. Such a measure cannot therefore be inconsistent with that legal system. The executive force of Community law cannot vary from one State to*

in the aforementioned judgment seem to be clear, a distinction needs to be made between decisions such as this, where a call for the primacy of EU law and its consistent interpretation and application throughout all Member States is with regard to a specific provision of EU law,[10] and cases where EU law should play a decisive role and overrule the interpretation and application of general constitutional principles in the fields where the EU has no specific competencies.

5.10. Similarly, the Kreil case[11] concerns Council Directive 76/207/ EEC of 09 February 1976 on the implementation of the principle of equal treatment for men and women as regards access to employment, vocational training and promotion, and working conditions. Under Article 2(1) of the Directive, the principle of equal treatment shall mean that there shall be no discrimination whatsoever on grounds of sex, either directly or indirectly, by reference in particular to marital or family status. Therefore, when the ECJ rules on the compliance of the German national law with the prohibition of any discrimination laid down by the Directive, its decision concerns the application of EU law to which the Member States voluntarily agreed to adhere. The considerations of the ECJ do not necessarily interfere with the competences that remain with the Member States.

5.11. It is correct that the limited access for women to military posts in the Bundeswehr stemmed from Article 12a of the German constitution (Grundgesetz für die Bundesrepublik Deutschland) in the wording effective at that time, which barred women outright from military posts involving the use of arms and which only allow women access to the medical and military-music services. Taking this fact into consideration, it would be easy to draw a conclusion that the ECJ took on the role of overruling the constitutional system of a Member State, but the interpretation of the judgment is not as simple as that.

5.12. Apart from the fact that – as explained above – the subject of the judgment is the implementation of very specific obligations arising from EU law, and not the examination and assessment of abstract constitutional values and the application thereof throughout a national legal system, it does not deal with the constitutional issue, or rather the precedence of EU law over

---

another in deference to subsequent domestic laws, without jeopardizing the attainment of the objectives of the Treaty set out in Article 5 (2) and giving rise to the discrimination prohibited by Article 7.

[10] The E.N.E.L. case mentioned above concerned the prohibition of discrimination as stipulated by Article 7 of the Treaty establishing the European Economic Community (the Rome Treaty or the EEC Treaty). This provision specifically refers to the prohibition of discrimination within the field of application of the EEC Treaty, and does not provide the EU with the power to make decisions and if necessary to take measures outside the scope of the competences conferred upon the EU.

[11] ECJ Judgment of 11 January 2000, C-285/98.

national constitutional system at all. It simply discusses the content of all relevant provisions of the German law (i.e. not exclusively the constitution), without suggesting that the EU has the authority to force changes to the national constitutional regime.

5.13. Moreover, the Directive in question does not require the Member States to provide women with instant access to any occupation, regardless of the potential underlying principles and values that their society may be based on.[12] Where appropriate, the Directive provided for the discretion of the Member States to let the national law provide for certain exceptions to the Directive, if and where considered appropriate (reasonable). It is clear that such exceptions may vary depending on the cultural and constitutional traditions and specific values on which their society may be based, as well as the individual circumstances of each Member State. Should the national legislature make use of the right to limit the scope of application of the Directive, it should be noted that such exception might impair the binding nature of EU law and its uniform application. This is just another argument against the notion that the judgment could be read as a clear declaration of the primacy of EU law over the constitutional systems of the Member States.

5.14. What the ECJ ruled is that when determining the scope of any derogation from a fundamental right, such as the equal treatment of men and women, the principle of proportionality, as one of the general principles of EU law, must also be observed.

5.15. In this particular case, it was held that an exclusion that applies to almost all military posts cannot be regarded as a derogating measure justified by the specific nature of the posts in question or by the particular context in which the activities in question are carried out. The breach of EU law was not found due to the limited access of women to military posts *per se*, but rather because of the general exclusion of women from military posts involving the use of arms without providing any reasoning and justification for this measure and limiting them to specific posts. Nevertheless, it clearly shows that collisions between EU law and the constitutional orders of the Member States exist.

---

[12] According to Article 2(2) of the Directive, it shall be without prejudice to the right of the Member States to exclude from its field of application occupations (as well as the training leading thereto) for which, by reason of their nature or the context in which they are carried out, the sex of the worker constitutes a determining factor.

Relationship between the EU Law and Constitutional System of Member States...

Czech Yearbook of International Law®

II.2.   Reaction of National Law of Member States

5.16.   Courts of the Member States took the (logically) opposite approach and argued in favour of the supremacy of the constitutional orders of the Member States. The most famous example is the constitutional court of Germany, which issued a decision[13] in which it retained its right to examine CJEU judgments as far as the protection of fundamental rights and freedoms is concerned, since the protection granted to individuals on the EU (then Community) level is not as strong as the protection provided by the constitutional system of Germany, until the EU guarantees a sufficient level of protection that will be maintained and that will provide German people with at least the same fundamental rights and freedoms afforded to them under the German constitution.

5.17.   The aforementioned decision is presented in academic discussions as an act of defiance against the primacy of the EU. However, looking at its reasoning, it is yet another example of a decision that effectively defines the borders between the competences of the EU and its Member States, but rather from a practical perspective. The issue is not the jurisdiction of the CJEU, but a doctrine according to which EU law cannot deprive German individuals of the fundamental rights and freedoms that they currently exercise under the German constitutional system.

5.18.   Even if the end effect is still the same, the argumentation is quite different to claiming that, regardless of the circumstances, the German Constitutional Court is generally not bound by EU law. The Solange I decision seems to suggest the direct opposite, and to imply that once it is satisfied that EU law guarantees the same fundamental rights and freedoms as German law, it will accept the primacy of EU law and the CJEU judgments.[14]

5.19.   At least from the side of the German Constitutional Court, there is no sign of defiance against the growth in the powers of the EU. In fact, it calls for closer integration of the EU and a defined list of fundamental rights and freedoms that would be interpreted and applied by EU institutions. It is therefore somehow paradoxical that the Solange I judgment is seen as inspiration for other constitutional courts that maintained the doctrine of supremacy of national constitutional law.[15]

---

[13]   Resolution of the German Constitutional Court (Bundesverfassungsgericht) of 29 May 1974, No. 2 BvL 52/71, known as Solange I.

[14]   Compare also the judgment of the German Constitutional Court of 12 October 1993, No. 2 BvR 2134, 2159/92, which deals (among others) with the constitutionality of the delegation of certain powers to the EU.

[15]   See also the Italian Constitutional Court in its judgment, No. 288/2010, of 04 October 2010, referenced in Michał Jerzy Dębowski, *EU and National Law: Which Is 'superior'?*, NEW EASTERN EUROPE (2021),

5.20. In its decision known as Solange II,[16] the German Constitutional Court acknowledged the development of EU law and its institutions as far as the protection of fundamental rights and freedoms is concerned, and stated that the conditions laid down in the Solange I decision had been met. As a result, it ruled that there is no further need for the review of the interpretation of EU law provided by the CJEU from the (national) constitutional point of view. This does not preclude the German Constitutional Court from returning to its former position expressed in the Solange I decision and taking back the right to review the CJEU judgments as far as their conformity with the German constitutional system is concerned.

5.21. Considering that, following the entry into force of the Lisbon Treaty in 2009, the Charter of Fundamental Rights of the European Union also became effective, which renders (at least from the German perspective) the return to the Solange I doctrine unlikely, if not impossible.[17]

II.3. Further Development of CJEU Case Law

5.22. Despite the fact that none of the decisions of the (national) state courts mentioned above directly refused to respect the CJEU´s decisions having constitutional aspects, the CJEU considered it necessary to repeatedly reaffirm the primacy of EU law, even if it contradicts the constitutional system of a Member State. To this effect, see the judgment of the CJEU of 26 February 2013 in Case C-399/11.[18]

---

available at: https://neweasterneurope.eu/2021/08/10/eu-national-law-which-is-superior/ (accessed on 24 March 2022) or the decision of the same court, No. 183/73, of 27 December 1973 (see Mart Cartabia, *The Italian Constitutional Court and the Relationship Between the Italian Legal System and the European Community*, 12(1) MICHIGAN JOURNAL OF INTERNATIONAL LAW (1990). Similarly, the decisions of the Czech Constitutional Court, No. Pl. ÚS 50/04 of 08 March 2006 and No. Pl. ÚS 19/08 of 26 November 2008. Despite the refusal of the interference of EU law with the very core of the Czech constitutional system, the direct effect and primacy of EU law is not directly called into question. It is held that, to the extent that the Czech constitutional law can be interpreted and applied in a way consistent with EU law, a duty exists to do so. At the same time, it can be seen that, should EU law – based on the individual circumstances – undermine the primary elements of the Czech constitutional system, the Czech Constitutional Court can overrule it. For a further comparison of the decisions rendered in this respect, see the decisions rendered by the Irish Supreme Court of 19 December 1989 (*Society for the Protection of Unborn Children (Ireland) Ltd.* v. *Grogan*) and of 05 March 1992 (*Attorney General* v. *X.*), judgment of the Polish Supreme Court of 29 May 2019, No. III CSK 209/17, and the decision of the Danish Supreme Court of 06 April 1998, No. I-361/1997.

[16]   Resolution of the German Constitutional Court No. 2 BvR 197/83 of 22 October 1986.

[17]   This conclusion cannot be interpreted too broadly and to the effect that the German Constitutional Court fully accepted the primacy of EU law over the German constitution and the CJEU´s role as the decisive body when it comes to the interpretation of the EU law, as well as the determination of the conformity of the national laws of the Member States with it. In fact, it is the German Constitutional Court that recently rendered a decision in which it retained the right to refuse any decision or other legal act issued by any of the EU institutions, should it exceed the scope of competences conferred upon the EU.

[18]   The following was held – paragraph 58 ff (quote): *That interpretation of Article 53 of the Charter would undermine the principle of the primacy of EU law inasmuch as it would allow a Member State to disapply EU legal rules that are fully in compliance with the Charter where they infringe the fundamental rights*

Relationship between the EU Law and Constitutional System of Member States...

Czech Yearbook of International Law®

5.23. Yet another decision dealt with a different situation, specifically with the obligations of the national courts - when it comes to a conflict between EU law and national rules that are contrary to the Charter of Fundamental Rights of the European Union – to disapply national norms that are contrary to the Charter.[19] It was held that the court´s duty to set aside national legislative provisions cannot be made conditional upon that infringement of the Charter being clear from its text or the case-law relating to it. It was argued that such requirement would withhold from the national court the power to fully assess (or in cooperation with the CJEU) whether the provision in question is compatible with the Charter. To withdraw these powers from the national court would then prevent EU law from having full force and effect.

5.24. The judgment does not specifically mention that this obligation of the national courts also comprises the need to disregard any of their constitutional norms. Such interpretation and conclusion to this effect can, however, be drawn tacitly from the judgment's wording. Considering the unambiguous declaration of the priority of the Charter, there is little doubt that it also takes precedence over any constitutional norms.

5.25. Another interesting point on the issue was (also implicitly) expressed in the CJEU judgment of 05 April 2016 in joined Cases C-404/15 and C-659/15 PPU. It does not explicitly confirm the primacy of EU law over the national legal systems of the Member States, including their constitutional law. Maybe even unintentionally, it opens some questions, mainly concerning the relationship between provisions of EU law that would form part of the constitutional system, had they been adopted by a Member State.

5.26. The case concerned Council Framework Decision 2002/584/ JHA of 13 June 2002 on the European arrest warrant and the surrender procedures between Member States. In short, the application of the Framework Decision is dependent on the court of the executing state being satisfied that the person who is the subject of the European arrest warrant won´t - following the surrender of that person to the issuing Member State - run

---

guaranteed by that State's constitution. It is settled case-law that, by virtue of the principle of the primacy of EU law, which is an essential feature of the EU legal order (see Opinion 1/91 [1991] ECR I-6079, paragraph 21, and Opinion 1/09 [2011] ECR I-1137, paragraph 65), rules of national law, even of a constitutional order, cannot be allowed to undermine the effectiveness of EU law on the territory of that State (see, to that effect, inter alia, Case 11/70 Internationale Handelsgesellschaft [1970] ECR 1125, paragraph 3, and Case C-409/06 Winner Wetten [2010] ECR I-8015, paragraph 61).

[19] See the CJEU judgment of 26 February 2013, C-617/10.

a real risk of being subjected in the issuing Member State to inhuman or degrading treatment.[20]

5.27. Generally, the executing judicial authority must rely on information that is objective, reliable, specific and properly updated on the detention conditions prevailing in the issuing Member State and that demonstrates that there are deficiencies. The question was whether the German authorities on their own have the authority to make a determination as to whether the conditions in the issuing state comply with the requirements set in Article 6 TEU, or whether the execution state must make the decision on the permissibility of surrender conditional upon assurances that detention conditions are in compliance with Article 6 TEU.

5.28. This question is not only a practical one. It goes to the point of whether the constitutional court of the executing state can on its own examine whether the person who is the subject of the European arrest warrant will be (following the surrender) detained in conditions that guarantee respect for human dignity, that the way in which detention is enforced does not cause the individual concerned distress or hardship of an intensity exceeding the unavoidable level, or whether it needs to request additional information from the issuing state as to the conditions in which it is envisaged that the individual concerned will be detained.[21]

5.29. While at first, an impression may arise that by giving the power to ultimately decide on the adherence to Article 6 TEU to the courts of the executing Member State without the issuing Member State being able to intervene, the CJEU would have accepted the role of the national constitutional system and its prevalence over EU law, such interpretation would be clearly wrong.

5.30. Even if the courts of the executing Member Stets were able to make the determination on their own, they would still be bound not to apply any constitutional doctrines that developed with

---

[20] This principle stems from Article 1(3) of the Framework Decision, according to which it is not to have the effect of modifying the obligation to respect fundamental rights as enshrined in Article 6 TEU (this provision refers to the Charter of Fundamental Rights of the European Union, which in Article 4 prohibits the use of inhuman or degrading treatment or punishment). The rights guaranteed under Article 4 of the Charter correspond to Article 3 ECHR (European Convention on Human Rights, as one of the most important instruments developed on the platform of the Council of Europe) and are considered to be absolute. By virtue of Article 52(3) of the Charter, it therefore has the same meaning and the same scope as the legal framework (regulation) provided by the ECHR (see the Explanations relating to the Charter of Fundamental Rights - OJ 2007 C 303, et. 17).

[21] Under Article 15(2) of the Framework Decision, authorities of the issuing state are entitled to do so if they find the information communicated by the issuing Member State to be insufficient to allow it to decide on surrender. In the end, the CJEU confirmed that the aforementioned provision is to be applied and that the issuing Member State needs to be provided with the possibility to provide evidence that, in the individual case at hand, there is no danger of a breach of Article 6 TEU.

regard to the prohibition of inhuman or degrading treatment or punishment. Article 51(1) of the Charter expressly provides that its provisions are addressed to the Member States, and that they are obliged to adhere to them only (sic!) when they are implementing EU law. Since, in this case, the priority of the Charter is expressly provided for, the conflict between EU law and the constitutional systems of the Member States does not even arise.[22]

5.31.   Disregarding the above, the decision can be seen as confirmation of the tendency of the German courts expressed in the Solange I decision to apply their own constitutional standards, should they feel that by adhering to the otherwise applicable law (including EU law) the standard of protection guaranteed to individuals would not reach that required by the German constitution.

5.32.   In a way, the decision shows some similarities to the judgment in the Kreil case. Both concern the application of principles that form part of the constitutional system, and in both situations, the need to apply them is based on a specific provision of EU law, rather than on the general requirement of adherence to the national constitutional system. In this respect, the decision only confirms the previous stance that, where EU law prescribes a certain course of action, the state courts cannot disregard it by referring to their own constitutional principles.

5.33.   This is where the similarity ends and where the CJEU began to deal with issues that the German Constitutional Court provided in its answer in the Solange I decision. While the German courts, by relying on national law,[23] argued that once the court is satisfied that the rights of a person who is the subject of the European arrest warrant guaranteed by Article 4 of the Charter are jeopardized, no additional steps need to be taken and the person in question cannot be surrendered, the CJEU reiterated the principle of the primacy of EU law, regardless of the content of the national law.[24]

---

[22]   In this particular situation, any such conflict could only be theoretical, because all 47 Member States of the Council of Europe, including all EU Member States, are signatories to the ECHR. Article 4 of the Charter is identical to Article 3 ECHR, and is to be interpreted in the same manner. From a practical point of view, the institutions of the EU Member State are bound to come to the same result, regardless of the form in which the aforementioned provisions will be formally applied.

[23]   The Framework Decision was transposed into the German legal system by Sections 78 to 83k of the Law on international mutual legal assistance in criminal matters (Gesetz über die internationale Rechtshilfe in Strafsachen).

[24]   Which – as far as the protection of fundamental rights and freedoms is concerned – is more favorable. From this perspective and unlike in the Kreil case, the German law was in compliance with the EU law but provided for a more favorable treatment to the individuals.

II.4. Charter of Fundamental Rights of European Union

5.34. What should further be taken into account is that, since the Charter became effective, the EU has a codified set of fundamental rights and freedoms, and the inevitable question arises as to the relationship between the Charter and the national constitutional systems. A strong case was made by the Members States when they claimed the superiority of the constitutional principles over EU secondary law.

5.35. The Charter is composed of the same fundamental rights and freedoms that are also part of the national constitutional systems. This could give the wrong impression that there is no actual clash between the two systems. Nothing could be further from the truth. The problem is not the set of rights that are protected, because they indeed overlap. Despite the insistence that these rights and freedoms are universally shared among all Member States,[25] this may to some extent be correct when it comes to the identification of the rights and freedoms *per se.* None of the Member States denies the need for the protection of principles such as the prohibition against discrimination or against the use of inhuman or degrading treatment, etc.

5.36. But every single national constitutional system may ascribe slightly different meaning to these rights, and may guarantee their protection in a different scope and using different tools. This means that one and the same right may be applied significantly differently in various Member States.[26] This is why the distinction between the competences of the EU and its Member States is so important. The application of one and the same right may vary depending on whether the interpretation by the CJEU or the one done by the state courts is considered to be decisive.

5.37. EU law specifically deals with this situation and stipulates limits within which the Charter, as an instrument providing for the guarantee of fundamental rights and freedoms, can be

---

[25] This is one of the reasons why the author is very critical to the concepts such as the EU *public ordre* and the attempt to create an EU constitution. The differences between the values on which the societies in the individual Member States are based are simply too big in order for them to be just disregarded. Much of the friction between the Member States comes down to the Member States´ understandable desire to keep their sovereignty and to be able to interpret and apply their constitutional systems autonomously and without any interference from the EU.

[26] An area where the differences are most significant is family law / family relationships. The concepts of what constitutes family and the view on other issues in connection herewith vary and show that the idea of universally shared values and principles on which society is based is an illusion used for political purposes, such us promoting and enhancing unity and federalization of the EU. Strangely enough, this is also an area where the sovereignty of the Member States and the acceptance of the differing views on family relationships has never been questioned, and the EU is purposefully avoiding the inclusion in its laws of specific rules on this matter, to which the Member States would have to adhere.

used.[27] Taking into account the clear wording of the respective provisions, a conclusion could be drawn that the Charter was never intended to be used outside the scope of the competences of the EU.

5.38.   This, on the other hand, would suggest that with regard to areas where the EU law does not play any role, the Charter should not be applied and the state courts are to proceed in accordance with their national constitutional systems.

5.39.   Areas in which the EU exercises its competences fall clearly within the scope of the Charter, which prevails over the national constitutional system. This is a matter of fact, because arguments can still be made that the principle of state sovereignty is inextricably linked with modern constitutional theory. The Charter does not (at least formally) possess any special effect that would enable it to override national constitutional systems, nor does it take such place within the hierarchy of the legal system that would justify its prevalence over the constitution (constitutional system) of the Member States. The idea that the EU constitution could potentially give rise to a discussion concerning the relationship between the national constitutional system and unified constitutional system of the EU was strictly rejected by the Member States - with reference to the principle of sovereignty, which would be severely impaired by the establishment of the EU´s own constitutional system.

5.40.   Based on the above, and from a legal point of view, the existence of the Charter does not settle the ongoing dispute concerning the relationship between EU law and the constitutional systems of its Member States. On the other hand, the debate is academic. It is widely recognised in practice that the Charter takes precedence over national constitutional systems within the scope of its applicability.

5.41.   The situation is remotely similar to the one that was the subject of examination in the Kreil case, i.e. the EU guarantees in its law that the Member States are bound to apply certain rights that have a constitutional dimension in the national legal system. Considering the Member States´ obligation to apply EU law, there is little doubt that the Charter is to be applied within the scope of competences of the EU.

5.42.   This creates little problems if EU law simply provides for new rights and freedoms of the individuals not foreseen by the

---

[27]   See Article 6(1) TEU, specifying that the provisions of the Charter shall not extend in any way the competences of the EU as defined in the Treaties. The same is stated in the Charter itself. Article 51(2) thereof provides that the Charter does not extend the field of application of EU law beyond the powers of the EU, and does not establish any new power or task for the EU. The same applies for any modification of powers and tasks as defined in the Treaties.

national legal system. While it gets a little more complicated if the new right or freedom collides with an existing national norm that does not form part of the constitutional system of the Member State, the primacy of the EU law is generally accepted. The real problem arises if a specific right provided for by EU law directly contradicts the national constitutional system, or if it guarantees a lesser standard than the national constitutional system.

5.43. This is where the Member States revert to their sovereignty and question the primacy of EU law. Based on the nature of EU law, the CJEU does not deviate from its argumentation and insists that EU law needs to take precedence over the national constitutional system even in these situations. The position of the Member States also did not change. They still reject that the EU can overrule their constitutional systems, at least with regard to issues that the Member States consider crucial and forming the core of the constitutional system.

II.5. Application of EU Law in Case It Falls Outside Powers Conferred upon EU

5.44. The German Constitutional Court recently issued an interesting decision[28] in which it reserved the right to review EU law and to refuse to apply it, despite the principle of primacy,[29] if it comes to the conclusion that the act to be applied is to be considered *ultra vires*. The reason behind this conclusion is the persuasion that if fundamental interests of the Member States are affected, it is imperative that the division of competences between the EU and its Member States be respected as a measure safeguarding the principle of democracy.

5.45. As a result, and in addition to the insistence that EU law cannot lower the level of protection provided by the German constitution,[30] the German Constitutional Court held that the primacy of EU law and the role of the CJEU under Article 19 TEU in its interpretation of the acts of the EU institutions cannot lead to the erosion of Member States´ competences and

---

[28] Judgment in the joint cases 2 BvR 859/15, 2 BvR 1651/15, 2 BvR 2006/15 and 2 BvR 980/16 of 05 May 2020.

[29] As is illustrated by the decision of the German Constitutional Court, it has never questioned the principle of the primacy of EU law. It identifies situations in which it feels justifiable (even taking into account EU law) to disregard this principle and to rely on the national constitutional principles.

[30] The coming into effect of the Charter has put the application of this principle to a test. As has been explained, the Charter needs to be interpreted and applied autonomously and can in certain instances provide a lesser degree of protection that the German Constitution. So far, it seems that Germany accepted the CJEU´s role in the interpretation of the Charter and the supremacy of the CJEU´s rulings in this respect – see also the aforementioned judgment of the CJEU of 05 April 2016 in joined cases C-404/15 and C-659/15 PPU.

to the silent conferral of additional powers on EU institutions. It was further held that in the event of a manifest and structurally significant exceedance of competences by institutions, bodies, offices and agencies of the EU, the constitutional organs must make use of the means at their disposal to actively take steps seeking to ensure adherence to the division of competences and respect for its limits. They should work towards the rescission of acts that fall outside the scope of competences of the EU,[31] and take suitable action to limit the domestic impact of such acts to the greatest extent possible.

5.46. The aforementioned should in no way undermine the primacy of EU law or the CJEU's role. To this effect, the German Constitutional Court confirmed that when assessing the validity or the interpretation of a measure taken by the EU institutions, it should base its review on the understanding and the assessment of such a measure provided by the CJEU.

5.47. At the same time, it was concluded that the CJEU exceeds its judicial mandate given to it by Article 19 TEU when an interpretation of the Treaties is not comprehensible and must thus be considered arbitrary from an objective perspective. Such decisions are no longer covered by Article 19(1). As far as the position of such acts in Germany is concerned,[32] a conclusion was reached that these decisions lack the minimum of democratic legitimation necessary for them to stand the review of the Constitutional Court. The German institutions are also not permitted to participate in the development, nor in the implementation, execution or operationalisation of *ultra vires* acts.

5.48. In case a question concerning the interpretation of the competences conferred upon the EU arises, the German Constitutional Court expressed its opinion that it is not sufficient to simply accept positions asserted by the respective EU institution without closer scrutiny. The broad discretion afforded the EU institutions, together with the limited standard of review applied by the CJEU, fails to give sufficient effect to the principle of conferral[33] and opens the door for the competences

---

[31] Here specifically, the EU integration agenda. The decision in question concerned the Decision of the Governing Council of the European Central Bank of 22 January 2015 and Decision (EU) 2015/774 of the European Central Bank of 04 March 2015 (ECB/2015/10) on a secondary markets public sector asset purchase programme in conjunction with (i) Decision (EU) 2015/2101 of the European Central Bank of 03 September/05 November 2015 (ECB/2015/33), (ii) Decision (EU) 2015/2464 of the European Central Bank of 03 December/16 December 2015 (ECB 2015/48), (iii) Decision (EU) 2016/702 of the European Central Bank of 10 March/18 April 2016 (ECB/2016/8) and (iv) Decision (EU) 2017/100 of the European Central Bank of 08 December 2016/11 January 2017 (ECB/2017/1), all amending Decision (EU) 2015/774.

[32] This conclusion will vary depending on the constitutional system of each individual Member State and cannot be seen as universal. The consequences can thus be different than in Germany.

[33] As one of the fundamental principles of the functioning of the EU.

of the Member States to be undermined. The principle of proportionality and the overall assessment and appraisal that it entails are of great importance with regard to the respect for democracy and the principle of sovereignty. Disregarding these requirements could potentially shift the bases for the division of competences in the EU, undermining the understanding of how the competences between the EU and the Member States are divided and the will of the Member States to confer certain competences upon the EU.

5.49. The German Constitutional Court, however, specifically emphasized that the aforementioned conclusions do not impact in any way the finality and legitimacy of the European integration agenda. In fact, it is implied that the adherence to the principal of conferral is necessary for the successful completion of further integration of the EU.

5.50. While it is clear that the decision does not aim to undermine the position of the EU and its integration,[34] it makes an interesting and in fact important point. It more or less confirms that when it comes to the assessment of the legitimacy of the acts of the EU institutions, the CJEU is not necessarily to be seen as impartial, and its considerations cannot be held to be reliable as far as its conclusions are concerned.[35]

5.51. The decision probably cannot be read as a direct declaration of supremacy of the national constitutional system over EU law, but then the author is of the opinion that such conclusion cannot be drawn from the Solange I decision either. And maybe it´s exactly the concept of the coexistence and cooperation between the two legal systems[36] applied by the German Constitutional Court that makes the decisions more or less acceptable and unchallenged (at least not openly).

5.52. In any case, it brings us to the actual question, which becomes more imminent every day. The discussion concerning the

---

[34] As just mentioned, the decision is purposefully worded so that the conclusions of the German Constitutional Court can actually be presented as being in the interests of the EU and being made with the aim of promoting the acceptance of the integration agenda. It can be inferred that the respect for the division of powers is a precondition for a successful integration. One can agree with this statement if it is understood as a general notion, but it seems to be a little out of place considering the context in which these allegations were made.

[35] Of course, when one reaches such a conclusion, the logical question is whether it only concerns the control exercised in order to ensure that the EU institutions don't overstep their competencies, or whether it applies universally. The politicization of the CJEU´s decision-making process has been the subject of discussion for a long time. It can definitely be said that the observations by the German Constitutional Court exceed the decision in which they were made. At the same time, it would be wrong to undermine the role of the CJEU by rejecting any and all decisions ever rendered. The achievements of the CJEU in the unification of the interpretation of EU law are both undeniable and indispensable to the functioning and application of EU law as a whole.

[36] As opposed to trying to pit them against each other and concluding the definite and overall supremacy of one over the other.

relationship between EU law and the national constitutional system can only remain factual and based on legal arguments if the principle of conferral is respected by the EU institutions, as well as the Member States. But can we still say that this is the case?

III.   Poland

5.53. The EU recently took an extremely proactive approach with regard to certain political decisions taken by its Member States. The interference by the EU institutions opened a completely new chapter in the discussion of whether a Member State has the right to disregard pieces of EU law if it comes to the conclusion that they are contrary to their constitutional system. Poland in particular has been embroiled in a dispute with the EU institutions with regard to the interpretation of some aspects of EU law.

5.54. Herein actually lies the first problem. The dispute is often presented as an attempt by the Polish (and also Hungarian) government to challenge the EU´s rule of law ideal by claiming that different interpretations of it are possible, and that illiberal democracies can co-exist with liberal ones within the EU constitutional framework.[37] Such description suggests that there is indeed only one universal interpretation of the values listed in Article 2 TEU. As mentioned several times, this is a misconception that causes most of the disputes.

5.55. It could probably be said that the Member States share the general concept of each of the aforementioned values; it in no way means that they are interpreted in exactly the same way when it comes to the particularities. The purpose of this article is not to judge whose interpretation is correct or better serves the ideal pursued by the EU. It should highlight the attempts to use these differences as a means to intervene with political decisions and laws of Member States outside the scope of the EU´s competencies.[38]

5.56. From the very beginning, Poland has been one of the Member States that refused to subject its constitutional principles to

---

[37] Michiel Luining, *The EU's rule of law: work is needed*, ACADEMIA (2021), available at: https://www.academia.edu/45681054/The_EUs_rule_of_law_work_is_needed (accessed on 24 March 2022).
[38] I.e. exactly what the German Constitutional Court rejected in the judgment concerning the joint cases 2 BvR 859/15, 2 BvR 1651/15, 2 BvR 2006/15 and 2 BvR 980/16 of 05 May 2020. The difference is that while the German judgment challenged specific decisions made by the ECB, in the case of Poland, the question is much broader and concerns the use of the CJEU´s interpretation of the values listed in Article 2 TEU as a criterion for the determination of the adherence of acts of the Polish government to EU law. Both situations deal with the question of whether decisions rendered by the CJEU when exceeding the competences conferred to it by Article 19 TEU can be subject to review by the (constitutional) courts of the Member States.

Czech Yearbook of International Law®

the power of the EU institutions.[39] Soon enough, some of the political decisions taken by the polish government became a point of controversy. Again, the point of this article is not to scrutinize the position that Poland took with regard to certain issues. The point to be made is that these disputes escalated, especially with regard to the judicial reform that Poland decided to implement. The disputes began on several fronts. On 03 April 2019, the Commission launched an infringement procedure on the grounds that the new disciplinary regime for judges undermines the judicial independence of Polish judges and does not ensure the necessary guarantees to protect judges from political control.[40]

5.57. The CJEU rendered a judgment in the matter on 15 July 2021.[41] It was argued by the Commission that, while in general terms the intervention of an executive body in the process for appointing judges does not, in itself, affect the independence or impartiality of those judges, the combination and simultaneous introduction of various legislative reforms prepared by the Polish government have given rise to a structural breakdown, which no longer makes it possible either to preserve the appearance of the independence and impartiality of justice and the trust that the courts must inspire.[42]

5.58. It was argued that the requirement of independence derives from Article 19(1) TEU, and must be met by national courts since they have to interpret and apply EU law. Therefore, it is necessary that the rules governing the disciplinary regime applicable to the judges who make up those courts provides for the involvement of bodies that themselves meet the requirements inherent in effective judicial protection.[43]

[39] In fact, the first decision in which the Polish Constitutional Court refused the full effects of the primacy of EU law was already rendered in May 2005 (see judgment K 18/04 released on 11 May 2005, English summary available at: http://www.proyectos.cchs.csic.es/euroconstitution/library/documents/Polish%20 Constitutional%20Tribunal_Judgment%20Polands%20accession%20to%20the%20EU.pdf (accessed on 24 March 2022)), in which it was asked to rule on the constitutionality of Poland's accession to the EU. The Polish Constitutional Court held that the Accession Treaty does not infringe the provisions of the Polish Constitution, and specifically emphasized that recognition of the Constitution as the supreme Polish law, which is not undermined by the accession to the EU. In this respect, it was concluded that the Constitution enjoys the precedence of binding force and the precedence of application. It was further confirmed that a possible collision between a constitutional norm and a provision of EU law may under no circumstances be resolved by assuming the supremacy of EU law (see Marta Lasek-Markey, *Poland's Constitutional Tribunal on the status of EU law: The Polish government got all the answers it needed from a court it controls*, EUROPEAN LAW BLOG (2021), available at: https://europeanlawblog.eu/2021/10/21/polands-constitutional-tribunal-on-the-status-of-eu-law-the-polish-government-got-all-the-answers-it-needed-from-a-court-it-controls/ (accessed on 24 March 2022).
[40] See the Commission´s press release - Rule of Law: Commission launches infringement procedure against Poland for violations of EU law by its Constitutional Tribunal, available at: https://ec.europa.eu/commission/presscorner/detail/en/ip_21_7070 (accessed on 24 March 2022).
[41] Case C-791/19.
[42] CJEU Judgment of 15 July 2021, C-791/19, paragraph 64. See also paragraphss 56 ff of the judgment.
[43] CJEU Judgment of 15 July 2021, C-791/19, paragraph 64.

Relationship between the EU Law and Constitutional System of Member States...

Czech Yearbook of International Law®

5.59. Finally, it was held that the preliminary ruling procedure provided for in Article 267 TFEU forms a key part of the judicial system, and provides sufficient scope of discretion for the national courts in referring matters to the CJEU.[44] It was held that national law (including rules under which judges are exposed to disciplinary proceedings when they have made a reference for a preliminary ruling to the CJEU) cannot prevent a national court from exercising that discretion or complying with that obligation to refer a preliminary question to the CJEU.[45]

5.60. Based on all the above, the CJEU concluded that Poland failed to fulfil its obligations under Article 19(1) TEU and Article 267 TFEU.[46]

5.61. Even before that, a request to issue a preliminary ruling concerning the disputed judicial reform was referred to the CJEU by Polish courts dealing with disputes with some judges affected by the judicial reform. On 19 November 2019, the CJEU rendered a judgment in joint cases C-585/18, C-624/18 and C-625/18 that already answered the questions mentioned above and effectively served as the basis for all future judgments in the matter, including the CJEU Judgment, of 15 July 2021, C-791/19.

5.62. The (so far) final judgment of the CJEU in the matter was rendered on 02 March 2021 in Case C-824/18. Apart from the repeated criticism of the judicial reform, it once again reiterated the principle of the primacy of EU law, and explained it as binding on all the bodies of a Member State, without, inter alia, provisions of domestic law relating to the attribution of jurisdiction, including constitutional provisions, being able to prevent that.[47]

5.63. Further, the CJEU argued that the principle of primacy of EU law must be interpreted as requiring national courts to disapply any rules of national law being contrary to EU law, whether they are of a legislative or constitutional origin.[48] This reaffirms

---

[44] CJEU Judgment of 15 July 2021, C-791/19, paragraphs 222 and 223.
[45] CJEU Judgment of 15 July 2021, C-791/19, paragraphs 225 ff.
[46] In the meantime, a further infringement procedure was initiated by the Commission on 29 April 2020. The Commission proceeded by requesting that the CJEU impose interim measures on Poland. This request was granted by an order dated 27 October 2021 in Case C-204/21 R. Because the Commission further concluded that Poland did not take measures necessary in order to implement the conclusions reached by the CJEU in its judgment in Case C-791/19 of 15 July 2021, on 07 September 2021, the Commission took the decision to request that financial penalties be imposed on Poland in order for it to comply with the aforementioned CJEU judgment ordering interim measures. Further, the Commission decided to send a letter of formal notice under Article 260(2) TFEU to Poland for not taking the necessary measures needed in order to fully comply with the judgment. For more details on this development, see the Commission's press release - Rule of Law: Commission launches infringement procedure against Poland for violations of EU law by its Constitutional Tribunal, available at: https://ec.europa.eu/commission/presscorner/detail/en/ip_21_7070 (accessed on 24 March 2022).
[47] CJEU Judgment of 02 March 2021, C-824/18, paragraph 148.
[48] See the CJEU Judgment of 02 March 2021, C-824/18, paragraph 150.

the position that EU law prevails even over the constitutional systems of the Member States.

5.64. The judgment resulted in an application to the Polish Constitutional Court, which on 07 October 2021 decided (Ref. No. K 3/21) that Articles 1, 2 and 19 TEU are partially unconstitutional insofar as they enable the EU institutions to act outside the scope of the competences conferred upon them, to promote the primacy of EU law over the Polish constitution, and to restrict Polish sovereignty as a result. It was held that Article 19 TEU in particular cannot be applied in order to allow the national courts to bypass the provisions of the Polish constitution by referring the matter to the CJEU and allowing the CJEU to rule on the legality and effectiveness of the procedure for appointment.

5.65. Apparently, when limiting the procedure for a preliminary ruling, the Polish Constitutional Court even exceeded the application by the Polish Prime Minister by challenging the preliminary ruling procedure laid down in Article 267 TFEU, and opened the door for the Polish courts to disregard the judgments rendered by the CJEU.[49]

5.66. While the latter clearly is a step too far that can only escalate the conflict, it is clear from the reasoning of the CJEU´s judgments that the EU is indeed using the aforementioned provisions of the TEU in order to be able to rule on issues that fall outside the scope of its competences and interfere with the political decisions of the Member States. What can further be seen is a double standard, since the EU (CJEU) only seems to revert to these alleged powers in case it disagrees with the steps taken by the Member State. The notion that the Member states voluntarily subjected themselves to the interpretation of the values and rights listed in Article 2 TEU provided by the EU and agreed to suspend the application of their national constitutional system has never been properly argued, and the EU (CJEU) simply takes it as a given fact.

5.67. The withholding of billions of euros of aid for post-pandemic rebuilding in Poland by the EU over concerns that the rule of law is being degraded in the country[50] also does not help. In this specific case, both sides have long ceased to use proper legal

---

[49]   Marta Lasek-Markey, *Poland's Constitutional Tribunal on the status of EU law: The Polish government got all the answers it needed from a court it controls*, EUROPEAN LAW BLOG (2021), available at: https:// europeanlawblog.eu/2021/10/21/polands-constitutional-tribunal-on-the-status-of-eu-law-the-polish-government-got-all-the-answers-it-needed-from-a-court-it-controls/ (accessed on 24 March 2022).
[50]   Poland's top court rules against primacy of EU law, available at: https://www.dw.com/en/polands-top-court-rules-against-primacy-of-eu-law/a-59440843 (accessed on 24 March 2022).

arguments and have made the collision between EU law and the constitutional systems of the Member States a political one.

5.68. This is exactly what hinders the possibility of reaching a solution that would respect the relevant positions of both sides. While it is clear that the member States cannot cherry-pick the pieces of EU law that they like and disregard any rules to which they have reservations, it is similarly unacceptable[51] for the EU to use the primacy of EU law for its own purposes and in order to obtain additional powers that were not conferred upon it.

| | |

Summaries

FRA [*Les rapports entre le droit de l'UE et les systèmes constitutionnels des États membres : l'UE a-t-elle dépassé les limites ?*]

Le droit de l'UE est fondé sur le principe de sa primauté. Un argument fréquent est qu'en adhérant à l'UE, les États membres ont volontairement accepté la restriction de leur souveraineté et le transfert de certains de leurs pouvoirs à l'UE. Ces principes sont incontestables dans la mesure où ils concernent l'interprétation et l'application du droit dérivé de l'UE en matière de droits et obligations concrètes qui doivent prendre effet dans tous les États membres. Dans cette perspective, le principe d'une interprétation autonome et uniforme du droit de l'UE paraît pleinement acceptable.

Au fil des années, l'UE est parvenue à la conclusion que le droit de l'UE non seulement prévaut sur le droit national des États membres, mais aussi ne peut être restreint par l'ordre constitutionnel d'un État membre. La CJUE a jugé que lorsque le système constitutionnel d'un État membre est en conflit avec le droit de l'UE, les juridictions nationales doivent faire abstraction des dispositions pertinentes du droit constitutionnel.

Cette position a provoqué une réaction de la part des cours constitutionnelles nationales. On peut trouver des décisions qui rejettent catégoriquement l'ingérence du droit de l'UE dans les valeurs et principes fondamentaux qui sont à la base du système constitutionnel. Il convient toutefois de noter qu'en adoptant cette position, les cours constitutionnelles n'ont pas rejeté la primauté du droit de l'UE en tant que telle : elles se

---

[51] Not mentioning the detrimental effect that it has on the reputation of the EU within the general public of the Member States and any potential attempts for further integration.

sont seulement réservé le droit d'examiner son interprétation par la CJUE dans des circonstances exceptionnelles, lorsque des principes constitutionnels fondamentaux sont en jeu.

Cette discussion est devenue particulièrement animée au moment où elle a dépassé le cadre juridique relatif à la question de compétence. Les institutions des Communautés européennes, invoquant le principe de la primauté du droit de l'UE, ont récemment commencé à interférer dans les décisions des États membres (en particulier la Pologne et la Hongrie) qui ne relèvent pas nécessairement de la compétence de l'UE, et ce sur le fondement des articles 1, 2 et 19 du TUE. Si une telle interprétation des compétences de l'UE devait être confirmée, l'UE serait dotée de la capacité de contrôler l'ensemble des décisions politiques de ses États membres.

CZE **[Vztah práva EU a ústavních systémů členských států - překročila EU hranice?]**

Právo EU je založeno na principu své nadřazenosti. Argumentuje se, že dobrovolným vstupem do EU souhlasily členské státy s omezením suverenity a přenosem určitých svých pravomocí na EU. Tyto zásady byly nesporné, dokud se týkaly výkladu a aplikace sekundárního práva EU ohledně konkrétních práv a povinností, jež by měly nabýt plných účinků ve všech členských státech. Z tohoto pohledu se zdá být zásada autonomního a jednotného výkladu práva EU plně akceptovaná.

Během let přistoupila EU k pozici, podle níž nejenže má právo EU přednost před národním právem členských států, ale nemůže být omezeno ani na základě ústavního pořádku členského státu. SDEU vydal rozhodnutí, podle něhož v případě, kdy ústavní systém členského státu koliduje s právem EU, národní soudy by se neměly opírat o příslušná ustanovení ústavního práva.

Tento postoj vyvolal reakci ze strany národních ústavních soudů. Lze nalézt příklady rozhodnutí, která jednoznačně odmítají zásah práva EU do základních principů a hodnot tvořících základ ústavního systému. Je nutné poznamenat, že ústavní soudy takto postupovaly bez toho, aniž by obecně odmítly přednost práva EU a vyhradily si právo přezkoumat jeho výklad provedený SDEU za výjimečných okolností, kdy jsou v sázce stěžejní ústavní principy. Tato diskuze se vyostřila v okamžiku, kdy došlo k jejímu přesunu z čistě právní perspektivy týkající se pravomoci. Instituce ES zaštiťující se principem přednosti práva EU začaly v nedávné době zasahovat do rozhodnutí členských států (zvláště Polska a Maďarska), která jednoznačně nespadají pod pravomoci EU. Učinily tak s odkazem na čl. 1, 2 a 19 SEU. Pokud by se měl takový výklad pravomocí EU potvrdit, vedlo by to ke schopnosti

Czech Yearbook of International Law®

EU kontrolovat veškerá politická rozhodnutí svých členských států.

| | |

POL   [*Stosunek prawa UE i systemów konstytucyjnych krajów członkowskich – czy UE przekroczyła granice?*]
Teoria konstytucyjna, według której konstytucję należy bezwzględnie postrzegać jako nadrzędną wobec wszystkich pozostałych przepisów prawa, mających zastosowanie w konkretnej sytuacji, przez wiele lat była niepodważalna. Jednak wraz z powstaniem prawa UE zasada nadrzędności konstytucji zaczęła być stopniowo kwestionowana. TSUE wielokrotnie potwierdzał prymat prawa UE i orzekł, że musi on być stosowany bez względu na ewentualne kolizje z krajowym porządkiem konstytucyjnym. Na początku ta dyskusja dotyczyła stosowania konkretnych zasad prawa UE, jednak późniejsza argumentacja TSUE stała się środkiem wykorzystywanym przez UE do wpływania na decyzje polityczne i legislacyjne krajów członkowskich i wymuszania własnej wykładni podstawowych praw i wartości wskazanych w art. 2 TUE.

DEU   [*Zur Beziehung zwischen dem EU-Recht und den Verfassungssystemen der Mitgliedsstaaten – ist die EU zu weit gegangen?*]
Über lange Jahre hinweg galt die Verfassungstheorie als unanfechtbar, wonach die Verfassung eines Staates notwendigerweise als allen übrigen auf die jeweilige Situation anzuwendenden Rechtsvorschriften übergeordnet zu betrachten war. Mit der Entstehung des EU-Rechts wurde allerdings dieses Prinzip des absoluten Vorrangs der Verfassung schrittweise untergraben. Der EuGH hat wiederholt den Vorrang des EU-Rechts bestätigt und beschlossen, das EU-Recht müsse seine vollen Wirkungen ungeachtet einer etwaigen Kollision mit dem Verfassungsrecht des jeweiligen Mitgliedsstaats entfalten. Anfangs betraf diese Diskussion die Anwendung konkreter Regeln des EU-Rechts, doch wurde die Argumentation des EuGH später zu einem Mittel der Beeinflussung politischer und gesetzgeberischer Entscheidungen der Mitgliedsstaaten seitens der EU, insofern als sie eine eigene Auslegung der in Art. 2 des Gründungsvertrags erwähnten Grundrechte und Werte erzwingt.

RUS [*Отношения между правом ЕС и конституционными системами государств-членов: перешел ли ЕС границы?*]
В течение длительного времени не подвергалась сомнению конституционная теория, согласно которой конституцию следует считать выше всех других законов, применяемых в той или иной ситуации. Однако с появлением права ЕС принцип верховенства конституции начал терять свое безусловное значение. Суд Европейского союза (СЕС) неоднократно подтверждал верховенство права ЕС и выносил решения, что оно должно действовать независимо от возможного конфликта с национальным конституционным порядком. В то время как вначале данное обсуждение касалось применения конкретных правил права ЕС, позже аргументация СЕС стала средством, с помощью которого ЕС оказывает влияние на политические и законодательные решения государств-членов, навязывая свое толкование основных прав и ценностей, перечисленных в Статье 2 Договора о Европейском союзе.

ESP [*¿Proporciona la jurisdicción incuestionable de los árbitros a las partes litigantes un mecanismo de control efectivo por parte de los tribunales nacionales?*]
El lugar del arbitraje como criterio principal para distinguir entre el arbitraje nacional y el extranjero no solo determina la lex arbitri aplicable, sino que también influye en el alcance de la jurisdicción de los tribunales en relación con el arbitraje. En una número creciente de casos, se hace necesaria la intervención (el ejercicio de funciones auxiliares) de los tribunales de otro Estado. La relación entre los tribunales nacionales y el arbitraje extranjero no siempre es sencilla. Además, las diferencias entre los regímenes nacionales de lex arbitri hacen que no exista una norma uniforme para ellos. Por lo tanto, es importante que las partes litigantes del arbitraje sean conscientes de los problemas prácticos a los que se pueden enfrentar, así como del impacto de la elección del lugar del arbitraje en el alcance de la jurisdicción de los tribunales.

| | |

Bibliography:

Mart Cartabia, *The Italian Constitutional Court and the Relationship Between the Italian Legal System and the European Community*, 12(1) MICHIGAN JOURNAL OF INTERNATIONAL LAW (1990).

Michał Jerzy Dębowski, *EU and National Law: Which Is 'superior'?*, NEW EASTERN EUROPE (2021).

Michiel Luining, *The EU's rule of law: work is needed*, ACADEMIA (2021).

Marta Lasek-Markey, *Poland's Constitutional Tribunal on the status of EU law: The Polish government got all the answers it needed from a court it controls*, EUROPEAN LAW BLOG (2021).

Czech Yearbook of International Law®

Albertas Šekštelo

Key words:
BIT | ECHR | ICSID |
investment arbitration | MIT
| Urbaser | VCLT

Jurisdictional Challenges Related to Investor-State Counterclaims Based on Breach of Human Rights

Abstract | No one could imagine that the international investment dispute settlement would evolve to the level that the States-respondents raise counterclaims for the breach of human rights.

Historically, international protection of human rights is vested exclusively upon the States. This is partially because the corporations do not have international personality in terms of public international law.

On the other hand, the international investment dispute settlement system was designed to give an option for the aggrieved investors to file international claims directly against the host States without using diplomatic protection.

However, no one could imagine that there would be a turn around and the States would start complaining against investors in the same investment arbitrations by filing counterclaims. As this dispute settlement system was not created to protect the States from breach of human rights by investors, the counterclaims raise serious jurisdictional concerns.

This Article will address the following hypotheses: (1) whether a Tribunal can discern investor's consent to resolve a State's counterclaim based on investment protection treaties, irrespective of the wording of the applicable treaty, and (2) whether the latter must impose obligations on Investors to protect human rights for such a counterclaim to succeed.

Consequently, the first hypothesis is that the investor's consent to a counterclaim must be expre-

Albertas Šekštelo is a counsel in PLP Motieka & Audzevičius. He has considerable experience in both international investment and commercial arbitrations under ICSID, ICC, SCC, UNCITRAL, LCIA, VIAC, MKAS, BelCCI, VCCA rules, as well as in complex cross-border litigations with a focus on international insolvency, asset-tracing proceedings and human rights. Šekštelo has a Master's Degree in Law from the Faculty of Law, Vilnius University (2005), and a PGDip (with distinction) in International Arbitration from Queen Mary University of London (2011) and LL.M (with distinction) in Comparative and International Dispute Resolution from Queen Mary University of London (2021). In 2013, he became a Fellow of the Chartered Institute of Arbitrators (FCIArb). He also is an individual observer of the European Law Institute (ELI). Šekštelo is the author of many publications in the field of arbitration and civil procedure. He is a lecturer in the Vilnius University where he teaches courses in civil law, business dispute resolution, and

Czech Yearbook of International Law®

ssly stated, should not be interpreted broadly, and should stem from the relevant BIT or MIT. The landmark case Urbaser v. Argentina sets the scene for further use of the counterclaims by the States-respondents. This hypothesis can be tested by checking the consent requirements generally and for the counterclaims. The investor's consent must also be analyzed as to whether it is implied or interpreted broadly for purposes of jurisdictional requirements set forth in the ICSID Convention and BITs.

international business transactions for LL.M students.
E-mail: albertas.sekstelo@motieka.com

The second hypothesis tested in this Article is that any broadly-worded BIT or MIT imposes an obligation on the investors to protect human rights. There should be little debate that, under international law, States have positive obligations to safeguard human rights. By testing this hypothesis, the question becomes whether the protection of human rights falls by default within the ambit of BITs or should be addressed expressly.

| | |

I. Introduction

6.01.   Counterclaims based on infringement of human rights by investors have become more popular in investment arbitration. This is because international corporations acting as investors gain more financial and regulatory power when dealing with the host States and could be in principle accountable for the breach of human rights. Moreover, investments quite often are substantial to the State's economy and interfere with human rights, for instance, with the right to water[1] or protection of the areas vital for indigenous people.[2]

6.02.   Consequently, the States started raising counterclaims in a number of recent investment arbitrations. This indicates a broader trend in asserting counterclaims more frequently and easily in investment arbitration or negotiating new treaties that expressly allow counterclaims and protects human rights infringed by the investors or their responsible investments.

6.03.   However, such counterclaims raise the following main serious jurisdictional issues to be addressed: (1) whether a Tribunal can discern investor's consent to resolve State's counterclaims based on investment protection treaties, irrespective of the wording of the applicable treaty, (2) whether the latter must

---

[1]   See, e. g., *Urbaser S.A. and Consorcio de Aguas Bilbao Bizkaia, Bilbao Biskaia Ur Partzuergoa* v. *the Argentine Republic*, ICSID Case no. ARB/07/26, Award of December 08, 2016.

[2]   *Burlington Resources Inc* v. Republic of Ecuador, ICSID Case no. ARB/08/5, Award of February 08, 2017.

impose obligations on Investors to protect human rights for such counterclaims to succeed.

6.04. Consequently, the first hypothesis is that the investor's consent to counterclaims must be expressly stated, should not be interpreted broadly, and should stem from the relevant BIT or MIT. The landmark case *Urbaser* v. *Argentina* sets the scene for further use of the counterclaim by the States-respondents. This hypothesis will be tested by checking the consent requirements generally and for the counterclaims. Finally, there will be an analysis of whether the investor's consent can be implied or interpreted broadly for the purposes of jurisdictional requirements set forth in the ICSID Convention and BITs.

6.05. The second hypothesis tested in this Article is that any broadly-worded BIT or MIT imposes an obligation on the investors to protect of human rights. There should be little debate that, under international law, States have positive obligations to safeguard human rights. By testing this hypothesis, the question becomes whether the protection of human rights falls by default within the ambit of BITs or should be addressed expressly. Finally, I will analyse whether the Tribunals have an obligation to apply the human rights law *ex offitio* because of *iura novit curia* or *ius cogens* implications.

II. Hypothesis 1: The Investor's Consent to a Counterclaim Must Be Expressly Stated, Should Not Be Interpreted Broadly, and Should Stem from the Relevant BIT or MIT

6.06. Like any other adjudicating body having the power to grant a *res judicata* judgment, a Tribunal must, first of all, make sure it has jurisdiction over a particular party (*ratione personae*) and subject matter of the dispute (*ratione materiae*). Such dispute must also meet the temporal requirements under a particular treaty or other instrument containing the parties' consent to arbitration (*ratione temporis*). No finding of jurisdiction is possible without establishing both parties' consent.

6.07. Case law analysis related to counterclaims in investment arbitration[3] tends to reveal that Tribunals are too eager to

---

[3] See e. g., *Saluka Investments B.V.* v. *Czech Republic*, Decision on Jurisdiction over the Czech Republic's Counterclaim, 07 May 2004; *Sergei Paushok, SJSC Golden East Company and SJSC Vostokneftegaz Company* v. *The Government of Mongolia*, Award on Jurisdiction and Liability, 28 April 2011; *Spyridon Roussalis* v. *Republic of Romania*, ICSID Case no. ARB/06/1, Award of December 07, 2011; *Urbaser S.A. and Consorcio de Aguas Bilbao Bizkaia, Bilbao Biskaia Ur Partzuergoa* v. *the Argentine Republic*, ICSID Case no. ARB/07/26, Award of December 08, 2016; *Bear Creek Mining Corporation* v. *Republic of Peru*, ICSID Case no. ARB/14/21, Award of November 30, 2017; *David Aven et al.* v. *Costa Rica*, DR-CAFTA and

interpret investors' consents to the jurisdiction over States' counterclaims overly broadly, thus disregarding not only the relevant language of the BIT or MIT, but also basic principles of public international law.

6.08. *Urbaser* v. *Argentina* is a perfect example. This section will begin with (**II.1.**) a brief summary of the case and the Tribunal's findings. (**II.2.**) Then it will address the important jurisdictional problems raised by the award: Tribunal's ignorance of lack of the investor's consent to jurisdiction over counterclaims, (**II.3.**) and overly broad interpretation of the applicable BIT that led to a wrong assumption of the existence of such consent. (**II.4.**) Following will be a critical analysis, because *Urbaser* v. *Argentina* sets the scene for prospective disputes over counterclaims and might instigate the Tribunals not to investigate properly the jurisdictional issues of the awards in question. (**II.5.**) Finally, there will be a conclusions on the first hypothesis whether the investor's consent to a counterclaim must be expressly stated, should not be interpreted broadly, and should stem from the relevant BIT or MIT.

II.1. Summary of the Facts and Tribunal's Findings in *Urbaser* v. *Argentina*

6.09. In the landmark *Urbaser* v. *Argentina* case⁴ the Investor entered into a concession agreement with Argentina. The agreement was related to the provision of drinking water and sewage services in Buenos Aires. When the investor brought claims before ICSID under the relevant Argentina-Spain BIT,⁵ Argentina launched a counterclaim. The counterclaim was based on the alleged violation by the investor of an international human rights obligation.

6.10. The claimant made jurisdictional objections on several main points: (1) the claimant did not consent to the counterclaim; (2) the asymmetric nature of Argentina-Spain BIT prevents the State from submitting the counterclaim; (3) the main goal of the BIT in question is to protect investments, but not a quasi-judicial review of national regulatory actions.⁶

6.11. In its 328-page award the Tribunal devotes only slightly over four pages to the jurisdictional issues related to the counterclaim.

UNCITRAL Case no. UNCT/15/3, Final Award of September 08, 2018.

⁴ *Urbaser S.A. and Consorcio de Aguas Bilbao Bizkaia, Bilbao Biskaia Ur Partzuergoa* v. *the Argentine Republic*, ICSID Case no. ARB/07/26, Award of December 08, 2016.

⁵ Agreement Between the Argentine Republic and the Kingdom of Spain on the Reciprocal Promotion and Protection of Investments (03 October 1991).

⁶ *Urbaser S.A. and Consorcio de Aguas Bilbao Bizkaia, Bilbao Biskaia Ur Partzuergoa* v. *the Argentine Republic*, ICSID Case no. ARB/07/26, Award of December 08, 2016, paragraph 1120.

The central provision of the Argentina-Spain BIT examined by the Tribunal was Article X(1) stating that

> [d]isputes arising between a Party and an investor of the other Party in connection with investments within the meaning of this Agreement shall, as far as possible, be settled amicably between the parties

6.12. The Tribunal disagreed with the claimant and explained that Article X(1) of the Argentina-Spain BIT does not prevent the counterclaims as it refers to 'parties'.[7] It concluded that '[t]he consent given by the Claimant on the basis of Article X [...] covers all disputes in connection with investments [...]'.[8] The Tribunal assumed that it had jurisdiction over the counterclaim.

6.13. However, with due respect, the Tribunal's reasoning is not persuasive.

II.2. *Urbaser* v. *Argentina* - Did the Investor Expressly or Otherwise Consent to Jurisdiction Over Counterclaim?

II.2.1. *Investor's Consent, Expressly or Otherwise to Counterclaim Jurisdiction*

6.14. It seems that the Tribunal relied on the implied claimant's consent for the respondent's right to file a counterclaim. The Tribunal even admitted that '[t]here had never been the slightest concern expressed in that regard.'[9]

6.15. The theory of implied consent has its foundation in the private, not public, law and may be employed in commercial arbitration 'to infer the parties' true intention through their behaviour.[10] However, there was no factual basis for such implied consent. The claimants argued that the counterclaim came as a surprise after over more than seven years of the respondent's silence and 'it is an unmistakable symptom of the completely unfounded nature of an improvised counterclaim entirely devoid of foundation.'[11] Thus, there are no factual implications of the implied claimants' consent to respondent's right to file a counterclaim.

---

[7] *Ibid.*, at 1143. Article X(1) of the BIT in question states that "[d]isputes arising between a Party and an investor of the other Party in connection with investments within the meaning of this Agreement shall, as far as possible, be settled amicably between the parties to the dispute".

[8] *Ibid.*, at 1147.

[9] *Urbaser S.A. and Consorcio de Aguas Bilbao Bizkaia, Bilbao Biskaia Ur Partzuergoa v. the Argentine Republic*, ICSID Case no. ARB/07/26, Award of December 08, 2016, paragraph 1146.

[10] Magnarelli Martina, *Privity of Contract in International Investment Arbitration: Original Sin or Useful Tool*, 52 KLUWER LAW INTERNATIONAL (2020), et. 97-98.

[11] *Urbaser S.A. and Consorcio de Aguas Bilbao Bizkaia, Bilbao Biskaia Ur Partzuergoa v. the Argentine Republic*, ICSID Case no. ARB/07/26, Award of December 08, 2016, paragraphs 1110-1111.

Czech Yearbook of International Law®

6.16. Based on this implied consent assumption, the Tribunal further noted that the claimants did not exclude counterclaims from their declaration or in the request for arbitration and thus consented to the respondent's right.[12] This reasoning is doubtful because it is the respondent's *onus probandi* to prove that the claimant consented to the counterclaim, not the claimants'. How can the investor prove a negative statement that the claimant gave no consent for the counterclaims?

6.17. Therefore, we must firstly address the question whether consent can be implied in such a scenario and then analyse the Tribunal's findings in *Urbaser* through the lenses of the consent issue.

II.2.1.1. Consent Cannot be Implied

6.18. The consent of the parties is a fundamental prerequisite for the Tribunal's jurisdiction in investment arbitration.[13] When the State wants to launch a counterclaim, the existence of the parties' consent for such action must be established. The form of consent in the international investment arbitration is specific because it is not necessarily contained in one document signed by both parties. Rather the States make an offer in the BITs, or MITs, or national legislation; and investors accept such an offer by launching the investment claims.[14]

6.19. In terms of international public law, there are four forms of State's consent for a dispute to be resolved before an International Tribunal:[15]

1. International treaty stipulates the resolution of the dispute before the Tribunal in question;[16] or
2. There is a special agreement between two States to resolve the dispute before the Tribunal;[17] or
3. State may agree to submit the dispute after the dispute has emerged;[18] and /or

---

[12]   *Ibid.*, at 1146.
[13]   STEINGRUBER MARCO, CONSENT IN INTERNATIONAL ARBITRATION, Oxford: Oxford University Press (2012), et. 1; Jourdain-Fortier Clotilde, *Access to Justice and Arbitration: Is Consent to Arbitrate Still at Stake?*, in LEONARDO DE OLIVEIRA, SARA HOURANI, ACESS TO JUSTICE IN ARBITRATION: CONCEPT, CONTEXT AND PRACTICE, London: Kluwer Law International (2020), et. 42.
[14]   STEINGRUBER MARCO, CONSENT IN INTERNATIONAL ARBITRATION, Oxford: Oxford University Press (2012), et. 190.
[15]   Michael Nolan and Frédéric Caivano, *Limits of Consent – Arbitration without Privity and Beyond*, in MIGUEL ANGEL FERNANDEZ-BALLESTER, DAVID ARIAS LOZANO, LIBER AMICORUM BERNARDO CREMADES, España: Wolters Kluwer (2010), et. 881.
[16]   Barcelona Traction, Light and Power Company, Limited (Preliminary Objections) (*Belgium* v. *Spain*), Judgment of July 24, I.C.J. Reports 1964, et. 6, 32.
[17]   *Ibid.*, at 6, 32. Thus, *ad hoc* agreements and treaties are two main sources of the Court's jurisdiction.
[18]   The Corfu Channel Case (Preliminary Objection) (*United Kingdom* v. *Albania*), Judgment on Preliminary Objection of 25 March 1948, I.C.J. Reports 1948.

4. State may submit the dispute with a declaration for compulsory jurisdiction.[19]

6.20. In fact, the methods of giving consent in international investment arbitration are quite similar, which means it is arbitration having its roots in international public law. The State's consent in international investment arbitration can be granted in the following ways:[20]

1. By an arbitration clause in an investor-State contract;[21]
2. By a provision in a national legislation (e.g., an investment law);[22]
3. Dispute resolution provision in the BIT or MIT; and
4. By a unilateral declaration given after the dispute has emerged (*compromis*).[23]

6.21. Thus, in terms of international investment arbitration, there is no conventional arbitration clause stipulated in one document, and the State-Respondent may give it in various ways. However, more controversial is the investor's consent for the State's counterclaim.

6.22. The general understanding is that by filing its request for arbitration, the Investor consents for arbitration. Thus, '[p]rocedurally speaking, investment agreements limit the jurisdiction of tribunals to consider originating claims of investors challenging state acts.'[24] As explained by Stefan Dudas,

> [t]he investor is not involved in the conclusion of investment treaties and is not party to such treaties. Therefore, meeting of the minds can only occur if the investor consents to arbitration by separately accepting the State's offer to arbitrate.[25]

6.23. In other words, if the Investor's consent is defined by its relief sought, the latter determines the *ratione materiae* of the Tribunal's jurisdiction. Hence, the Investor consents to resolve before the Tribunal a particular dispute, not any further possible counterclaims. But 'consent by the foreign investor must be

---

[19]   Anglo-Iranian Oil Co. Case (Jurisdiction) (*United Kingdom* v. *Iran*), Judgment, I.C. J. Reports 1952, et. 93.

[20]   STEINGRUBER MARCO, CONSENT IN INTERNATIONAL ARBITRATION, Oxford: Oxford University Press (2012), et. 196.

[21]   See e.g., *Mobil* v. *New Zeland*, ICSID Case no. ARB/87/2, Award of May 04, 1989; *Vacuum Salt* v. *Ghana*, ICSID Case no. ARB/92/1, Award of February 16, 1994.

[22]   See e.g., *SPP* v. *Egypt*, ICSID Case no. ARB/84/3, Award of April 14, 1988; *Tradex* v. *Albania*, ICSID Case no. ARB/94/2, Awards of December 24, 1996.

[23]   See e.g., *Compañía del Desarrollo de Santa Elena* v. *Costa Rica*, ICSID Case no. ARB/96/1, Award of February 17, 2000.

[24]   Farrugia Bree, *The human right to water: defences to investment treaty violations*, 31(2) OXFORD UNIVERSITY PRESS (2015), et. 281.

[25]   See also Stefan Dudas, *Treaty Counterclaims under the ICSID Convention*, in CRINA BALTAG, ICSID CONVENTION AFTER 50 YEARS: UNSETTLED ISSUES, Alphen aan den Rijn: Kluwer Law International (2016), et. 403.

expressed in some positive way and cannot be [...] simply assumed.[26]

6.24. Prior to *Urbaser*, this procedural issue emerged in *Roussalis v. Romania*[27] where the Tribunal held that it lacked jurisdiction.[28] The Tribunal decided by majority that Article 9 of the Greece-Romania BIT 'undoubtedly limit jurisdiction to claims brought by investors about obligations of the host State'[29] and found that it lacked jurisdiction over the State's counterclaim because of a lack of the investor's consent for such claims.[30]

6.25. Consequently, the wording of the treaty in question[31] becomes very important to the existence of counterclaims' jurisdiction.

II.2.2. Consent for the Jurisdiction on the Counterclaim in Urbaser

6.26. There was no Investor's express consent to jurisdiction over counterclaims in *Urbaser*. The Tribunal wrongly implied that
1. it is the claimant who carries the burden of establishing that jurisdiction does not exists,
2. the Urbaser Tribunal did not provide full analysis on its jurisdiction under Articles 46 and 25 of the ICSID Convention, and, finally,
3. the Tribunal assumed, without proper analysis of applicable public international law, the existence of the investor's consent to jurisdiction over counterclaims under the applicable BIT.

---

[26] STEINGRUBER MARCO, CONSENT IN INTERNATIONAL ARBITRATION, Oxford: Oxford University Press (2012), et. 207.

[27] *Spyridon Roussalis v. Republic of Romania*, ICSID Case no. ARB/06/1, Award of December 07, 2011, paragraph 866.

[28] Article 9 of the BIT between Greece and Romania provided as far as relevant: '[d]isputes between an investor [...] and the other Contracting Party concerning an obligation of the latter under this Agreement, in elation to an investment of the former [...] shall [...] be settled [...] in an amicable way. If such disputes cannot be settled [...] *the investor concerned may submit the dispute* [...] *to international arbitration*' [emphasis added]. Tribunal in *Urbaser* stressed though that '[i]n the *Roussalis* case, the counterclaim was based on domestic law; the Tribunal therefore observed that in order to extend the Tribunal's competence to a State counterclaim, the arbitration agreement should refer to disputes brought under domestic law [...]. This is equally irrelevant in the instant case to the extent the Counterclaim is not based on domestic law but on alleged obligations of Claimants under international law'; *Urbaser S.A. and Consorcio de Aguas Bilbao Bizkaia, Bilbao Biskaia Ur Partzuergoa v. the Argentine Republic*, ICSID Case no. ARB/07/26, Award of December 08, 2016, paragraph 424. However, the majority Tribunal in *Roussalis* put emphasis not on domestic law, but on the wording or applicable Article 9(1) of the BIT limiting 'jurisdiction to claims brought by investors about obligations of the host State'; *Spyridon Roussalis v. Republic of Romania*, ICSID Case no. ARB/06/1, Award of December 07, 2011, paragraph 869.

[29] *Spyridon Roussalis v. Republic of Romania*, ICSID Case no. ARB/06/1, Award of December 07, 2011, paragraphs 869, 871.

[30] Popova Ina, Poon Fiona, *From Perpetual Respondent to Arising Counterclaimant? State Counterclaims in the New Wave of Investment Treaties*, 2(2) BCDR INTERNATIONAL ARBITRATION REVIEW (2015), 229.

[31] Or national investment law if the jurisdiction stems from there.

II.2.2.1. Onus Probandi of Jurisdiction

6.27. It is general rule that the party making factual or legal assertion must prove it. Such basic rule is reflected in a Latin phrase *actori incumbit onus probandi*. This principle is accepted by the Permanent Court of International Justice, the International Court of Justice, and the World Trade Organization dispute settlement panels.[32] The principle is recognized also by the international investment arbitration tribunals.[33]

6.28. In terms of jurisdictional burden of proof, the Tribunal in *Roussalis* expressly stated that 'the Respondent carries the burden of establishing that jurisdiction exists.'[34] However, the Tribunal in *Urbaser* chose a different path. The Tribunal based, *inter alia*, its decision on jurisdiction over counterclaims on the fact that the claimants were silent on their acceptance of the jurisdiction over counterclaims. The Tribunal held:

> [t]he Tribunal notes that Claimants admit that their acceptance did not comprise any specific exclusion of potential counterclaims by the respondent State.

6.29. There had never been the slightest concern expressed in that regard. Therefore, it cannot be assumed that the exclusion of a counterclaim on part of the Argentine Republic had not been made one of the purposes of Claimants' acceptance of international arbitration. Claimants' declaration observe complete silence on the issue that has not been addressed, neither explicitly, or implicitly.[35]

6.30. In other words, the Tribunal shifted the *onus probandi* from the Respondent on to the Claimant by assuming the opt-out concept of the claimants' consent: the claimants by default gave their consent unless they prove *vice versa*. It is doubtful whether such an approach is correct. The investor's consent, as one of the prerequisites for jurisdiction, must be given in line with the ICSID Convention (when applicable) and with the applicable BIT.

---

[32] For more details see SOURGENS FREDERIC, DUGGAL KABIR, EVIDENCE IN INTERNATIONAL INVESTMENT ARBITRATION, Oxford: Oxford University Press (2018), et. 24.

[33] See, *e. g.*, *Hussein Nuaman Souflaki* v. *United Arab Emirates*, ICSID Case no. ARB/02/7, Award of July 07, 2004, paragraph 58; *Waguih Elie George Siad and Clorinda Vecchi* v. *Arab Republic of Egypt*, ICSID Case no. ARB/05/15, Award of June 01, 2009, paragraph 315; *Saipem SpA* v. *People's Republic of Bangladesh*, ICSID Case no. ARB/05/7, Award of June 30, 2009, paragraph 113; *RosInvestCo UK Ltd* v. *Russian Federation*, SCC Case no. V079/2005, Award of September 12, 2010, paragraph 250.

[34] *Spyridon Roussalis* v. *Republic of Romania*, ICSID Case no. ARB/06/1, Award of December 07, 2011, paragraph 860.

[35] *Urbaser S.A. and Consorcio de Aguas Bilbao Bizkaia, Bilbao Biskaia Ur Partzuergoa* v. *the Argentine Republic*, ICSID Case no. ARB/07/26, Award of December 08, 2016, paragraph 1146.

II.2.2.2. Jurisdiction Under ICSID Convention

6.31. The Tribunal in *Urbaser* did not perform a thorough analysis of the counterclaim's jurisdiction under the ICSID Convention. Before analyzing the Tribunal's finding in this regard, the general requirements for jurisdiction must be recalled briefly.

6.32. Article 46 of the ICSID Convention[36] allows the Tribunal to determine 'any counterclaims arising directly out of the subject-matter of the dispute provided that they are within the scope of the consent of the parties and are otherwise within the jurisdiction of the Centre'.

6.33. Mere linguistic analysis of this provision reveals that there is three-prong test:[37] the counterclaim must arise directly from the subject matter of the dispute; the counterclaim is within the scope of the consent of the parties; and is otherwise within the jurisdiction of the Centre in accordance with Article 25 of the ICSID Convention.[38] The Tribunal in *Urbaser* failed to apply this test correctly.

II.2.2.2.i. Counterclaim Must Be Directly and Closely Linked to the Main Subject Matter

6.34. Non-binding, though authoritative, note B(A) to the ICSID Arbitration Rule 40 explains that

> [t]o be admissible such claims must arise 'directly' out of the 'subject-matter of the dispute' (French version: *'l'objet du différend'*; Spanish version: *'la diferencia'*).

6.35. The test to satisfy this condition is whether the factual connection between the original and the ancillary claim is so close as to require the adjudication of the latter in order to achieve the final settlement of the dispute, the object being to dispose of all the grounds of dispute arising out of the same subject matter.[39]

6.36. Thus, beside the directness, the Note introduces the close connection test which should also be met when establishing the Tribunal's jurisdiction over the counterclaims under Article 46

---

36 See also Rule 40(1) of the ICSID Arbitration Rules.
37 This provision is not mandatory, and the parties can derogate from it by mutual agreement. This expressly allowed by wording "except as the parties otherwise agree" provided in the very beginning of Article 46.
38 See also Stefan Dudas, *Treaty Counterclaims under the ICSID Convention*, in CRINA BALTAG, ICSID CONVENTION AFTER 50 YEARS: UNSETTLED ISSUES, Alphen aan den Rijn: Kluwer Law International (2016), et. 389-390.
39 ICSID Regulations and Rules, paragraph 105, available at: https://icsid.worldbank.org/sites/default/files/ICSID%20Regulations%20and%20Rules%201968%20-%20ENG.pdf (accessed on 27 November 2021).

of the ICSID Convention.[40] This is the standard test for systems of international dispute resolution.[41]

6.37. The Tribunals often struggle to find the necessary connection with the subject matter of the dispute. The Tribunal in *Klöckner* v. *Cameroon* stressed the need for the subject matter of the counterclaim to be immanently connected with the subject matter of the primary claim: they were, as the tribunal put it, 'indivisible' and 'interdependent'.[42] In non-ICSID arbitration *Saluka* v. *Czech Republic,* the Tribunal ruled that the counterclaim should share the same legal basis with the main claim, and the counterclaim based on domestic law does not meet such standard.[43] The same view was followed in *Paushok* v. *Mongolia*.[44]

II.2.2.2.ii. Counterclaim Must Be Within the Scope and Consent

6.38. The second leg of the test in Article 46 of the ICSID Convention requires parties' consent for the counterclaim. This issue is generally discussed elsewhere.[45] More specifically, the due account should be made on the wording of the agreement to arbitrate[46] and asymmetric nature of the investment treaty arbitration 'in sense that it is aimed solely at promoting foreign investment and protecting foreign investors from any potentially abusive exercise of sovereign power'[47] being a *raison d'être* of this regime.

---

[40] SCHREUER CHRISTOPH, THE ICSID CONVENTION A COMMENTARY, Cambridge: Cambridge University Press (2nd ed 2011), et. 752-754.

[41] See e.g., Article 80 of the Rules of the International Court of Justice; Article 19(3) of the UNCITRAL Arbitration Rules.

[42] *Klöckner* v. *Cameroon*, ICSID Case no. ARB/81/2, Award of October 21, 1983.

[43] *Saluka Investments B.V.* v. *Czech Republic* (UNCITRAL), Decision on Jurisdiction over the Czech Republic's Counterclaim, 07 May 2004, paragraphs 79-80.

[44] *Sergei Paushok, SJSC Golden East Company and SJSC Vostokneftegaz Company* v. *The Government of Mongolia*, Award on Jurisdiction and Liability, 28 April 2011, paragraph 694.

[45] See Part *II.2.2.2.*of the Article.

[46] For instance, in *Saluka* v. *Czech Republic* the Tribunal found that the language of relevant BIT 'in referring to 'All disputes,' is wide enough to include disputes giving rise to counterclaims', *Saluka Investments B.V.* v. *Czech Republic*, Decision on Jurisdiction over the Czech Republic's Counterclaim, 7 May 2004, paragraph 39.

[47] Stefan Dudas, *Treaty Counterclaims under the ICSID Convention,* in CRINA BALTAG, ICSID CONVENTION AFTER 50 YEARS: UNSETTLED ISSUES, Alphen aan den Rijn: Kluwer Law International (2016), et. 386.

II.2.2.2.iii. Counterclaim Must Be Within General Jurisdiction Under Article 25 of the ICSID Convention

6.39. The counterclaim also must be 'otherwise within the jurisdiction of the Centre', i.e., within the jurisdiction under Article 25 of the ICSID Convention. Article 25 is one of the fundamentals of the ICISD Convention and its detailed analysis could be an object of another Article.[48]

6.40. Importantly, Article 25(1) also requires that any legal dispute must arise directly out of the investment. In other words, '[t] he requirement of directness is one of the objective criteria for jurisdiction [...] [and] the dispute must not only be connected to an investment but must be also reasonably closely connected.'[49] Directness stems from the investment dispute, not the investment.[50] However, a different approach might be found in jurisprudence. e.g., in *Goetz v. Burundi (II)* the Tribunal states

> '[l']article 25 exige une relation directe avec un investissement, l'article 46 un rapport direct avec l'objet du différend.'[51]

6.41. Consent of the parties is also a vital element of the jurisdiction.[52]

6.42. In light of the foregoing, the counterclaims may only be admitted under the ICSID Convention regime when they comply with these fundamental requirements: the counterclaims arise directly out of the subject matter of the underlying dispute and when the parties gave their express consent for that type of dispute. Moreover, the subject matter of the counterclaims must be in line with Article 25 of the ICSID Convention. Thus, it is not an easy test to meet.

II.2.2.2.iv. The Urbaser Tribunal did not appy the ICSID Test for Jurisdiction

6.43. The Urbaser Tribunal avoided scrutinized the application of Articles 46 and 25 of the ICSID Convention in the Award. It only deducted that

---

[48] For example, prof. Schreuer dedicates 277 pages of his treatise to analysis of Article 25, see SCHREUER CHRISTOPH, THE ICSID CONVENTION A COMMENTARY, Cambridge: Cambridge University Press (2nd ed 2011), et. 71-347.

[49] *Ibid.*, at 106.

[50] See, e. g., *Fedax v. Venezuela*, Decision on Jurisdiction, 11 July 1997, paragraph 28; *CSOB v. Slovakia*, Decision on Jurisdiction, 24 May 1999, paragraphs 71, 72; *CMS v. Argentina*, Decision on Jurisdiction, 17 July 2003, paragraph 52; *Siemens v.* Argentina, Decision on Jurisdiction, 03 August 2004, paragraph 150.

[51] *Antoine Goets and others v. Republic of Burundi (II)*, ICSID Case no. ARB/01/2, Award of June 21, 2012, paragraph 283.

[52] SCHREUER CHRISTOPH, THE ICSID CONVENTION A COMMENTARY, Cambridge: Cambridge University Press (2nd ed 2011), et. 190.

> Article X(4) of the BIT offers submission of 'disputes between the parties within the meaning of this article' either to an ICSID arbitral proceeding or to an *ad hoc* UNCITRAL arbitral tribunal. There is no indication given that such submission, including its offer and its acceptance, could be split into parts of the dispute based on the origin *ratione personae* of claims or on the basis of other criteria of determination. [...] Article 46 of the ICSID Convention cannot be understood otherwise.[53]

6.44. Such Tribunal's deduction was based on the assumption that the applicable BIT contains the claimants' consent for the jurisdiction over counterclaims. Such deduction, as we will see later, might be wrong. More importantly, the Tribunal did not apply the test set forth in Article 46 of the ICSID Convention. It did not check in the jurisdiction part of the Award whether counterclaims arise directly from the subject matter of the underlying dispute. The Tribunal did not check whether it has jurisdiction over counterclaims under the general requirements of Article 25. Instead, it devoted its jurisdictional reasoning to the consent of the parties allegedly arising out of the applicable BIT. This might not be the case.

6.45. The *Urbaser* Tribunal did not establish the claimants' consent for the Tribunal's jurisdiction over the counterclaims. As the right to counterclaim is outside of the protection of investments granted by the BIT, right to the counterclaim must be expressly stated in the BIT.

6.46. Generally speaking, in the BITs, 'consent by both parties is an indispensable condition for the exercise of the tribunal's jurisdiction.'[54] Especially when the ICSID Convention is not applicable.[55] Because, in Reisman' words, 'when the States Parties to a BIT contingently consent, *inter alia*, to ICSID jurisdiction, the consent component of Article 46 of the Washington Convention is *ipso facto* imported into any ICSID arbitration which an investor then elects to pursue.'[56]

6.47. If the ICSID Convention is not applicable, then the consent for a counterclaim should be expressly mentioned in the BIT

---

[53] *Urbaser S.A. and Consorcio de Aguas Bilbao Bizkaia, Bilbao Biskaia Ur Partzuergoa* v. *the Argentine Republic*, ICSID Case no. ARB/07/26, Award of December 08, 2016, paragraph 1147.
[54] *Zin Shahrizal, Chapter 11: Reappraising Access to Justice in ISDS: A Critical Review on State Recourse to Counterclaim*, in ALAN ANDERSON, BEN BEAUMONT, THE INVESTOR-STATE DISPUTE SETTLEMENT SYSTEM: REFORM, REPLACE OR STATUS QUO?, Alphen aan den Rijn: Kluwer Law International (2020), et. 232.
[55] See e.g., with disputes with Russia as the latter has not ratified the ISCID Convention.
[56] *Spyridon Roussalis* v. Romania, ICSID Case no. ARB/06/1, Declaration of W. Michael Reisman, Award of November 28, 2011.

in question. Practice in this regard varies. Some modern model BIT include this option. Article D(2)(a)(ii) of Model BIT of Belgium-Luxembourg Economic Union states 'that the Host State may pursue any defense, counterclaim, right of set off or other similar claim [...]'.[57] Other countries limit the right to counterclaim. Article 44 of Canada does not allow State's counterclaims under insurance or guarantee contracts:

> [i]n an arbitration under this [Investor-State Dispute] Section, a respondent Party may not assert as a defence, counterclaim [...] that the claimant has received or will receive, under an insurance or guarantee contract, indemnification or other compensation for all or part of its alleged damages.[58]

6.48. Other BITs do not prescribe any express consent for the counterclaims. Article 46 of Russia's Model BIT stipulates that a:

> [d]ispute arising from the written arrangements **between an investor** of one Party to the Agreement **and the other Party** to the Agreement and that are not in breach of the provisions of the Agreement that the **investor** refers to, are submitted to arbitration [...]. [Emphasis added].

6.49. Wording of this Russia's Model BIT provision implies that it is the investor who is entitled to launch the claims, not the State.

6.50. Thus, BITs opt for different options; however, consent of the Parties for the States' counterclaims must be expressly given in the BIT.

6.51. In the context of ECT as MIT, the counterclaim issue was examined in the *AMTO LLC* v. *Ukraine* case where Ukraine filed a counterclaim for non-material injury to the respondent's reputation as a result of the claimant's wrongful allegations.[59] The Tribunal did not answered in a clear way whether the counterclaims were admissible under the ECT regime. The Tribunal only declared that

> '[t]he jurisdiction of an Arbitral Tribunal over a State party counterclaim under an investment treaty, the nature of the counterclaim, and the relationship of

---

[57] See also Article 17(2)(a)(i) in conjunction with Article 15(4) of Slovakia's Model BIT; Article 19/2 of Southern African Development Community Model BIT Template, available at: ttps://investmentpolicy. unctad.org/international-investment-agreements/model-agreements (accessed on 27 November 2021).
[58] See also Article 28(7) of the US Model BIT, available at https://investmentpolicy.unctad.org/ international-investment-agreements/model-agreements (accessed on 27 November 2021).
[59] Yaroslav Petrov, *AMTO LLC* v. *Ukraine*, Award, SCC Case no. 080/2006, 26 March 2008, contribution by ITA Board of Reporters (Kluwer Law International), paragraph 116.

the counterclaims with the claims in the arbitration' must be assessed.[60]

6.52. Interestingly, the Tribunal dismissed the counterclaim not because it lacked jurisdiction, but because there was no substantial basis for the counterclaim.[61] Thus, it can be implied that the Tribunal somehow found jurisdiction over the counterclaim but failed to substantiate its findings.

6.53. The respondent in the *AMTO LLC* v. *Ukraine* case raised and interesting issue. They asserted that the SCC Rules applicable to the dispute allowed counterclaims. The Tribunal, however, did not answer this argument. Mere reference to the counterclaim in the SCC Rules however is not sufficient for the investment-related counterclaims because such claims (1) must be related to the investment (*ratione materiae*) and (2) the investor must have given the consent for the counterclaims related to the particular investments under the relevant investment treaty.

6.54. In *Urbaser*, Argentina-Spain BIT did not expressly allow the counterclaims as a State's defense. Article X(1) of the applicable BIT neutrally states that;

> [d]isputes arising between a Party and an investor of the other Party **in connection with investments within the meaning of this Agreement** shall, as far as possible, be settled amicably between the parties to the dispute. [Emphasis added].

6.55. Importantly, this provision gave indications that the dispute must be connected with the investments. Article I(2) gives a broad notion of investments that comprise any kind of assets. But, more importantly, the scope of the BIT in question is revealed in recital 3 and intends 'to create favorable conditions for **investments made by investors** of either State in the territory of the other State.' [Emphasis added].[62] Thus, the notion of investments is linked to investors who are not the States.[63] Article X(1) of the applicable BIT does not state that 'any dispute' may be settled amicably. Thus, the BIT does not give a broad content for the dispute. In turn, disputes must be connected with investments made by investors. More importantly, the BIT in question does not contain human rights as a protected value.[64]

---

[60] *Ibid.*, at 118.
[61] *Ibid.*, at 118.
[62] The recital further reflects in Article II(1) which states that '[e]ach party shall, to the extent possible, promote investments made in its territory by investors of the other Party and shall accept those investments in accordance with its legislation.'
[63] See Article I(1) of the Argentine-Spain BIT.
[64] I will address this issue in more details in Part III of the Article.

6.56. In fact, the *Urbaser* Tribunal also agrees that that provision of Article X(1) 'is completely neutral as to the identity of the claimant or respondent in an investment dispute arising between the parties'.[65] The Tribunal further states that this provision does not indicate that a State party cannot sue the investors.[66] In the same vein, this provision does not state that the State is entitled to file the counterclaim against the investors. The provision of Article X(1) of the BIT in question must be interpreted in line with the object and purpose of the BIT which is reflected in recitals 2-4: to intensify economic cooperation by creating favorable conditions for investments and protecting those investments.[67] Nothing in the applicable Argentina-Spain BIT says that the BIT protects human rights or the individuals' right to water. Nor does the BIT in question or any applicable international law impose any obligations in this regard on the investor.[68]

6.57. As the right to counterclaim is outside of the protection of investments granted by the BIT, the right to the counterclaim must be expressly stated in the BIT as, for example, in Article D(2)(a)(ii) of Model BIT of Belgium-Luxembourg Economic Union. One may argue that the consent for the jurisdiction over counterclaims may be implied and, consequently, the relevant BIT provision could be interpreted broadly. This will be addressed in the next section.

II.3. Broad or Narrow Interpretation of the Investor's Consent Over Jurisdiction of the Counterclaims

6.58. If the consent is not express, the next issue is whether the provisions of relevant MIT or BIT can be interpreted broadly in favor of the existence of the consent. Consent should not be interpreted in a broad sense because of the *in dubio mitius* principle applicable in public international law, and, consequently, consent cannot be implied.

6.59. Investment arbitration is a treaty-based dispute resolution method. However, it is used as a platform for international commercial arbitration.[69] This could lead to some confusion

---

[65] *Urbaser S.A. and Consorcio de Aguas Bilbao Bizkaia, Bilbao Biskaia Ur Partzuergoa* v. *the Argentine Republic*, ICSID Case no. ARB/07/26, Award of December 08, 2016, paragraph 1143.

[66] *Urbaser S.A. and Consorcio de Aguas Bilbao Bizkaia, Bilbao Biskaia Ur Partzuergoa* v. *the Argentine Republic*, ICSID Case no. ARB/07/26, Award of December 08, 2016, paragraph 1143.

[67] Article 31(1) of the VCLT.

[68] Interestingly, after confirming its jurisdiction, the Tribunal dismissed the counterclaim on the same basis that there were obligations upon the investor to ensure the right to water, *ibid.*, at 1206 et seq.

[69] For instance, when the ICSID Convention is not applicable, the New York Convention is the basis for recognition and enforcement of the BIT-based arbitral awards.

as to which primary source of law - national, conflict of laws or public international law - should be applied to determine principles of jurisdiction.

6.60. Although some commentators think that international investment arbitration is autonomous with public international law,[70] the prevailing view is that the principles of public international law are *prima facie* applicable to investment arbitration.[71] Briefly speaking, this is because such dispute resolution methods are based on treaties and '[t]reaties are the most important source of obligation in international law.'[72] Thus, when establishing the treaty-based jurisdiction, the relevant principles of public international law should be considered.

6.61. Generally speaking, from the contractual point of view, 'if the entity against which the counterclaim is proposed does not coincide with the claimant, the counterclaim has to be dismissed if the doctrine of privity of contract is applied strictly.'[73] But from the public international law view, restrictive interpretation seems to be more balanced in this situation.

6.62. One of the usual means for treaty interpretation is the principle *in dubio mitius*, or the principle of restrictive interpretation according to which, where 'a treaty's provisions are open to doubt, the interpretation that entails the lesser obligation [...] should be selected, and if an obligation is not clearly expressed, its less onerous extent is to be preferred.'[74]

6.63. Although there are examples of extensive or 'effective' interpretation, of States' consents,[75] scholars have also observed that in investment arbitration, due to the circumstances that consent has to be constructed from the standing consent given by the host State through the treaty and the subsequent consent given by the foreign investor at the time the claim is submitted

---

[70]   See e.g., Bentolila Dolores, *Arbitrators as lawmakers*, 43 KLUWER LAW INTERNATIONAL (2017), et. 53.

[71]   See e.g., CRAWFORD JAMES, BROWNLIE'S PRINCIPLES OF PUBLIC INTERNATONAL LAW, Oxford: Oxford University Press (9th ed. 2018), et. 690; Bishop Doak, Crawford James, Reisman Michael, *Foreign Investment Disputes Cases, Materials and Commentary*, KLUWER LAW INTERNATIONAL (2005), et. 13; LIM CHIN LENG, HO JEAN, PAPARINSKIS MARTINS, INTERNATIONAL INVESTMENT LAW AND ARBITRATION COMMENTARY, AWARDS AND OTHER MATERIALS, Cambridge: Cambridge University Press (2019), et. 22; DÖRR OLIVER, SCHMALENBACH KIRSTEN, VIENNA CONVENTION ON THE LAW OF TREATIES: A COMMENTARY (Springer 2nd ed., 2018), et. 37.

[72]   CRAWFORD JAMES, BROWNLIE'S PRINCIPLES OF PUBLIC INTERNATONAL LAW, Oxford: Oxford University Press (9th ed. 2018), et. 28. Recent awards also remind us that investor-state arbitrations are public international law disputes; see Robert Volterra, Álvaro Nistal, *What the award in Interocean v Nigeria tells us*, Global Arbitration Review (10 November 2020), available at: https://globalarbitrationreview.com/public-international-law/what-the-award-in-interocean-v-nigeria-tells-us(accessed 9 August 2021).

[73]   Magnarelli Martina, *Privity of Contract in International Investment Arbitration: Original Sin or Useful Tool*, 52 KLUWER LAW INTERNATIONAL (2020), et. 8.

[74]   DÖRR OLIVER, SCHMALENBACH KIRSTEN, VIENNA CONVENTION ON THE LAW OF TREATIES: A COMMENTARY (Springer 2nd ed., 2018), et. 577.

[75]   See e.g., *Tradex* v. *Albania*, ICSID Case no. ARB/94/2, Award of December 24, 1996; *SGS Société de Surveillance SA* v. *Republic of the Philippines*, ICSID Case no. ARB/02/6, Award of January 29, 2004.

to arbitration, it is particularly important to construe the ambit of the host State's consent strictly.[76]

6.64. The same restrictive interpretation should be applied to the Investor's consent on equal arms as well.

6.65. In *Urbaser*, however, the Tribunal interpreted too broadly the provision of Article X(1) of the BIT in question. It concluded that this provision encompasses the Tribunal's jurisdiction over the counterclaims. The danger of such broad interpretation is that the Tribunals assume obligations that the investor has not consented to. This is a serious issue which can be avoided either by the express wording of the applicable BIT, or by the subsequent Parties agreement as was done in *Burlington v. Republic of Ecuador*.

II.4. *Urbaser* v. *Argentina* Has Set the Scene for Prospective Disputes Over Counterclaims

6.66. Nevertheless, *Urbaser* inspired subsequent further case law. For instance, the *Bear Creek Mining Corporation v. Peru*[77] case concerned investments into the mining project in Peru. The local indigenous community strongly opposed the project, and Peru revoked the authorization for the mining activity. The investor then referred to the ICSID, claiming that such revocation is tantamount to the unlawful indirect expropriation. The Tribunal significantly reduced the claimed damage. In his partial dissenting opinion, a co-arbitrator prof. Philippe Sands stated that, in his view, the mining activity of the investor caused the local protests and unrest. The arbitrator disagreed with the majority's assessment of the amount of damages and 'the failure to reduce that amount by reason of the fault of the Claimant in contributing to the unrest.'[78] The arbitrator referred to the provisions of ILO Indigenous and Tribal Peoples Convention. Although admitting that 'the Convention may not impose obligation directly on a private foreign investor,'[79] he quoted some passages of *Urbaser* v. *Argentina* award and asserted that 'ILO Convention 169 is a rule of international law applicable to the territory of Peru.'[80] Thus, the *Urbaser* v. *Argentina* award inspired the dissenting arbitrator in *Bear*

---

[76] STEINGRUBER MARCO, CONSENT IN INTERNATIONAL ARBITRATION, Oxford: Oxford University Press (2012), et. 237; MCLACHLAN CAMPBELL, SHORE LAURENCE, WEINIGER MATTHEW, INTERNATIONAL INVESTMENT ARBITRATION SUBSTANTIVE PRINCIPLES, Oxford: Oxford University Press (2008), paragraph 7.168.

[77] *Bear Creek Mining Corporation v. Republic of Peru*, ICSID Case no. ARB/14/21, Award of November 30, 2017.

[78] *Ibid.*, Partial Dissenting Opinion of Prof. Philippe Sanders, at 4.

[79] *Ibid.*, at 10.

[80] *Ibid.*, at 11.

Creek Mining Corporation v. *Peru* to apply broadly the ILO Convention, which is not applicable to the private investor and rather imposes obligations on the State.[81]

6.67. *Urbaser* also had a huge impact on the Tribunal's reasoning in the *David Alen* v. *Costa Rica case*.[82] A different situation that could be a cure for the inherent lack of the Tribunal's jurisdiction over a counterclaim was in the *Burlington case*. Discussion of both cases follows.

II.4.1. David Alen v. Costa Rica Case

6.68. The *David Alan* case is a perfect example demonstrating that by relying on *Urbaser* the Tribunal can simply avoid the lack of fundamental prerequisites for the jurisdiction investor's consent to arbitrate the counterclaims.

6.69. The dispute arose out of investment in parcels of land and a tourism project. However, Costa Rican authorities closed the project when damage to protected wetlands and forest areas was revealed. The claimants then brought a claim under the Dominican Republic-Central America Free Trade Agreement (DR-CAFTA). In turn, Costa Rica filed a counterclaim in respect of environmental harm. The respondent argued that the claimants undertook works that adversely impacted the Las Olas project site considerably, affecting the environment. The Tribunal confirmed its jurisdiction but rejected the counterclaim on procedural grounds.

6.70. Costa Rica affirmed the Tribunal's jurisdiction on three main grounds. Firstly, it alleged that 'DR-CAFTA neither excludes nor prohibits an investment tribunal from exercising its jurisdiction over counterclaims.'[83] DR-CAFTA 'provisions are completely neutral as to identity of the claimant or respondent in an investment dispute arising between the parties, allowing a State Party to sue an investor in relation to a dispute concerning an investment in that country.'[84] Secondly, on reasons of procedural economy and efficiency, Costa Rica referred to prof. Michael Reisman's Declaration in the *Roussalis case*. Thirdly, the respondent invoked the *Urbaser case*.[85] Claimant was opposed to these allegations.

---

[81] Article 2(1) of the Convention is clear in this regard: 'Governments shall have the responsibility for developing, with the participation of the peoples concerned, co-ordinated and systematic action to protect the rights of these peoples and to guarantee respect for their integrity', available at: https://www.ilo.org/dyn/normlex/en/f?p=NORMLEXPUB:12100:0::NO::P12100_ILO_CODE:C169 (accessed on 31 August 2021).

[82] *David Aven et al.* v. *Costa Rica*, DR-CAFTA and UNCITRAL Case no. UNCT/15/3, Final Award, Award of September 08, 2018.

[83] *Ibid.*, at 691.

[84] *Ibid.*, at 692.

[85] *Ibid.*, at 728.

6.71. The Tribunal agreed that dispute settlement under DR-CAFTA is conceived for claims against host States.[86] The Tribunal held that

> '[s]ection A of Article 10 sets out only State's obligations, so it may be deducted that only States can be sued and that the investors cannot be respondents even in the counterclaim.'[87]

6.72. However, the Tribunal noted that Article 10.11 allows the States to enforce measures to protect the environment.[88] Then the Tribunal raised a question: if this provision imposes obligations on investors and the latter can be found in breach of a treaty obligation, '[d]oes it mean that host States may sue investors before an international arbitral tribunal under [...] DR-CAFTA?'[89]

6.73. Although the Tribunal admitted that the answer to this question is not simple,[90] it answered in affirmative relying, *inter alia*, on *Urbaser* v. *Argentina* and *Burlignton* v. *Ecuador* findings. The Tribunal found that environmental law is integrated in many ways to international law, including DR-CAFTA:

> [i]t is true that the enforcement of environmental law is primarily to the States, but it cannot be admitted that a foreign investor could not be subject to international law obligations in this field [...].[91]

6.74. Then the Tribunal shared the views of the *Urbaser* Tribunal that it can no longer be admitted that investors operating internationally are immune from becoming subjects of international law.[92] The Tribunal concluded that '[t]here are no substantive reasons to exempt foreign investor of the scope of claims for breaching obligations [...] in the field of environmental law.'[93] Moreover, admission of counterclaims, in the Tribunal words, has several practical advantages on procedural economy and efficiency.[94]

6.75. However, this Tribunal's reasoning raises some concerns. Firstly, there is no customary international law stating that private

---

[86] *Ibid.*, at 731.

[87] *Ibid.*, at 732.

[88] *Ibid.*, at 734. Article 10.11 of the DR-CAFTA prescribes that '[n]othing in this Chapter shall be construed to prevent a Party from adopting, maintaining, or enforcing any measure otherwise consistent with this Chapter that it considers appropriate to ensure that investment activity in its territory is undertaken in a manner sensitive to environmental concerns'.

[89] *Ibid.*, at 735.

[90] *Ibid.*, at 736.

[91] *Ibid.*, at 737.

[92] *Ibid.*, at 738.

[93] *Ibid.*, at 739.

[94] *Ibid.*, at 740.

companies have on equal footing with the States, international legal personality in terms of public international law. Such admission would be far-reaching today despite developments of corporate social responsibility and, '[i]n principle, however, corporations do not have international legal personality.'[95] Thus, the assumption that an investor has an international legal personality in terms of public international law is not correct. Secondly, the Tribunal ignored the lack of claimant's consent to admit the counterclaim. It is alarming that the investor's consent had been ignored. The consent is the fundamental prerequisite for the arbitration. In the investment arbitration parties' consents are usually given by the State in the relevant BIT (as an offer) and by the investor in the relevant request for arbitration (as an acceptance). It should be stressed that the claimant heavily opposed the Tribunal's jurisdiction over the counterclaims and did not agree to such mechanism in its request for arbitration. Although the Tribunal relied, inter alia, on the *Burlington* v. *Ecuador* decision, the latter had a different *ratio decidendi*, because, in the *Burlington case*, the parties expressly agreed that the Tribunal had jurisdiction to hear the counterclaims. This was not the case in the *Davd Aven* situation.

6.76. Interestingly, the Tribunal dismissed the counterclaim not on merits but on procedural grounds stating that the Costa Rican counterclaim did not meet requirements stipulated in Articles 20(2) and 20(4) of the UNCITRAL Arbitration Rules.[96] This decision is a bit surprising as well. After going so far and admitting its jurisdiction over the counterclaim, stressing the importance of procedural economy and efficiency, the Tribunal denied the counterclaim simply because the respondent failed to specify the subject matter of the claims.[97] It seems that the Tribunal was not ready to examine the counterclaim but wanted to express its modern view on the counterclaims and to grant a trendy award that supports *Urbaser*. The question remains whether such Tribunal's behavior was in line with procedural economy and efficiency.

6.77. A completely different outcome emerged in the *Burlington case*.

---

[95]   CRAWFORD JAMES, BROWNLIE'S PRINCIPLES OF PUBLIC INTERNATONAL LAW, Oxford: Oxford University Press (9th ed. 2018), et. 111; WOLFRUM RUDIGER, THE MAX PLANCK ENCYCLOPEDIA OF PUBLIC INTERNATIONAL LAW, Oxford: Oxford University Press (2012), 549.
[96]   *Ibid.*, at 745.
[97]   *Ibid.*, at 745.

II.4.2. Burlington v. Republic of Ecuador Case

6.78.   In *Burlington* v. *Ecuador*,[98] the learned Tribunal rendered a separate 470-pages decision on counterclaims and awarded over USD 39 million in favor of Ecuador.

6.79.   Burlington lodged an ICSID claim against Ecuador under the US-Ecuador BIT. The investor challenged the State's imposition of a 'windfall tax' on excess profits from oil exploitation. In turn, Ecuador brought a counterclaim, *inter alia*, for the breaches of environmental law.

6.80.   Analysis of this case is relevant because of one fundamental difference with the *Urbaser* v. *Argentina* case. In *Burlington* v. *Ecuador* the investor initially stated that it would challenge the Tribunal's jurisdiction over the counterclaims, but later the Parties executed an agreement by which Burlington accepted the jurisdiction.[99] In this agreement, Burlington and Ecuador agreed that the arbitration is the 'appropriate forum for the final resolution of the Counterclaims arising out of the investments made by Burlington Resources and its affiliates [...] so as to ensure maximum judicial economy and consistency'.[100] The parties also agreed that (i) the Tribunal's jurisdiction would be final and binding; (ii) Ecuador waived its rights to file the counterclaims against Burlington and its subsidiaries and affiliates before 'any jurisdiction whatsoever whether arbitral or judicial, national or international except for this Arbitration.'[101] Even though the parties expressly accepted the Tribunal's jurisdiction, the latter nevertheless referred to Article 46 of the ICSID Convention and stated that all the jurisdictional conditions for the counterclaim are met:

> (i) the counterclaims arise directly out of the subject matter of the dispute, namely Burlington's investment [...]; (ii) they are within the scope of the Parties' consent to ICSID arbitration which is manifested in the agreement just referred to; and (iii) they also fall within the jurisdiction of the Centre as circumscribed by Article 25 of the ICSID Convention (legal dispute arising out of an investment, and nationality requirement).[102]

6.81.   *Burlington* v. *Ecuador* is a very good example how the counterclaims should be dealt with. Firstly, it confirms that

---

[98]   *Burlington Resources Inc* v. *Republic of Ecuador*, ICSID Case no. ARB/08/5, Award of February 07, 2017.
[99]   *Ibid.*, at 6.
[100]   *Ibid.*, at 60.
[101]   *Ibid.*, at 61.
[102]   *Ibid.*, at 62.

the parties', and in particular, the investor's consent for the jurisdiction over counterclaims is necessary and vague provisions of the BITs are not sufficient. Secondly and more importantly, such consent must be express and in writing. Therefore, when the BIT in question is silent on the possibility to bring counterclaims related e.g. to the environmental damage made by investments, the Tribunal must strive for the parties' relevant consent. Thirdly, mere consent is not sufficient for jurisdiction over counterclaims. Besides, the jurisdictional test set forth in Article 46 of the ICSID Convention must still be met and, in addition to the consent, the counterclaims must have a direct link with the dispute and be within jurisdictional requirements further prescribed in Article 25.

II.5.   Conclusions on the first hypothesis

6.82. In summary, the first hypothesis that investor's consent to a counterclaim must be expressly stated, should not be interpreted broadly, and should stem from the relevant BIT or MIT, should be answered in the affirmative because of the following main reasons.

6.83. *Firstly*, the parties' consent is one of the fundamental elements for the investment Tribunal's jurisdiction. Usually, such consent is contained in the applicable BIT or MIT.

6.84. *Secondly*, the State's right for the counterclaim must be expressly stated in the BIT or MIT. If a BIT or MIT in question does not contain provisions constituting consent to counterclaims, parties to a specific investment dispute can separately agree on Tribunal's jurisdiction over certain claims already raised or future claims by a host-State.

6.85. *Thirdly*, public international law is applicable when, *inter alia*, establishing the Tribunal's jurisdiction over the counterclaims. As the investment arbitration is a treaty-based dispute resolution method, public international law does not allow broad interpretation of the investor's consent as this may distort the true will of the parties. Therefore, particular BIT or MIT provisions related to the scope and content of the parties' consent must be interpreted narrowly.

III.   Hypothesis 2: BITs or MITs Cover *Ipso Facto* Protection of Human Rights, and IMpose AN Obligation on the Investors

6.86. In order to establish the Tribunal's jurisdiction, the latter must not only identify the parties' consent; it must also determine whether a counterclaim falls within the scope of the consent instrument – the BIT or MIT (*ratione materiae*).

6.87. The Tribunals should not assume that by default the relevant BIT or MIT covers protection of human rights. There must be an analysis of whether the relevant investment regime opts for a direct application of the human rights law.

6.88. Historically, international investment treaties were designed to avoid diplomatic protection and give to the investors, whose rights were infringed by the States, a tool to sue the State directly before the forum, chosen by the investor as a claimant.[103] This system was not designed to give the States the same options of suing the investors. The majority in *Roussalis* stressed in this regard that 'the BIT imposes no obligations on investors, only on contracting States'.[104] This was logical because States have regulatory and administrative power as a sovereign to argue with the investors.

6.89. In addition, the purposes of the international investment treaties are to promote, and only then safeguard investments. These treaties were not construed to protect human rights. However, the investment law, as any other law, evolves and some modern BIT models include human rights into the ambit of protection, often through a corporate social responsibility mechanism.[105] Despite this trend of including reference to human rights into the BITs, the question remains who has an obligation to protect human rights – the State or the investor?

6.90. Under the ECHR regime, principle of subsidiarity embodied in recital 6 of the ECHR, it is the State who has the primary obligation to comply with the ECHR provisions.[106] In other words,

> [t]he obligation to respect human rights has both negative and positive dimensions. In a negative sense, States are under an obligation not to violate articles 2 to 14 [of the ECHR], as well as the substantive provisions of the Protocols to the extent these have been ratified. But they must also ensure respect for the [ECHR] […] through, for example, establishing

---

103 Bishop Doak, Crawford James, Reisman Michael, Foreign Investment Disputes Cases, Materials and Commentary, KLUWER LAW INTERNATIONAL (2005).

104 *Spyridon Roussalis* v. *Republic of Romania*, ICSID Case no. ARB/06/1, Award of December 07, 2011, paragraph 871.

105 See e.g., Article 16 of the Canada Model BIT; Article 2(11) of the Belgium-Luxembourg Economic Union Model BIT; Article 5(3) of the Netherlands Model BIT; Recital 5 of the Slovakia Model BIT; Article 12 of the India Model BIT; Article 31 of Norway Model BIT; Article 14 of the Brazil Model BIT; Article 8(3)(c) (ii) of the US Model BIT; Article 4(1)(a) of the Turkey Model BIT.

106 SCHABAS WILLIAM, THE EUROPEAN CONVENTION ON HUMAN RIGHTS A COMMENTARY, Oxford: Oxford University Press (2015), et. 74.

a legal framework for the protection of these rights and enforcing measures to ensure its observance. This is what it meant by the positive dimension.[107]

6.91. This raises an issue of 'horizontal application': where the State has a positive obligation to protect human rights within its jurisdiction. This would indirectly affect private conduct with the State as 'guarantor'.[108] If so, can the international human rights law have a horizontal effect, or the States have a monopoly over human rights responsibility? Although debates on this issue are ongoing,[109] there is a trend to include norms related to the human rights law into the Model BITs.[110] The States do this through the corporate social responsibility provisions. For instance, Article 16(1) of the Canada's Model BIT prescribes that

> [t]he Parties reaffirm that investors and their investments shall comply with domestic laws and regulations of the host State, including laws and regulations on human rights [...].

6.92. Brazil Model BIT goes even further imposing in Article 14 further obligations on investors:

> [i]nvestors and their investments shall strive to achieve the highest possible level of contribution to the sustainable development of the Host State and the local community, through the adoption of a high degree of socially responsible practices [...]. The investors and their investments shall endeavor to comply with the following voluntary principles and standards for responsible business conduct and consistent with the laws adopted by the Host State receiving the investment: [...]. Respect the internationally recognized human rights of those involved in the companies' activities.

6.93. Some of the Countries even made references to instruments such as OECD Guidelines for Multinational Enterprises and the United Nations Guiding Principles on Business and Human Rights.[111]

---

107   *Ibid.*, at 91.
108   CRAWFORD JAMES, BROWNLIE'S PRINCIPLES OF PUBLIC INTERNATONAL LAW, Oxford: Oxford University Press (9th ed. 2018), et. 629.
109   *Ibid.*, at 629-630.
110   *Supra* note 106.
111   See e.g., Article 16(2) of the Canada Model BIT; Article 7(3) of the Netherlands Model BIT; Recital 6 of the Slovakia Model BIT; Article 31 of the Norway Model BIT.

6.94. Such trend also signals that the scope of human rights protection shall be included in the relevant BIT to make it effective against the investors. However, can the Tribunal exercise its power to hear the counterclaim based on human rights infringements when the BITs are silent on this point?

6.95. In *Urbaser* the Tribunal answered positively. The Tribunal held that

> the Tribunal is reluctant to share Claimant's principled position that guaranteeing the human right to water is a duty that may be born solely by the State, and never borne also by private companies like the Claimants. When extended to human rights in general, this would mean that private parties have no commitment or obligation for compliance in relation to human rights, which are on the States' charge exclusively [Footnotes omitted].[112]

6.96. With due respect, the Tribunal's position is not supported. Firstly, as explained elsewhere, corporations do not (yet) have international legal personality in terms of public international law and, therefore, cannot assume obligations vested to the States under public international law. Secondly, it is the duty of the States to safeguard compliance with the human rights law. It does not mean that the corporations do not have any commitments towards compliance with human rights. However, such obligations stem from domestic or international human rights law and is outside the scope of the investment protection, unless expressly stated otherwise in the applicable BIT or MIT. In other words, the host States have their own domestic regulation of the human rights law disputes. Thirdly, no one can deny that the scope of the BIT or MIT primarily is to protect investments from the States' unlawful behavior, not *vice versa*. Thus, there is a certain asymmetry between scope of protected Investors' rights and that of the States. Finally, the Tribunals must establish whether the investors are bound by the BITs or MITs to protect human rights. Even the *Urbaser* Tribunal did not answer this question in the affirmative. It concluded that '[t]he human right to water entails an obligation of compliance on the part of the State, but it does not contain an obligation for performance on part of any company providing the contractually required service.'[113] The Tribunal further stated that

---

[112] *Urbaser S.A. and Consorcio de Aguas Bilbao Bizkaia, Bilbao Biskaia Ur Partzuergoa* v. *the Argentine Republic*, ICSID Case no. ARB/07/26, Award of December 08, 2016, paragraph 1193.

[113] *Urbaser S.A. and Consorcio de Aguas Bilbao Bizkaia, Bilbao Biskaia Ur Partzuergoa* v. *the Argentine Republic*, ICSID Case no. ARB/07/26, Award of December 08, 2016, paragraph 1208.

> '[i]ndeed, the enforcement of the human right [...] represents an obligation to perform. Such obligation is imposed upon States. It cannot be imposed on any company [...].'[114]

6.97. This was the main reason why the *Urbaser* Tribunal dismissed the State's counterclaims.

6.98. After analysis of jurisdiction regimes under the ICSID Convention and BITs and, the importance of the investor's consent to the counterclaim which must be express and interpreted narrowly, we need to look into the question whether alleged infringements of human rights make the states' counterclaims available. The answer seems to be negative. The Tribunal does not have an obligation to apply human rights law *ex officio* and only the fundamental human rights, such as prohibition of slavery, torture, and due process, falls within the scope of *ius cogens*. Moreover, asymmetric regimes under the investment treaties suggests that the BITs *per se* does not impose the positive obligations upon the investors to protect human rights. This is primarily the States' obligation under international public law.

6.99. In light of the foregoing, it is clear that the BIT or MIT in question do not cover the protection of human rights and, that obligation can not be imposed on the investors. This is based on several main reasons.

6.100. Firstly, if the applicable BIT or MIT does not expressly cover obligations related to the protection of human rights, such an obligation cannot be implied from this instrument. This conclusion also stems from the asymmetric nature of the BIT or MIT, whose primary scope of protection is foreign investment, not the human rights.

6.101. Secondly, by virtue of the public international law, the ambit of BIT or MIT protection must be interpreted narrowly and should not be extended to the protection of human rights.

6.102. Thirdly, the BIT or MIT in question must expressly impose a relevant obligation upon the investor or, as in *Burlington*, the parties could agree upon the Tribunal's jurisdiction over the counterclaims.

IV.   Conclusions

6.103. In this article, two principal hypotheses relevant for the jurisdictional challenges related to investor-State counterclaims

---

[114]   *Urbaser S.A. and Consorcio de Aguas Bilbao Bizkaia, Bilbao Biskaia Ur Partzuergoa v. the Argentine Republic*, ICSID Case no. ARB/07/26, Award of December 08, 2016, paragraph 1210.

based on breach of human rights have been raised: (1) whether the investor's consent to counterclaim must be expressly stated, interpreted narrowly, and stem from the applicable BIT or MIT; (2) whether the BIT or MIT in question cover the protection of human rights and if so, whether such obligation can be imposed on the investors.

6.104. In terms of the first hypothesis, it should be answered in the affirmative. An express investor's consent for the jurisdiction of the counterclaim must be clearly stipulated in the applicable BIT or MIT. The parties may subsequently agree on such jurisdiction. Scope and content of such consent must be interpreted narrowly. Tribunals tend to ignore these fundamentals in order to grant trendy awards that allow counterclaims.

6.105. In terms of the second hypothesis, the answer is negative, because when the applicable BIT or MIT does not expressly protect the human rights, such protection cannot be implied. This conclusion also stems from the asymmetric nature of the BIT or MIT, whose primary scope of protection is investments, not the State's rights. Moreover, the BIT or MIT in question must expressly impose relevant obligation upon the investor or, as in *Burlington*, the parties could agree upon the Tribunal's jurisdiction over the counterclaims.

6.106. The current trend of including the rights for counterclaims into the model BITs, as well as expanding their scope towards protection of human rights law and establishing the corporate social responsibility, demonstrate that some States want to include the human rights law protection through the counterclaims in the international investment arbitration. This could be instigated by proper administration of justice and the wish to hear all related disputes before one international forum. However, full protection of such human rights is only possible through legislative and treaty reforms that are on the way. Otherwise, separate attempts to stretch the BIT or MIT protection towards the safeguard of human rights could indeed bring more confusion and disappointment with such investor-State dispute settlement regime and could even cause a backlash in investment arbitration.

Summaries

FRA [*La contestation de la compétence arbitrale dans le cadre d'un arbitrage d'investissement en cas de demande reconventionnelle fondée sur la violation des droits de l'homme*]

À la surprise de tous, le règlement des litiges internationaux en matière d'investissements a progressivement atteint un stade où les États, parties défenderesses, déposent des demandes reconventionnelles fondées sur la violation des droits de l'homme. Historiquement, la protection internationale des droits de l'homme appartient exclusivement aux États. Ceci découle, entre autres, du fait que les sociétés commerciales ne sont pas dotées de la personnalité internationale au sens du droit international public.

Cependant, le système de règlement des litiges internationaux en matière d'investissements a été créé afin de permettre aux investisseurs lésés d'introduire des demandes internationales directement contre les États d'accueil, sans être obligés de recourir à la protection diplomatique.

On n'imaginait pas alors que la situation allait se retourner et que les États se mettraient à introduire, dans le cadre des arbitrages d'investissement, des recours contre les investisseurs sous forme de demandes reconventionnelles. Comme ce système de règlement des litiges n'a pas été créé pour protéger les États contre les violations des droits de l'homme par les investisseurs, ces demandes reconventionnelles soulèvent de graves doutes au regard des pouvoirs et de la compétence du tribunal arbitral.

Dans le présent article, l'auteur examine les questions suivantes : 1) Le tribunal arbitral peut-il conclure au consentement de l'investisseur à l'examen de la demande reconventionnelle de l'État sur le seul fondement du traité d'investissement, sans tenir compte des dispositions de la convention en question ? 2) Est-il nécessaire, pour que ces demandes reconventionnelles soient accueillies, que ces traités imposent aux investisseurs des obligations en matière de protection des droits de l'homme ?

La première hypothèse est que le consentement de l'investisseur à la demande reconventionnelle doit être explicite, ne doit pas faire l'objet d'une interprétation extensive et doit découler du traité d'investissement en question, qu'il soit bilatéral (TBI) ou multilatéral (TMI). La décision historique rendue dans l'affaire Urbaser contre Argentine a ouvert la voie aux demandes reconventionnelles introduites par les États défendeurs. Cette hypothèse peut être vérifiée en examinant les conditions de consentement en général, puis dans le contexte d'une demande reconventionnelle. Lors de l'analyse du consentement de l'investisseur, il convient également de vérifier s'il s'agit d'un consentement tacite, ou si le consentement est interprété de manière extensive, au vu des dispositions régissant les pouvoirs et compétence énoncées dans la Convention CIRDI et dans les traités bilatéraux d'investissement.

La seconde hypothèse que l'auteur examine dans le présent article consiste à supposer que tous les traités bilatéraux ou multilatéraux d'investissement formulés de manière extensive obligent les investisseurs à sauvegarder les droits de l'homme. Il est incontestable que les États sont liés par l'obligation de sauvegarder les droits de l'homme en vertu du droit international. L'examen de cette hypothèse amène l'auteur à la question de savoir si cette obligation relève par défaut des traités bilatéraux d'investissement, ou si elle doit être formulée explicitement.

CZE   *[**Námitky proti pravomoci rozhodců související s protinároky v investičním rozhodčím řízení vycházejícími z porušení lidských práv**]*

Nikdo si nedovedl představit, že se řešení mezinárodních sporů z investic postupem času dostane až do fáze, kdy budou státy v postavení žalovaných podávat protinároky z důvodu porušování lidských práv.

Z historického hlediska náleží mezinárodní ochrana lidských práv výlučně státům. Jedním z důvodů je skutečnost, že obchodní společnosti nemají mezinárodněprávní subjektivitu ve smyslu mezinárodního práva veřejného.

Na druhou stranu, smyslem systému řešení mezinárodních sporů z investic bylo umožnit poškozeným investorům podávat mezinárodní žaloby přímo proti hostitelským státům, aniž by byli nuceni využívat diplomatické ochrany.

Nikdo si však nedovedl představit, že se situace obrátí a státy začnou podávat stížnosti proti investorům v týchž investičních rozhodčích řízeních formou protinároků. S ohledem na skutečnost, že tento systém řešení sporů nebyl vytvořen za účelem ochrany států proti porušování lidských práv investory, vyvolávají tyto protinároky vážné pochybnosti z hlediska pravomoci a příslušnosti.

V tomto článku se autor věnuje následujícím hypotézám: 1) zda může rozhodčí soud dovodit souhlas investora s projednáním a rozhodnutím o protinároku státu na základě dohod o ochraně investic, bez ohledu na znění příslušné dohody, a 2) zda je podmínkou vyhovění těmto protinárokům to, aby tyto dohody ukládaly investorům povinnosti v oblasti ochrany lidských práv. První hypotézou tedy je, že souhlas investora s protinárokem musí být výslovně vyjádřen, neměl by být vykládán extenzivně a měl by vyplývat z příslušné dvoustranné (BIT) nebo mnohostranné (MIT) dohody o ochraně investic. Přelomové rozhodnutí ve věci Urbaser v. Argentina položilo základy dalšímu využívání institutu protinároku žalovaných států. Tuto hypotézu je možno přezkoumat ověřením požadavků kladených na souhlas obecně a ve vztahu k protinárokům zvlášť. Souhlas investora je rovněž nutno analyzovat z toho pohledu, zda se jedná o souhlas konkludentní, nebo zda je vykládán extenzivně pro účely požadavků na pravomoc a příslušnost zakotvených v Úmluvě ICSID a ve dvoustranných dohodách o ochraně investic.

Druhou hypotézou, kterou autor v tomto článku ověřuje, je předpoklad, že všechny extenzivně formulované dvoustranné či mnohostranné dohody o ochraně investic ukládají investorům povinnost ochrany lidských práv. Není sporu o tom, že podle mezinárodního práva jsou povinnostmi ochrany lidských práv vázány státy. Na základě prověřování této hypotézy přechází autor k otázce, zda ochrana lidských práv spadá standardně do rámce dvoustranných dohod o ochraně investic, nebo zda musí být řešena výslovně.

| | |

POL [*Sprzeciw wobec kompetencji arbitrów związany z powództwem wzajemnym w inwestycyjnym postępowaniu arbitrażowym z tytułu naruszenia praw człowieka*]

Tryb rozpatrywania międzynarodowych sporów inwestycyjnych został opracowany w celu wsparcia ochrony inwestycji, m.in. przez umożliwianie inwestorom zaskarżenia kraju jako pozwanego nie tylko przed sądami krajowymi, ale przede wszystkim przed sądami międzynarodowymi.

Z drugiej strony, aktywna ochrona praw człowieka to obowiązek nałożony na państwa, nie na inwestorów.

Nikt nie podejrzewał, że system rozstrzygania sporów inwestycyjnych z czasem dostanie się do fazy, gdzie po stronie państwa przyjmującego pojawi się konieczność ochrony praw człowieka, których naruszenia rzekomo dopuścili się inwestorzy. Nikt nie wyobrażał sobie nawet, że kraje mogą podejść do gwarantowania ochrony praw człowieka przez zastosowanie instrumentu powództwa wzajemnego w międzynarodowych arbitrażach inwestycyjnych.

Powództwo wzajemne z tytułu naruszania praw człowieka wzbudza jednak poważne wątpliwości co do kompetencji i właściwości. Autor analizuje je postulując i reagując na dwie hipotezy.

DEU [*Einwendungen gegen die Zuständigkeit von Schiedsrichtern im Zusammenhang mit auf Menschenrechtsverletzungen beruhenden Gegenansprüchen im Investitionsschiedsverfahren*]

Das System der Beilegung von internationalen Investitionsstreitigkeiten wurde deshalb geschaffen, um den Schutz von Investitionen zu stärken, und zwar u.a. dadurch, dass Investoren die Möglichkeit an die Hand gegeben wurde, direkt den Staat als Anspruchsgegner zu verklagen, nicht nur vor nationalen Gerichten, sondern auch und vor allem vor internationalen Gerichten.

Auf der anderen Seite handelte es sich beim aktiven Schutz der Menschenrechte um eine Pflicht, die Staaten und nicht Investoren auferlegt wurde.

Niemand rechnete damit, dass das System für die Beilegung von Investitionsstreitigkeiten im Laufe der Zeit in eine Phase gelangt, in der auf Seiten des Gastlands ein Bedarf entsteht, Menschenrechte zu schützen, an deren Verletzung Investoren angeblich beteiligt sein sollen. Niemand konnte sich vorstellen, dass Staaten zur Gewährleistung des Schutzes der Menschenrechte zum Rechtsinstitut des Gegenanspruchs in internationalen Investitionsschiedsverfahren greifen würden.

Gegenansprüche, mit denen die Verletzung der Menschenrechte eingewandt wird, rufen allerdings ernsthafte Zweifel in Sachen der Zuständigkeit auf den Plan. Der Autor analysiert diese Frage, indem er zwei Hypothesen aufstellt und sodann beantwortet.

RUS [*Возражения против компетенции арбитров в связи со встречными исками в инвестиционном арбитраже о нарушениях прав человека*]

Режим рассмотрения и разрешения международных инвестиционных споров был создан в целях защиты инвестиций, в том числе путем предоставления инвесторам возможности напрямую предъявлять иски государству как ответчику не только в национальных судах, но и, прежде всего, в международных судах.

С другой стороны, обязанность активно защищать права человека была возложена на государства, а не на инвесторов.

Никто не предполагал, что система рассмотрения и разрешения инвестиционных споров со временем достигнет такой стадии, когда у принимающей страны возникнет потребность в защите прав человека, якобы нарушаемых инвесторами. Никто не мог себе даже представить, что государства будут вынуждены прибегнуть к обеспечению защиты прав человека посредствам встречных исков в международных инвестиционных арбитражах.

Однако встречные иски о возможных нарушениях прав человека вызывают серьезные сомнения в отношении компетенции и юрисдикции. Автор анализирует этот вопрос, выдвигая две гипотезы и проверяя их.

ESP [***Objeciones a la competencia de los*** árbitros ***en relación con las reconvenciones en los arbitrajes de inversión que alegan violaciones de los derechos humanos***]

El régimen de la resolución de los litigios en materia de inversiones internacionales se estableció para promover la protección de las inversiones, ofreciendo a los inversores, además de otros instrumentos, la posibilidad de demandar al Estado en calidad de demandado no solo ante los tribunales nacionales sino, lo que es más importante, ante los tribunales internacionales.

Por otro lado, la protección activa de los derechos humanos es una obligación impuesta a los Estados y no a los inversores.

No se preveía que el sistema de resolución de litigios en materia de inversiones llegara a la fase en la que el Estado anfitrión tendría que proteger los derechos humanos, supuestamente violados por los inversores. Nadie imaginaba que los Estados recurrieran a las reconvenciones en los arbitrajes de inversión internacionales para garantizar la protección de los derechos humanos.

Sin embargo, las reconvenciones que alegan las violaciones de los derechos humanos plantean serias cuestiones sobre la jurisdicción y la competencia de los árbitros. El autor analiza estas cuestiones postulando dos hipótesis y respondiendo a las preguntas que estas plantean.

| | |

Bibliography:

Dolores Bentolila, *Arbitrators as lawmakers*, 43 KLUWER LAW IN-TERNATIONAL (2017).

DOAK BISHOP, JAMES CRAWFORD, MICHAEL REISMAN, FOR-EIGN INVESTMENT DISPUTES CASES, MATERIALS AND COM-MENTARY, Alphen aan den Rijn: Kluwer Law International (2005).

JAMES CRAWFORD, BROWNLIE'S PRINCIPLES OF PUBLIC IN-TERNATONAL LAW, Oxford: Oxford University Press (9th ed., 2018).

OLIVER DÖRR, SCHMALENBACH KIRSTEN, VIENNA CONVEN-TION ON THE LAW OF TREATIES: A COMMENTARY (Springer 2nd ed., 2018).

Stefan Dudas, *Treaty Counterclaims under the ICSID Convention*, in CRINA BALTAG, ICSID CONVENTION AFTER 50 YEARS: UNSET-TLED ISSUES, Alphen aan den Rijn: Kluwer Law International (2016).

Bree Farrugia, *The human right to water: defences to investment treaty violations*, 31(2) OXFORD UNIVERSITY PRESS (2015).

Clotilde Jourdain-Fortier, *Access to Justice and Arbitration: Is Consent to Arbitrate Still at Stake?*, in LEONARDO DE OLIVEIRA, SARA HOU-RANI, ACESS TO JUSTICE IN ARBITRATION: CONCEPT, CON-TEXT AND PRACTICE, London: Kluwer Law International (2020).

LENG LIM CHIN, JEAN HO, MARTINS PAPARINSKIS, INTERNA-TIONAL INVESTMENT LAW AND ARBITRATION COMMEN-TARY, AWARDS AND OTHER MATERIALS, Cambridge: Cambridge University Press (2019).

Martina Magnarelli, *Privity of Contract in International Investment Ar-bitration: Original Sin or Useful Tool*, 52 KLUWER LAW INTERNA-TIONAL (2020), 97.

CAMPBELL MCLACHLAN, SHORE LAURENCE, WEINIGER MAT-THEW, INTERNATIONAL INVESTMENT ARBITRATION SUB-STANTIVE PRINCIPLES, Oxford: Oxford University Press (2008).

Nolan Michael and Caivano Frédéric, *Limits of Consent – Arbitration without Privity and Beyond*, in MIGUEL ANGEL FERNANDEZ-BAL-LESTER, DAVID ARIAS LOZANO, LIBER AMICORUM BERNARDO CREMADES, España: Wolters Kluwer (2010).

Petrov Yaroslav, *AMTO LLC v. Ukraine*, Award, SCC Case no. 080/2006, contribution by ITA Board of Reporters (Kluwer Law International).

Ina Popova, Fiona Poon, *From Perpetual Respondent to Arising Counter-claimant? State Counterclaims in the New Wave of Investment Treaties*, 2(2) BCDR INTERNATIONAL ARBITRATION REVIEW (2015), 229.

WILLIAM SCHABAS, THE EUROPEAN CONVENTION ON HU-MAN RIGHTS A COMMENTARY, Oxford: Oxford University Press

(2015).

CHRISTOPH SCHREUER, THE ICSID CONVENTION A COMMENTARY, Cambridge: Cambridge University Press (2nd ed., 2011).

FREDERIC SOURGENS, KABIR DUGGAL, EVIDENCE IN INTERNATIONAL INVESTMENT ARBITRATION, Oxford: Oxford University Press (2018).

MARCO STEINGRUBER, CONSENT IN INTERNATIONAL ARBITRATION, Oxford: Oxford University Press (2012).

Robert Volterra, Álvaro Nistal, *What the award in Interocean v Nigeria tells us*, Global Arbitration Review (10 November 2020).

RUDIGER WOLFRUM, THE MAX PLANCK ENCYCLOPEDIA OF PUBLIC INTERNATIONAL LAW, Oxford: Oxford University Press (2012).

Shahrizal Zin, *Chapter 11: Reappraising Access to Justice in ISDS: A Critical Review on State Recourse to Counterclaim*, in ALAN ANDERSON, BEN BEAUMONT, THE INVESTOR-STATE DISPUTE SETTLEMENT SYSTEM: REFORM, REPLACE OR STATUS QUO?, Alphen aan den Rijn: Kluwer Law International (2020).

Guangjian Tu | Zeyu Huang

Inter-Regional Judicial Assistance: Achievements, Problems and Suggestions

Key words:
conflict of laws | Hong Kong |
judicial assistance | Macau |
Mainland China

Abstract | *Since the handovers of Hong Kong and Macau in 1997 and 1999 respectively, China has become a country with multiple legal systems. This has allowed the problem of inter-regional conflict of laws to surface. Compared with others, the Chinese problem of inter-regional conflict of laws has its own distinctive features. This is due to the unique political structure resulting from the policy of 'One Country, Two Systems.' In the past two decades, China has made great achievements in inter-regional conflict of laws in the field of judicial co-operations despite shortcomings and in the hope of further possible improvements. Looking to the future, with a sound legal basis, deeper integration of conflict of laws including jurisdiction and choice of law, even substantive private laws among the three regions should/could be achieved in a tri-lateral way.*

| | |

Guangjian Tu is a Full Professor of Law in the University of Macau; a researcher for Southern Marine Science and Engineering Guangdong Laboratory (Zhuhai). He holds the Qualifications of Judge and Lawyer (PRC); LLM, PhD (UK). Prof. Dr. Guangjian Tu is a life member of Clare Hall (Cambridge University), an elected associate member of the International Academy of Comparative Law and a Standing Member of the Chinese Society of Private International Law. He is an editor for the Chinese Journal of International Law and the global blog of www.conflictoflaws.net. E-mail: tuguangjian@yahoo.co.uk

Zeyu Huang is an Attorney at Law in the Hui Zhong Law Firm, Shenzhen Office. He is a PhD Candidate & LLM at the Faculty of Law in University of Macau, LLB at the Renmin University of China Law School. E-mail: huangzeyu@huizhonglaw.com

I. Introduction

7.01. As a sovereign country with one powerful central government, the People's Republic of China (PRC or China) seemingly should not have been a candidate puzzled with conflict of laws issues.[1] However, since the return of Hong Kong and Macau respectively on 1 July 1997 and 20 December 1999, inter-regional conflict of laws has come into being within China, due to the 'One Country, Two Systems' policy.[2] Under this policy, China has become one sovereign country with the concurrent existence of multiple legal systems.[3] To find feasible solutions for Chinese inter-regional conflict of laws is thus necessary and pressing, especially when the intercourses among the Mainland China, Hong Kong SAR and Macau SAR after the handovers have been increasing more rapidly than ever. Ever since the handovers, Chinese scholars have been diligently exploring legal issues around this problem and they have made useful suggestions.[4] Indeed, certain official achievements have been made in this area during the past two decades.[5] Despite these intellectual efforts and practical achievements, the job is far from being completed.

7.02. Any measure to be taken or suggestion to be made for this problem, however, must be based on and compatible with the political structure constructed under two Basic Laws.[6] As indicated, this political structure is rather unique indeed, compared with other countries adopting a system of federalism

---

[1]   For a discussion of the historic background to the emergence of conflict of laws within China, see ZHENG SOPHIA TANG, YONGPING XIAO & ZHENGXIN HUO, CONFLICT OF LAWS IN THE PEOPLE'S REPUBLIC OF CHINA, Edward Elgar 352-356 (2016). See also GUANGJIAN TU, PRIVATE INTERNATIONAL LAW IN CHINA, Springer 10 (2016).

[2]   See Jin Huang, Andrew Xuefeng Qian, *"One Country, Two Systems," Three Law Families, and Four Legal Regions: The Emerging Interregional Conflicts of Law in China*, 5 DUKE JOURNAL OF COMPARATIVE & INTERNATIONAL LAW 289, 290 (1995).

[3]   Since the handovers from the UK and Portugal to China, Hong Kong and Macau have been incorporated as two Special Administrative Regions (SARs) i.e. Hong Kong SAR and Macau SAR. The situation of Taiwan is now quite different from the two SARs in terms of inter-regional conflict of laws so that this article will not touch upon Taiwan unless necessary.

[4]   See e.g., TANG, XIAO & HUO, *supra* note 1, at 357-394; Depei Han, *An Analysis of Chinese Inter-regional Conflict of Laws: A New Subject in Chinese International Conflict of Laws*, 6 CHINA LEGAL SCIENCE 3 (1988); Huang & Qian, *supra* note 2; Guobin Zhu, *Inter-regional Conflict of Laws under "One Country, Two Systems": Revisiting Chinese Legal Theories and Chinese and Hong Kong Law, with Special Reference to Judicial Assistance*, 32 HONG KONG LAW JOURNAL 615 (2002); Xianglin Zhao & Yinghong Liu, *A Comparative Study on the Inter-State Conflict of Laws in the United States and China's Inter-Regional Conflict of Laws*, 1 JOURNAL OF COMPARATIVE LAW 66 (2000); Jie Huang, *Interregional Recognition and Enforcement of Civil and Commercial Judgments: Lessons for China from US and EU Laws*, 6 JOURNAL OF PRIVATE INTERNATIONAL LAW 109 (2010); Meirong Zhang, *Developments in Inter-Regional Conflict of Laws within China*, 48 HONG KONG LAW JOURNAL 1097 (2018).

[5]   For detailed discussions of this, see *infra* Section III.

[6]   See the Basic Law of the Hong Kong Special Administrative Region of the People's Republic of China (the Hong Kong Basic Law) which was promulgated by the National People's Congress on 4 April 1990 and entered into force on 1 July 1997, and the Basic Law of the Macau Special Administrative Region of the People's Republic of China (the Macau Basic Law) which was promulgated by the National People's Congress on 31 March 1993 and entered into force on 20 December 1999.

such as the United States, Canada and Australia. Thus, before initiating any action, one has to be clear about the distinctive features of Chinese inter-regional conflict of laws:[7] (1) the conflict of laws within China takes place between three legal districts of two different social systems i.e. socialism vis-à-vis capitalism;[8] (2) the conflict happens between common law tradition and civil law tradition;[9] (3) there is no solidly-reliable constitutional basis for resolving the conflict;[10] (4) the conflict occurs among the three legal districts, each of which enjoys independent legislative power and judicial power including the power of final adjudication;[11] (5) each legal district can have the freedom of joining international agreements without the others.[12]

7.03.   Bearing in mind these features, the present article firstly aims to have a systematic review on the problem of Chinese inter-regional judicial assistance in civil and commercial matters to see what the *status quo* is. Thereafter, it would reflect the current situation and make suggestions for future developments. The issues of legal basis and coordination models for Chinese inter-regional judicial assistance are explored in Section II. Section III examines the practical achievements that have been made so far. Section IV reflects the current situations from comparative perspectives and makes suggestions for improvements. Given the experiences in the past two decades, Section V concludes this article positively with great expectation for the future.

II.   Legal Basis and Coordination Models for Inter-regional Judicial Assistance

II.1.   Legal Basis

7.04.   In the Constitution of the PRC there is only one provision, Article 31, that can be directly applicable with uniform binding

---

[7]   See Depei Han & Jin Huang, *An Exploration on Inter-Regional Conflict of Laws within China*, 1 CHINA LEGAL SCIENCE 117, 121-123 (1989); Xianwei Meng, *On the Characteristics of Inter-Regional Conflict of Laws and its Settlement in China*, 2 LAW SCIENCE 43, 43-45 (1989).

[8]   See Article 1 of the Constitution of the PRC; Article 5 of the Hong Kong Basic Law and Macau Basic Law.

[9]   The legal systems of Mainland China and of the Macau SAR are basically of civil law tradition whereas the Hong Kong SAR is a common law jurisdiction. Hong Kong has basically received English law and Macau has largely inherited Portuguese law which belongs to the civil law family.

[10]   This situation results from the reality that there is no uniform national constitution that can have a direct binding force over all the three legal districts. In the Constitution of the PRC, only one provision, namely Article 31 is directly applicable to the Hong Kong SAR and the Macau SAR, which says *"The State may establish Special Administrative Regions when necessary. The systems to be instituted in Special Administrative Regions shall be prescribed by law enacted by the National People's Congress in the light of specific conditions."*

[11]   See Article 2 of the Hong Kong Basic Law and Macau Basic Law.

[12]   See Article 153 of the Hong Kong Basic Law and Article 138 of the Macau Basic Law.

force to all the three legal districts.[13] Regrettably, Article 31 says nothing about Chinese inter-regional conflict of laws. Although it is still controversial whether the two Basic Laws are 'Mini-Constitutions' having constitutional status within each region,[14] they are indeed enacted to implement Article 31. In each Basic Law, there is only one article, Article 95 of the Hong Kong Basic Law and Article 93 of the Macau Basic Law respectively which does, in tandem with Article 31, prescribe legal basis for inter-regional conflict of laws. The two articles identically provide: "The Hong Kong (Macau) Special Administrative Region may, through consultations and in accordance with law, maintain juridical relations with the judicial organs of other districts of the Country, and they may render assistance to each other."[15]

7.05. According to the wording, it seems that these two provisions could provide a legal basis for coordinating judicial assistance but nothing else. The two articles in the Basic Laws also appear impractical by virtue of the lack of technical regulation thereof which can make them more workable.[16] For instance, it is unclear about the legislative procedure for Hong Kong or Macau SAR to reach bi- or tri-lateral arrangements or other types of legal instruments with 'other districts of the Country' and if such instruments need to be submitted to the National People's Congress (NPC) for final approval or for the purpose of depositary only.[17] In addition, some terms used in the two articles have to be further clarified. First, commentators have argued different understandings for the term of 'other districts of the Country'. While some consider that it may refer to the provinces, autonomous regions and municipalities in the Mainland China, others say it could only denote an independent jurisdiction i.e. the Mainland China, Hong Kong SAR or Macau SAR.[18] In order to make Articles 95 and 93 more workable, a clear-cut clarification of 'other districts of the Country' should be given.[19]

[13] See Article 31 of the Constitution of the PRC, *supra* note 10; Jin Huang, *Constitutional Law and Inter-Regional Conflict of Laws*, 18 LEGAL FORUM 54, 57 (2003).
[14] See Huang, *ibid*, at 57. Cf. Guiguo Wang & Priscilla M.F. Leung, *One Country, Two Systems: Theory into Practice*, 7 PACIFIC RIM LAW & POLICY JOURNAL 279, 297 (1998); FAQIANG YUAN, CONSTITUTION AND COORDINATION OF CHINESE INTERREGIONAL CONFLICT OF LAWS, Law Press China 34, 35, 255 (2009).
[15] See Article 95 of the Hong Kong Basic Law and Article 93 of the Macau Basic Law.
[16] See Shudian Zhang, *The Breakthrough in Coordination Models of the Judicial Assistance in the Hong Kong and Macau SARs and their Deficiencies*, 35 JINAN JOURNAL (PHILOSOPHY AND SOCIAL SCIENCES) 66, 67 (2013).
[17] See Zhang, *ibid*, at 67; Xixiang Song, *The Achievements, Problems, and Suggestions in the Judicial Assistance between Mainland China and the Macau SAR in Civil and Commercial Matters*, 8 POLITICAL SCIENCE AND LAW 91, 99 (2011).
[18] See Likun Dong, *On the Pattern of China's Interregional Judicial Assistance and Its Characteristics*, 17 JOURNAL OF SHENZHEN UNIVERSITY (HUMANITIES & SOCIAL SCIENCES) 45, 48 (2000).
[19] See Zhang, *supra* note 16, at 67.

Secondly, the term of 'judicial organs' is also ambiguous. It may raise the doubt as to which level of judicial organs in each legal district is authorized to conclude agreements regarding inter-regional judicial assistance.[20] More concretely, is the Supreme People's Court (SPC) of the PRC the only authorized judicial organ in the Mainland China that has the power to sign such agreements? Is a local judicial organ in the Mainland China such as the High People's Court of Guangdong Province authorized to sign such agreements with either SAR?[21] A clarification on this term is also needed to make the two provisions in the Basic Laws more practical with certainty.

7.06.   In the past two decades or so, the two provisions in the two Basic Laws, however, have successfully acted as the legal basis for concluding a series of bilateral arrangements for inter-regional judicial assistance within China.

II.2.   Coordination Models

7.07.   Chinese scholars have also explored various coordination models for resolving the problem of inter-regional conflict of laws.[22] These models are based on comparative research of other countries with non-unified legal systems. Learning from foreign experiences, they have attempted to spell out ideal models for the Chinese problem. Their proposed models can be generally categorized into two groups. The first group adopts the uniform substantive law approach while the second follows the conflictual approach.[23] As proposed by Chinese commentators like Jin Huang and Andrew Xuefeng Qian, these two approaches are not mutually exclusive but rather could be adopted selectively at the different development stages.[24]

7.08.   As summarized by Huang & Qian, to adopt the uniform substantive law approach, China might have several possible models to opt from.[25] The same authors, however, acknowledged that each of these models may encounter insurmountable obstacles by virtue of the unique characteristics of Chinese

---

[20]   See Zhu, *supra* note 4, at 642; Yuan, *supra* note 14, at 263.

[21]   Indeed, prior to the handover, in 1985 the High People's Court of Guangdong Province once reached an agreement on service of documents in civil and commercial matters with Hong Kong, which had been operating during the period from 1986 to 1999. See the Reply of the Supreme People's Court Concerning the Preliminary Agreement for Mutual Assistance on Service of Judicial Documents in Civil and Commercial Matters between the High People's Court of Guangdong Province and the Supreme Court of Hong Kong, which was promulgated and entered into force on 3 January 1986, repealed in 1999.

[22]   See Huang & Qian, *supra* note 2, at 307; Zhu, *supra* note 4, at 637; Han, *supra* note 4, at 7-10; Tu, *supra* note 1, at 12-15; TANG, XIAO & HUO, *supra* note 1, at 363-365; Zhang, *supra* note 4, at 1100-1107.

[23]   See Zhu, *supra* note 4, at 637.

[24]   See Huang & Qian, *supra* note 2, at 312-313.

[25]   See Huang & Qian, *supra* note 2, at 307-309; Zhu, *supra* note 4, at 638.

inter-regional conflict of laws.[26] The uniform substantive law approach is thus idealistic but unrealistic, at least for the time being when the policy of 'One Country, Two Systems' is still in force.[27] Rather, it is more realistic and practical to have recourse to the conflictual approach at this stage. Likewise, different models are proposed to apply the conflictual approach: (1) to establish a uniform set of national conflict rules governing inter-regional cases among the three legal regions (the uniform conflict rules model); (2) each region may formulate specific inter-regional conflict rules (the respective inter-regional conflict rules model); (3) conflict rules of each region dealing with private international law cases may be applied to private inter-regional cases (the quasi-private international law model); (4) a model law or statute making provision for inter-regional conflict rules could act as a benchmark for each region, and international conventions or treaties concerning conflict of laws rules may provide effective paradigms for unification (the model law model).[28]

7.09.   In the past two decades, China has adopted the quasi-private international law model to pragmatically resolve the inter-regional conflict of laws problem 'step by step and item by item'.[29] The three legal districts within China have been concluding judicial assistance arrangements with one another in a piece-meal way rather than making a 'one-stop' arrangement for all conflict issues.[30] It would probably also be the most pragmatic and useful way to harmonize the conflict of laws rules within China in the future.[31] The following section will explore in detail the legal status and practical operation of these arrangements made in such a piece-meal way.

III.   The Achievements That Have Been Made

III.1.   Service of Documents

7.10.   The first achievement that has been made in judicial assistance among the three sister legal districts happened to be in inter-regional service of judicial documents in civil and commercial matters. In 1999 and 2001, the SPC of the Mainland China reached two Arrangements for mutual service of judicial documents

---

[26]   See Huang & Qian, *supra* note 2, at 308-309; *supra* notes 7-12 and accompanying text.
[27]   See Han, *supra* note 4, at 8; Zhu, *supra* note 4, at 638, 639.
[28]   See Huang & Qian, *supra* note 2, at 309-310.
[29]   See Zhu, *supra* note 4, at 643.
[30]   See TANG, XIAO & HUO, *supra* note 1, at 364; Zhang, *supra* note 4, at 1106-1107.
[31]   See the discussions about the arrangements made in such a piece-meal way in *infra* Section III; Zhu, *supra* note 4, at 643.

with the Hong Kong SAR and the Macau SAR respectively.[32] The entry into force of the two judicial assistance arrangements on service of process officially ended the lack of a workable legal framework for inter-regional service of documents between Mainland China and Hong Kong/Macau in the post-handover era.[33] It was not until recently that the Hong Kong SAR and the Macau SAR signed and activated the Arrangement for Mutual Service of Judicial Documents in Civil and Commercial Cases (the Hong Kong-Macau Service Arrangement).[34]

7.11. In practice, the implementation of the Mainland-Hong Kong Service Arrangement cannot be said to be satisfactory because of the low success rate of service under this Arrangement.[35] It is particularly the case for the service of judicial documents rendered through the High People's Courts of the Mainland to the High Court of the Hong Kong SAR.[36] The success rate of service of judicial documents rendered through the High Court of the Hong Kong SAR to the High People's Courts of the Mainland is relatively higher than the other way around albeit the number is still not impressive.[37] Given the fact that the people's courts in the Mainland are burdened with much larger caseloads needing

---

[32] See the Arrangement for Mutual Service of Judicial Documents between the Courts of the Mainland and the Hong Kong SAR in Civil and Commercial Matters, which was signed on 14 January 1999 and entered into force on 30 March 1999 (the Mainland-Hong Kong Service Arrangement); the Arrangement for Mutual Service of Judicial Documents and Taking of Evidence between the Courts of the Mainland and the Macau SAR, which was signed on 29 August 2001 and entered into force on 15 September 2001 (the Mainland-Macau Service and Evidence Arrangement).

[33] Prior to the respective handovers in 1997 and 1999 and after China acceded to the Hague Convention on the Service Abroad of Judicial and Extrajudicial Documents in Civil or Commercial Matters (the Hague Service Convention) in 1991, this Convention could be directly applied to service of documents between Mainland China and Hong Kong or Macau.

[34] See the Arrangement for Mutual Service of Judicial Documents in Civil and Commercial Matters between the Hong Kong SAR and the Macau SAR, signed in Macau on 5 December 2017, which came into force on 1 August 2020.

[35] See the Speech by Mr. Erxiang Wan, the then Vice President of the Supreme People's Court, given in the National Working Conference Concerning Hong Kong- and Macau-Related Commercial Trials, cited in Xixiang Song & Hongyan Wang, *On Achievements, Problems and Suggestions for Improvement of the Inter-Regional Evidence-Obtaining System Among the Mainland and Hong Kong and Macao*, 11 ACADEMIC JOURNAL OF ONE COUNTRY TWO SYSTEMS 123, 124 (2012).

[36] See e.g. The High People's Court of the Guangdong Province, *The Main Problems in the Contemporary Civil and Commercial Trials Involving Hong Kong and Macau*, 8 PEOPLE'S JUDICATURE 6, 8 (2005), (In 2003, the High People's Courts in the Mainland entrusted 187 judicial documents to the High Court of the Hong Kong SAR, but 81 of them failed to reach the recipient and the success rate of service was only 56 percent).

[37] See e.g. Xia Feng, *An Exploration of the Judiciary on Inter-Regional Service of Documents in Civil and Commercial Matters in Mainland China*, 8 PEOPLE'S JUDICATURE 79 (2006), at 10 (In 2003, the success rate of service from the Mainland to Hong Kong was 45 percent with 849 documents served in total whereas the success rate of service from Hong Kong to the Mainland was 51 percent with 72 documents served in total.); Xixiang Song, *Reflections on Status Quo and Improvement of Inter-Regional Service of Judicial Documents in Civil and Commercial Cases between the Mainland and Hong Kong and Macau*, 15 ACADEMIC JOURNAL OF ONE COUNTRY TWO SYSTEMS 121, 124 (2013), (From 2002 to 2004, the success rate of service from the High People's Court of the Guangdong Province to the High Court of the Hong Kong SAR was 31.2 percent with 554 documents served in total, while the success rate from the latter to the former was 60.7 percent with 89 documents served in total.).

to serve judicial documents to Hong Kong than the courts of the Hong Kong SAR to the Mainland China,[38] the people's courts of the Mainland China have much more pressure because the low success rate has resulted in a backlog of cases that are pending before the Mainland courts. Responses from several Chinese people's courts in the Guangdong Province that often made use of this Arrangement are negative with respect to its efficiency as well.[39] In contrast, the feedback from the Hong Kong SAR is, however, positive regarding the operation and efficiency of the Mainland-Hong Kong Service Arrangement.[40] In addition, the courts of the two legal districts have taken similar attitudes towards the nature of this Arrangement in its application. The people's courts in the Mainland tend to consider the application of the Mainland-Hong Kong Service Arrangement as merely optional,[41] or non-mandatory.[42] The Hong Kong courts adopted the same approach by rejecting the argument that "on a proper construction of O 11 r 5A [implementing the Arrangement], substituted service may not be ordered by the Hong Kong court because this provision is mandatory and exhaustive".[43] Instead, Hong Kong courts held that substituted service of a writ is permissible to effect the service on a defendant residing in the Mainland China.[44] Besides, there are clearly alternative means for inter-regional service as provided respectively under the law of each legal district. For example, a judicial interpretation issued by the SPC in 2009 expressly stipulates that the service of judicial documents on the Hong Kong and Macau recipients who have no domicile in Mainland China *may* be rendered through the

---

[38] See Zhonglin He, *The Status Quo and Prospects of Judicial Cooperation and Communication between the Courts of Mainland, Hong Kong, Macau and Taiwan*, 8 PEOPLE RULE OF LAW 18, 21 (2015), (Between 1999 and 2014, the people's courts in the Mainland had 15,127 judicial documents needing to be served by requesting the courts of Hong Kong, while the courts of Hong Kong entrusted 1,959 judicial documents to the people's courts in the Mainland.).

[39] See Research Group of the Foreign-Related Commercial Tribunal on Foreign-Related Service, *Research Report on the Issue of Service of Documents in Foreign-Related and Hong Kong- and Macau-Related Cases*, which was published on 28 July 2014. In this Report, one basic people's court in the Guangzhou City criticized that the procedure of service through the Arrangement by submitting the documents to the High People's Court of the Guangdong Province was time-consuming and tedious so that it normally had to reserve ten more months for this procedure to be finished. See also Intermediate People's Court of the Shenzhen City, *The White Paper on Foreign-Related Commercial Trials by the Shenzhen People's Court (2008-2013)* (27 December 2014). All these documents are on file with the authors.

[40] See paragraph 10 of the Speech by Mr. Frank Poon Ying-kwong, the then Solicitor General delivered on the Sixth Legal Seminar for the Regions of Guangdong, Hong Kong and Macau on 20 December 2014, available at: https://www.doj.gov.hk/en/community_engagement/speeches/pdf/lo20141220c.pdf (accessed on 02 June 2021).

[41] See e.g. *Guangdong BBK Electronics Corp Ltd* v. *Taiwan Cheong Ming Press Factory Ltd*, the High People's Court of the Guangdong Province (2004) Yue Gao Fa Min San Zhong Zi No. 152.

[42] See e.g. *Yanming Zhu* v. *Hong Kong Wen Wei Po Ltd*, unreported and quoted in KAIYUAN TAO, CASE SELECTIONS ON INTELLECTUAL PROPERTY RIGHTS IN THE GUANGDONG PROVINCE, Series No. 2, Law Press China 57-63 (2014).

[43] See *Deutsche Bank AG Hong Kong Branch* v. *Zhang Hong Li* [2016] HKCU 1177, paragraph 50.

[44] See *ibid*, paragraph 57.

court-to-court channel of the two Arrangements on service of process (emphasis added).[45] Under certain circumstances, some other means of effecting the service of documents to the Hong Kong and Macau recipients may, however, also be adopted.[46]

7.12.   The operation of the Mainland-Macau Service (and Evidence) Arrangement is relatively more satisfactory than that of the Mainland-Hong Kong Service Arrangement. According to the latest statistics provided by the judiciary of the Macau SAR in its annual report,[47] by the end of 2018 the people's courts of the Mainland had entrusted the Court of Final Appeal of the Macau SAR with 1140 applications (1093 applications concerning the service of documents, and only 47 related to taking of evidence). Under this Arrangement, 744 had been served effectively with a success rate of 67.15 percent.[48] For the reverse, a total of 455 letters of entrustment (390 letters concerning service of documents, 65 related to taking of evidence) had been transferred from the courts of the Macau SAR to various High Courts of the Mainland, 199 out of which were performed effectively with a success rate of 45.96 percent.[49] Thus, it can be seen that the success rate of service from the Mainland to the Macau SAR is relatively higher than service from the Mainland to the Hong Kong SAR under the relevant Arrangements.[50] However, like the Mainland-Hong Kong Service Arrangement it is time-consuming to deliver judicial documents from one legal district to another under this Arrangement. According to the statistics provided by the People's Court of Hengqin New Area in the Zhuhai City of the Guangdong Province,[51] from 2014-2016 the average time needed to complete the service of documents from this court through the Macau court to the person to be served is 151 days[52] and 57 percent of all the cases

---

[45]   See Article 6 of the Several Provisions of the Supreme People's Court on Service of Judicial Documents in Hong Kong- and Macau-Related Cases, Fa Shi [2009] No. 2, which was promulgated on 9 March 2009 and entered into force on 16 March 2009 (the 2009 SPC's Provisions on Service).

[46]   See Articles 3-5, 7-11 of the 2009 SPC's Provisions on Service, *ibid.*

[47]   See the Macau SAR Judiciary Annual Report, Tribunais da Região Administrativa Especial de Macau, Relatório do Ano Judiciário (2017-2018), at 88-92, available at: http://www.court.gov.mo/ebook/2017-2018/index.html#_2017-2018/page/92-93 (accessed on 27 May 2021).

[48]   See *ibid*, at 88, 91.

[49]   See *ibid.*

[50]   See the statistics in *supra* notes 37 and 48 and accompanying text.

[51]   The new court was set up with the approval of the SPC (Reply of the SPC [2012] No. 277) on 26 December 2013 and began to hear cases on 21 March 2014 in the Hengqin New Area of the Zhuhai City, which is separated from the Macau SAR only by a strip of water and acts as the bridgehead for deepening cooperation between the Zhuhai City and the Macau SAR. Since 1 September 2014, the People's Court of the Hengqin New Area is the sole basic people's court that has exclusive jurisdiction over the Macau-related and other foreign-related cases at first instance within the Zhuhai City.

[52]   See *White Paper on Judgments over the Civil and Commercial Cases Involving Macao by the People's Court of Hengqin New Area, Zhuhai (2014-2016)*, Tribunal Popular da Nova Área de Hengqin em Zhuhai Livro, Branco Sobre Julgamento de Causas de Naturezas Civil e Comercial que Envolvem Macau (2017), at 41, available at: http://www.hqcourt.gov.cn/list/144.html (accessed on 02 June 2021) (hereinafter "the White

in this period were served in 3 to 6 months.[53] Negative responses from the people's courts in the Mainland on the operation of this Arrangement are similar to those for the Mainland-Hong Kong Service Arrangement.[54] Although the judiciary of the Macau SAR did not negatively comment on the operation of the Mainland-Macau Service (and Evidence) Arrangement in its annual report, it seems certain that the Macau side could not be satisfied with the operation either, especially when considering the lower success rate of service from Macau to the Mainland than that of service from the Mainland to Macau. In order to improve the efficiency of the Arrangement, several amendments have recently been made in 2020 to the Mainland-Macau Service (and Evidence) Arrangement through the consultations between the SPC and the Macau SAR.[55] Two noteworthy points need to be mentioned here. Firstly, the method of serving documents by electronic means via the Mainland-Macau judicial assistance network platform has been adopted in the Arrangement.[56] Secondly, the SPC may authorize certain lower courts i.e. intermediate people's courts and basic people's courts to directly render mutual service with the Court of Final Appeal of the Macau SAR.[57]

7.13. As regards the nature of the Mainland-Macau Service (and Evidence) Arrangement in its application, the non-use of the word 'may' suggests that its provisions are mandatory.[58] However, the existence of alternative channels other than the court-to-court channel in practice appears to indicate that the application of the Mainland-Macau Service (and Evidence) Arrangement is optional rather than mandatory.[59]

7.14. Both parties to the Hong Kong-Macau Service Arrangement are optimistic about its implementation.[60] It is, however, foreseeable

---

Paper"). The longest one was 268 days while the shortest one was 25 days.

[53] See *ibid*.

[54] See Caixia Lei & Jiang Hu, *A Discussion on the Reasonable Approach to Service of Judicial Documents in Hong Kong- and Macau- Related Cases in Civil and Commercial Matters*, Hui Zhou Intermediate People's Court (9 May 2017), available at: https://hzzy.gov.cn/web/content?gid=2256&lmdm=1006 (accessed on 02 June 2021).

[55] See the Decision of the Supreme People's Court on Revising the Arrangement for Mutual Service of Judicial Documents and Taking of Evidence between the Courts of the Mainland and the Macau SAR, Fa Shi [2020], which was promulgated on 14 January 2020 and entered into force on 1 March 2020 (the SPC's Decision on Revision (2020).

[56] See Article 2 of the SPC's Decision on Revision (2020) and Article 3 of the Mainland-Macau Service (and Evidence) Arrangement, which was amended in 2020.

[57] See Article 1 of the SPC's Decision on Revision (2020) and Article 2 of the Mainland-Macau Service (and Evidence) Arrangement, which was amended in 2020.

[58] See Article 1 of the Mainland-Macau Service and Evidence Arrangement.

[59] See *supra* notes 45-46 and accompanying text.

[60] See *Macau and Hong Kong Ink Judicial Mutual Service Deal*, MACAU NEWS (6 December 2017), available at: https://macaonews.org/politics/macau-hong-kong-ink-judicial-mutual-service-deal/ (accessed on 02 June 2021).

that just like the two other inter-regional Arrangements on service, this Arrangement would face similar problems in its implementation in the two jurisdictions sticking to different legal traditions and values.

III.2.   Taking of Evidence

7.15.   Right after the return of Hong Kong, the Hague Convention on the Taking of Evidence Abroad in Civil or Commercial Matters (the Hague Evidence Convention) was ratified by China on 3 July 1997.[61] Like service of documents, although all the three legal districts within China are parties to the Hague Evidence Convention, this Convention does not and cannot apply among them directly.[62] As a result, the three districts have to resort to conclude inter-regional arrangements to resolve the problem. In 2001, the Mainland-Macau (Service and) Evidence Arrangement came into being and became applicable to mutual taking of evidence between Mainland China and the Macau SAR. This Arrangement was the first inter-regional arrangement on reciprocal taking of evidence, which had produced positive influence and provided abundant experiences for later reaching the Mainland-Hong Kong Evidence Arrangement.[63] No such bilateral arrangement has ever been reached between the Hong Kong SAR and the Macau SAR so far.

7.16.   The implementation of the Mainland-Macau (Service and) Evidence Arrangement can be said to be satisfactory in general.[64] Between 2001 and 2017, the courts in the Macau SAR received 47 Letters of Request for taking of evidence from the people's courts of the Mainland while the latter received 65 Letters of Request from the former.[65] Its implementation regarding taking of evidence, however, has encountered the same problem as the mutual service of documents between Mainland China and Macau.[66] Between 3 July 2001 and 31 December 2008, various

---

[61]   See the Decision of the Standing Committee of the National People's Congress on China's Accession to the Convention on the Taking of Evidence Abroad in Civil or Commercial Matters, which was promulgated on 3 July 1997 and entered into force on 3 July 1997; the Hague Convention of 18 March 1970 on the Taking of Evidence Abroad in Civil or Commercial Matters. The status table of this Convention can be found at: https://www.hcch.net/en/instruments/conventions/status-table/?cid=82 (accessed on 27 May 2021).

[62]   See the Legislative Council of the Hong Kong SAR, *Arrangement on Mutual Taking of Evidence in Civil and Commercial Matters between the Courts of the Mainland and the Hong Kong Special Administrative Region*, LC Paper No. CB(4)333/16-17(01) (The Hong Kong 2016 Legislative Council Paper on Evidence) (2016), available at: https://www.legco.gov.hk/yr16-17/english/panels/ajls/papers/ajlscb4-333-1-e.pdf (accessed on 27 May 2021).

[63]   See the Arrangement on Mutual Taking of Evidence in Civil and Commercial Mattes between Courts of the Mainland and the Hong Kong SAR, which was signed on 29 December 2016 and entered into force on 1 March 2017 (the Mainland-Hong Kong Evidence Arrangement).

[64]   See TANG, XIAO & HUO, *supra* note 1, at 379; Song & Wang, *supra* note 35, at 126.

[65]   See the Macau SAR Judiciary Annual Report (2017-2018), *supra* note 47, at 91-92.

[66]   See *supra* notes 47-54 and accompanying text.

courts in the Mainland entrusted 9 Letters of Request to the courts in the Macau SAR, and the success rate of execution was about 89%. The courts in the Macau SAR entrusted 28 Letters of Request to various people's courts in the Mainland, and the success rate of execution was only 57.14%.[67] It is easy to tell from the statistics that the Letters of Request from the Mainland China to Macau enjoy higher success rate of execution than those from Macau to the Mainland China.[68] The underlying reason for this disparity is unclear. With respect to the time it normally takes to finish executing a Letter of Request for obtaining evidence, a look into the statistics provided by the People's Court of Hengqin New Area may give us a clue. From 2014 to 2016, the average time for evidence-gathering in Macau was 170 days; the longest case was 268 days while the shortest one was 25 days.[69] Among the 41 cases of obtaining evidence in Macau from 2014 to 2016, only 12 percent of them were completed within 3 months; 46 percent were executed within 3 to 6 months, and 42 percent of them needed 6 to 12 months to be finished.[70] As countermeasures to the inefficiency of cross-border taking of evidence, the recent amendments made to the Mainland-Macau (Service and) Evidence Arrangement have incorporated the use of video-link or audio-link technology and transmission by electronic means via internet.[71]

7.17. After the handover of Hong Kong and before the Mainland-Hong Kong Evidence Arrangement was made, in practice mutual taking of evidence between Mainland and Hong Kong was primitive and rare. The method for mutual taking of evidence lacked certainty and efficiency because the Letters of Request delivered between the two jurisdictions had to be transmitted through intermediary bodies before the executing authority on each side could ultimately receive and execute them.[72] From 1997 to 2015, there were only three reported cases in which the people's court helped the Hong Kong court in taking of evidence and the Hong Kong court provided judicial assistance in taking of evidence to the people's court in only one case.[73]

---

[67] See Song & Wang, *supra* note 35, at 126.
[68] See *ibid*.
[69] See the White Paper, *supra* note 52, at 42.
[70] See *ibid*.
[71] See Articles 2 and 8 of the SPC's Decision on Revision (2020); Articles 3 and 23 of the Mainland-Macau (Service and) Evidence Arrangement, which was amended in 2020.
[72] See the Hong Kong 2016 Legislative Council Paper on Evidence, *supra* note 62, paragraph 4. The only one case in which the Hong Kong court helped the Mainland people's court in taking of evidence refers to *Yan Liying* v. *Xu Wei, Xu Jing, Xu Hongxi & Shi Xiuying*, the Nanjing Xuanwu District People's Court of Jiangsu Province (2013) Xuan Suo Min Chu Zi No. 231.
[73] See Xiaoli Gao, *A Look at the Development of the Arrangements between Mainland China and Hong Kong/Macau from the Perspective of the Judicial Assistance Practices by the Mainland Courts*, 6 CHINA

Moreover, litigants were not entirely clear about the types of mutual assistance in obtaining evidence that could be provided under Chinese law and Hong Kong law and the requirements of content to be included in a Letter of Request.[74] Given the fact that litigation between residents of Mainland China and Hong Kong had become a daily routine,[75] it is surprising that there was only one reported case in which a people's court in the Mainland successfully requested a Hong Kong court to obtain evidence before the Mainland-Hong Kong Evidence Arrangement was made in 2016.[76] As a result, absent a bilateral arrangement between the two districts, execution of a Letter of Request for mutual taking of evidence is time-consuming, inefficient and non-transparent.[77] But will this new Arrangement between the Mainland and Hong Kong in mutual taking of evidence end the dilemma? It is hard to give a clear-cut answer and still too early to say whether the channel provided in this Arrangement can be effective, due to the short term of operation of this Arrangement. As said, the Mainland-Macau (Service and) Evidence Arrangement has produced positive influence and given us abundant experiences. It is believed and hoped that the Mainland-Hong Kong Evidence Arrangement could effectively act as the counterpart between Mainland China and Macau.

7.18. As with the nature of the Hague Evidence Convention,[78] it is debatable whether the bilateral Arrangements concluded between one another among Mainland China, Hong Kong and Macau are mandatory in character. A literal reading of the Arrangements suggests that the channels thereof seem to be mandatory in character for inter-regionally obtaining cross-border evidence. First, to them, the non-use of word "may" in Article 1 of the Mainland-Macau (Service and) Evidence Arrangement and of the Mainland-Hong Kong Evidence Arrangement implicitly suggests their mandatory nature.[79] Secondly, in the Mainland China other channels have been implicitly rejected already. The Notice issued by the SPC in 2011 generally forbids the direct taking of evidence by the judicial personnel of the requesting court, unless relevant central authorities of the PRC and the SPC grant an approval on a case-

---

LAW 72, 73 (2015).

[74] See the Hong Kong 2016 Legislative Council Paper on Evidence, *supra* note 62, paragraph 4.

[75] See *Deutsche Bank AG Hong Kong Branch* v. *Zhang Hong Li* [2016] HKCU 1177, paragraph 76.

[76] See *Yan Liying* v. *Xu Wei, Xu Jing, Xu Hongxi & Shi Xiuying*, *supra* note 72.

[77] See TANG, XIAO & HUO, *supra* note 1, at 376-378; Song & Wang, *supra* note 35, at 126.

[78] See the Permanent Bureau of HCCH, *The Mandatory/Non-Mandatory Character of the Evidence Convention*, Preliminary Doc. No 10 of December 2008 (2008).

[79] See Article 1 of the Mainland-Macau Service and Evidence Arrangement and of the Mainland-Hong Kong Evidence Arrangement. Cf. Article 1 of the Hague Evidence Convention, and Article 27 of the same Convention.

by-case basis.[80] Before the conclusion of the Mainland-Hong Kong Evidence Arrangement, the practice by which some High People's courts in the Mainland had tried to directly contact the court in Hong Kong for judicial assistance in obtaining evidence was halted by the 2013 SPC's Notice on Evidence.[81] On the side of the Macau SAR which is also a civil law jurisdiction, it is believed that the Macau courts are also inclined to accept that the application of the Mainland-Macau (Service and) Evidence Arrangement is mandatory.[82] The courts of Mainland China and Macau are thus inclined to interpret the Arrangement(s) as the sole mechanism to obtain evidence in the other region(s). However, the Hong Kong side contemplates the Mainland-Hong Kong Evidence Arrangement as add-ons to the existing Hong Kong law on court-to-court assistance in taking of evidence.[83] It shows that foreseeably Hong Kong courts would consider the application of this Arrangement as optional and discretionary, depending on a case-by-case basis. With the entry into force of the Mainland-Hong Kong Evidence Arrangement, the primitive practice of transmitting letters of request through intermediary bodies will be superseded by the approach adopted in the Mainland-Hong Kong Evidence Arrangement.

III.3.   Recognition and Enforcement of Judgments

7.19.   As for inter-regional recognition and enforcement of judgments (REJs), the Mainland China has signed three arrangements with the Hong Kong SAR and one with the Macau SAR after the resumption of sovereignty.[84] These substantial achievements

---

[80]   See paragraphs 1-4 of the Notice of the Supreme People's Court on Further Regulation of Taking of Evidence by People's Courts in Hong Kong-, Macau- and Taiwan-Related Cases, Fa [2011] No. 243, which was promulgated and entered into force on 7 August 2011 (the 2011 SPC's Notice on Evidence).

[81]   See the Notice of the Supreme People's Court on Further Regulation of Taking of Evidence and Judicial Assistance by People's Courts in Hong Kong-Related Cases, Fa [2013] No. 26, which was promulgated and entered into force on 4 February 2013 (the 2013 SPC's Notice on Evidence).

[82]   Under Macau law, cross-border taking of evidence could only be taken by a letter of request based on a treaty or a regional arrangement, see Article 126(1) of the Macau CPC.

[83]   See the Hong Kong 2016 Legislative Council Paper on Evidence, *supra* note 62, paragraph 6.

[84]   See the Arrangement on Reciprocal Recognition and Enforcement of Judgments in Civil and Commercial Matters by the Courts of the Mainland and the Hong Kong SAR Pursuant to Choice of Court Agreements between the Parties Concerned, which was signed on 14 July 2006 and entered into force on 1 August 2008 (the Mainland-Hong Kong Choice of Court Arrangement); the Arrangement on Reciprocal Recognition and Enforcement of Judgments in Civil and Commercial Matters between the Mainland and the Macau SAR, which was signed on 28 February 2006 and entered into force on 1 April 2006 (the Mainland-Macau Judgments Arrangement); the Arrangement on Reciprocal Recognition and Enforcement of Civil Judgments in Matrimonial and Family Cases by the Courts of the Mainland and of the Hong Kong Special Administrative Region, which was signed on 20 June 2017 and has not yet entered into force (the Mainland-Hong Kong Matrimonial and Family Arrangement); the Arrangement on Reciprocal Recognition and Enforcement of Judgments in Civil and Commercial Matters by the Courts of the Mainland and of the Hong Kong Special Administrative Region, which was signed on 18 January 2019 and has not yet entered into force (the Mainland-Hong Kong Judgments Arrangement).

Czech Yearbook of International Law®

have drawn heavily on international experiences of REJs.[85] In the following part, only the operation of the Mainland-Macau Judgments Arrangement and the Mainland-Hong Kong Choice of Court Judgments Arrangement will be explored, due to the fact the other two REJ Arrangements between Mainland and Hong Kong have not come into force yet.

III.3.1. The Mainland-Macau Judgments Arrangement

7.20. Prior to the handover of Macau, the recognition and enforcement of non-local judgments in Macau were subject to the then Portuguese Civil Procedure Law that was applicable in Macau.[86] After the handover, the current Macau regime has generally followed the suit of its predecessor and adopted quite liberal attitudes towards recognition and enforcement of non-local judgments, including Mainland judgments.[87] However, the recognition and enforcement of Macau judgments in Mainland China was treated less favorably by Mainland Chinese courts because of the generally less liberal attitude adopted by Mainland Chinese law for recognition and enforcement of foreign judgments including those judgments from Macau (and Hong Kong).[88] Fortunately, the implementation of the Mainland-Macau Judgments Arrangement would facilitate the free circulation of judgments between the two regions, especially for Macau judgments.[89]

7.21. Although it is expressly provided that the scope of the Mainland-Macau Judgments Arrangement shall cover civil and commercial matters in the broadest sense, divorce judgments rendered by

---

[85] See e.g. the Hague Convention of 30 June 2005 on Choice of Court Agreements (the Hague Choice of Court Convention); the 1968 Brussels Convention on Jurisdiction and the Enforcement of Judgments in Civil and Commercial Matters, OJ L 299, 31 December 1972 (the 1968 Brussels Convention); the Lugano Convention on Jurisdiction and the Recognition and Enforcement of Judgments in Civil and Commercial Matters, OJ L 147/5, 10 June 2009 (the Lugano Convention); the Council Regulation (EC) No 44/2001 of 22 December 2000 on Jurisdiction and the Recognition and Enforcement of judgments in Civil and Commercial Matters (the Brussels I Regulation), replaced by Regulation (EC) No 1215/2012 (the Brussels I Regulation Recast); the Council Regulation (EC) No 2201/2003 of 27 November 2003 Concerning Jurisdiction and the Recognition and Enforcement of Judgments in Matrimonial Matters and the Matters of Parental Responsibility, Repealing Regulation (EC) No 1347/2000 (the Brussels IIa Regulation); the Hague Convention of 2 July 2019 on the Recognition and Enforcement of Foreign Judgments in Civil or Commercial Matters (the 2019 Hague Judgments Convention).

[86] See Guangjian Tu, *Recognition and Enforcement of Non-Local Judgments in Macau: A Critical Review*, 42 HONG KONG LAW JOURNAL 633, 642 (2012).

[87] See Guangjian Tu, *Arrangement on Mutual Recognition and Enforcement of Judgments in Civil and Commercial Matters between China and Macau: Inherent Problems, Six Years' Experience and the Way Forward*, 43 HONG KONG LAW JOURNAL 349, 373 (2013).

[88] See Articles 281 and 282 of the Civil Procedure Law of PRC. See TANG, XIAO & HUO, *supra* note 1, at 386; Tu, *ibid*, at 370-371. See also Ramon E. Reyes Jr., *The Enforcement of Foreign Court Judgments in the People's Republic of China: What the American Lawyer Needs to Know?*, 23 BROOKLYN JOURNAL OF INTERNATIONAL LAW 241 (1997).

[89] See TANG, XIAO & HUO, *supra* note 1, at 386.

Czech Yearbook of International Law®

the Mainland courts, in practice, make up the largest portion of REJs applications submitted to the Intermediate Court of the Macau SAR.[90] From 2006 to 2018, about 170 Mainland judgments have been recognized by the Intermediate Court of the Macau SAR, while the Court of Frist Instance of the Macau SAR have successfully enforced no more than 17 Mainland judgments.[91] According to the statistics given by Judge Xiaoli Gao from the SPC, from 2008 to 2014 the Mainland courts have received 17 applications for recognition and enforcement of Macau judgments.[92] Considering the huge differences between the Mainland China and the Macau SAR in terms of population, territory and court numbers, it is quite understandable that there have been far more judgments made by Mainland courts that need to be addressed to Macau for recognition/enforcement than the other way around.

7.22. On the Mainland side, a mature regime of recognition and enforcement of foreign judgments has never been established. Without the historic burden of legal tradition, once there is an inter-regional Arrangement, its implementation could be achieved with few difficulties, whereby the Arrangement may effectively facilitate the recognition and enforcement of Macau judgments in the Mainland China. On the Macau side, the application of the Mainland-Macau Judgments Arrangement may, however, encounter the problem of its compatibility with more liberal and mature rules in the Macau CPC.[93] An empirical research finds that Macau courts still prefer to apply Macau domestic rules in the Macau CPC to deal with the recognition and enforcement of Mainland judgments and ignore the Arrangement, totally or partially.[94] From 2012 to 2017, the Macau courts totally ignored the Arrangement in 10 cases (about 22 percent of all cases) in which they applied the relevant provisions stipulated in the Macau CPC only.[95] In 3 cases (about 7 percent), the Macau judges merely mentioned the Arrangement but thereafter paid all attention to the provisions of Macau CPC to determine whether to recognize/enforce the Mainland judgments or not.[96] In 33 cases (about 72 percent), the Macau courts referred to the Arrangement first in juxtaposition

---

[90] See the Macau SAR Judiciary Annual Report (2017-2018), *supra* note 47, at 88.
[91] See *ibid.*
[92] See Gao, *supra* note 73, at 74.
[93] See *supra* notes 86-87 and accompanying text.
[94] See Tu, *supra* note 87, at 373-374.
[95] See the cases of the Intermediate Court of the Macau SAR: Case 1013/2012, Case 414/2013, Case 602/2012, Case 638/2013, Case 825/2013, Case 126/2014, Case 698/2014, Case 31/2015, Case 62/2016, Case 666/2016.
[96] See cases of the Intermediate Court of the Macau SAR: Case 544/2013, Case 55/2015, Case 463/2016.

with the rules in the Macau CPC, then dealt with the cases more like applying Macau Law rather than the Arrangement.[97] The Macau courts, thus, have generally followed their previous approach and the Arrangement has largely not been applied by Macau courts in practice.[98]

III.3.2. The Mainland-Hong Kong Choice of Court Arrangement

7.23. Before the enactment and implementation of this Arrangement, recognition and enforcement of Mainland judgments in Hong Kong was governed by a set of common law principles,[99] distinguished from those foreign judgments subject to the statutory regime.[100] After its entry into force, currently the recognition and enforcement of Mainland judgments is subject to the statutory regime implementing the Arrangement i.e. the Mainland Judgments Ordinance[101] and common law principles.[102] However, under the common law, Hong Kong courts are reluctant to recognize and enforce the Mainland judgments for want of finality,[103] due to the existence of the adjudicatory supervision regime in Chinese law.[104] One the side of Mainland China, prior to the Arrangement with the Hong Kong SAR recognition and enforcement of Hong Kong judgments was subject to the rigid legal framework.[105] Still, the people's courts would very possibly refuse to recognize and enforce Hong Kong judgments falling outside the scope of the

---

[97] See cases of the Intermediate Court of the Macau SAR: Case 956/2012, Case 800/2012, Case 26/2013, Case 375/2013, Case 301/2013, Case 405/2013, Case 826/2013, Case 616/2013, Case 116/2014, Case 361/2014, Case 119/2014, Case 562/2014, Case 289/2014, Case 459/2014, Case 770/2014, Case 587/2014, Case 481/2014, Case 287/2015, Case 455/2015, Case 77/2015, Case 444/2015, Case 567/2015, Case 371/2016, Case 469/2016, Case 636/2016, Case 22/2016, Case 552/2016, Case 791/2016, Case 19/2017, Case 332/2017, Case 284/2017, Case 420/2017, Case 831/2017.

[98] See Tu, *supra* note 87, at 369.

[99] See GRAEME JOHNSTON & PAUL HARRIS SC, THE CONFLICT OF LAWS IN HONG KONG, Sweet & Maxwell 590 (2017).

[100] See the Foreign Judgments (Reciprocal Enforcement) Ordinance (Cap. 319).

[101] See the Mainland Judgments (Reciprocal Enforcement) Ordinance (Cap. 597).

[102] The essential conditions for recognition and enforcement of non-local judgments under common law principles include e.g. that the judgment is given by a court with competent jurisdiction for payment of money; that it is final and conclusive on the merits of the case between the same parties as those before the Hong Kong court. The party seeking recognition and enforcement must initiate a fresh action to plead and prove that the essential conditions are satisfied. See Johnston & Harris SC, *supra* note 99, at 595.

[103] See e.g. *Chiyu Bank Corp Ltd* v. *Chan Tin Kwun* [1996] 2 HKLR 395; *Wuhan Zhong Shuo Hong Real Estate Co Ltd* v. *Kwong Sang Hong International Ltd* [2000] HKCFI 708. For a commentary, see Philip St. John Smart, *Finality and the Enforcement of Foreign Judgments under the Common Law in Hong Kong*, OXFORD UNIVERSITY COMMONWEALTH LAW JOURNAL 301, 303-307 (2005). For the latest Hong Kong case law on this issue, see *Wu Zuocheng* v. *Liang Li & Other* [2016] HKCFL 261; *Bank of China Ltd* v. *Yang Fan* [2016] HKCFI 708.

[104] See Articles 198, 199 and 208 of the Civil Procedure Law of PRC.

[105] See *supra* note 88 and accompanying text. See also Qingjiang Kong, *Enforcement of Hong Kong SAR Court Judgments in the People's Republic of China*, 50 INTERNATIONAL & COMPARATIVE LAW QUARTERLY 867, 867-875 (2000).

Arrangement.[106] The implementation of the Arrangement in the Mainland China, thus, has broken the ice for the recognition and enforcement of Hong Kong judgments in the Mainland.

7.24. When the Arrangement was just made, some commentators showed a pessimistic attitude towards its practical usefulness[107] while others reposed great expectation upon it.[108] In practice, the operation of this Arrangement is actually frustrated by its narrow scope of application. From 2008 to 2014, the people's courts in the Mainland had accepted only 6 applications for recognition and enforcement of judgments rendered by the Hong Kong courts under this Arrangement.[109] On the side of the Hong Kong SAR, during the same time period, no Mainland judgment was ever recognized (and enforced) in accordance with the Mainland Judgments Ordinance implementing the Arrangement. The first Mainland judgment recognized and enforced under the Arrangement in Hong Kong was not reported until 2016.[110] Therefore, the Mainland-Hong Kong Choice of Court Arrangement cannot be considered as successful in practice, due to its narrow scope of application. In contrast, the Mainland-Macau Judgments Arrangement with broad scope of application appears to be more successful. There had been a pressing call to negotiate Arrangements for recognition and enforcement of judgments between Mainland China and Hong Kong to cover as the broad scope as the Mainland-Macau Judgments Arrangement i.e. in civil and commercial matters in the broadest sense[111] which would also cover matrimonial and family matters.[112]

III.3.3. The Mainland-Hong Kong Judgments Arrangement and the Mainland-Hong Kong Matrimonial and Family Arrangement

7.25. The pressing call for a 'broad' Arrangement in civil and commercial matters but excluding matrimonial and family matters was crystalized in early 2019. A bilateral Arrangement

---

[106] See Huang, *supra* note 4, at 127.
[107] See e.g. Xianchu Zhang & Philip Smart, *Development of Regional Conflict of Laws: On the Arrangement of Mutual Recognition and Enforcement of Mutual Recognition and Enforcement of Judgments in Civil and Commercial Matters between Mainland China and Hong Kong SAR*, 36 HONG KONG LAW JOURNAL 553, 580 (2006).
[108] See e.g. Stephen Kai Yi Wong, *Reciprocal Enforcement of Court Judgments in Civil and Commercial Matters between Hong Kong SAR and the Mainland*, HONG KONG LAWYER OCTOBER ISSUE 31, 31 (2006).
[109] See Gao, *supra* note 73, at 74.
[110] See *Wu Zuocheng* v. *Liang Li & Other* [2016] HKCFL 261.
[111] See Rimsky Yuen, *Two Decades' Judicial Assistance in Civil and Commercial Matters between Mainland China and Hong Kong: Look Back and Look Ahead*, People's Court Daily (30 June 2017).
[112] See Gao, *supra* note 73, at 74.

to supposedly replace the Mainland-Hong Kong Choice of Court Arrangement and extend the scope to cover all other civil and commercial matters but excluding matrimonial and family matters was signed between the Mainland China and Hong Kong on 18 January 2019.[113] This Arrangement will complement and work alongside the Mainland-Hong Kong Matrimonial and Family Arrangement which was signed on 20 June 2017.[114] Although the two new Arrangements have not yet entered into force, it is believed by the authors that both Arrangements would definitely enrich the jurisprudence of inter-regional assistance in recognition and enforcement of judgments for both sides.

IV.   Reflections and Suggestions

IV.1.   Legal Basis and Coordination Model

7.26.   Legal basis and coordination model are intertwined with each other and closely connected with the political structure. They all shall be taken together when one ponders the way to resolve the problem of Chinese inter-regional conflict of laws. The unique political structure of 'One Country, Two Systems' within one sovereignty is distinctive, which renders the conflict of laws within China quite different from that in the United States (US) and the European Union (EU). However, the value of making references to the experiences in the US and EU is obvious. Going together with the US, Chinese inter-regional conflict of laws occurs within one sovereign country among the different territorial parts of local governments with highly independent legislative power in private laws. As in the EU, Chinese inter-regional conflict of laws develops among different jurisdictions in the process of their ever-closer economic and political integration. On the other hand, the value of relying on the experiences in the US and EU might be limited. Unlike the US, China, strictly speaking, does not have a uniform constitution applicable to the whole land that could provide uniform constitutional basis for the harmonization of its conflict of laws.[115] In addition, the SPC is only the highest court for the Mainland so that China does not have a supreme court that could make a decision or interpretation of law for the whole country.[116] Different from the EU, China does not have a common court and a uniform legislative body that could

---

[113]   See *supra* note 84.
[114]   See *supra* note 84.
[115]   See *supra* notes 10 and 13 accompanying text.
[116]   See *supra* note 11 and accompanying text.

legislate on conflict of laws for the whole territory.[117] Thus, the re-examination of the legal basis and coordination model for the problem of Chinese inter-regional conflict of laws should be based on these political realities.

7.27.　As said earlier, the legal basis only consists of two almost identical provisions in the two Basic Laws.[118] With some ambiguous concepts still to be clarified, it has only provided for Chinese inter-regional judicial co-operations.[119] Indeed, in the past two decades or so, on this legal basis, many achievements have been made in the field of Chinese inter-regional judicial cooperation, but for this field only. Rather, the United States Constitution has laid down a solid 'Federal Article' which defines in American conflict of laws "the relations of the state entities to one another and of the national government to the states".[120] On the basis of constitutional provisions such as the Full Faith and Credit Clause as well as the Due Process Clause,[121] the US Supreme Court has developed series of case law defining the 'lowest common factors' to be observed by states so that private inter-state law rules can be broadly harmonized across the country.[122] In the EU, after the entry into force of the Treaty of Lisbon in 2009, Article 81 of the Treaty on the Functioning of the European Union (TFEU), succeeding to and extending for the previous counterparts,[123] began to act as the legal basis for measures for the harmonization of conflict rules at the EU level.[124] This Article in one of the two treaties forming the constitutional basis of the EU provides legal basis for a full-scale harmonization of legal rules in civil matters having cross-border implications.[125] Indeed, on the predecessors of this Article and this Article itself, private international law rules have been comprehensively harmonized in the EU.[126] Looking

---

[117]　See *ibid*. Cf. Article K.3 of the Treaty on European Union ("the Treaty of Maastricht"), 24 December 2002, OJ C 325/5. See also Zhang, *supra* note 4, at 1125.

[118]　See Article 95 of the Hong Kong Basic Law and Article 93 of the Macau Basic Law.

[119]　See *supra* notes 15-21 and accompanying text.

[120]　See the Full Faith and Credit Clause in the United States Constitution, Article IV, §1. See also Edwards S. Corwin, *The Full Faith and Credit Clause*, 81 UNIVERSITY OF PENNSYLVANIA LAW REVIEW 371, 371 (1933).

[121]　See generally Frederic L. Kirgis Jr., *The Roles of Due Process and Full Faith and Credit in Choice of Law*, 64 CORNELL LAW REVIEW 94 (1976).

[122]　See SYMEON C. SYMEONIDES, AMERICAN PRIVATE INTERNATIONAL LAW, Kluwer Law International 18-19 (2008).

[123]　See the Treaty Establishing the European (Economic) Community (1957 Treaty of Rome), Article 220, 25 March 1957, 298 U.N.T.S. 11, at 87, Article 220 EEC Treaty, subsequently Article 293 EC Treaty, now repealed; the Treaty of Maastricht, Article K.1; the Treaty of Amsterdam, Article 65. See GEERT VAN CALSTER, EUROPEAN PRIVATE INTERNATIONAL LAW, Hart Publishing 9-13 (2013).

[124]　See PETER STONE, EU PRIVATE INTERNATIONAL LAW, Edward Elgar 4-6 (2nd ed. 2010).

[125]　See Article 81 of the Treaty on the Functioning of the European Union (consolidated version), [2012] OJ C 326/47. The other EU Treaty forming constitutional basis refers to the Treaty on European Union (consolidated version), [2002] OJ C 325/5.

[126]　See Calster, *supra* note 123, at 12-13; Stone, *supra* note 124, at 4.

to the future, the comparatively limited legal basis comprising Article 95 of the Hong Kong Basic Law and Article 93 of the Macau Basic Law is far from enough if measures for fields other than judicial co-operations e.g. jurisdiction and choice of law are to be taken for Chinese inter-regional conflict of laws, which is surely a 'must'. One way is to adopt an expansive, even excessively, interpretation of the current legal basis; another to revise the two Basic Laws. Here, comparative insights could be drawn from the progressive evolution of the legal basis in the EU. At the early stage of development, Article 220 of the 1957 Treaty of Rome only provided for a limited legal basis for mutual recognition and enforcement of judgments and arbitral awards[127] but the 1980 Rome Convention on contractual obligations was made on this Article.[128] Not until the entry into force of the Treaty of Amsterdam in 1999 which prescribed a much broader legal basis was the European Community empowered to comprehensively adopt rules in conflict of laws.[129] It would certainly be more realistic and politically easier to embrace a broad interpretation of the current Article 95 of the Hong Kong Basic Law and Article 93 of the Macau Basic Law for the future development of Chinese inter-regional conflict of laws.[130] Alternatively, the two Basic Laws could be amended to broaden the legal basis, on which future Chinese inter-regional conflict of laws developments could comfortably rely, including jurisdiction, choice of law and other issues beyond.[131]

7.28. When it comes to the coordination model, as analysed, the political reality is that China has neither a uniform legislative body that can legislate conflict of laws for the whole country as in the EU nor a common supreme court that can unify conflict of laws by 'interpreting' the provisions in the uniform constitution as in the US although the three regions share the same Chinese language and largely the same Confucian culture.[132] It is rational for China to resolve its problems of inter-regional conflict of laws in a semi-international way for now.[133] In the meantime, as

---

[127]   See Article 220 of the 1957 Treaty of Rome.
[128]   See the Convention on the law applicable to contractual obligations (consolidated version), 26 January 1998, OJ C 027 (the 1980 Rome Convention).
[129]   See Article 61 of the Treaty of Amsterdam. Also see Aude Fiorini, *The Evolution of European Private International Law*, 57 INTERNATIONAL & COMPARATIVE LAW QUARTERLY 969, 973 (2008).
[130]   The broad interpretation of Article 95 of the Hong Kong Basic Law and Article 93 of the Macau Basic Law could be made according to Article 158 of the Hong Kong Basic Law and Article 143 of the Macau Basic Law respectively.
[131]   The two Basic Laws could be amended according to Article 159 of the Hong Kong Basic Law and Article 144 of the Macau Basic Law.
[132]   Due to the colonial history, Hong Kong and Macau largely share the Confucian culture but with western taste.
[133]   See *supra* notes 28-31 and accompanying text.

what happened in the past, China should adopt the piece-meal approach by concluding 'Arrangements' item-by-item. However, bilateral Arrangements between every two regions for the same subject matters are not the ideal way.[134] On the one hand, it takes the three regions resources to negotiate the Arrangements; on the other, it would add complexity to each region's law and lead to confusion for private parties in practice. It is believed that 'tri' rather than 'bi'-lateral Arrangements should be made among the three regions in the future.

7.29. Furthermore, since every region has its own power of final adjudication and there is no common court that can make autonomous interpretations for the Arrangements, the application of Chinese inter-regional Arrangements in the three regions could be inconsistent.[135] To ensure the even application of the Arrangements, it is suggested that the SPC of Mainland China, the Court of Final Appeal of the Macau SAR and that of the Hong Kong SAR shall jointly be responsible and coordinate with each other with a view to strengthening the consistent application of Arrangements in each legal district. As proposed by some Chinese scholars, establishing a common case reporting system that is open to the courts in the Mainland China, Hong Kong and Macau could contribute to the convergences of their approaches to applying domestic laws incorporating the inter-regional Arrangements.[136] At the international level, the Case Law on the UNCITRAL Texts (CLOUT), which has been developed to ensure the consistent application of the UNCITRAL instruments in differing jurisdictions around the globe, may be a useful reference for China, too.[137] Indeed, in practice, except for the Case Guidance system put forward by the SPC,[138] a local Chinese people's court in the Mainland China has invented a set of internal rules called 'Similar-Case Debate Regime' to apply to Macau-related cases in which the application of the laws is uncertain.[139] Under

---

[134] See Huang, *supra* note 4, at 127, 128.

[135] For example, as to the nature of the Mainland-Hong Kong Evidence Arrangement there are different understandings, see *supra* notes 78-83 and accompanying text.

[136] See Jianhua Zhong, *The Role of Case Law in the Course of Settling Inter-Regional Conflict of Laws in China from Comparative Law Perspective*, 2-3 JOURNAL OF COMPARATIVE LAW 62 (1992), cited in Zhu, *supra* note 4, at 637.

[137] The Clout, which is the UNCITRAL's legal database, is available at: https://www.uncitral.org/clout/search.jspx (accessed on 27 May 2021).

[138] See the Notice of the Supreme People's Court on Issuing the Provisions on Case Guidance [2010] Fa Fa No. 51, which entered into force on 26 November 2010; the Detailed Rules for the Implementation of the Provisions of the Supreme People's Court on Case Guidance [2015] Fa No. 130, which entered into force on 13 May 2015.

[139] See the People's Court of Hengqin New Area in Zhuhai City of the Guangdong Province, *Measures for the Implementation of the Similar-Case Debate System (Trial)*, which was promulgated on 11 December 2017 and available in Chinese at: http://www.hqcourt.gov.cn/list/info/608.html#anchor (accessed on 02 June

Czech Yearbook of International Law®

this set of rules, the parties concerned are allowed to provide certain cases with similar factual matrix before the court to restrain judges' exercise of discretion over controversial issues regarding application of the laws, including that implementing the inter-regional Arrangements.[140] Macau also has a system of publicizing judgments in civil and commercial matters,[141] while Hong Kong is a common law jurisdiction with historically developed case report system adhering to the doctrine of *stare decisis*. Thus, it is believed that consistent interpretation and application of domestic rules incorporating the inter-regional Arrangements could be assured by having reference to relevant case law publicized by the courts in each jurisdiction on a common database or website. In such a way, the courts would tend to interpret the Arrangements consistently and judges' discretion may also be properly constrained even though their statutory interpretation methodologies and legal traditions are drastically different from each other. Moreover, a regular report monitoring the application of these Arrangements may also collectively be prepared by the authorities in Mainland China, Hong Kong and Macau to help courts to appropriately interpret the Arrangements or their domestic laws implementing them.

IV.2.   Service of Documents

7.30.   As discussed above, compared with the Hague Service Convention and the EU Service Regulation, the bilateral Arrangements with one another among Mainland China, Hong Kong and Macau on service of documents are neither mandatory nor exclusive in nature i.e. the channels provided under the Arrangements are merely optional.[142] In practice, it is, however, submitted that prior considerations should be paid to the application of these Arrangements and the use of the channels provided therein when inter-regional service of process needs to be conducted. This could, on the one hand, strengthen the authority of the judiciaries making/implementing the Arrangements in the three regions; on the other hand, enhance the eventual free circulation of judgments among the three regions once service could be done not by a unilateral way probably only existing in the domestic law of the court hearing the case but by the way both (the court hearing the case and the court requested to

---

2021).

[140]   See the White Paper, *supra* note 52, at 47.

[141]   The judgments made by the various Macanese courts can be searched and downloaded at: http://www.court.gov.mo/zh/ (accessed on 27 May 2021).

[142]   See the discussions in *supra* section III.1.

recognize and enforce the eventual judgment) have agreed in advance in the relevant Arrangement.

7.31.   The Court-to-Court channel for inter-regional service of judicial documents is the cornerstone of these Arrangements. It does not follow the step of the Central Authority channel under the Hague Service Convention or the Central Body channel under the EU Service Regulation, which requires the Contracting (Member) States to designate a Central Authority/Body for the purpose of processing service of documents requests.[143] However, it is believed that the Court-to-Court channel under the Arrangements can bypass a Central Authority/Body and instead resort to a direct, quick and efficient communication for service of judicial documents between the concerned courts of the three regions without involving any third party and excessive intermediary.[144] Therefore, the operation of inter-regional service under the bilateral Arrangements should have been comparatively more successful and less costly than that under the Hague Service Convention and the EU Service Regulation. Nevertheless, the responses from the courts regarding the practical implementation of the inter-regional Arrangements on service have shown that the performance of the Court-to-Court channel is not as satisfactory as expected.[145] Thus, how to make better use of the Arrangements and the channels provided therein deserves special attention.

7.32.   Some reasons might explain the awkward situation. First, before the amendment in 2020 made to the Mainland-Macau Service and Evidence Arrangement, in the Mainland China, only the High People's Courts at the provincial level were authorized to process requested outgoing and incoming services. Most inter-regional cases are, however, heard by lower people's courts who have to transmit service requests first to the High People's Courts for the purpose of service in the SARs.[146] The other way around, services requested by the SARs will have to be transmitted by the High People's Courts to lower people's courts for execution in the Mainland China.[147] Under the Court-to-Court channel in the Arrangements, the High People's Courts at the provincial level are thus *de facto* mainly acting as the transmitting agencies

---

[143]   See e.g. Article 2 of the Hague Service Convention.

[144]   It should be noted that the direct Court-to-Court service channel by judicial officers, officials and other competent persons is also allowed under the Hague Service Convention (Article 10(b)) and the EU Service Regulation (Article 15).

[145]   See the discussions in *supra* Section III.1.

[146]   Cases heard by the SPC and High People's Courts are exception to this procedure, see Article 2 of the Mainland-Macau Service and Evidence Arrangement.

[147]   See Article 3(1) of the Mainland-Macau Service and Evidence Arrangement; Article 6 of the Mainland-Hong Kong Service Arrangement.

between the lower people's courts in the Mainland and the Hong Kong/Macau courts, which might have caused the delay for inter-regional services. To improve this situation, the unnecessary intermediate nodes could be cut off and the channel could be made straight and direct because service entrusted by the other region is not a difficult issue that must be screened by the High People's Courts and it can generally be well managed by lower courts. It is, therefore, submitted that lower people's courts in the Mainland having jurisdiction hearing inter-regional cases should be able to make a direct request of service to the relevant courts in the SARs, and vice versa.[148] This proposition has been accepted in the recent amendment to the Mainland-Macau Service (and Evidence) Arrangement in 2020.[149]

7.33. Secondly, the method of transmitting judicial documents is rather primitive under the Arrangements. It only refers to Court-to-Court transmission of letters of entrustment sealed with official stamps in hard copies. The lack of multiple methods for transmission renders the inter-regional framework overly rigid. During the modern era of Internet, it is unreasonable not to adopt methods of electronic means when it comes to the transmission of judicial documents between the courts of separate legal districts. Furthermore, if permissible under the law of the place where the service is sought, the electronic means should be incorporated into the implementation of the Arrangements in order to increase efficiency.[150] As mentioned above, this proposition has also been accepted in the amendment to the Mainland-Macau Service (and Evidence) Arrangement in 2020.[151]

7.34. Moreover, except for the Court-to-Court channel, more others could be added to the Arrangements for future development, namely service by post and direct service by judicial officers/ officials/lawyers without compulsion.[152] The concerns around 'judicial sovereignty' might have led to the exclusion of service by post and direct service by judicial officers, officials or lawyers from the bilateral Arrangements. It is still debatable whether the concept of judicial sovereignty should be considered in coping with inter-regional service of judicial documents under

---

[148] See Guangjian Tu, *Service of Process (Documents) in International Civil and Commercial Proceedings: A Critical Review of the Chinese Approach*, 13(3) CHINESE JOURNAL OF INTERNATIONAL LAW 577, 599 (2014).
[149] See *supra* note 57 and accompany text.
[150] See Permanent Bureau of HCCH, *Use of Information Technology in the Transmission of Requests under the Service and Evidence Conventions*, Preliminary Doc. No 9 of January 2019 (2019). See also Tu, *supra* note 148, at 601.
[151] See *supra* note 56 and accompanying text.
[152] Cf. Article 10(b) of the Hague Service Convention and Article 15 of the EU Service Convention.

one single and indivisible sovereignty in the sense of public international law.[153] The present authors believe that since the return of Hong Kong and Macau, the concept of separate judicial sovereignty should be downplayed. Given the frequent use and importance of service by post in practice, the formal addition of this channel to the Arrangements can reflect the reality and streamline judicial activities in this respect among the regions.[154] The judicial authorities in the three regions can further jointly develop a common digital postal platform that exclusively facilitates service by post. Alternatively, for now the Express Mail Service (EMS) can be the candidate as a traditional postal platform for service by post, which definitely would reduce the cost of time and money for inter-regional service of process.[155] As to direct service conducted by competent persons, if not over-sensitive to judicial sovereignty and local public order would not be disturbed because of compulsion, it could also be added to the Arrangements because this channel has the great advantage of efficiency.

IV.3.   Taking of Evidence

7.35.   As a common law jurisdiction, Hong Kong adopts quite a liberal attitude towards cross-border taking of evidence, either incoming or outgoing.[156] However, under Chinese law and Macau law, just like in other civil law jurisdictions, the taking of evidence is largely conducted by courts and viewed as exercising public power of judicial sovereignty.[157] Cross-border taking of evidence could only be achieved by inter-governmental treaties (agreements) except the diplomatic channel.[158] Due to these divergent attitudes resulting from the different legal traditions, the nature of the Arrangements on taking of evidence could thus be understood differently.[159] Considering that after many years' practice the Hague Evidence Convention has gradually been

---

[153]   See e.g. Andrew Law, *The Law and Practice of Serving Legal Documents on Mainland Parties*, Deacons, Litigation & Dispute Resolution, Newsletter (3 May 2016), available at: https://www.deacons.com.hk/news-and-insights/publications/the-law-and-practice-of-serving-legal-documents-on-mainland-parties.html (accessed on 27 May 2021).

[154]   See Tu, *supra* note 148, at 599-600.

[155]   Also see the Permanent Bureau of HCCH, *supra* note 150, footnote 6 in paragraph 6, where it is suggested that the 'electronic postal services' as provided under Article 37 of the Universal Postal Union Convention (as revised by the 2016 Istanbul Congress) can further facilitate the application of Article 10(a) of the Hague Evidence Convention. For information about the EMS as an international postal express network, see https://www.ems.post/en/global-network (accessed on 27 May 2021).

[156]   See Johnston & Harris SC, *supra* note 99, at 723.

[157]   See Comments, *Hague Convention on the Taking of Evidence Abroad in Civil or Commercial Matters: The Exclusive and Mandatory Procedures for Discovery Abroad*, 132 UNIVERSITY OF PENNSYLVANIA LAW REVIEW 1461, 1464 (1984).

[158]   See Articles 276 and 277 of the Civil Procedure Law of PRC; Article 126(1) of the Macau CPC.

[159]   See *supra* notes 79-83 and accompanying text.

accepted as optional and non-exclusive despite still existing debates,[160] the authors would suggest to interpret the bilateral Arrangements on taking of evidence as optional and non-exclusive in that only this interpretative approach can reconcile the disparity between Hong Kong and Mainland/Macau. Moreover, even if the Arrangements are considered optional and non-exclusive in nature, they should be given the status of 'first–resort' in practice, as analysed for the Arrangements for service of documents.[161]

7.36.   Yet, there are still improvements to be made. As said already, within one single and indivisible sovereignty country, concerns arising from potentially infringing 'judicial sovereignty' of the other regions should be downplayed in inter-regional cross-border taking of evidence.[162] Otherwise, it would impede the effective implementation of the 'One Country, Two Systems' policy with the aim of promoting the great unity within One-China. Therefore, more channels of taking of evidence may be added to the Arrangements except the one of transmission and execution of Letters of Request between designated authorities/courts. For example, the direct taking of evidence extraterritorially on voluntary witnesses is feasible under the EU Evidence Regulation while the Arrangements have not provided for such a way.[163] It is submitted that Mainland China and Macau should accept this method for the Arrangements as what has been done under the EU Evidence Regulation by Member States of the EU such as Germany who is a typical country of civil law tradition and sensitive to judicial sovereignty in cross-border taking of evidence. Furthermore, more and more Chinese scholars are advocating the incorporation of direct taking of evidence by duly appointed commissioners into the inter-regional Arrangements.[164] There is much to commend in their arguments. The authors agree that direct taking of evidence in the other regions by duly appointed commissioners, either a member of judicial personnel or a lawyer/expert, could provide alternative ways and increase efficiency for taking of evidence, especially in cases where no coercive measures need to be taken.

7.37.   In addition, if legally allowed, for cross-border taking of evidence under the Arrangements, modern communication technology such as videoconference and teleconference can be used to

---

[160]   See the Permanent Bureau of HCCH, *supra* note 78.
[161]   See the discussions in *supra* Section III.1.
[162]   See *supra* note 153 and accompanying text. See also Huang, *supra* note 4, at 137.
[163]   Cf. Article 17 of the EU Evidence Regulation.
[164]   See e.g. Li Chen, *Application of the Hague Evidence Convention in Chinese Foreign-Related Trials in Civil and Commercial Matters*, 1 ORIENTAL LAW 138, 147 (2010); Fei Yu, *Inter-Regional Direct Taking of Evidence in China*, 35 MACAU LAW REVIEW 5, 11 (2017).

enhance efficiency, in particular in situation where the witness cannot physically be present with justification.[165] The use of information technology in inter-regional taking of evidence will unquestionably reduce the cost and time that are needed.[166] The gradual change of mindset of domestic courts regarding the use of modern technology such as video-link in trial proceedings make this suggestion possible.[167] For instance, despite the fundamental rule of Hong Kong civil procedure that the facts shall be proved by the examination of witnesses 'orally and in open court',[168] the use of Video-Conference Facilities has readily been accepted by Hong Kong courts.[169] In the Macau SAR, in addition to communication by post, it has been accepted that communication methods by fax, long-distance communication technology, telegraph, telephone and other efficient and safe methods can be employed by courts to facilitate cross-border taking of evidence.[170] In Mainland China, people's courts have become open-minded towards using remote video technology and other modern technologies to facilitate proceedings in foreign-related cases.[171] Fortunately, in the amendment to the Mainland-Macau (Service and) Evidence, the method of obtaining evidence by using video link or audio-link technology is allowed.[172]

7.38. Lastly, the three legal districts should encourage more interactions with each other in the hope of learning different legal culture and traditions. More specifically, Hong Kong law adopts the pretrial discovery regime, under which Hong Kong courts also generally follow the English approach of preventing non-specific fishing expeditions for evidence. However, such regime is unknown in most civil law jurisdictions including Mainland China and Macau. Litigants from the Mainland China are unfamiliar with and therefore concerned about the scope and application of the pretrial discovery regime under Hong Kong law when performing inter-regional taking of evidence. Such concern is in fact unnecessary in that under Hong Kong

---

[165]   Cf. Articles 10(4) and 17(4) of the EU Service Regulation.

[166]   See the Permanent Bureau of HCCH, *supra* note 150.

[167]   Also see HCCH, *Report of the Experts' Group on the Use of Video-Link and Other Modern Technologies in the Taking of Evidence Abroad (2-4 December 2015, The Hague, the Netherlands)*, Preliminary Doc. No 8 of December 2015 (2015).

[168]   See Order 38, rule 1 of the Hong Kong Rules of the High Court (Cap. 4A).

[169]   See *Chow Kam Fai, David ex p Rambas Marketing Co, LLC* [2004] 2 HKLRD 260, CA, *per* Rogers V-P.

[170]   See Article 126(4) of the Macau CPC.

[171]   See e.g. Sophie Hunter, *China's Innovative Internet Courts and Their Use of Blockchain Backed Evidence*, Conflictoflaws.net, Views and News in Private International Law (28 May 2019), available at: http://conflictoflaws.net/2019/chinas-innovative-internet-courts-and-their-use-of-blockchain-backed-evidence/ (accessed on 27 May 2021).

[172]   See *supra* note 71 and accompanying text.

law any discovery order issued by the Hong Kong court must not be unduly wide and should be restricted to those classes of documents that are necessary.[173] Therefore, the pretrial discovery regime in Hong Kong law actually will not bring any striking challenge to the operation of the Mainland-Hong Kong Evidence Arrangement. To reduce such kind of misunderstandings, the three separate legal jurisdictions should enhance mutual legal education and practical training.

IV.4. Recognition and Enforcement of Judgments

7.39. All the inter-regional Arrangements for this aspect within the PRC are 'simple' ones, which address only the issue of recognition and enforcement of judgments, but not those of jurisdiction and parallel proceedings at the jurisdictional stage directly.[174] Theoretically and seemingly, if the political will is strong enough and jurisdictional concern could be diminished, the simple Arrangements could be highly efficient and successful because the addressed region will just simply recognize and enforce judgments from the other regions without checking jurisdictional basis except where its own exclusive jurisdiction might be offended. However, the simple Arrangements are more likely to produce forum shopping than *arrangements double*, which regulate both assumption of jurisdiction and the recognition and enforcement of the resulting judgment.[175] Without dealing with jurisdictional issues and unifying them upstream, the courts in each region would determine whether exercising and taking up a case by their own rules, parallel proceedings would necessarily entail and have to be handled downstream as evidenced in the Arrangements. To 'cleverly' make use of the rules, 'race to courts' and 'race to judgments' would happen.[176] In the future, if there is a chance of amendment, direct jurisdictional rules and a mechanism of dealing with parallel proceedings should ideally be provided in the Arrangements as done under the Brussels I Regulation of the EU.

7.40. As to the Mainland-Macau Judgments Arrangement, some empirical studies have already demonstrated that conflicts of jurisdiction and parallel proceedings in inter-regional cases between the Mainland China and the Macau SAR would be

---

[173] See *A Co* v. *B Co* [2002] 3 HKLRD 111, paragraph 13, per Ma J.
[174] For the concepts of "simple", "double" and "mixed" convention for recognition and enforcement of foreign judgments, see Arthur T. von Mehren, *Recognition and Enforcement of Foreign Judgments: A New Approach for the Hague Conference?*, 57 LAW & CONTEMPORARY PROBLEMS 271, 282 (1994).
[175] See von Mehren, *ibid*, at 282, 286.
[176] See Tu, *supra* note 87, at 357-361.

a serious problem.[177] Besides the problem of jurisdiction, a special issue that might be worth mentioning in this context is whether the judgments arising out of gambling debts rendered by Macau courts should be recognized and enforced under the Arrangement. Owing to the strict moral standard demanded by the socialism policy practiced in the Mainland China, judgments related to gambling debts rendered by Macau courts will very probably be denied for recognition and enforcement on the ground of public policy by Mainland Courts.[178] Some commentators support this approach for the reason that although gambling debts are legally protected in the Macau SAR they are illegal in the Mainland China.[179] It is quite obvious that a conflict exists between Chinese law and Macau law as to the legality of gambling debts and whether judgments of gambling debts should fall into the 'civil and commercial matters' in the Arrangement.[180] Although there is no direct case report in which the people's court in Mainland China has refused to recognize and enforce a gambling debts judgment rendered by a Macau court, it is inferable from the current judicial practice that the people's courts tend to employ the device of public policy to do so.[181] However, the current authors contend that gambling debts judgments from the Macau SAR should be recognized and enforced by the Mainland courts under the Arrangement in the future. In *Kai Song* v. *Shilong Li,* the SPC did not invoke the ground of offending public policy and instead applied Macau law as the governing law for the loan relationship involving gambling debts.[182] This liberal approach should be maintained in future for the reason that 'vested rights' that have been created legally in other jurisdictions could be recognized in the

---

[177] See Chengzhi Wang, *Some Legal Problems Arising Out of the Trial of Civil and Commercial Cases Related to Hong Kong and Macau: with Special Reference to the Judicial Practice in Guangdong Province,* in PROCEEDINGS OF CHINESE ANNUAL CONFERENCE OF PRIVATE INTERNATIONAL LAW 774, 774-776 (2008), on file with the authors; The Fourth Civil Division of the Guangdong High Court, *The Main Problems at Present: Existing in the Trial of Civil and Commercial Cases Related to Macau and Hong Kong,* 8 PEOPLE'S JUDICATURE 6, 6-7 (2015).

[178] See Tu, *supra* note 87, at 367, 371.

[179] See e.g. Huang, *supra* note 4, at 124.

[180] See Tu, *supra* note 87, at 362-363; Article 1 of the Mainland-Macau Judgments Arrangement.

[181] See Changbin Wang, *Collection of Macau's Gambling Debts in Greater China Area,* 3 MACAU LAW REVIEW 43, 55-56 (2011). In practice, some people's court refused to apply Macau law as the applicable law to recognize the legality of gambling debts on the ground of public policy doctrine. See the case of *the Dispute between Wen Xu and Guisheng Hu as to Determining the Validity of the Contract,* the High People's Court of the Guizhou Province (2015) Qian Gao Min San Zhong Zi No. 7; the appeal case of *the Dispute between Huahan Feng and Guangshui Zhu on the Loan Contract,* the High People's Court of the Shandong Province (2011) Lu Min Si Zhong Zi No. 162. For a commentary written by the judge engaged in deciding the dispute between *Huahan Feng* and *Guangshui Zhu,* see Yuntao Zhu, *Determining the Validity of the Gambling Debts Contract in the Context of Interregional Conflict of Laws,* 12 THE PEOPLE'S JUDICATURE (CASES) 60, 62-63 (2014).

[182] See the appeal case of *the Dispute between Kai Song and Shilong Li Concerning a Share Transfer Agreement,* the Supreme People's Court (2016) Zui Gao Fa Min Zhong No. 152.

local region although the same rights cannot be created to be protected locally.[183]

7.41. As for the Mainland-Hong Kong Choice of Court Arrangement, as said already, it has no uniform rules on the treatment of exclusive choice of court agreements. The Arrangement *simple* does not deal with the issue of exclusive choice of court agreement itself. Instead, the questions around an exclusive choice of court agreement are left to domestic laws, under which the Mainland courts and the Hong Kong courts may unilaterally decide them.[184] It is believed that this insufficiency and uncertainty would discourage the parties from concluding exclusive choice of court agreements for their inter-regional cross-border disputes.[185] Even if this Agreement will be superseded by the 'broad' Mainland-Hong Kong Judgments Arrangement later on, those concerns are still there, real and true. Therefore, unified rules for exclusive choice of court agreements should be provided for both sides in their Arrangement in the future.

V. Conclusion

7.42. Although what would happen after 2047 to Hong Kong and 2049 to Macau is far unknown, the existence of multiple legal systems within China is presumed to last at least for 50 years. Thus, for the next three decades, the conflict of laws within China with its own distinctive features will surely remain a problem to be resolved. In the past two decades or so, on the limited legal basis by a realistic piece-meal approach, a series of inter-regional Arrangements have been made for judicial co-operations between one another among the three regions. These Arrangements may have shortcomings and disadvantages as revealed by practice and compared with corresponding international and other inter-regional instruments. The experiences of and lessons learned from them are still invaluable assets to Chinese legislators, judges and scholars who endeavour to improve the *status quo* of inter-regional judicial assistance within China. It is anticipated that the legal basis would be expanded or broadly interpreted; deeper integration of conflict of laws including jurisdiction and choice of law, even substantive private laws among the three regions would be achieved. It is also submitted that future Arrangements shall be done in a tri-

---

[183]   See Tu, *supra* note 87, at 372. See also PAUL GRU TORREMANS, CHESHIRE, NORTH AND FAWCETT, PRIVATE INTERNATIONAL LAW, Oxford University Press 24-26 (14th ed., 2008).
[184]   See Guangjian Tu, *Recognition and Enforcement of Mainland China's Civil and Commercial Judgments in Hong Kong – An Update*, 25 ASIA PACIFIC LAW REVIEW 190 (2017), at 194.
[185]   See Zhang & Smart, *supra* note 107, at 579, 580.

lateral way and an effective mechanism shall be developed to ensure a uniform interpretation and application of the Chinese inter-regional Arrangements.

| | |

Summaries

FRA [*La coopération judiciaire interrégionale : avancées, problèmes, propositions*]
Depuis la rétrocession de Hong Kong en 1997 et de Macao en 1999, la Chine est un pays doté de plusieurs systèmes juridiques. De ce fait, elle fait face à des conflits de lois au niveau interrégional. Par rapport à d'autres pays, ces conflits de lois se caractérisent par certaines spécificités, qui découlent de la structure politique unique du pays, fondée sur le principe « un pays, deux systèmes ». Au cours des deux dernières décennies, la Chine a réalisé des avancées importantes en matière de coopération judiciaire répondant à des conflits de lois interrégionaux, et ce malgré certaines complications et avec l'espoir de réaliser d'autres améliorations potentielles. À l'avenir, une approche tripartite, fondée sur une solide base juridique, pourrait et devrait mener à une plus profonde intégration des règles de conflit entre ces trois régions, y compris les règles de compétence et le choix de la loi applicable, voir les règles matérielles du droit privé.

CZE [*Meziregionální justiční spolupráce: úspěchy, problémy a návrhy*]
Od předání Hongkongu v roce 1997 a Macaa v roce 1999 je Čína zemí s několika právními řády. V důsledku této skutečnosti se objevil problém meziregionálních kolizí právních úprav. V porovnání s jinými zeměmi se tento čínský problém meziregionálních kolizí vyznačuje jistými specifiky. Příčinou je ojedinělá politická struktura vzniklá na základě politiky „jedna země, dva systémy". V průběhu uplynulých dvou desetiletí dosáhla Čína významných úspěchů na poli justiční spolupráce v oblasti meziregionálního kolizního práva, a to navzdory jistým nedostatkům a s nadějí na dosažení dalších potenciálních zlepšení. V budoucnu by se na základě solidní právní základny mohlo a mělo podařit dosáhnout trojstrannou cestou hlubší integrace kolizních norem mezi těmito třemi regiony, včetně

Czech Yearbook of International Law®

norem upravujících pravomoc a příslušnost a volbu práva, a dokonce i hmotněprávních norem soukromého práva.

| | |

POL   [*Międzyregionalna współpraca wymiaru sprawiedliwości: sukcesy, problemy, sugestie*]
Niniejszy artykuł omawia kwestie związane z prawem kolizyjnym między Hongkongiem, Makau i kontynentalnymi Chinami, w szczególności problematykę międzyregionalnej współpracy wymiaru sprawiedliwości. W ciągu dwóch minionych dekad, pomimo pewnych niedociągnięć, osiągnięto znaczne sukcesy. Jest również co ulepszać. Być może w przyszłości uda się drogą trójstronną pogłębić integrację prawa kolizyjnego między tymi trzema regionami.

DEU   [*Interregionale Gerichtszusammenarbeit: Erfolge, Probleme, Vorschläge*]
Der Artikel widmet sich Fragen des Kollisionsrechts zwischen Hongkong, Macau und Festlandchina, und insbesondere dann dem Problem der interregionalen justiziellen Zusammenarbeit. Im Laufe der letzten zwei Jahrzehnte wurden hier ungeachtet bestimmter Mängel große Erfolge erzielt, wobei noch weitere Verbesserungsmöglichkeiten bestehen. Künftig machbar und wünschenswert erscheint eine mehr tiefgreifende Integration des Kollisionsrechts zwischen diesen drei Regionen auf trilateralem Wege.

RUS   [*Межрегиональное сотрудничество в области юстиции: успехи, проблемы и предложения*]
В данной статье рассматриваются вопросы коллизионного права между Гонконгом, Макао и материковым Китаем, прежде всего, вопрос межрегионального сотрудничества в области юстиции. Несмотря на некоторые недостатки, в течение последних двух десятилетий были достигнуты большие успехи, причем имеются возможности для дальнейших улучшений. В будущем на трехсторонней основе может и должна быть достигнута более глубокая интеграция коллизионного права в этих трех регионах.

ESP   [*La cooperación judicial interregional: éxitos, problemas y propuestas*]
Este artículo se centra en la cuestión del conflicto de leyes entre Hong Kong, Macao y la China continental, en particular, en el problema de la cooperación judicial interregional. En las dos

últimas décadas se han conseguido grandes logros a pesar de algunas deficiencias que dejan un margen para mejoras. En el futuro, podría y debería lograrse, de forma trilateral, una mayor integración de las normas de conflicto entre las tres regiones.

| | |

Bibliography:

GEERT VAN CALSTER, EUROPEAN PRIVATE INTERNATIONAL LAW, Hart Publishing (2013).

Comments, *Hague Convention on the Taking of Evidence Abroad in Civil or Commercial Matters: The Exclusive and Mandatory Procedures for Discovery Abroad*, 132 UNIVERSITY OF PENNSYLVANIA LAW REVIEW 1461 (1984).

Li Chen, *Application of the Hague Evidence Convention in Chinese Foreign-Related Trials in Civil and Commercial Matters*, 1 ORIENTAL LAW 138 (2010).

Edwards S. Corwin, *The Full Faith and Credit Clause*, 81 UNIVERSITY OF PENNSYLVANIA LAW REVIEW 371 (1933).

Likun Dong, *On the Pattern of China's Interregional Judicial Assistance and Its Characteristics*, 17 JOURNAL OF SHENZHEN UNIVERSITY (HUMANITIES & SOCIAL SCIENCES) 45 (2000).

Xia Feng, *An Exploration of the Judiciary on Inter-Regional Service of Documents in Civil and Commercial Matters in Mainland China*, 8 PEOPLE'S JUDICATURE 79 (2006).

Aude Fiorini, *The Evolution of European Private International Law*, 57 INTERNATIONAL & COMPARATIVE LAW QUARTERLY 969 (2008).

Fourth Civil Division of the Guangdong High Court, *The Main Problems at Present: Existing in the Trial of Civil and Commercial Cases Related to Macau and Hong Kong*, 8 PEOPLE'S JUDICATURE 6 (2015).

Xiaoli Gao, *A Look at the Development of the Arrangements between Mainland China and Hong Kong/Macau from the Perspective of the Judicial Assistance Practices by the Mainland Courts*, 6 CHINA LAW 72 (2015).

Depei Han, *An Analysis of Chinese Inter-regional Conflict of Laws: A New Subject in Chinese International Conflict of Laws*, 6 CHINA LEGAL SCIENCE 3 (1988).

Depei Han & Jin Huang, *An Exploration on Inter-Regional Conflict of Laws within China*, 1 CHINA LEGAL SCIENCE 117 (1989).

HCCH, *Report of the Experts' Group on the Use of Video-Link and Other Modern Technologies in the Taking of Evidence Abroad (2-4 December*

2015, The Hague, the Netherlands), Preliminary Doc. No 8 of December 2015 (2015).

Zhonglin He, *The Status Quo and Prospects of Judicial Cooperation and Communication between the Courts of Mainland, Hong Kong, Macau and Taiwan*, 8 PEOPLE RULE OF LAW 18 (2015).

High People's Court of the Guangdong Province, *The Main Problems in the Contemporary Civil and Commercial Trials Involving Hong Kong and Macau*, 8 PEOPLE'S JUDICATURE 6 (2005).

Jin Huang, *Constitutional Law and Inter-Regional Conflict of Laws*, 18 LEGAL FORUM 54 (2003).

Jie Huang, *Interregional Recognition and Enforcement of Civil and Commercial Judgments: Lessons for China from US and EU Laws*, 6 JOURNAL OF PRIVATE INTERNATIONAL LAW 109 (2010).

Jin Huang, Andrew Xuefeng Qian, *"One Country, Two Systems," Three Law Families, and Four Legal Regions: The Emerging Interregional Conflicts of Law in China*, 5 DUKE JOURNAL OF COMPARATIVE & INTERNATIONAL LAW 289 (1995).

Sophie Hunter, *China's Innovative Internet Courts and Their Use of Blockchain Backed Evidence*, Conflictoflaws.net, Views and News in Private International Law (28 May 2019).

Intermediate People's Court of the Shenzhen City, *The White Paper on Foreign-Related Commercial Trials by the Shenzhen People's Court (2008-2013)* (2014).

GRAEME JOHNSTON & PAUL HARRIS SC, THE CONFLICT OF LAWS IN HONG KONG, Sweet & Maxwell (2017).

Frederic L. Kirgis Jr., *The Roles of Due Process and Full Faith and Credit in Choice of Law*, 64 CORNELL LAW REVIEW 94 (1976).

Qingjiang Kong, *Enforcement of Hong Kong SAR Court Judgments in the People's Republic of China*, 50 INTERNATIONAL & COMPARATIVE LAW QUARTERLY 867 (2000).

Andrew Law, *The Law and Practice of Serving Legal Documents on Mainland Parties*, Deacons, Litigation & Dispute Resolution, Newsletter (3 May 2016).

Legislative Council of the Hong Kong SAR, *Arrangement on Mutual Taking of Evidence in Civil and Commercial Matters between the Courts of the Mainland and the Hong Kong Special Administrative Region*, LC Paper No. CB(4)333/16-17(01) (The Hong Kong 2016 Legislative Council Paper on Evidence) (2016).

Caixia Lei & Jiang Hu, *A Discussion on the Reasonable Approach to Service of Judicial Documents in Hong Kong- and Macau- Related Cases in Civil and Commercial Matters*, Hui Zhou Intermediate People's Court (2017).

Macau SAR Judiciary Annual Report, Tribunais da Região Administrativa Especial de Macau, Relatório do Ano Judiciário (2017-2018).

Macau and Hong Kong Ink Judicial Mutual Service Deal, MACAU NEWS (6 December 2017).

Arthur T. von Mehren, *Recognition and Enforcement of Foreign Judgments: A New Approach for the Hague Conference?*, 57 LAW & CONTEMPORARY PROBLEMS 271 (1994).

Xianwei Meng, *On the Characteristics of Inter-Regional Conflict of Laws and its Settlement in China*, 2 LAW SCIENCE 43 (1989).

Permanent Bureau of HCCH, *The Mandatory/Non-Mandatory Character of the Evidence Convention*, Preliminary Doc. No 10 of December 2008 (2008).

Permanent Bureau of HCCH, *Use of Information Technology in the Transmission of Requests under the Service and Evidence Conventions*, Preliminary Doc. No 9 of January 2019 (2019).

Research Group of the Foreign-Related Commercial Tribunal on Foreign-Related Service, *Research Report on the Issue of Service of Documents in Foreign-Related and Hong Kong- and Macau-Related Cases* (28 July 2014).

Ramon E. Reyes Jr., *The Enforcement of Foreign Court Judgments in the People's Republic of China: What the American Lawyer Needs to Know?*, 23 BROOKLYN JOURNAL OF INTERNATIONAL LAW 241 (1997).

Philip St. John Smart, *Finality and the Enforcement of Foreign Judgments under the Common Law in Hong Kong*, OXFORD UNIVERSITY COMMONWEALTH LAW JOURNAL 301 (2005).

Xixiang Song, *Reflections on Status Quo and Improvement of Inter-Regional Service of Judicial Documents in Civil and Commercial Cases between the Mainland and Hong Kong and Macau*, 15 ACADEMIC JOURNAL OF ONE COUNTRY TWO SYSTEMS 121 (2013).

Xixiang Song, *The Achievements, Problems, and Suggestions in the Judicial Assistance between Mainland China and the Macau SAR in Civil and Commercial Matters*, 8 POLITICAL SCIENCE AND LAW 91 (2011).

PETER STONE, EU PRIVATE INTERNATIONAL LAW, Edward Elgar (2nd ed. 2010).

SYMEON C. SYMEONIDES, AMERICAN PRIVATE INTERNATIONAL LAW, Kluwer Law International (2008).

ZHENG SOPHIA TANG, YONGPING XIAO & ZHENGXIN HUO, CONFLICT OF LAWS IN THE PEOPLE'S REPUBLIC OF CHINA, Edward Elgar (2016).

KAIYUAN TAO, CASE SELECTIONS ON INTELLECTUAL PROPER-

TY RIGHTS IN THE GUANGDONG PROVINCE, Series No. 2, Law Press China (2014).

PAUL GRU TORREMANS, CHESHIRE, NORTH AND FAWCETT, PRIVATE INTERNATIONAL LAW, Oxford University Press (14th ed., 2008).

Guangjian Tu, *Arrangement on Mutual Recognition and Enforcement of Judgments in Civil and Commercial Matters between China and Macau: Inherent Problems, Six Years' Experience and the Way Forward*, 43 HONG KONG LAW JOURNAL 349 (2013).

GUANGJIAN TU, PRIVATE INTERNATIONAL LAW IN CHINA, Springer (2016).

Guangjian Tu, *Recognition and Enforcement of Mainland China's Civil and Commercial Judgments in Hong Kong – An Update*, 25 ASIA PACIFIC LAW REVIEW 190 (2017).

Guangjian Tu, *Recognition and Enforcement of Non-Local Judgments in Macau: A Critical Review*, 42 HONG KONG LAW JOURNAL 633 (2012).

Guangjian Tu, *Service of Process (Documents) in International Civil and Commercial Proceedings: A Critical Review of the Chinese Approach*, 13(3) CHINESE JOURNAL OF INTERNATIONAL LAW 577 (2014).

Erxiang Wan, *The Speech given in the National Working Conference Concerning Hong Kong- and Macau-Related Commercial Trials*, cited in Xixiang Song & Hongyan Wang, *On Achievements, Problems and Suggestions for Improvement of the Inter-Regional Evidence-Obtaining System Among the Mainland and Hong Kong and Macao*, 11 ACADEMIC JOURNAL OF ONE COUNTRY TWO SYSTEMS 123 (2012).

Changbin Wang, *Collection of Macau's Gambling Debts in Greater China Area*, 3 MACAU LAW REVIEW 43 (2011).

Chengzhi Wang, *Some Legal Problems Arising Out of the Trial of Civil and Commercial Cases Related to Hong Kong and Macau: with Special Reference to the Judicial Practice in Guangdong Province*, in PROCEEDINGS OF CHINESE ANNUAL CONFERENCE OF PRIVATE INTERNATIONAL LAW 774 (2008).

Guiguo Wang & Priscilla M.F. Leung, *One Country, Two Systems: Theory into Practice*, 7 PACIFIC RIM LAW & POLICY JOURNAL 279 (1998).

White Paper on Judgments over the Civil and Commercial Cases Involving Macao by the People's Court of Hengqin New Area, Zhuhai (2014-2016), Tribunal Popular da Nova Área de Hengqin em Zhuhai Livro, Branco Sobre Julgamento de Causas de Naturezas Civil e Comercial que Envolvem Macau (2017).

Stephen Kai Yi Wong, *Reciprocal Enforcement of Court Judgments in Civil and Commercial Matters between Hong Kong SAR and the Main-*

land, HONG KONG LAWYER OCTOBER ISSUE 31 (2006).

Frank Poon Ying-kwong, The Speech delivered on the Sixth Legal Seminar for the Regions of Guangdong, Hong Kong and Macau (20 December 2014).

Fei Yu, Inter-Regional Direct Taking of Evidence in China, 35 MACAU LAW REVIEW 5 (2017).

FAQIANG YUAN, CONSTITUTION AND COORDINATION OF CHINESE INTERREGIONAL CONFLICT OF LAWS, Law Press China (2009).

Rimsky Yuen, Two Decades' Judicial Assistance in Civil and Commercial Matters between Mainland China and Hong Kong: Look Back and Look Ahead, People's Court Daily (30 June 2017).

Meirong Zhang, Developments in Inter-Regional Conflict of Laws within China, 48 HONG KONG LAW JOURNAL 1097 (2018).

Shudian Zhang, The Breakthrough in Coordination Models of the Judicial Assistance in the Hong Kong and Macau SARs and their Deficiencies, 35 JINAN JOURNAL (PHILOSOPHY AND SOCIAL SCIENCES) 66 (2013).

Xianchu Zhang & Philip Smart, Development of Regional Conflict of Laws: On the Arrangement of Mutual Recognition and Enforcement of Mutual Recognition and Enforcement of Judgments in Civil and Commercial Matters between Mainland China and Hong Kong SAR, 36 HONG KONG LAW JOURNAL 553 (2006).

Xianglin Zhao & Yinghong Liu, A Comparative Study on the Inter-State Conflict of Laws in the United States and China's Inter-Regional Conflict of Laws, 1 JOURNAL OF COMPARATIVE LAW 66 (2000).

Jianhua Zhong, The Role of Case Law in the Course of Settling Inter-Regional Conflict of Laws in China from Comparative Law Perspective, 2-3 JOURNAL OF COMPARATIVE LAW 62 (1992).

Yuntao Zhu, Determining the Validity of the Gambling Debts Contract in the Context of Interregional Conflict of Laws, 12 THE PEOPLE'S JUDICATURE (CASES) 60 (2014).

Guobin Zhu, Inter-regional Conflict of Laws under "One Country, Two Systems": Revisiting Chinese Legal Theories and Chinese and Hong Kong Law, with Special Reference to Judicial Assistance, 32 HONG KONG LAW JOURNAL 615 (2002).

Czech Yearbook of International Law®

Julia Cirne Lima Weston

The International Tribunal for the Law of the Sea: Its Wide Jurisdiction and Potential to Analyse Current Law of the Sea Topics

Key words:
International Tribunal
for the Law of the Sea |
Jurisdiction | Law of the Sea

Abstract | *This article seeks to identify how the International Tribunal for the Law of the Sea (IT-LOS) could contribute towards the development of the current Law of the Sea topics such as sea-level rise, Biodiversity Beyond National Jurisdiction (BBNJ) and Law of the Sea and Human Rights. First, the dispute settlement provisions of the United Nations Convention on the Law of the Sea (LOSC) are explained in order to provide a better understanding of the ITLOS' jurisdiction. Second, the ITLOS' jurisdiction is analysed. Third, the aforementioned current issues are briefly contextualized. Fourthly, an analysis taking into consideration the ITLOS' jurisdiction and the contextualization of the current topics is pursued in order to conclude on how the ITLOS could contribute to their development. The article concludes that the ITLOS can have an important role to play in all of the analysed current issues, and further developments should be observed in this sense.*

Julie Cirne Lima Weston
received her LL.M degree
in International Law at
University College London.
She is a Brazil-qualified
lawyer, Columnist and
English Language Editor
at the Brazilian Institute
for the Law of the Sea
(BILOS).
E-mail: j.clweston@gmail.
com

| | |

I. Introduction

8.01.   The International Law of the Sea's foundational document, the United Nations Convention for the Law of the Sea (LOSC), established the International Tribunal for the Law of the Sea (ITLOS) amongst its forms of dispute settlement.[1] Known as the 'Constitution for the Oceans', the LOSC, although having been signed in 1982, still covers current themes and references treaties signed before and after it, should they be related to its main theme – the Law of the Sea.[2] Since establishment in 1992, the ITLOS has had the chance to hear interesting cases, touching upon issues of environmental law and marine delimitation, among others.[3] This article aims to analyse the International Tribunal for the Law of the Sea's jurisdiction, its limits and its statute, in order to determine how it can be further used to cover current topics that affect the Law of the Sea. For the sake of objectivity, the topics chosen for this specific analysis are sea-level rise, Biodiversity Beyond National Jurisdiction (BBNJ), and the interface between the International Law of the Sea and International Human Rights Law. This choice was due to the fact that the author considers them some of the most pressing issues within the Law of the Sea debate at the moment. As such, this article will be organised in the following way. Firstly, the Part XV of the LOSC will be better explained, in order to best understand the ITLOS' jurisdiction, which will then be (secondly) analysed. Thirdly, the aforementioned current issues will be briefly contextualized in order to conclude on whether they can be submitted to the appreciation of the ITLOS, taking into account its jurisdiction and past case law.

II. Part XV of the UNCLOS

8.02.   Before we can understand the ITLOS, it is important that we understand the LOSC and how its dispute settlement mechanism works. The LOSC, also referred to by one of its negotiators, Ambassador Tommy Koh, as the 'Constitution for the Oceans', established a progressive and stable rule of Law within Law of

---

[1]   United Nations Convention on the Law of the Sea, 1982 (Signed 10 December 1982, Entered into force 16 November 1994), Annex VI.

[2]   Tommy Koh, *A Constitution for The Oceans*, Centre for International Law National University of Singapore, (6 December 1982), available at: https://www.un.org/depts/los/convention_agreements/texts/koh_english.pdf (accessed on 28 June 2021).

[3]   See for example *Southern Bluefin Tuna (New Zealand* v. *Japan; Australia* v. *Japan)*, Provisional Measures, Order of 27 August 1999, ITLOS Reports 1999, et. 280; ITLOS Report, *Responsibilities and obligations of States with respect to activities in the Area, Advisory Opinion, 1 February 2011*, ITLOS Reports 2011, et. 10.

the Sea matters.[4] Although the LOSC was signed in 1982 at Montego Bay, it does not limit its content solely to its Articles, but also makes reference to other treaties in provisions such as those related to environmental law and dispute settlement.[5] This means that the LOSC is able to stay updated on current trends, even if they are covered within other treaties negotiated after it, as long as they are compatible with it.[6] The LOSC's robust dispute settlement is no exception to this.

8.03.　The dispute settlement system is considered as one of the Convention's main achievements.[7] After all, the panorama that previously existed did not allow for the compulsory settlement of disputes related to the Law of the Sea.[8] The LOSC's complex dispute settlement mechanism was the result of many negotiations, and '[...] attempts to strike a delicate balance between states that argued in favor of a judicial and binding dispute settlement procedure and those that preferred diplomatic and nonbinding means.'[9] But what does this so-called balance mean, in practice?

8.04.　The first Article of Part XV of the LOSC, Article 279 obligates parties to settle any disputes between them by peaceful means, referring to Article 2, paragraph 3, and Article 33, paragraph 1 of the Charter of the United Nations (UN Charter).[10] Turning to the UN Charter, this means that disputes shall be solved by peaceful means, safeguarding international peace, security and justice.[11] It also means that, when parties to disputes, States must try to seek a solution through '[...] negotiation, enquiry, mediation, conciliation, arbitration, judicial settlement, resort to regional agencies or arrangements, or other peaceful means of their own choice.'[12] Accordingly, the LOSC's system will not apply when parties agree to seek settlement by any peaceful means of their choice, and even makes reference to other existing general, bilateral or regional agreements for peaceful dispute settlement.[13]

8.05.　However, when no such settlement through peaceful means is achieved, Part XV obliges parties to a dispute to submit

---

[4]　Tommy Koh, *supra* note 2.
[5]　United Nations Convention on the Law of the Sea, *supra* note 1; Tullio Treves, *Human Rights and the Law of the Sea*, 28(1) BERKELEY JOURNAL OF INTERNATIONAL LAW 1, 6 (2010).
[6]　United Nations Convention on the Law of the Sea, *supra* note 1, Article 311.
[7]　IGOR V. KARAMAN, DISPUTE RESOLUTION IN THE LAW OF THE SEA, Leiden: Brill 1 (2012).
[8]　Ibid.
[9]　Cesare Romano, *The Southern Bluefin Tuna Dispute: Hints of a World to Come... Like it or not*, 32(4) OCEAN DEVELOPMENT AND INTERNATIONAL LAW 313, 320 (2001).
[10]　United Nations Convention on the Law of the Sea, 1982, *supra* note 1, Article 279.
[11]　Charter of the United Nations, Article 2(3).
[12]　Ibid., Article 33(1).
[13]　United Nations Convention on the Law of the Sea, *supra* note 1, Articles 281, 282.

the dispute, at the request of any of the parties, to any court or tribunal with jurisdiction under the LOSC.[14] These are the ITLOS, the International Court of Justice (ICJ) and arbitral tribunals constituted in accordance with Annex VII or VIII of the LOSC.[15] What decides to which of these courts or tribunals a case will be submitted is the choice by a State, which can be done by means of written declaration to be submitted to the Secretary-General for publicity, or whether there is otherwise an agreement regarding the forum of choice between both parties.[16] As such, when States signed, ratified or acceded to the LOSC, or at any time after that, they have been given the space to express, in a written declaration, what their forum of choice is.[17] Up until this article was drafted, 54 States, out of 168 Parties to the LOSC have made such declarations regarding the fora listed in Article 287.[18] Out of those, 42 have chosen the ITLOS as one of their dispute settlement fora.[19]

8.06. If both parties to a dispute have chosen the same forum, the dispute will be submitted to that forum, unless there is an agreement otherwise.[20] What happens in the case that two States have chosen different fora, or if one or more States involved in a dispute have not chosen any forum at all? If the fora chosen are different, or if no forum at all has been selected, the dispute will necessarily need to be submitted to an arbitral tribunal, unless there is an agreement otherwise.[21]

8.07. In sum, the LOSC's system is innovative as it establishes a binding dispute settlement system, in which States are bound to solve disputes through peaceful means and, in case other forms of settlement do not work, a solution by adjudication is mandatory.[22] Out of the 54 States who have submitted their declarations under the LOSC, 42, a significant majority, have listed the ITLOS as one of their dispute settlement options.[23] As for those who have not made any declarations, disputes will be pointed straight to arbitration, unless both parties agree on submitting their disputes to the ITLOS. This means that the role

---

[14] Ibid., Articles 286.
[15] Ibid., Article 287.
[16] Ibid.
[17] Ibid.
[18] United Nations, *United Nations Convention on the Law of the Sea*, available at: https://treaties.un.org/Pages/ViewDetailsIII.aspx?src=TREATY&mtdsg_no=XXI-6&chapter=21&Temp=mtdsg3&clang=_en (accessed on 28 June 2021).
[19] Ibid.
[20] United Nations Convention on the Law of the Sea, *supra* note 1, Article 287.
[21] Ibid.
[22] Howard S. Schiffman, *The Dispute Settlement Mechanism of UNCLOS: A Potentially Important Framework for Marine Wildlife Management*, 1 JOURNAL OF INTERNATIONAL LAW WILDLIFE AND POLICY 293, 294 (1998).
[23] United Nations, *supra* note 18.

The International Tribunal for the Law of the Sea: Its Wide Jurisdiction...

Czech Yearbook of International Law®

of the ITLOS has a space to grow, as more countries can still opt for it via declarations, or agree to it as a forum for their specific disputes over time.

III. The ITLOS: Its Jurisdiction and Limits

8.08. As previously seen, the ITLOS was a creation of the LOSC and it is one of the dispute settlement alternatives presented to member States by the LOSC's Part XV.[24] The reasons for its creation are multiple, such as the political distrust of certain States in the ICJ at the time and the potential lack of jurisdiction of the ICJ over certain cases.[25] It is a specialised body, as it only hears cases related to the Law of the Sea, and appears to be more representative of the international community as a whole: out of its 21 judges, the majority comes from developing States, due to geographic requirements.[26] These requirements are that there shall be no fewer than three members from each geographical group established by the United Nations General Assembly (UNGA).[27] The regional groups established by the UNGA are: the Group of Asian States, Group of African States, Group of Latin American and Caribbean States, Group of Western European and other States and the Group of Eastern European States.[28] It does not require much analysis to say that most of the members elected to the ITLOS by following these rules would be of developing States, as of the writing of this article.

8.09. The ITLOS' jurisdiction comprises '[...] all disputes and all applications submitted to it in accordance with this Convention and all matters specifically provided for in any other agreement which confers jurisdiction on the Tribunal.'[29] This, aligned with the requirement that other agreements or treaties concern the same 'subject-matter' of the LOSC, within Article 22 of the Statute, leads one to conclude that the ITLOS' jurisdiction is restricted to the Law of the Sea.[30]

8.10. There are other important things to note regarding the ITLOS' jurisdiction which end up enlarging its range of action within the current matters analysed in this article. Article 20 of its Statute opens the ITLOS not only to States Parties, but also to entities

---

[24]   United Nations Convention on the Law of the Sea, *supra* note 1.
[25]   IGOR V. KARAMAN, DISPUTE RESOLUTION IN THE LAW OF THE SEA, Leiden: Brill 4 (2012).
[26]   Susanne Wasum-Rainer & Daniela Schlegel, *The UNCLOS Dispute Settlement System - Between Hamburg and the Hague*, 48 GERMAN YEARBOOK OF INTERNATIONAL LAW 187, 203-204 (2005).
[27]   United Nations Convention on the Law of the Sea, *supra* note 1, Annex VI, Article 3.
[28]   United Nations General Assembly, A/RES/33/138, (18 December 1978), available at: https://undocs.org/en/A/RES/33/138 (accessed on 15 July 2021); United Nations, Regional groups of member States, available at: https://www.un.org/dgacm/en/content/regional-groups (accessed on 15 July 2021).
[29]   United Nations Convention on the Law of the Sea, *supra* note 1, Annex VI, Article 21.
[30]   Ibid., Article 22.

other than States, in cases provided for in Part XI (the Area) or in cases in which other agreements confer jurisdiction to it.[31] This means that, unlike in the ICJ, entities who are not States can access the Tribunal in specific cases. This can potentialize the ITLOS' action in the upcoming years, should we have more treaties and agreements which grant it jurisdiction.

8.11. This brings us to another important aspect which potentializes the ITLOS' room for action in the international plane. Article 21 confers jurisdiction to the ITLOS to '[...] all disputes and all applications submitted to it in accordance with this Convention and all matters specifically provided for in any other agreement which confers jurisdiction on the Tribunal.'[32] Additionally, parties to existing conventions or treaties can submit disputes regarding their application or interpretation to the ITLOS through an agreement.[33] This clearly does not limit the ITLOS' cases to those regarding the LOSC, but also other agreements regarding the Law of the Sea which can have the ITLOS as their dispute resolution forum of choice. This is particularly important in the context of the BBNJ negotiations, in which we still do not have chosen means of dispute settlement.[34]

8.12. Besides giving the ITLOS compulsory jurisdiction over contentious cases, the tribunal is also granted advisory jurisdiction under two circumstances. The LOSC confers advisory jurisdiction to the ITLOS's Seabed Disputes Chamber, at the request of the Assembly or the Council of the International Seabed Authority (ISA), on legal issues under the scope of the ISA.[35] The Rules of the ITLOS also grant it the power to grant advisory opinions '[...] if an international agreement related to the purposes of the Convention specifically provides for the submission to the Tribunal of a request for such an opinion.'[36]

8.13. Not only is the ITLOS empowered to do so, it has actually issued two advisory opinions, each of those based on one of these justifications. The first advisory opinion was requested to the Seabed Disputes Chamber, regarding the responsibilities of sponsoring States in activities in the Area, based on the LOSC, and was delivered in 2011.[37] The second and latest opinion, delivered in 2015, dealt with the issue of illegal, unreported

---

31   Ibid., Article 20.
32   Ibid., Article 21.
33   Ibid., Article 22.
34   Joanna Mossop, *Dispute Settlement in the New Treaty on Marine Biodiversity in Areas beyond National Jurisdiction*, (23 December 2019), available at: https://site.uit.no/nclos/2019/12/23/dispute-settlement-in-the-new-treaty-on-marine-biodiversity-in-areas-beyond-national-jurisdiction/ (accessed 20 June 2021).
35   United Nations Convention on the Law of the Sea, *supra* note 1, Article 191.
36   Rules of the International Tribunal for the Law of the Sea, Article 138.
37   ITLOS Report, *Responsibilities and obligations of States with respect to activities in the Area, Advisory Opinion, 1 February 2011*, ITLOS Reports 2011, et. 10.

and unregulated fishing (IUU fishing), and was requested by the Sub-Regional Fisheries Commission, based on a regional agreement conferring advisory jurisdiction upon the ITLOS.[38]

8.14. As such, the ITLOS, although a Law of the Sea tribunal, is not solely a LOSC tribunal. Its jurisdiction is not restricted to disputes concerning the LOSC, and disputes from other treaties or conventions may be submitted to it, either by default, should it be the means of dispute settlement chosen by these legal documents, or through an agreement of both parties to other agreements. This is important to note when considering current themes and issues within the Law of the Sea, for which answers are not yet clearly defined.

IV. Limited Current Issues within the Law of the Sea

IV.1. Sea-level Rise

8.15. According to the latest report published by the Intergovernmental Panel on Climate Change, sea-level rise is a problem, and the global mean sea level has been increasing faster today than it previously did.[39] Sea-level rise varies regionally and is fomented by anthropogenic drivers.[40] As a consequence, low-lying States are set to feel considerable effects from this climatic event.[41]

8.16. The topic is relevant for the Law of the Sea because, if previsions are correct, we will have the complete submersion of certain States if no measures are taken.[42] Sea-level rise is one of the most discussed topics within the Law of the Sea and general International Law, as it surpasses the LOSC and the Law of the Sea itself, and touches upon issues such as migration and statehood.[43] It is currently the topic of a working group at the International Law Commission (ILC) and of a study group at

---

[38] ITLOS Report, *Request for Advisory Opinion submitted by the Sub-Regional Fisheries Commission, Advisory Opinion, 2 April 2015, ITLOS Reports 2015*, et. 4.

[39] The Intergovernmental Panel on Climate Change, *Sea Level Rise and Implications for Low-Lying Islands, Coasts and Communities*, Chapter 4 (14 July 2019), available at: https://www.ipcc.ch/srocc/chapter/chapter-4-sea-level-rise-and-implications-for-low-lying-islands-coasts-and-communities/ (accessed on 19 June 2021).

[40] Ibid.

[41] Ibid.

[42] DAVOR VIDAS & DAVID FREESTONE & JANE MCADAM, INTERNATIONAL LAW AND SEA LEVEL RISE: REPORT OF THE INTERNATIONAL LAW ASSOCIATION COMMITTEE ON INTERNATIONAL LAW AND SEA LEVEL RISE, Brill Research Perspectives in the Law of the Sea (2019).

[43] See DAVOR VIDAS & DAVID FREESTONE & JANE MCADAM, *supra* note 42, and Bogdan Aurescu & Nilufer Oral: *First issues paper by Bogdan Aurescu and Nilüfer Oral, Co-Chairs of the Study Group on sea-level rise in relation to international law*, (28 February 2020), available at: https://documents-dds-ny.un.org/doc/UNDOC/GEN/N20/053/91/PDF/N2005391.pdf?OpenElement (accessed on 15 June 2021).

the International Law Association (ILA) regarding its effects on International Law.[44]

8.17. Although the effects of sea-level surpass the scope of the LOSC, the most intrinsically connected point of this event to the Law of the Sea is the issue of baselines.[45] The territorial sea and other maritime zones are to be calculated from baselines established by States, with the normal baseline being the low-water line.[46] With sea-level rise, normal baselines and other baselines thereof would likely shift landwards in low-lying States and island nations.[47] It is the current challenge of the ILC and the ILA to tackle the Law of the Sea impacts and challenges to this matter.

8.18. For that, both the ILA and the ILC present alternatives as to what can happen to the regime of baselines for sea-level rise. One possibility is to maintain the baseline regime as it is in the LOSC, even if baselines may, indeed, retract.[48] Another option is to freeze baselines where they were established by States, even if the coastline may end up retracting.[49] This is, however, not a preferred alternative, as some say it goes against the logic of the LOSC.[50] This is argued because the low-water line chosen by the LOSC as its main baseline would not correspond to the low-water line in practice.[51] Finally, another option is to 'freeze' the baselines only when they were deposited with the Secretary-General under the due publicity obligation, according to the LOSC.[52] This is, however, an ongoing study that will need to have its outcomes more thoroughly analysed in order for a conclusion to be reached.

8.19. As such, there is not yet a conclusion on how the issue will be approached. It may be that the LOSC will have the answers to that, but it may also be that the LOSC's guidance will not be enough to answer the question of sea-level rise, and new rules may have to be put in place, perhaps as a matter of exception.

---

[44] International Law Commission, *Report of the International Law Commission*, Seventieth Session (August 2018), available at: https://legal.un.org/ilc/reports/2018/english/annex_B.pdf (accessed 15 June 2021).
[45] DAVOR VIDAS & DAVID FREESTONE & JANE MCADAM, *supra* note 42 and Bogdan Aurescu & Nilufer Oral, *supra* note 43.
[46] United Nations Convention on the Law of the Sea, *supra* note 1, Article 5.
[47] Bogdan Aurescu & Nilufer Oral, *supra* note 43.
[48] DAVOR VIDAS & DAVID FREESTONE & JANE MCADAM, *supra* note 42, and Bogdan Aurescu & Nilufer Oral, *supra* note 43.
[49] Ibid.
[50] Ibid.
[51] Ibid.
[52] Ibid.

The International Tribunal for the Law of the Sea: Its Wide Jurisdiction...

Czech Yearbook of International Law®

IV.2.   Biodiversity Beyond National Jurisdiction

8.20.   The issue of areas beyond national jurisdiction and biodiversity beyond national jurisdiction is vast, complex, and, as it is not the main issue of this article, will only be briefly contextualised in this subsection. The interest in the conservation of areas beyond national jurisdiction comes from the various threats to the marine environment posed by the advance of technology, the overexploitation and exploration of marine living resources within the high seas, and the reflections of other anthropogenic activity, such as shipping.[53] While the LOSC regime has put some areas under the jurisdiction and conservation obligations of certain States, some are still left out of this protection, even though they contain important biodiversity for the maintenance of a healthy marine ecosystem.[54] The LOSC does not regulate these activities, as they are within the regime of the high seas.[55] There is, thus, a call for an international system to regulate said areas of protection within the high seas.[56]

8.21.   Biodiversity Beyond National Jurisdiction (BBNJ), concerns the ongoing discussions at the Preparatory Committee established by General Assembly resolution 69/292 for the Development of an international legally binding instrument under the United Nations Convention on the Law of the Sea on the conservation and sustainable use of marine biological diversity of areas beyond national jurisdiction.[57] Seeking to draft a new instrument regarding the conservation of biological diversity within areas beyond national jurisdiction, a preparatory committee was established, in order to produce a draft legal instrument under the LOSC in this respect.[58]

8.22.   The meetings of the Committee have, this far, focused on issues such as marine genetic resources, marine protected areas,

---

[53]   Robin Warner, *Conserving Marine Biodiversity in Areas Beyond National Jurisdiction: Co-Evolution and Interaction with the Law of the Sea* in DONALD ROTHWELL; ALEX OUDE ELFERINK; KAREN SCOTT; TIM STEPHENS, THE OXFORD HANDBOOK OF THE LAW OF THE SEA, Oxford: OUP (2015).
[54]   International Union for Conservation of Nature, *Governing areas beyond national jurisdiction*, available at: https://www.iucn.org/resources/issues-briefs/governing-areas-beyond-national-jurisdiction (accessed 25 June 2021).
[55]   United Nations Convention on the Law of the Sea, *supra* note 1, Article 87.
[56]   International Union for Conservation of Nature, *supra* note 54.
[57]   United Nations Division for Ocean Affairs and the Law of the Sea, Preparatory Committee established by General Assembly resolution 69/292: Development of an international legally binding instrument under the United Nations Convention on the Law of the Sea on the conservation and sustainable use of marine biological diversity of areas beyond national jurisdiction, available at: https://www.un.org/depts/los/biodiversity/prepcom.htm (accessed 25 June 2021).
[58]   United Nations General Assembly, *Development of an international legally-binding instrument under the United Nations Convention on the Law of the Sea on the conservation and sustainable use of marine biological diversity of areas beyond national jurisdiction* (06 July 2015), available at: https://undocs.org/en/a/res/69/292 (accessed on 25 June 2021).

environmental impact assessment, transfer of technology, etc.[59] This is because we are dealing with valuable resources, including for scientific use. Another aspect currently in consideration by the Committee has been that of dispute settlement. Within the third meeting, there was a convergence on the fact that the new BBNJ agreement's dispute settlement provisions should draw from the UN Charter and the LOSC, and that the dispute settlement modalities would be set out in the agreement.[60]

8.23. The recently published 'draft text' of the agreement, elaborated at the third meeting of the conference, applies Part XV of the LOSC to dispute settlement under the BBNJ agreement.[61] A novelty introduced by the draft is the possibility for States who are not parties to the LOSC, but who are parties to the BBNJ Agreement, to choose among the dispute settlement fora set out in Part XV.[62] If adopted as such, this would clearly put ITLOS in a favourable light to address disputes arising not solely between LOSC parties, but also between parties and non-Parties, or hypothetically even two non-Parties, as long as they so agree to choose ITLOS through the BBNJ agreement.

IV.3.   The Law of the Sea and Human Rights

8.24. The issue of the interaction between the Law of the Sea and Human Rights is also vast and comprises many unanswered questions. It is, thus, not the goal of this article to exhaust it, or to provide any complex answer to this matter. It is, however, to briefly present the issue in its current context. There are many threats to Human Rights at sea, that is undeniable, ranging from issues such as abuse of seafarers, fishers, and fisheries observers, to human trafficking and the distress faced by migrants at sea and many others.[63]

8.25. The LOSC is not regarded as a Human Rights treaty.[64] In fact, there are not many provisions to it which spark a person's

---

[59]   United Nations General Assembly, *Report of the Preparatory Committee established by General Assembly resolution 69/292: Development of an international legally binding instrument under the United Nations Convention on the Law of the Sea on the conservation and sustainable use of marine biological diversity of areas beyond national jurisdiction* (31 July 2017), available at: https://www.un.org/ga/search/view_doc.asp?symbol=A/AC.287/2017/PC.4/2 (accessed 25 June 2021).

[60]   Ibid.

[61]   United Nations General Assembly, *Draft text of an agreement under the United Nations Convention on the Law of the Sea on the conservation and sustainable use of marine biological diversity of areas beyond national jurisdiction* (17 May 2019), available at: https://undocs.org/a/conf.232/2019/6 (accessed on 25 June 2021), Article 54.

[62]   Ibid., Article 55.

[63]   Tafsir Malick Ndiaye, *Human Rights at Sea and the Law of the Sea*, 10 BEIJING LAW REVIEW 261, 262 (2019).

[64]   Bernard H. Oxman, *Human Rights and the United Nations Convention on the Law of the Sea*, 36 COLUMBIA JOURNAL OF TRANSNATIONAL LAW 399, 401 (1998).

The International Tribunal for the Law of the Sea: Its Wide Jurisdiction...

Czech Yearbook of International Law®

attention regarding Human Rights, although former ITLOS Judges Tafsir Malick Ndiaye and Tullio Treves point out that there are many provisions in the LOSC which are intrinsically related to the protection of Human Rights.[65] As examples of that, ITLOS cases such as *M/V Saiga* and *Juno Trader* are mentioned, arguing that prompt release cases are intrinsically related to Human Rights protection.[66] Among other examples given by commentators are the obligation not to detain people in the EEZ and the high seas, and the obligation of rescue at sea.[67]

8.26. Indeed, the ITLOS did mention in the case of *M/V Saiga*, the issue of 'considerations of humanity'.[68] The case concerned the arrest of a vessel by Guinea due to illegal bunkering (transfer of fuel at sea) in its EEZ.[69] The issue of 'considerations of humanity' appeared when the ITLOS analysed the use of force by Guinea in the arrest of the M/V Saiga, saying that although it was not an issue directly covered by the LOSC, it should be considered due in light of such considerations.[70] The specific wording used by the ITLOS was 'Considerations of humanity must apply in the law of the sea, as they do in other areas of international law'.[71] The understanding was echoed later in the *Juno Trader* case.[72]

8.27. Although used in the specific context of the use of force, it can be presumed that the ITLOS, through the employment of such wording, may have demonstrated itself as available for considering Human Rights, or such 'considerations of humanity' in further cases submitted to it.[73] It also demonstrates a will of the ITLOS to engage in other international law issues which are not excluded by the LOSC, as per the LOSC's terms.

8.28. So far, there are no means for individuals to access the Law of the Sea regarding Human Rights violations pursued onboard ships. There is, however, a reflection that could be done when looking at Human Rights violations at sea, which is the issue of jurisdiction, which, in the high seas, pertains to flag States. Ships, in order to sail, must be registered in States, which then

---

[65] Irini Papanicolopulu, *The Law of the Sea Convention: No Place for Persons*, 27(4) INTERNATIONAL JOURNAL OF MARINE & COASTAL LAW, 867, 867 (2012); Tafsir Malick Ndiaye, *supra* note 63, 269-271; Tullio Treves, *supra* note 5, 3-5.

[66] Ibid.

[67] Bernard H. Oxman, *supra* note 64.

[68] *M/V "SAIGA" (No. 2) (Saint Vincent and the Grenadines* v. *Guinea)*, Judgment, ITLOS Reports 1999, et. 10.

[69] Ibid.

[70] Ibid.

[71] Ibid.

[72] *"Juno Trader" (Saint Vincent and the Grenadines* v. *Guinea-Bissau)*, Prompt Release, Judgment, ITLOS Reports 2004, et. 17.

[73] Tafsir Malick Ndiaye, *supra* note 63, 271; Tullio Treves, *supra* note 5, 5.

become flag States.[74] The LOSC gives jurisdiction to flag States over '[...] administrative, technical and social matters over ships flying its flag [...]'.[75]

8.29. The LOSC's regime is still one centred on flag State jurisdiction, even if a vessel is going through territorial waters of another State, save for specific situations in which coastal States are called to action by the flag State or ship authorities.[76] This means that, as far as we maintain this regime, the only means to 'enforce' these protections would be via the notification of flag States in order for the flag States themselves to conduct due investigations over their flagged vessels.[77] Such is the case contained in the Human Rights at Sea (HRAS) report on the human rights violations of fisheries observers, analysing a situation in which a fisheries observer from Kiribati disappeared during his work in a Taiwanese-flagged vessel.[78] The flag State in the case was duly notified of the incident by Kiribati, and promised to undertake due investigations.[79] Although in this case there was a favourable ending, the need to notify flag States, who will then decide whether to conduct investigations, is arguably still a very feeble framework for Human Rights protection. That, of course, if we consider Human Rights to be applicable both in land territory and vessels, which this article presumes as such due to the lack of geographical and territorial limitations imposed to treaties such as the International Covenant on Civil and Political Rights, among others.[80]

8.30. As such, the issue of Human Rights is still far from being solved within the realm of the Law of the Sea. While there are no such provisions within the LOSC which are obvious to the 'naked eye', there are provisions which arguably have Human Rights content, as argued by former ITLOS Judges Treves and Ndiaye. We also live in a context where two implementing agreements, complementing the LOSC were negotiated: the implementing agreement on seabed mining and one on high seas fish stocks.[81] With a new implementing agreement underway with regards

---

[74]   United Nations Convention on the Law of the Sea, *supra* note 1, Article 91.
[75]   Ibid., Article 94.
[76]   Ibid., Article 217.
[77]   Ibid.
[78]   Human Rights at Sea, *Fisheries Observer Deaths at Sea, Human Rights & the Role & Responsibilities of Fisheries Organisations* (01 July 2020), available at: https://www.humanrightsatsea.org/wp-content/uploads/2020/07/HRAS_Abuse_of_Fisheries_Observers_REPORT_JULY-2020_SP_OPTIMISED.pdf (accessed on 10 July 2021).
[79]   Ibid.
[80]   Luciana Fernandes Coelho & Julia Cirne Lima Weston, *Who Observes the Onboard Observers Working in the Waters Adjacent to the Pacific Small Islands Developing States? The Flag State Responsibility for Violation of Human Rights at Sea* in DIREITO DO MAR: REFLEXÕES, TENDÊNCIAS E PERSPECTIVAS, V. 4, Belo Horizonte: Editora D'Plácido (André de Paiva Toledo et al ed., 2020).
[81]   Irini Papanicolopulu, *supra* note 65, 867.

The International Tribunal for the Law of the Sea: Its Wide Jurisdiction...

Czech Yearbook of International Law®

to the BBNJ issue, it is not to rule out that new agreements regarding Human Rights be negotiated in the future.[82] As such, Human Rights discussions are not yet done with, and can, and will likely be approached in the future.

V. The ITLOS and Current Issues: A Promising Way Forward

8.31. As shown above, there are many contemporary issues within the Law of the Sea including sea-level rise, the BBNJ agreement and Human Rights issues. Part XV of the LOSC is innovative and complex and, most importantly, it brings forward compulsory dispute settlement for issues in which agreement is not reached by its States Parties.[83] Besides contentious jurisdiction, the ITLOS also enjoys advisory jurisdiction in two cases: that enjoyed by its Seabed Disputes Chamber and in cases where an agreement grants the ITLOS such power.[84]

8.32. These three issues continue to present practical issues. First, sea-level rise is currently being analysed by committees within both the ILA and the ILC. This far there are unanswered questions on whether the LOSC will be ultimately used as a basis for the shifting of baselines, for maintaining baselines, or whether progressive codification will need to be done to address this specific issue.[85] There is thus some room to speculate, and two possible hypotheses.

8.33. Should any dispute arise regarding some States' decision to 'freeze', or move their baselines in case of sea-level rise, Part XV would definitely apply, as that concerns a disagreement over the interpretation of the LOSC and its provisions, specifically those concerning baselines. In this sense, ITLOS would have a say should States have opted for it, or should the disputing States agree to its jurisdiction.[86] In the case of a new specific codification, either the dispute settlement provisions under the LOSC will be kept, or those could be negotiated or established by the ILC in its draft regulation. In this case, should the new text refer to Part XV, the same procedure would apply. If it only referred to the ITLOS, which may be unlikely, then of course, ITLOS would also have sole jurisdiction over issues related to it. For stability and predictability reasons sought after by parties

---

[82] Ibid.

[83] United Nations Convention on the Law of the Sea, *supra* note 1, Part XV.

[84] United Nations Convention on the Law of the Sea, *supra* note 1, Annex VI, Article 21; Rules of the International Tribunal for the Law of the Sea, Article 138.

[85] See DAVOR VIDAS & DAVID FREESTONE & JANE MCADAM, *supra* note 42, and Bogdan Aurescu & Nilufer Oral, *supra* note 43.

[86] United Nations Convention on the Law of the Sea, *supra* note 1, Part XV.

and the ILC alike, reference to Part XV LOSC and its robust dispute settlement will probably be made. Unless a new treaty or agreement is reached, it is unlikely that the ITLOS will have advisory jurisdiction over this specific issue.

8.34. Regarding the BBNJ agreement, there is clearly an intention to give Part XV the spotlight, and that does include the ITLOS. Should the draft be followed and approved as it currently stands, Part XV would apply by reference. This means that, should both States have opted for the ITLOS as their chosen mechanism, or should they agree upon it afterwards, the Tribunal could have a role to play in BBNJ-related disputes. If the draft is kept as it currently is, the ITLOS would lack advisory jurisdiction on this matter. It is important to keep in mind that discussions are still ongoing and that could change, should negotiating Parties find it interesting to give ITLOS advisory powers.

8.35. Nonetheless, it is important that the ITLOS have a role and a say in the BBNJ-related disputes, due to its involvement in judging cases which relate to environmental law, such as the Southern Bluefin Tuna case, among others.[87] Since the BBNJ is a Law of the Sea matter, it will be interesting that it is decided on by a specialised Tribunal and the ITLOS, as we know, is the only specialised Law of the Sea tribunal there is.[88]

8.36. Regarding Human Rights, all will depend on whether new agreements are negotiated, or whether disputes between States of nationality of injured nationals will go to the ITLOS for incidents involving nationals. Although incidents involving nationals could be submitted to the ITLOS for analysis, as it would pertain to Article 94, it is unlikely that this will surface. Even though flag State jurisdiction is a constant in the LOSC regime, it shall be hard to attribute liability to a flag State for a specific event of a Human Rights violation. This is because the flag State has jurisdiction over a vessel, but it is not necessarily the perpetrator of a Human Rights violation onboard a vessel. However, should there be a poor trend of the flag State in terms of implementing Human Rights legislation, that fact itself could be challenged in a dispute. This is because the ITLOS itself has connected the concept of due diligence with flag State jurisdiction in its advisory opinion on IUU Fishing. In it, the tribunal said that the flag States must do all they can to stop IUU

---

[87] See for example *Southern Bluefin Tuna (New Zealand v. Japan; Australia v. Japan)*, Provisional Measures, Order of 27 August 1999, ITLOS Reports 1999, et.280; ITLOS Report, *Responsibilities and obligations of States with respect to activities in the Area, Advisory Opinion, 1 February 2011*, ITLOS Reports 2011, et. 10.

[88] Hugo Caminos, *The Jurisdiction and Procedure of the International Tribunal for the Law of the Sea: an overview*, in GOVERNING OCEAN RESOURCES NEW CHALLENGES AND EMERGING REGIMES: A TRIBUTE TO JUDGE CHOON-HO PARK, Leiden: Brill (Jon M. Van Dyke; et al ed. 2013).

The International Tribunal for the Law of the Sea: Its Wide Jurisdiction...

Czech Yearbook of International Law®

Fishing activities from taking place within their flagged vessels.[89] The obligation of due diligence, as per the understanding of the ITLOS, is one of conduct, not of result.[90]

8.37.	Due diligence in International Law is a broad term, and as such we need to look at it from a Human Rights Law perspective. According to the ILA's report on Due Diligence, some of the due diligence obligations of States under International Human Rights Law would be to have a system to ensure Human Rights protection and adequate means of investigation and remedies.[91] In this specific case, the due diligence obligation would likely concern having in place legislation that could prevent the problem, an investigative organ, as well as a system providing for adequate recourse.[92] In the case of Human Rights, for instance adequate labour or Human Rights regulations, as well as applicable courts and judicial recourse, for instance, could serve as proof. What could be harder for States to prove, however, would be the efficacy of those available means for investigation and remedying a Human Rights violation, as it is a requisite that institutions must function 'diligently'.[93]

8.38.	Regarding upcoming issues and agreements, there has been a trend to negotiate implementing agreements for issues which are lacking regulation.[94] Should an implementing agreement be negotiated, it would most likely refer to Part XV and, as a consequence, to the ITLOS. This could mean expanding the Tribunal's line of action to a whole new world of disputes concerning not only issues contained in the LOSC, but those related to it, as its scope of jurisdiction refers to. Considering the ITLOS' decision-making in line with 'considerations of humanity', it is not impossible that the Tribunal be referred a Human Rights case. It is important to consider, however, that the ICJ may be a more 'popular' alternative in such a scenario, as it deals with both Law of the Sea and Human Rights Law issues within its case law, and has a more established track record in this sense.[95]

---

[89]	Advisory Opinion on IUU Fishing, *supra* note 38.
[90]	Advisory Opinion on IUU Fishing, *supra* note 38; Advisory Opinion on the Area, *supra* note 37.
[91]	International Law Association, *ILA Study Group on Due Diligence in International Law First Report* (07 March 2014), available at: https://ila.vettoreweb.com/Storage/Download.aspx?DbStorageId=1429&StorageFileGuid=fd770a95-9118-4a20-ac61-df12356f74d0 (accessed on 10 July 2021).
[92]	Ibid.
[93]	Ibid.
[94]	Irini Papanicolopulu, *supra* note 65.
[95]	Ibid.

VI.   Conclusion

8.39.   The dispute settlement provisions under Part XV of the LOSC were surely ground-breaking in International Law, by allowing for compulsory dispute settlement under a complex system. The creation of the ITLOS as a specialised Law of the Sea forum by the LOSC is also something worthy of praise. This article has sought to bring to the analysis the potential contributions of the ITLOS in certain current developments within the Law of the Sea.

8.40.   Due to the ITLOS' wide scope of jurisdiction, there is a potentially wide space for it to occupy within future dispute settlement in the Law of the Sea, within the aforementioned topics. While the LOSC was drafted in the 1970s and approved in the 1980s, its reference to other treaties, as well as the possibility to negotiate implementing agreements under it, still make it able to cope with current challenges.

8.41.   The ITLOS, in the way that it is organised by the LOSC, can surely be an ally in further developing the Law of the Sea within these aforementioned current issues. As this analysis has tried to indicate, the ITLOS still has a large role to play within such analyses in the future, and further developments should be observed in this sense.

| | |

Summaries

FRA   [*Le Tribunal international du droit de la mer : sa large compétence et son potentiel pour analyser les questions actuelles du droit de la mer*]

Le présent article se propose de réfléchir sur les manières dont le Tribunal international du droit de la mer (TIDM) pourrait contribuer à des avancées sur les questions actuelles du droit de la mer, telles que la montée du niveau des océans, la biodiversité des zones ne relevant pas de la juridiction nationale (Biodiversity Beyond National Jurisdiction – BBNJ), ou la relation entre le droit de la mer et les droits de l'homme. Tout d'abord, l'article explique les dispositions relatives au règlement des différends prévues par la Convention des Nations Unies sur le droit de la mer (CNUDM), afin de mieux cerner les pouvoirs et la compétence du TIDM. Ensuite, il examine ces pouvoirs et compétence. Troisièmement, il met les questions abordées dans leur contexte. Quatrièmement, l'auteur procède à une analyse

The International Tribunal for the Law of the Sea: Its Wide Jurisdiction...

Czech Yearbook of International Law®

conjointe de la compétence du TIDM et du contexte dans lequel s'inscrivent les questions débattues, afin d'arriver à des conclusions sur la manière dont le TIDM pourrait contribuer à leur approfondissement. En conclusion, l'auteur estime que le TIDM pourrait jouer un rôle important à tous les niveaux envisagés et qu'on peut s'attendre à de nouvelles avancées en ce sens.

CZE [*Mezinárodní tribunál pro mořské právo: široká pravomoc tohoto soudu a potenciál analyzovat aktuální témata mořského práva*]

Cílem tohoto článku je odpovědět na otázku, jakým způsobem by mohl Mezinárodní tribunál pro mořské právo (International Tribunal for the Law of the Sea – ITLOS) přispět k pokroku, pokud jde o aktuální témata mořského práva, jako je zvyšování hladiny moře, biodiverzita za hranicemi národních jurisdikcí (Biodiversity Beyond National Jurisdiction – BBNJ), jakož i vztah mořského práva a lidských práv. V článku jsou zaprvé jsou vysvětlena ustanovení o řešení sporů zakotvená v Úmluvě Organizace spojených národů o mořském právu (United Nations Convention on the Law of the Sea – UNCLOS), aby bylo možno lépe porozumět pravomoci a příslušnosti ITLOS. Zadruhé článek tuto pravomoc a příslušnost ITLOS analyzuje. Zatřetí jsou výše zmíněné aktuální otázky stručně uvedeny ve vzájemném kontextu Začtvrté autorka provádí analýzu s přihlédnutím k pravomoci a příslušnosti ITLOS a ke kontextu, v němž jsou aktuální témata zasazena, aby bylo možno dospět k závěru o tom, jakým způsobem by mohl ITLOS přispět k jejich rozvinutí. Na závěr autorka v článku uvádí, že ITLOS by mohl hrát významnou roli ve všech analyzovaných rovinách a lze očekávat, že v tomto smyslu budeme svědky dalšího pokroku.

| | |

POL [*Międzynarodowy Trybunał Prawa Morza: szerokie kompetencje sądu i analityczny potencjał w odniesieniu do aktualnej problematyki prawa morskiego*]

Międzynarodowy Trybunał Prawa Morza (International Tribunal for the Law of the Sea – ITLOS) to jedna z instytucji założonych na gruncie Konwencji Narodów Zjednoczonych o prawie morza z 1982 roku. Już od momentu powstania przyczynia się do kształtowania międzynarodowego prawa morza. Niniejszy artykuł przedstawia analizę kompetencji i właściwości ITLOS w celu ustalenia, w jaki sposób ITLOS może wpływać na rozwój wiedzy prawniczej w zakresie wybranych aktualnych kwestii, takich jak podnoszący się poziom wód morskich, morska różnorodność biologiczna na obszarach znajdujących się poza jurysdykcją krajową (Biodiversity Beyond National Jurisdiction – BBNJ) i stosunek prawa morza do praw człowieka.

DEU **[*Der Internationale Seegerichtshof: zu den breiten Kompetenzen dieses Gerichts und dem vorhandenen Potenzial für die Analyse aktueller Seerechtsfragen*]**

Beim Internationalen Seegerichtshof (International Tribunal for the Law of the Sea – ITLOS; deutsche Abkürzung ISGH) handelt es sich um eine der Institutionen, die mit dem Seerechtsübereinkommen der Vereinten Nationen von 1982 geschaffen wurden. Seit seiner Entstehung trägt er zur Entwicklung des Internationalen Seerechts bei. Ziel dieses Artikels ist es, die Kompetenzen und Zuständigkeiten des ISGH auszuloten, um festzustellen, auf welche Art und Weise dieser zur Entwicklung der Rechtswissenschaften im Bereich ausgewählter aktueller Fragen beitragen könnte: Anstieg des Meeresspiegels, Biodiversität in Gebieten der hohen See und des Tiefseebodens (Biodiversity Beyond National Jurisdiction – BBNJ), und die Beziehung zwischen Seerecht und Menschenrechten.

RUS [*Международный трибунал по морскому праву: широкая компетенция этого суда и потенциал в области анализа текущих вопросов морского права*]

Международный трибунал по морскому праву (International Tribunal for the Law of the Sea – ITLOS) был одной из организаций, созданных Конвенцией Организации Объединенных Наций по морскому праву (1982 год). С момента своего создания трибунал вносит вклад в развитие международного морского права. В данной статье анализируются компетенции и юрисдикция ITLOS с целью определить, как ITLOS может способствовать развитию юридической науки в области выбранных текущих вопросов, в частности, повышения уровня моря, биоразнообразия за пределами действия национальной юрисдикции (Biodiversity Beyond National Jurisdiction – BBNJ) и взаимосвязи морского права и прав человека.

ESP **[*Tribunal Internacional del Derecho del Mar: la amplia jurisdicción de este tribunal y su potencial para analizar las cuestiones actuales del derecho del mar*]**

El Tribunal Internacional del Derecho del Mar (International Tribunal for the Law of the Sea – ITLOS) es una de las instituciones

The International Tribunal for the Law of the Sea: Its Wide Jurisdiction...

Czech Yearbook of International Law®

creadas por la Convención de las Naciones Unidas sobre el Derecho del Mar de 1982. Desde su creación, ha contribuido al desarrollo del derecho internacional del mar. El objetivo de este artículo es analizar la jurisdicción y la competencia del ITLOS con el fin de identificar cómo podría contribuir la institución al desarrollo de la jurisprudencia sobre algunas cuestiones actuales como el aumento del nivel del mar, la biodiversidad en áreas fuera de la jurisdicción nacional (Biodiversity Beyond National Jurisdiction – BBNJ) y la relación entre el derecho del mar y los derechos humanos.

| | |

Bibliography:

Bogdan Aurescu & Nilufer Oral, *First issues paper by Bogdan Aurescu and Nilüfer Oral, Co-Chairs of the Study Group on sea-level rise in relation to international law* (28 February 2020), available at: https://documents-dds-ny.un.org/doc/UNDOC/GEN/N20/053/91/PDF/N2005391.pdf?OpenElement (accessed on 15 June 2021).

Hugo Caminos, *The Jurisdiction and Procedure of the International Tribunal for the Law of the Sea: an overview*, in GOVERNING OCEAN RESOURCES NEW CHALLENGES AND EMERGING REGIMES: A TRIBUTE TO JUDGE CHOON-HO PARK, Leiden: Brill (Jon M. Van Dyke; et al ed. 2013).

Luciana Fernandes Coelho & Julia Cirne Lima Weston, *Who Observes the Onboard Observers Working in the Waters Adjacent to the Pacific Small Islands Developing States? The Flag State Responsibility for Violation of Human Rights at Sea*, in DIREITO DO MAR: REFLEXÕES, TENDÊNCIAS E PERSPECTIVAS, V. 4, Belo Horizonte: Editora D'Plácido (André de Paiva Toledo et al ed., 2020).

Human Rights at Sea, *Fisheries Observer Deaths at Sea, Human Rights & the Role & Responsibilities of Fisheries Organisations* (01 July 2020), available at: https://www.humanrightsatsea.org/wp-content/uploads/2020/07/HRAS_Abuse_of_Fisheries_Observers_REPORT_JULY-2020_SP_OPTIMISED.pdf (accessed on 10 July 2021).

International Law Association, *ILA Study Group on Due Diligence in International Law*

First Report (07 March 2014), available at: https://ila.vettoreweb.com/Storage/Download.aspx?DbStorageId=1429&StorageFileGuid=fd770a95-9118-4a20-ac61-df12356f74d0 (accessed on 10 July 2021).

International Law Commission, *Report of the International Law Com-*

mission, Seventieth Session (August 2018), available at: https://legal.un-.org/ilc/reports/2018/english/annex_B.pdf (accessed 15 June 2021).

International Union for Conservation of Nature, *Governing areas beyond national jurisdiction*, available at: https://www.iucn.org/resources/issues-briefs/governing-areas-beyond-national-jurisdiction (accessed 25 June 2021).

ITLOS Report, *Responsibilities and obligations of States with respect to activities in the Area, Advisory Opinion, 1 February 2011*, ITLOS Reports 2011, et. 10.

IGOR V. KARAMAN, DISPUTE RESOLUTION IN THE LAW OF THE SEA, Leiden: Brill (2012).

Tommy Koh, *A Constitution for The Oceans*, Centre for International Law National University of Singapore, (06 December 1982), available at: https://www.un.org/depts/los/convention_agreements/texts/koh_english.pdf (accessed on 04 August 2021).

Joanna Mossop, *Dispute Settlement in the New Treaty on Marine Biodiversity in Areas beyond National Jurisdiction*, (23 December 2019), available at: https://site.uit.no/nclos/2019/12/23/dispute-settlement-in-the-new-treaty-on-marine-biodiversity-in-areas-beyond-national-jurisdiction/ (accessed 20 June 2021).

Tafsir Malick Ndiaye, *Human Rights at Sea and the Law of the Sea*, 10 BEIJING LAW REVIEW 261 (2019).

Bernard H. Oxman, *Human Rights and the United Nations Convention on the Law of the Sea*, 36 COLUMBIA JOURNAL OF TRANSNATIONAL LAW 399 (1998).

Irini Papanicolopulu, *The Law of the Sea Convention: No Place for Persons*, 27(4) INTERNATIONAL JOURNAL OF MARINE & COASTAL LAW 867 (2012).

Cesare Romano, *The Southern Bluefin Tuna Dispute: Hints of a World to Come... Like it or not*, 32(4) OCEAN DEVELOPMENT AND INTERNATIONAL LAW 313 (2001).

Howard S. Schiffman, *The Dispute Settlement Mechanism of UNCLOS: A Potentially Important Framework for Marine Wildlife Management*, 1 JOURNAL OF INTERNATIONAL LAW WILDLIFE AND POLICY 293 (1998).

The Intergovernmental Panel on Climate Change, *Sea Level Rise and Implications for Low-Lying Islands, Coasts and Communities*, Chapter 4 (14 July 2019), available at: https://www.ipcc.ch/srocc/chapter/chapter-4-sea-level-rise-and-implications-for-low-lying-islands-coasts-and-communities/ (accessed on 19 June 2021).

Tullio Treves, *Human Rights and the Law of the Sea*, 28(1) BERKELEY

The International Tribunal for the Law of the Sea: Its Wide Jurisdiction...

Czech Yearbook of International Law®

JOURNAL OF INTERNATIONAL LAW 1 (2010).

United Nations General Assembly, *Draft text of an agreement under the United Nations Convention on the Law of the Sea on the conservation and sustainable use of marine biological diversity of areas beyond national jurisdiction* (17 May 2019), available at: https://undocs.org/a/conf.232/2019/6 (accessed on 25 June 2021).

United Nations General Assembly, *Report of the Preparatory Committee established by General Assembly resolution 69/292: Development of an international legally binding instrument under the United Nations Convention on the Law of the Sea on the conservation and sustainable use of marine biological diversity of areas beyond national jurisdiction* (31 July 2017), available at: https://www.un.org/ga/search/view_doc.asp?symbol=A/AC.287/2017/PC.4/2 (accessed 25 June 2021).

United Nations General Assembly, *Development of an international legally-binding instrument under the United Nations Convention on the Law of the Sea on the conservation and sustainable use of marine biological diversity of areas beyond national jurisdiction* (06 July 2015), available at: https://undocs.org/en/a/res/69/292 (accessed on 25 June 2021).

DAVOR VIDAS & DAVID FREESTONE & JANE MCADAM, INTERNATIONAL LAW AND SEA LEVEL RISE: REPORT OF THE INTERNATIONAL LAW ASSOCIATION COMMITTEE ON INTERNATIONAL LAW AND SEA LEVEL RISE, Brill Research Perspectives in the Law of the Sea (2019).

Robin Warner, *Conserving Marine Biodiversity in Areas Beyond National Jurisdiction: Co-Evolution and Interaction with the Law of the Sea*, in DONALD ROTHWELL; ALEX OUDE ELFERINK; KAREN SCOTT; TIM STEPHENS, THE OXFORD HANDBOOK OF THE LAW OF THE SEA, Oxford: OUP (2015).

Susanne Wasum-Rainer & Daniela Schlegel, *The UNCLOS Dispute Settlement System - Between Hamburg and the Hague*, 48 GERMAN YEARBOOK OF INTERNATIONAL LAW 187 (2005).

Czech Yearbook of International Law®

Selected Case Law of Czech Courts and of Constitutional Court of Czech Republic Concerning Jurisdiction of Courts and Enforceability of Judicial Decisions on Basis of International Treaties and EU Law

Alexander J. Bělohlávek

ORCID iD 0000-0001-5310-5269
https://orcid.org/0000-0001-5310-5269

[Unless stipulated otherwise or unless the context clearly indicates otherwise, all references to specific national laws constitute references to the laws of the Czech Republic]

9.01.   **Judgment of the Constitutional Court of the Czech Republic, Case No. I. ÚS 1964/19 of 01 June 2021:**[1] **[prejudging the procedure; binding interpretation of EU law; power to interpret EU law; *acte clair*; competences of the Constitutional Court; right to be heard; preliminary reference] (1)** The competences of the Constitutional Court do not include a binding interpretation of EU law. Consequently, if the Constitutional Court sets aside a decision of a lower court, the former cannot prejudge further steps that the latter shall take in the case based on the need to interpret EU law. Hence, the Constitutional Court of the Czech Republic cannot interfere with the lower court's independent decisions. Should the opinion of the lower court expressed during the new hearing of the case differ from the opinion of the Constitutional Court, the case could not be deemed *acte clair*. In this case, the lower court would be obliged to make a preliminary reference to the EU Court of Justice in order to prevent any conflict between the court's decision and EU law and, in turn, a breach of obligations binding on the Czech Republic as a result of its membership in the EU. **(2)** If the appellate court applies a legal assessment of the case that differs from the legal assessment performed by the first-instance court, as well as the legal reasoning outlined

---

[1]   Preceding decisions in the case: (i) Instruction of the District Court in Znojmo [Czech Republic], Case No. 8 EXE 120/2018-15 of 05 September 2018, and (ii) Resolution of the Regional Court in Brno [Czech Republic], Case No. 20 Co 329/2018 of 02 April 2019.

by the parties, and if the appellate court denies the parties the opportunity to express their opinion on the appellate court's standpoint, the appellate court breaches the right to be heard under Article 38(2) of the Charter of Fundamental Rights and Freedoms. This shall not apply if the reasons for the court's decision indicate sufficiently clearly the reasons why the arguments presented in the constitutional complaint cannot stand, i.e. if they are merely an expression of the party's disagreement with the relevant conclusions made by the court that introduces no "new" elements in the assessment of the case.

9.02.   **Resolution of the Supreme Court of the Czech Republic, Case No. 30 Cdo 2784/2016 of 28 February 2017:**[2] **[payment order; parties to court proceedings; Brussels Ia Regulation; enter an appearance; first pleading on the merits; radio broadcasting; admissibility]** An appeal against a payment order cannot be deemed to constitute the respondent's appearance in the proceedings in terms of **Article 26(1) of the Brussels Ia Regulation**, whether or not the respondent puts forth any defence on the merits. [*From the factual and legal findings*] The claimant has claimed payment of an amount corresponding to the paid purchase price for heating systems, which the respondent should refund to the claimant as a result of the claimant's rescission of their contract. The court has issued a payment order, which was challenged by the respondent's appeal. The respondent has filed a pleading arguing that the court lacks **international jurisdiction**. The respondent claims that the respondent's business terms and conditions are a part of the contract and that they stipulate that the jurisdiction to hear and resolve the case rests with the Commercial Court in Mechelen [Belgium].

9.03.   **Resolution of the Constitutional Court of the Czech Republic, Case No. I ÚS 1744/20 of 28 July 2020:**[3] **[P.O. BOX; jurisdiction; admissibility of a cassation appeal; client centre]**[4] **(1)** As concerns the objection to the extent that "the location of the appellant's P.O. BOX in Hodonín [Czech Republic], which is not the appellant's property or any personal representation, but only a mailbox for delivery, cannot constitute grounds for the transfer of the territorial jurisdiction

---

[2]   Preceding decisions in the case: (i) Resolution of the District Court in Vsetín [Czech Republic], Case No. 8 C 69/2015-156 of 10 December 2015, and (ii) Resolution of the Regional Court in Ostrava [Czech Republic], Case No. 8 Co 54/2016 of 26 February 2016.

[3]   The *ratio decidendi* has been adopted from: www.aspi.cz; JUD451814CZ.

[4]   Preceding decisions in the case: (i) Resolution of the Supreme Court of the Czech Republic, Case No. 27 Cdo 3363/2018 of 26 March 2020, (ii) Resolution of the High Court in Olomouc [Czech Republic], Case No. 4 Co 5/2018-129 of 26 April 2018, and (iii) Resolution of the Regional Court in Brno [Czech Republic], Case No. 23 C 3/2017 of 26 January 2018.

from the Municipal Court in Prague [Czech Republic] to the Regional Court in Brno [Czech Republic]", the Cassation Court has argued that the applicant has fails to mention and explain whether the requirements for the admissibility of the cassation appeal are fulfilled. Having perused the cassation appeal, the Constitutional Court has no reason to question the assessment performed by the Supreme Court. The applicant's objection concerning the establishment of territorial jurisdiction of the first-instance court in consequence of the application of **Article 7(5) of the Brussels Ia Regulation** actually contests the appellate court's finding of fact that the applicant has its client centre in the district of the first-instance court and meets the hypothesis of the said provision. As concerns its interpretation, however, the applicant indeed presents no premise of the admissibility of the cassation appeal in terms of Sections 241a and 237 of the Code of Civil Procedure – i.e. a question of substantive or procedural law, the resolution of which is necessary for the contested decision of the appellate court and (a) in the resolution of which, the appellate court has departed from the consistent case-law of the Cassation Court, or (b) which has not yet been resolved in the case-law of the Cassation Court, or (c) in respect of which the case-law of the Cassation Court is not consistent, or (d) if the legal issue resolved by the Cassation Court ought to be assessed differently.

9.04. **Resolution of the Constitutional Court of the Czech Republic, Case No. II. ÚS 2356/2019 of 30 July 2019:**[5] **[interpretation of EU law; fair trial; (absence of a) request for a preliminary reference; principles of EU law; forum selection (choice of court)]**[6] **(1)** The Constitutional Court respects **the discretion of the courts of general jurisdiction in the interpretation of EU law**, and only imposes on them such requirements that are based on constitutional laws, i.e. primarily the respect for the rights of the parties to a fair trial in terms of Article 36(1) of the Charter of Fundamental Rights and Freedoms.[7] **The absence of a request for a preliminary ruling from the Court of Justice** shall only constitute a breach of the rights guaranteed by the constitutional laws if the court fails to provide an explanation in instances in which a party requests such explanation or in which

---

[5]   The *ratio decidendi* has been adopted from: Aspi.cz; JUD429060CZ, title: Preliminary reference – ECJ; business.

[6]   Preceding decisions in the case: (i) Resolution of the High Court in Prague, Case No. 5 Cmo 310/2016-135 of 08 February 2017, and (ii) Resolution of the Municipal Court in Prague, Case No. 56 Cm 182/2015 of 26 July 2016.

[7]   Article 36(1) of the Charter of Fundamental Rights and Freedoms (cit., approximate translation): *"Everyone may assert, through the legally prescribed procedure, his or her rights before an independent and impartial court or, in specified cases, before a different authority."*

it is *prima facie* clear that the interpretation of EU law in the relevant case is questionable. Indeed, Czech constitutional laws only demand that the justification be sustainable (defendable and persuasively supported by arguments) and not manifestly contrary to the **fundamental principles of EU law**.[8] **(2)** The Constitutional Court is not called upon to examine whether the contested judgment stands up to scrutiny from the perspective of the standards derived from EU law; but the contested decisions undoubtedly stand up to scrutiny from the perspective of the standards derived from the constitutional laws. [***From the factual and legal findings***] The claimant demanded that the applicant pay a certain amount as compensation for damage and losses caused by the applicant's breach of contractual obligations arising from trading in currency pairs. The applicant has challenged the jurisdiction of the Municipal Court in Prague [Czech Republic], arguing that the claimant and the applicant have entered into a **choice-of-court agreement (clause) whereby the parties agreed on the jurisdiction of a Danish court**.

9.05. **Judgment of the Constitutional Court of the Czech Republic, Case No. IV. ÚS 2042/19-1 of 08 February 2021:**[9] **[competences of the Constitutional Court;** *acte clair*; **preliminary reference; right to be heard; scope of reasons; binding interpretation of EU law; authority in the interpretation of EU law; enforcement of a foreign decision]**[10] **(1) The competences of the Constitutional Court do not include a binding interpretation of EU law.** Consequently, if the Constitutional Court sets aside a decision of a lower court, the former cannot prejudge further steps that the latter shall take in the case based on the need to interpret EU law. Hence, the Constitutional Court of the Czech Republic cannot interfere with the lower court's independent decisions. Should the opinion of the lower court expressed during the new hearing of the case differ from the opinion of the Constitutional Court, the case could not be deemed *acte clair*. In this case, the lower court would be obliged to make a preliminary reference to the **EU Court of Justice** in order to prevent any conflict between the court's decision and EU law and, in turn, a breach of obligations binding on the Czech Republic as a result of its

---

[8]   See also Judgment of the Constitutional Court of the Czech Republic, Case No. I. ÚS 1434/17 of 11 June 2018.

[9]   The *ratio decidendi* has been adopted from: Aspi.cz; JUD511626CZ.

[10]   The Constitutional Court invoked the following case-law in its reasoning: (i) Judgment of the Constitutional Court of the Czech Republic, Case No. I. ÚS 777/07 of 31 July 2008, and (ii) Judgment of Constitutional Court of the Czech Republic, Case No. I. ÚS 2502/09 of 15 March 2010.

membership in the EU. **(2)** If the appellate court applies a legal assessment of the case that differs from the legal assessment performed by the first-instance court, as well as the legal reasoning outlined by the parties, and if the appellate court denies the parties the opportunity to express their opinion on the appellate court's standpoint, the appellate court breaches the right to be heard under Article 38(2) of the Charter of Fundamental Rights and Freedoms.[11] This shall not apply if the reasons for the court's decision indicate sufficiently clearly the reasons why the arguments presented in the constitutional complaint cannot stand, i.e. if they are merely an expression of the party's disagreement with the relevant conclusions made by the court that introduces no "new" elements in the assessment of the case. [*From the factual and legal findings*] The District Court in Znojmo [Czech Republic], in enforcement proceedings initiated by the applicant (as the judgment creditor) versus the intervenor (as the judgment debtor), charged a private bailiff with the enforcement of a financial claim awarded by a judgment of the Labour and Social Court in Vienna [Austria]. The District Court has also given the order to the private bailiff, subsequently challenged by the constitutional complaint, to dismiss the part of the applicant's motion for enforcement in which the applicant requests authorisation to enforce the payment of default interest, because that part of the enforceable instrument is not materially enforceable, as it lacks any indication of the day until which the intervenor is obliged to pay such interest.

9.06. **Judgment of the Supreme Court of the Czech Republic, Case No. 20 Cdo 2302/2017 of 17 July 2018:[12] [enforcement of a foreign court's decision; recognition of foreign decisions; enforcement; translation of a document by the court; right to written communication; public policy proviso][13/14] (1)** The right to written communication (i.e. the translation of documents by the court that the party presents in their native language) has no basis in international human rights treaties or in Czech law. This does not exclude the possibility, though, that the statutory provisions in any particular State may guarantee a higher standard of protection. The second sentence of Section

---

[11] Article 38(2) of the Charter of Fundamental Rights and Freedoms (cit., approximate translation): "*Everyone has the right to have his or her case considered in public, without unnecessary delay, and in his or her presence, as well as to express his or her opinion on all examined evidence. The public may only be excluded in cases specified by law.*"
[12] The *ratio decidendi* has been adopted from: Aspi.cz; JUD381706CZ.
[13] Adopted from the case-law database of the Supreme Court.
[14] Preceding decisions in the case: (i) Judgment of the Regional Court in Hradec Králové – Pardubice Office [Czech Republic], Case No. 27 Co 259/2016 of 07 December 2016.

18(1) of the Code of Civil Procedure[15] cannot be interpreted as imposing an obligation on the court to secure a translation of its decision to the language of a party that does not speak Czech. (2) The requirement of a written communication in the native language of a party can also not be subsumed under the right to a fair trial. (3) The situation can also not become so serious as to justify the triggering of the public policy proviso in terms of Article 26 of the EC Insolvency Regulation (EC) 1346/2000.[16]

9.07. Resolution of the Supreme Court of the Czech Republic, Case No. 20 Cdo 1152/2020 of 16 June 2020:[17] [impediments to the recognition of judgments; right to a fair trial; violation of public policy; a foreign decision on the enforcement of a third country's decision cannot be recognised][18] (1) A declaration of the enforceability of an Austrian writ of execution would result in a situation in which a foreign decision that is subject to the provisions of Section 14 of the Private International Law Act[19] would be recognised without any special proceedings, and the person against whom the enforcement is targeted would have no opportunity to invoke the impediments to recognition under Section 15 of the Private International Law Act,[20] the

---

[15] The second sentence of Section 18(1) of the Code of Civil Procedure (cit., approximate translation): [The parties] *"[h]ave the right to appear and state their case in court in their native language."*

[16] In the reasoning of its decision, the Constitutional Court invoked the judgment of the Constitutional Court of the Czech Republic in Case No. II. ÚS 186/05 of 08 August 2005.

[17] The *ratio decidendi* has been adopted from: case-law database of the Supreme Court of the Czech Republic.

[18] Preceding decisions in the case: (i) Resolution of the District Court for Prague 4 [Czech Republic] of 18 April 2019, Case No. 13 EXE 1004/2015-250, and (ii) Resolution of the Municipal Court in Prague [Czech Republic] of 29 November 2019, Case No. 12 Co 185/2019-305.

[19] Section 14 of the Private International Law Act (cit., approximate translation): *"Judgments of the courts of a foreign State and rulings of the authorities of a foreign State concerning any rights and obligations whose private-law nature would, in the Czech Republic, subject them to the jurisdiction of courts, as well as foreign judicial settlements and foreign notarial or other authentic instruments concerning these matters (hereafter referred to as 'foreign judgments') will have effects in the Czech Republic, provided that they have become final according to a confirmation issued by the competent foreign authority and have been recognised by Czech public authorities."*

[20] Section 15 of the Private International Law Act (cit., approximate translation):
"(1) Unless the following provisions of this Act stipulate otherwise, a final foreign judgment cannot be recognised (a) if the matter falls within the exclusive jurisdiction of Czech courts or no authority of a foreign State would have had jurisdiction to conduct the proceedings if the provisions on the jurisdiction of Czech courts had been applied to the assessment of the foreign authority's jurisdiction, unless the party to the proceedings against whom the foreign judgment is made has voluntarily submitted to the jurisdiction of the foreign authority, (b) if any proceedings are pending in a Czech court concerning the same legal relationship and those proceedings had been opened earlier than the foreign proceedings in which the judgment was issued whose recognition is sought, (c) if a Czech court has already issued a final judgment regarding the same legal relationship or if a final judgment of a third State's authority has already been recognised in the Czech Republic, (d) if a party to the proceedings against whom the recognition of the judgment is sought was deprived of the opportunity to duly enter an appearance by the acts of the foreign authority, primarily if the party was not served with a summons or a petition to open the proceedings, (e) if the recognition were clearly contrary to public policy, or (f) if no reciprocity is guaranteed; reciprocity is not required if the foreign judgment is not directed against a citizen of the Czech Republic or a Czech legal entity. (2) The impediment set out in Subsection 1(d) shall only be taken into account if invoked by the party

scope of which is broader than the scope of the impediments to recognition under Article 34 of Council Regulation (EC) No 44/2001 of 22 December 2000 (Brussels I Regulation) on jurisdiction and the recognition and enforcement of judgments in civil and commercial matters. This would undermine the right of the judgment debtor to a fair trial and, consequently, be contrary to public policy of the Czech Republic, which constitutes grounds for a refusal to recognise the decision pursuant to Article 34(1) of the Brussels I Regulation. [*From the factual and legal findings*] The Austrian decision allowed enforcement to be conducted only in the Austrian Republic, on the basis of judgments issued by a court of the Principality of Liechtenstein. Hence, it constitutes a writ of execution in an EU Member State on the basis of a court decision issued in a third (non-EU) country.

9.08. **Resolution of the Supreme Court of the Czech Republic, Case No. 20 Cdo 4725/2017 of 09 May 2018: [enforcement proceedings; failure to serve the judgment on the respondent; impediments to the recognition and enforcement of a decision]**[21] The indicative list of circumstances preventing the recognition and enforcement of a foreign decision may also include other circumstances, if invoked by the parties. One such impediment may be the fact that the respondent was not served with the judgment, provided that the respondent was thereby denied the opportunity to participate properly in the proceedings. [*From the factual and legal findings*] The judgment creditor requested a writ of execution against the judgment debtor pursuant to a judgment of the Superior Court of Arizona in order to satisfy the claim of the judgment creditor for USD 100,000, whereby the judgment creditor was ordered to reimburse the judgment debtor for the costs of the proceedings, but it did not award the reimbursement of the costs of the enforcement proceedings. The judgment debtor was served with the action, the summons to a hearing, the court's notice and the attorney's statement. The judgment debtor was also served with the action and the summons to a hearing. However, the judgment debtor was not served with the enforceable instrument on the basis of which the enforcement was to be conducted.

---

to the proceedings against whom the recognition of the foreign judgment is sought. This also applies to the impediments set forth in Subsection 1(b) and (c), unless the authority that should make a decision on the recognition is otherwise aware that such impediments exist."

[21] Preceding decisions in the case: (i) Resolution of the Municipal Court in Prague [Czech Republic], Case No. 18 Co 147/2017 of 23 June 2017, and (ii) Resolution of the District Court for Prague 4 [Czech Republic], Case No. 72 EXE 3449/2012-481 of 28 February 2017.

9.09. **Resolution of the Supreme Court of the Czech Republic, Case No. 29 Cdo 3306/2018 of 27 May 2020:**[22] **[arbitration; court jurisdiction; doubts about the formation of the contract; claim under a contract pursuant to Article 5(1)(a) of the Brussels I Regulation]**[23] **(1)** The jurisdiction to resolve disputes concerning the existence of a contractual obligation must be determined in compliance with Article 5(1) of the Convention of 27 September 1968 on Jurisdiction and the Enforcement of Judgments in Civil and Commercial Matters ("Brussels Convention"). This provision is also applicable if the formation of the contract that impelled the action is a matter of dispute between the parties. **(2)** The concept of "matters relating to a contract" (claims under a contract) in terms of Article 5(1)(a) of Council Regulation (EC) No 44/2001 of 22 December 2000 on jurisdiction and the recognition and enforcement of judgments in civil and commercial matters ("Brussels I Regulation") cannot be interpreted as covering a situation in which no freely accepted commitment of one party to the other exists. **(3)** Hence, the application of the rule on special jurisdiction prescribed for matters relating to a contract or claims under a contract requires the finding of a legal commitment freely accepted by one person vis-à-vis another, underlying the action.

9.10. **Resolution of the Supreme Court of the Czech Republic, Case No. 29 Nd 130/2016 of 25 August 2016: [international jurisdiction; territorial jurisdiction; failure to comment on the court's jurisdiction] (1)** Article 26(1) of Regulation (EU) No 1215/2012 of the European Parliament and of the Council of 12 December 2012 on jurisdiction and the recognition and enforcement of judgments in civil and commercial matters ("Brussels Ia Regulation") sets forth rules regulating international jurisdiction, as well as the territorial jurisdiction of the court in which the action was lodged. **(2)** If the respondent replies to the action, but fails to challenge the jurisdiction of the said court in the reply or before filing the reply, then – unless the case concerns exclusive jurisdiction provided for in the provisions of Article 24 of the Brussels Ia Regulation – the court acquires (international and territorial) jurisdiction on or before that moment.

9.11. **Judgment of the Regional Court in Ostrava [Czech Republic], Case No. 56 Co 190/2017-340 of 25 August 2017:**

---

[22] The *ratio decidendi* has been adopted from: Aspi.cz; JUD451547CZ.
[23] Preceding decisions in the case: (i) Resolution of the Regional Court in Pilsen [Czech Republic], Case No. 41 Cm 43/2016 of 20 November 2017, and (ii) Resolution of the High Court in Prague [Czech Republic], Case No. 12 Cmo 5/2018 of 26 April 2018.

[international jurisdiction; residence][24] **(1)** International jurisdiction of Czech courts to hear and resolve a case in which the respondent is a citizen of the Hellenic Republic, with his place of residence in the territory of the Czech Republic, is established under Article 2(1) of the Brussels I Regulation. Subject to this Regulation, persons domiciled in a Member State shall, whatever their nationality, be sued in the courts of that Member State, in conjunction with Article 66(1) of the Brussels Ia Regulation. *[From the factual and legal findings]* The respondent's vehicle was damaged in a traffic accident that occurred as a result of unlawful conduct caused by the acts of a third party. The parties have verbally agreed on a contract for the repairs of the damaged vehicle belonging to the respondent. The respondent handed over the vehicle to the claimant for repairs. The insurance company paid out to the aggrieved party – respondent – an indemnification of CZK 15,100 for the total damage to the vehicle. The invoice was delivered to the respondent in an annex to the letter of formal notice (before action), and the respondent has not yet paid to the claimant the amount of CZK 14,120. The claimant has failed to prove that the parties agreed on the price of the repairs to the vehicle.

9.12. **Judgment of the Supreme Court of the Czech Republic, Case No. 30 Nd 27/2018 of 26 September 2018: [territorial jurisdiction; Lugano Convention; prohibition of making dispositions with shareholdings; interim measure]**[25] Pursuant to Article 31 of the Lugano Convention, Czech courts lack the international jurisdiction to adjudicate on a motion for an interim measure that is supposed to prohibit a person residing in Switzerland from making dispositions with their shareholdings in business companies established in Switzerland and in Georgia, because there is no close connection between the subject matter of the proposed interim measure and the territorial jurisdiction of Czech courts. *[From the factual and legal findings]* The claimant extended certain loans to the respondent. The respondent, however, failed to meet their obligation. The claimant thus filed a petition with a court in Horgen (Switzerland), and the court ordered the respondent to refund to the claimant the amount of CHF 1,122,848.50. The respondent has filed an action against the judgment in compliance with Swiss law. The claimant is concerned that the enforcement of the said judgment could be jeopardised, and

---

[24]   Preceding decision in the case: (i) Judgment of the District Court in Frýdek – Místek [Czech Republic], Case No. 41 C 136/2013-319 of 27 April 2017.

[25]   Preceding decision in the case: (i) Judgment of the Court in Horgen [Switzerland], Case No. EB160015-F/UB/KH/Sta of 05 October 2016.

consequently, the claimant has filed a motion for an interim measure pursuant to Section 102 of the Code of Civil Procedure that would prohibit the respondent from making dispositions with the respondent's assets in Switzerland and in Georgia. The claimant was a citizen of the Russian Federation with a permanent residence permit in the Czech Republic, while the respondent was a citizen of Georgia permanently residing in Switzerland.

9.13.   **Judgment of the Supreme Court of the Czech Republic, Case No. 27 Cdo 3456/2019 of 15 April 2020:**[26] **[compensation for damage and losses as a result of a breach of a contractual obligation; claim from a contract; court jurisdiction; action against an Executive Officer of a company; real seat of a company] (1)** An action for compensation for damage and losses caused by a breach of a contractual obligation is an action from a contract in terms of Article 5(1) of the Brussels I Regulation / Article 7(1) of the Brussels Ia Regulation. The jurisdiction to hear the case is vested in the court in the district in which the contractual obligation was to be fulfilled, the breach of which has caused damage and losses suffered by the claimant. **(2)** A company's action against its former Executive Officer due to alleged non-fulfilment of the obligation to properly discharge one's office, which is binding on the person under the law of business corporations, falls within the concept of "matters relating to a contract" in terms of Article 5(1) of the Brussels I Regulation / Article 7(1) of the Brussels Ia Regulation. **(3)** The claim for which the action was lodged corresponds to the concept of "matters relating to a contract" in terms of Article 7(1) of the Brussels Ia Regulation, not the concept of "matters relating to tort, delict or quasi-delict" in terms of Article 7(2) of that Regulation (as the claim was classified by the appellate court). **(4)** Hence, the court with jurisdiction to hear and resolve the dispute over the claim (apart from the generally competent court under Article 4 of the Brussels Ia Regulation) is the court of the place in which the contractual obligation was to be fulfilled (the obligation to discharge the office of Executive Officer with due managerial care). This must be the place of the **real seat of the company**, i.e. the place in or from which the Executive Officer actually managed the company.[27/28]

---

[26]   Preceding decisions in the case: (i) Resolution of the Municipal Court in Prague, Case No. 74 Cm 162/2018 of 21 November 2018, and (ii) Resolution of the High Court in Prague, Case No. 6 Cmo 2/2019 of 27 May 2019.

[27]   In this connection, the Supreme Court of the Czech Republic recalled Article 7(1) of the Brussels Ia Regulation and explicitly mentioned the jurisdiction of a Czech court.

[28]   Concerning a similar matter, see also the next decision (Resolution of the Supreme Court of the Czech Republic, Case No. 27 Cdo 3456/2019 of 15 April 2020).

9.14. **Judgment of the Supreme Court of the Czech Republic, Case No. 30 Cdo 3344/2019 of 18 May 2021:**[29] **[commercial agency; place of provision of services; residence of the commercial agent] (1)** In the case of a commercial agency contract where the agency services are to be performed in the territory of multiple States, the important factor for the purposes of the requirement of international and territorial jurisdiction pursuant to Article 7(1)(b) of the Brussels Ia Regulation is the place where the services were to be or predominantly were provided according to the contract. **(2)** It is necessary to have regard to the time spent on such places and the importance of the activity performed there. **(3)** If no such place can be determined, the relevant place is the commercial agent's place of residence.

9.15. **Resolution of the Supreme Court of the Czech Republic, Case No. 30 Cdo 4402/2017 of 20 June 2019:**[30] **[contractual interest; compensation for damage and losses]** Claims from a breach of contract, whether compensation for damage and losses sustained in connection with the contract or an obligation to pay contractual default interest, also constitute claims in matters relating to a contract in terms of the Brussels Ia Regulation.

9.16. **Resolution of the Supreme Court of the Czech Republic, Case No. 25 Nd 168/2016 of 22 July 2016:**[31] **[court with responsibility for enforcement; assets in the territory of the Czech Republic; economy of proceedings] (1)** Whether or not the judgment debtor has any seisable assets in the territory of the Czech Republic that could be seised by the private bailiff and sold after the enforcement is opened, will only become clear after the court-appointed private bailiff embarks on their activities in the implementation of the enforcement. **(2)** Hence, the court with responsibility for enforcement does not inquire into the judgment debtor's assets (or lack thereof) before the enforcement is opened and the private bailiff is charged with the implementation thereof. If the Supreme Court proceeds pursuant to Section 11(3) of the Code of Civil Procedure,[32] it determines the competent court with responsibility for enforcement in

---

[29] Preceding decisions in the case: (i) Resolution of the District Court in Liberec [Czech Republic], Case No. 23 C 92/2016 of 25 September 2018, and (ii) Resolution of the Regional Court in Ústí and Labem – Liberec Office [Czech Republic], Case No. 35 Co 183/2018 of 19 December 2018.

[30] Preceding decisions in the case: (i) Resolution of the District Court in Liberec [Czech Republic], Case No. 8 C 69/2015 of 10 December 2015, and (ii) Resolution of the Regional Court in Ústí and Labem – Liberec Office [Czech Republic], Case No. 8 Co 54/2016 of 26 February 2016.

[31] Preceding decision in the case: (i) Resolution of the District Court for Prague 5 [Czech Republic], Case No. 33 EXE 584/2016 of 11 April 2016.

[32] Section 11(3) of the Code of Civil Procedure (cit., approximate translation): *"If the case falls within the jurisdiction of Czech courts, but the conditions for territorial jurisdiction are absent or cannot be established, the Supreme Court shall determine which court shall hear and resolve the case."*

compliance with the principle of economy. [*From the factual and legal findings*]: The courts have established in the said case that the judgment debtor was granted a visa for a stay of over 90 days in the territory of the Czech Republic. He was registered at a particular address until 1 July 2020. The judgment debtor's assets (or lack thereof) in the territory of the Czech Republic had not been inquired into before the private bailiff was appointed.[33]

9.17. **Resolution of the High Court in Olomouc [Czech Republic], Case No. 5 Cmo 3/2017 of 17 January 2017:[34] [FOREX market; application of rules on consumer contracts] (1)** If a natural person traded on the international FOREX market in the form of Contracts For Difference (CFDs), the person did not act as a consumer. In such case, Article 17 of the Brussels Ia Regulation on consumer contracts shall not apply. **(2)** The person thus does not have the right to file an action with the court of the place where the person resides, i.e. in the Czech Republic.[35]

9.18. **Resolution of the Supreme Court of the Czech Republic, Case No. 30 Cdo 3918/2017 of 26 November 2019:[36] [FOREX contracts; consumer; court jurisdiction][37]** Article 17(1) of the Brussels Ia Regulation must be interpreted as meaning that a natural person who enters into a contract with a brokerage company, such as a Contract For Difference (CFD), and performs transactions on the international FOREX (Foreign Exchange) market through the company, must be qualified as a "consumer" in terms of the said provision, unless the execution of the contract falls within the professional or business activities of the person.

9.19. **Resolution of the Supreme Court of the Czech Republic, Case No. 25 Nd 266/2017 of 31 August 2017:[38] [economy of proceedings; enforcement proceedings] (1)** In view of the principles of the expeditiousness and economy of the proceedings pursuant to Section 11(3) of the Code of Civil Procedure,[39] the Supreme Court shall determine that the court

---

[33] In the reasoning supporting its decision, the court has held that, pursuant to Article 24(5) of the Brussels Ia Regulation, in proceedings concerned with the enforcement of judgments, the courts of the Member State in which the judgment has been or is to be enforced shall have exclusive jurisdiction.

[34] Preceding decision in the case: (i) Resolution of the Regional Court in Ostrava [Czech Republic], Case No. 42 Cm 242/2015 of 29 September 2016.

[35] An entirely opposite opinion was voiced by the Supreme Court in the next annotated decision (Resolution of the Supreme Court of the Czech Republic, Case No. 30 Cdo 3918/2017 of 26 November 2019).

[36] Preceding decision in the case: (i) Resolution of the Regional Court in Ostrava [Czech Republic], Case No. 42 Cm 242/2015 of 29 September 2016.

[37] Preceding decisions in the case: (i) Resolution of the High Court in Olomouc [Czech Republic], Case No. 5 Cmo 3/2017 of 17 January 2017, and (ii) Resolution of the Regional Court in Ostrava [Czech Republic], Case No. 42 Cm 242/2015 of 29 September 2016.

[38] The enforcement case was enrolled at the District Court in Rakovník [Czech Republic] under Case No. 28 EXE 1199/2017.

[39] Section 11(3) of the Code of Civil Procedure (cit., approximate translation): *"If the case falls within the*

with territorial jurisdiction will be the court in which the enforcement proceedings were opened.[40]/[41] *[From the factual and legal findings]* As it transpired during the enforcement proceedings, the judgment debtor was a natural person with no permanent residence in the Czech Republic and no registration for residence in the databases of the Foreign National Information System. Whether or not the person had any seisable assets in the Czech Republic has not yet been inquired into.

9.20. **Resolution of the Regional Court in Hradec Králové – Pardubice Office [Czech Republic]:[42] Case No. 18 Co 137/2016 of 29 April 2016: [request for a reply; failure to challenge the international jurisdiction of the court] (1)** The District Court (as the first-instance court) should have served the respondent with the claimant's action and a request to reply before applying Article 6 of the Brussels Ia Regulation in terms of Article 26(1) of the same Regulation. **(2)** Provided that the respondent presents a reply on the merits and fails to challenge the jurisdiction of the Czech court, the Czech court's jurisdiction to hear the case is thereby established. **(3)** The law applicable to the dispute would then be determined in compliance with the applicable bilateral international treaty.

9.21. **Resolution of the Supreme Court of the Czech Republic, Case No. 30 Cdo 5019/2017 of 11 December 2018:[43]/[44] [dependency; Isle of Man; application of EU law]** For the purposes of an assessment of international jurisdiction according to the Brussels Ia Regulation, a respondent with their place of residence on the Isle of Man must be regarded as a person with their place of residence outside the EU Member States.

---

jurisdiction of Czech courts, but the conditions for territorial jurisdiction are absent or cannot be established, the Supreme Court shall determine which court shall hear and resolve the case."

[40] The court has recalled in the said case that, pursuant to Article 24(5) of the Brussels Ia Regulation, in proceedings concerned with the enforcement of judgments, the courts of the Member State in which the judgment has been or is to be enforced shall have exclusive jurisdiction, regardless of the domicile of the parties.

[41] The court has also noted in the reasons that the Supreme Court of the Czech Republic, sitting as the Grand Chamber of the Civil and Commercial Division, in its resolution in Case No. 31 Nd 316/2013 of 12 November 2014, published as No. 11/2015 in Sbírka soudních rozhodnutí a stanovisek [Court Reports], presented and substantiated a legal opinion that if the Supreme Court is requested to determine the court with territorial jurisdiction pursuant to Section 11(3) of the Code of Civil Procedure on the basis of a final decision, whereby the first-instance court had denied its territorial jurisdiction and referred the case to the Supreme Court for determination of the court with territorial jurisdiction, the Supreme Court shall make such determination without examining (without being entitled to examine) whether or not Czech courts have jurisdiction to hear and resolve the case.

[42] Preceding decision in the case: Resolution of the District Court in Svitavy [Czech Republic], Case No. 12 C 31/2016 of 19 February 2016.

[43] Adopted from: Soudní judikatura z oblasti občanského, obchodního a pracovního práva [Court Case-Law Concerning Civil, Commercial and Labour Law], 5th edition (volume), 2020, p. 321. Published under Reg. No. 47/2020.

[44] Preceding decisions in the case: (i) Resolution of the District Court, Case No. 60 C 24/2015 of 27 December 2016.

9.22. **Resolution of the Supreme Court of the Czech Republic, Case No. 30 Cdo 1860/2015 of 24 February 2016:**[45] **[forum selection]** Unless the agreement on court jurisdiction in a case with a foreign (cross-border) dimension clearly indicates that the parties only intended to agree on the territorial jurisdiction of a particular court, the agreement must be regarded as an agreement on the choice of the international jurisdiction of the court or courts of a particular State.

9.23. **Resolution of the Supreme Court of the Czech Republic, Case No. 30 Cdo 3215/2016 of 28 February 2018:**[46] **[forum selection (choice of court); framework agreement; purchase contract]** An agreement on the jurisdiction of Czech courts entered into pursuant to Article 25(1) of the Brussels Ia Regulation, contained in a framework agreement and covering "disputes arising from and in connection with the agreement", also applies to a dispute from a purchase contract that was entered into on the basis of the framework agreement. *[From the factual and legal findings]* The claimant petitioned for a European payment order, requiring the respondent to pay a particular amount due to the respondent's failure to pay the price under a purchase contract for the delivery of goods. The District Court, as the first-instance court, discontinued the proceedings, ordered the claimant to reimburse the respondent for the costs of the proceedings, and issued a resolution on the refund of the court fee. The court argued that the respondent had appealed against the issued European payment order, arguing, *inter alia*, that the European payment order had not been properly served on the respondent. In the respondent's subsequent reply to the action, the respondent challenged the jurisdiction of the courts of the Czech Republic under the Brussels I Regulation, because the respondent's registered office was in the Federal Republic of Germany, with reference to Article 5(1) of the Brussels I Regulation, because the goods that were the subject matter of the purchase contract entered into by the claimant and the respondent were to be supplied and distributed in the territory of Germany.

9.24. **Resolution of the Supreme Court of the Czech Republic, Case No. 29 Nd 359/2017 of 26 March 2018: [forum selection (choice of court); agreement of the parties] (1)**

---

[45]   Adopted from: Soudní judikatura z oblasti občanského, obchodního a pracovního práva [Court Case-Law Concerning Civil, Commercial and Labour Law], 1st edition (volume), 2017, p. 15. Published under Reg. No. 4/2017.

[46]   Preceding decisions in the case: (i) Resolution of the District Court in České Budějovice [Czech Republic], Case No. 15 EVC 1/2015 of 28 December 2015, and (ii) Resolution of the Regional Court in České Budějovice [Czech Republic], Case No. 22 Co 367/2016 of 22 March 2016.

Unless the case meets the criteria of the exclusive jurisdiction of courts under Article 24 of the Brussels Ia Regulation, and if the parties agreed on the international jurisdiction of Czech courts following the procedure envisaged in Article 25(1) of the Brussels Ia Regulation, the courts of the Czech Republic are vested with international jurisdiction.

9.25. **Resolution of the Supreme Court of the Czech Republic, Case No. 29 Cdo 330/2017 of 27 June 2018:**[47] **[international jurisdiction clause; forum selection (choice of court); scope of the choice-of-court agreement]** The international jurisdiction clause may only cover disputes that have arisen or that arise in the future in connection with a particular legal relationship. This limits the scope of the agreement on jurisdiction to those disputes arising from the legal relationship in connection with which the court jurisdiction was agreed. This requirement aims to prevent a party from being surprised that a particular court will be seised of all disputes that arise from the party's relationships with its contract partner and that originate from other relationships than the one in connection with which the court jurisdiction was agreed.

9.26. **Resolution of the Supreme Court of the Czech Republic, Case No. 30 Cdo 2084/2019-292 of 26 May 2020:**[48/49] **[foreign professional; no branch; insurance] (1)** The interpretation of the words "directs such activities" in terms of Article 17(1)(c) of the Brussels Ia Regulation must also have regard to the fact that a foreign professional who supplied investment services to a consumer residing in the Czech Republic and has no branch in the territory of the Czech Republic launched the provision of such services after the requirements stipulated in Section 25(1) and (2) of Act No. 256/2004 Coll., the Capital Market Undertakings Act, were fulfilled.[50/51]

---

[47]   Preceding decisions in the case: (i) Resolution of the Regional Court in Ostrava [Czech Republic], Case No. 17 Cm 45/2015 of 14 March 2016, and (ii) Resolution of the High Court in Olomouc [Czech Republic], Case No. 7 Cmo 162/2016 of 28 July 2016.

[48]   Adopted from: Sbírka soudních rozhodnutí a stanovisek Nejvyššího soudu České republiky [Czech Supreme Court Reports]. 2021, No. 1.

[49]   Preceding decision in the case: Resolution of the Regional Court in Ústí and Labem – Liberec Office [Czech Republic], Case No. 38 EVCm 1/2017 of 08 February 2018.

[50]   An identical decision was made by the Supreme Court of the Czech Republic in Case No. 30 Cdo 4162/2019 of 04 September 2020.

[51]   Section 25(1) and (2) of Act No. 256/2004 Coll., Capital Market Undertakings Act (cit., approximate translation): *"(1) A foreign person authorised by the supervisory authority of another EU Member State to provide investment services may, in compliance with EU law, provide investment service in the Czech Republic, temporarily or occasionally, without establishing a branch in the Czech Republic, provided that it has an authorisation of the supervisory authority of its home State to provide such services; this shall not apply to investment services provided to professional clients pursuant to Section 2a, to whom investment services can be provided in such manner, even permanently. The Czech National Bank shall inform this person without undue delay that it has received data from the supervisory authority of its home State concerning the intended provision of investment services by this person in the Czech Republic. (2) A foreign person authorised by the*

9.27. Resolution of the Regional Court in Hradec Králové [Czech Republic], Case No. 26 Co 210/2020-145 of 14 September 2020:[52/53] [liability for harm; traffic accident] (1)

If the proceedings concern a claim under Section 10 of Act No. 168/1999 Coll., on Liability Insurance for Damage and Losses Caused by Operation of Vehicles,[54] made by the insurance company against the respondent, who has no residence in the territory of the Czech Republic, but resides in the territory of another EU Member State, and if the traffic accident occurred in the territory of the Czech Republic, Czech courts have the

supervisory authority of another EU Member State to provide investment services may launch the provision of such investment services in the Czech Republic without establishing a branch from the date on which the Czech National Bank receives data related to the provision of services by that person in the Czech Republic from the supervisory authority of its home State or after the expiry of one month from the date when the data was received by the supervisory authority of the home State."

[52] Adopted from: Sbírka soudních rozhodnutí a stanovisek Nejvyššího soudu České republiky [Czech Supreme Court Reports]. 2021, No. 1.

[53] Preceding decision in the case: Resolution of the District Court in Jičín, Case No. 5 C 153/2019 of 18 October 2019.

[54] Section 10 of Act No. 168/1999 Coll., on Liability Insurance for Damage Caused by Operation of Vehicles (cit., approximate translation): *(1) The insurer has a claim against the insured party for compensation of the performance provided by the former on behalf of the latter if the insurer proves that the insured party (a) caused the damage wilfully, (b) without a good reason failed to fulfil the obligation stipulated by the Act Regulating Road Traffic to draw up a joint record of the traffic accident or report the traffic accident that constitutes the insured event, in consequence of which the insurer's opportunity to duly investigate pursuant to Section 9(3) of this Act or the insurer's right to assert this right for compensation of the indemnification was impaired or entirely frustrated, (c) without good reason left the place of the traffic accident or otherwise prevented the determination of the actual cause of the traffic accident, (d) caused damage by operating a vehicle that the insured party used without proper authorisation, (e) without good reason failed to meet the obligation under Section 8(1) to (3), in consequence of which the insurer's opportunity to duly investigate pursuant to Section 9(3) was impaired or entirely frustrated, (f) as a driver of the vehicle refused, without good reason, to obey a request of a police officer to submit to a test for alcohol, narcotic drugs and psychotropic substances or medication labelled as incompatible with the driving of a motor vehicle, (g) was driving the vehicle without having the required driver's license, unless the insured party is a learner driver or a person taking a driving test, always supervised by the authorised teacher or trainer during individual tuition, (h) was driving the vehicle despite and before the expiration of a prohibition to drive vehicles, (i) was driving the vehicle under the influence of alcohol, narcotic drugs and psychotropic substances or medication labelled as incompatible with the driving of a motor vehicle, or (j) allowed a person identified under (g), (h), or (i) to drive the vehicle. (2) The insurer has a claim against the insured party for compensation of the performance provided by the former on behalf of the latter if the insurer proves that the insured party breached a fundamental obligation concerning road traffic by operating a vehicle (a) the chassis or technical condition of which failed to meet the requirements of safe road traffic or the safety of servicing personnel, passengers and transported things, or (b) the technical operability of which was not approved, and there was a causal connection between the breach and the damage or losses that the insured party is obliged to reimburse. (3) The operator of the vehicle assumes joint and several liability with the person under Subsection (1) for the insurer's claim for compensation of the amount paid out pursuant to Subsection (1)(g), (h), (i), and (j), unless the operator proves that the operator could not influence the acts of the person. (4) The insurer has a claim against the policyholder for compensation of the amount paid out by the former as a result of the damage and losses caused by the operation of the vehicle if the cause consisted in a fact that the insurer could not discover during the negotiation of the insurance due to wilfully false or incomplete answers and which was material for the execution of the insurance contract. (5) If the insured party breached any of the obligations stipulated in Section 8(1) to (3), the insurer has the right to claim compensation of the costs connected with the investigation of the insured event or any other costs caused by the breach of the obligations, without prejudice to the insurer's claim for reimbursement of the amount paid out pursuant to Subsection (1)(e). (6) The sum total of the requested compensation under Subsections (1) to (5) may not exceed the indemnification paid out by the insurer in consequence of the insured event to which the insurer's right is related."*

international jurisdiction to hear and resolve the case in terms of Section 2 – Article 7(2) of the Brussels Ia Regulation.

9.28. **Resolution of the Supreme Court of the Czech Republic, Case No. 27 Cdo 12/2019-156 of 15 April 2020: [active participation in the proceedings; guardian** *ad litem*]^[55] If the court appoints a guardian *ad litem* for a respondent with unknown residence pursuant to Section 29(3) of the Code of Civil Procedure,[56] the appointed guardian's reply to the claimant's action on the merits cannot be interpreted as meaning that the respondent enters an appearance in terms of Article 26(1) of the Brussels Ia Regulation.

9.29. **Decision of the Supreme Court of the Czech Republic, Case No. 30 Cdo 3157/2013 of 22 August 2014:**[57] **[protection of personality rights; court jurisdiction; territorial jurisdiction of the court; enforcement of a foreign court's decision;** *punitive damages*] **(1)** A dispute arising from the protection of personality rights is not subject to the exclusive jurisdiction of Czech courts. Consequently, the recognition of a judgment issued by an Arizona court could only be refused on the grounds that the court (and any other authority in the territory of Arizona) would lack the jurisdiction to hear and resolve the case if the court's jurisdiction were subject to the rules of jurisdiction applicable to Czech courts. **(2)** A decision on whether or not the second impediment specified in Section 64(a) of the Private International Law Act[58] prevents the recognition of the particular judgment entails the projection of Czech rules on court jurisdiction onto a foreign law.[59] **(3)** Hence, it is necessary

---

[55] Preceding decisions in the case: (i) Judgment of the Municipal Court in Prague [Czech Republic], Case No. 79 Cm 59/2015-94 of 29 January 2018, and (ii) Resolution of the High Court in Prague [Czech Republic], Case No. 12 Cmo 163/2018 of 29 August 2018.

[56] Section 29(3) of the Code of Civil Procedure (cit., approximate translation): *"Unless other measures are taken, the presiding judge may also appoint a guardian to unknown heirs of a deceased person if the deceased's heirs have not yet been identified in the inheritance proceedings, to a party whose place of residence is unknown or if an attempted delivery to a known address abroad failed, to a party suffering from a mental illness or a party who cannot participate in the proceedings for other medical reasons, unless such incapacity is merely temporary, or a party who is unable to express oneself clearly."*

[57] Preceding decisions in the case: (i) Resolution of the Municipal Court in Prague [Czech Republic], Case No. 18 Co 49/2013-170 of 17 June 2013, (ii) Resolution of the District Court for Prague 4 [Czech Republic] of 02 January 2013, Case No. 72 EXE 3449/2012-106, and (iii) Judgment of the Superior Court of Arizona in and for Maricopa County, U.S., Case No. CV2009-092456 of 30 September 2011.

[58] Section 64(a) of Act No. 97/1963 Coll., on Private International Law and Procedure (cit., approximate translation): *"A foreign decision cannot be recognized or enforced if:*
(a) the matter falls within the exclusive jurisdiction of Czechoslovak authorities or if no authority of a foreign State would have had jurisdiction to conduct the proceedings if the provisions on the jurisdiction of Czechoslovak courts had been applied to the assessment of the foreign authority's jurisdiction" This Act was replaced by Act No. 91/2012 Coll., on Private International Law, with effect from 01 January 2014.

[59] See also ZDENĚK KUČERA, LUBOŠ TICHÝ, ZÁKON O MEZINÁRODNÍM PRÁVU SOUKROMÉM A PROCESNÍM. KOMENTÁŘ [title in translation – ACT ON PRIVATE INTERNATIONAL LAW AND PROCEDURE. A COMMENTARY], Prague: Panorama (1989), et. 309.

to assess whether any authority of a foreign State had jurisdiction to hear and resolve the case if the applicable criteria of jurisdiction were the criteria applied in the Czech Republic. These criteria include not only the rules on jurisdiction stipulated in Act No. 97/1963 Coll., on Private International Law,[60] in conjunction with the Code of Civil Procedure, but also the rules incorporated in EU laws, which form an integral part of Czech law, as well as any jurisdictional rules contained in international treaties binding on the Czech Republic.[61] **(4)** The purpose of the rules is to prevent recognition and enforcement in those cases in which the foreign authority attracts jurisdiction to resolve matters that lack a sufficiently close connection to the authority's State. [*From the conclusions of the Supreme Court*]: **(i)** The concept of *"punitive damages"* represents compensation for non-material damage in U.S. law, which does not aim to indemnify the claimant (aggrieved party), but punish the wrongdoer.[62] **(ii)** *Punitive damages* are usually imposed if the defendant harmed the claimant intentionally, or if the defendant manifestly, grossly and wilfully ignored the claimant's fundamental rights.[63] **(iii)** The U.S. Supreme Court has defined punitive damages as a private-law sanction imposed by civil juries as a penalty for contemptible behaviour and a deterrent to the repetition of such conduct.[64] **(iv)** In the said decision, however, the U.S. Supreme Court has also limited the application of *punitive damages* in freedom of speech and protection of personality rights cases to situations in which the injured party proves that the defendant acted in bad faith, in that the defendant was aware of the information disseminated by the defendant being false, or at least failed to properly verify the truthfulness of the information. *Punitive damages* can be perceived as a penal sanction imposed in civil proceedings.[65] **(v)** In proceedings for the protection of personality rights and freedom of speech, the defendant (respondent) may claim that the award of *punitive damages* is contrary to the defendant's freedom of speech and is

---

[60]   This Act was applicable in the Czech Republic until 31 December 2013; it was replaced by Act No. 91/2012 Coll., on Private International Law, as a result of the recodification of Czech civil law, with effect from 01 January 2014.

[61]   See also PETR BŘÍZA, TOMÁŠ BŘICHÁČEK, ZUZANA FIŠEROVÁ, PAVEL HORÁK, LUBOMÍR PTÁČEK, JIŘÍ SVOBODA, ZÁKON O MEZINÁRODNÍM PRÁVU SOUKROMÉM. KOMENTÁŘ [title in translation – PRIVATE INTERNATIONAL LAW ACT. A COMMENTARY], Prague: C. H. Beck (2014), et. 105.

[62]   See also Clarence Morris, *Punitive Damages in Tort Cases*, 44 HARRVARD LAW REVIEW 1184 (1931).

[63]   Anthony Sebok, *Punitive Damages in the United States*, in HELMUT KOZIOL, VANESSA WILCOX, PUNITIVE DAMAGES: COMMON LAW AND CIVIL LAW PERSPECTIVES, Springer: Vienna (2009), et. 155.

[64]   *Gertz v. Robert Welch*, 4218 U. S. 323 (1974).

[65]   See also *Kelite Prods.*, Inc. v. *Binzel*, 224 F.2d 131, 5th Cir. 1955.

prohibited in consequence of its paralysing (deterrent) effect (*chilling effect*). **(vi)** Recently, the general trend in the United States is to limit the discretion of the individual States in awarding *punitive damages.* Compliance of the concept as such with the constitutional laws has been subject to review by the Federal Supreme Court in six cases; one of the most important cases was *State Farm Mutual Automobile Insurance Co.* v. *Campbell,* in which the Supreme Court has held that *punitive damages* can only be constitutional if a balance is struck between the element of satisfaction and the element of repression.[66] **(vii)** The Supreme Court has held that an excessive amount of *punitive damages* violates the Due Process Clause of the Fourteenth Amendment. **(viii)** The award of aggravated (but not punitive) damages for non-material harm was thus construed by the Court as a justified exception applicable to the protection against interference in the most intimate sphere of a publicly-known person's private life, which makes his or her situation comparable to a private person, where such interference is, moreover, committed by entities whose business is based on, or frequently accompanied by, clearly provable, wilful and serious interference in the fundamental rights of individuals, even undermining their human dignity.[67] **(ix)** Indeed, as the Constitutional Court of the Czech Republic has held, the degree of protection must be necessarily diminished, if not entirely eliminated, if the purpose of the subject's existence, their activity and marketing strategy are based predominantly on the publishing of defamatory and slanderous information that debases human dignity about publicly active or well-known people in order to reap property benefits and increase the publicity of the employed media.[68] **(x)** The courts of the Member States may, in exceptional circumstances, invoke the public policy proviso and overriding mandatory provisions on grounds of public interest. The violation of public policy in the place of the court seised of the dispute could primarily occur should the application of the law determined according to this Regulation result in the award of non-compensatory excessive damages of an exemplary or repressive nature, depending on the circumstances of the case and the law of the Member State whose court is seised of the dispute.[69] **(xi)** The case-law of the Court of Justice of the European Union concerning

---

[66]   *State Farm Mut. Auto. Is.*, 538 U.S. 422.
[67]   Judgment of the Constitutional Court of the Czech Republic, Case No. I. ÚS 1586/09 of 06 March 2012.
[68]   Judgment of the Constitutional Court of the Czech Republic, Case No. I. ÚS 1586/09 of 06 March 2012.
[69]   See Helmut Koziol, Vanessa Wilcox, *Punitive Damages: Common Law and Civil Law Perspectives. Tort and Insurance Law,* 25 SPRINGER 198–199 (2009).

discrimination in employment relationships is based on the principle that the system of sanctions applicable to infringements of the national provisions adopted pursuant to Directives concerning the implementation of the principle of equal opportunities and equal treatment for men and women in employment and occupation, must be effective, proportional and dissuasive.[70] **(xii)** European courts usually refuse the enforcement of U.S. decisions awarding *punitive damages* for being contrary to public policy, for violating the prohibition of unjust enrichment and for the fact that damages in private law do not have the nature of a sanction.[71] **(xiii)** The Federal Court of Justice (*Bundesgerichtshof*) refused to recognize the judgment of a U.S. court concerning punitive damages, which awarded the claimant damages for the sexual abuse of a fourteen-year-old boy, arguing that the modern concept of German private law dictates that damages may only serve to restore the situation before the damage occurred, but may not punish the wrongdoer or enrich the victim. The enforcement of the decision was denied for a violation of public policy in terms of Article 328(1) of the Zivilprozessordnung [Germany]. The Federal Court of Justice [Germany] based the refusal of recognition and enforcement on the violation of public policy and of the constitutional principles of the State (disproportionate amount of the awarded damages). In the said case, the perpetrator was imprisoned in the United States and, on top of that, was ordered to pay to the victim USD 750,260, consisting of USD 350,260 in compensation and USD 400,000 in *punitive damages*. The German Federal Court of Justice only recognised the part of the judgment awarding compensatory damages.[72] **(xiv)** Italian courts also refuse the enforcement of decisions awarding *punitive damages* as violating public policy, arguing that the aim of civil-law compensation for damage and losses is to compensate the damage or losses sustained by the injured party.[73] **(xv)** In proceedings for the recognition and enforcement of a decision issued by the Superior Court of California (County of Alameda), which awarded damages in the amount of USD 3,253,734.45, consisting of USD 1,391,650.12 as compensatory damages, USD 402,084.33 as legal fees and USD 1,460,000 as *punitive damages*, the French Supreme Court has held that foreign decisions

---

[70] See also Judgment of the Court of Justice of the EU, Case C-81/12, *Asociatia Accept* v. *Consilul National pentru Combbaterea Discriminaii.*

[71] See Csongor István Nagy, *Recognition and enforcement of U.S. judgments involving punitive damages in continental Europe*, 30(1) NEDERLANDS INTERNATIONAAL PRIVAATRECHT 4–11 (2012).

[72] Judgment of the German Federal Court of Justice (BGH) 118, 312, of 04 June 1992.

[73] Judgment of the Italian Supreme Court No. 1183/2007 of 19 January 2007.

awarding *punitive damages* are not principally contrary to public policy and, as such, are enforceable in France. However, the awarded amount of the *punitive damages* must be proportionate to the breached commitment and the actual damage. In the said case, the Court has held that the *punitive damages* exceeded the limit of reasonability. **(xvi)** The recognition of a foreign decision awarding *punitive damages* cannot be *eo ipso* refused under Czech law as violating public policy, despite the fact that Czech law is unfamiliar with the concept of private-law *punitive damages*. In this regard, the case-law of the Constitutional Court[74] must be interpreted as meaning that a higher degree of fault always increases the unlawfulness of the interference in personality rights (increases the injustice that requires satisfaction) and the form and amount of the awarded satisfaction must be determined accordingly; see also Paragraph 37 of the Constitutional Court's reasoning. Hence, the aim is to determine satisfaction, the form and amount of which will be proportionate to the harm suffered by the injured party, exacerbated by exceptional circumstances, not to allow private-law punishments. **(xvii)** Indeed, the currently applicable Civil Code is based on the same concept. Section 2957 of the Civil Code[75] lists circumstances that increase the intensity and seriousness of the harm sustained by the injured party and that must be reflected in the determination of the damages, such as causing intentional harm, including, without limitation, causing harm by trickery, threat, abuse of the victim's dependence on the tortfeasor, multiplying the effects of the interference by making it publicly known or as a result of discriminating against the victim with regard to the victim's sex, health condition, ethnicity, creed, or other similarly serious reasons. Account is also taken of the victim's concerns of loss of life or serious damage to health if such concerns were caused by threat or other causes. **(xviii)** Indeed, the violation of public policy does not occur merely for the fact that Czech law is unfamiliar with any particular concept of a foreign law underlying the foreign decision whose recognition is sought. The violation of public policy only occurs if the recognition of

---

[74] Especially Judgment of the Constitutional Court of the Czech Republic, Case No. I. ÚS 1586/09 of 06 March 2012.

[75] Section 2957 of Act No. 89/2012 Coll., Civil Code (cit., approximate translation): *"The manner and amount of adequate satisfaction must be determined so as to include compensation for circumstances deserving special consideration. Such circumstances shall include wilfully caused harm, especially, without limitation, harm by trickery, threat, abuse of the victim's dependence on the tortfeasor, multiplying the effects of the interference by making it publicly known, or harm resulting from discrimination against the victim with regard to the victim's sex, health condition, ethnicity, creed, or other similarly serious reasons. Account is also taken of the victim's concerns of loss of life or serious injury if such concerns were caused by the threat or other causes."*

the foreign decision were contrary to the overriding mandatory principles of the social and State system of the Czech Republic and its legal system, to which no exceptions are permitted.[76] **(xix)** Hence, the effects of the decision would have to be contrary to any of the fundamental principles underlying the Czech legal system. The principle must be a specific and existing principle.[77] **(xx)** Consequently, when the recognition of a decision awarding *punitive damages* is sought, the violation of Czech public policy can only be invoked if the amount of the punitive damages is clearly disproportionate to the harm that is to be indemnified. In such case, the decision conflicts with Article 11(1) of the Charter of Fundamental Rights and Freedoms,[78] because it constitutes a disproportionate interference in the right to property.[79] **(xxi)** The assessment of whether or not the underlying decision awarding *punitive damages* constitutes a disproportionate interference in the right to property thus requires a diligent examination of the seriousness of the harm that is to be compensated by the underlying decision, as greater (more intensive) harm justifies higher damages, and an examination of whether or not the compensatory component of the damages is disproportionately suppressed by the punitive component (i.e. whether or not the compensatory component of the damages is clearly smaller than the punitive component), and whether or not the amount of the damages constitutes an impermissible interference in the judgment debtor's property rights (i.e. does or does not entail complete elimination, have stifling effects). An assessment of whether or not the recognition of such a decision complies with public policy can only be made after these criteria are weighed.

9.30. **Resolution of the Supreme Court of the Czech Republic, Case No. 20 Cdo 665/2010 of 26 October 2011:**[80] **[enforcement proceedings, enforcement of a foreign court's**

---

[76]   See Section 36 of Act No. 97/1963 Coll., on Private International Law and Procedure (cit., approximate translation): *"Laws and regulations of a foreign State cannot be applied where the effects of such application would be contrary to the overriding mandatory principles of the social and State system of the Czechoslovak Socialist Republic and its legal system to which no exceptions are permitted."* This Act was replaced by Act No. 91/2012 Coll., on Private International Law, with effect from 01 January 2014.

[77]   See also *per analogiam*, Judgment of the Court of Justice of the EU, Case C-420/907, *Meletis Apostolides* v. *David Charles Orams, Linda Elizabeth Orams*.

[78]   Constitutional Act No. 2/1993 Coll., as amended by Constitutional Act No. 162/1998 Coll., Charter of Fundamental Rights and Freedoms.

[79]   See also Article 4(4) of the Charter of Fundamental Rights and Freedoms.

[80]   Preceding decisions in the case: (i) Resolution of the Regional Court in Brno [Czech Republic] of 25 September 2009, Case No. 20 Co 876/2008, 20 Co 877/2008–128, (ii) Resolution of the Municipal Court in Brno [Czech Republic] of 26 May 2008, Case No. 96 Nc 3139/2008–7, and (iii) Resolution of the Regional Court in Bratislava [Slovak Republic], Case No. 38 Cb 83/01–286 of 07 December 2004, and Case No. 38 Cb 83/01–299 of 18 January 2005, in conjunction with judgment of the Supreme Court of the Slovak Republic, Case No. 2 Obo 259/2007 of 19 March 2008, and a supplemental judgment of the Supreme Court of the Slovak Republic, Case No. 2 Obo 259/2007 of 16 April 2008.

decision, enforcement of decisions] (1) Section 238a(1) of the Code of Civil Procedure stipulates that a cassation appeal (as an exceptional remedy submitted to the Supreme Court of the Czech Republic) shall be admissible against a resolution of the appellate court upholding or overruling a resolution of the first-instance court that was rendered (a) in insolvency proceedings; (b) on an action for annulment; (c) in a case in which the discontinuation of enforcement proceedings is sought, unless the enforcement proceedings concern the return of a child in matters of international child abduction pursuant to an international treaty that forms a part of the legal system, or pursuant to a directly applicable law of the European Communities; (d) on approval of a sale at auction in enforcement proceedings; (e) on the distribution of an estate in enforcement proceedings; (f) on the duties of the bidder referred to in Section 336m(2) (Section 336n) and in Section 338za(2). Section 237(1) and (3) of the Code of Civil Procedure apply *per analogiam* (Subsection 2). **(2)** Section 68a(1) of Act No. 97/1963 Coll., on Private International Law,[81] stipulates that the provisions of this Part apply in proceedings for the recognition and enforcement of foreign decisions, other authentic instruments and court settlements that are governed by the law of the European Communities or a promulgated international treaty, the ratification of which has been approved by the Parliament and which is binding on the Czech Republic. **(3)** Section 68c(1) of the Private International Law Act[82] stipulates that a petition for the declaration of enforceability may be accompanied by a petition for the enforcement of a decision in enforcement proceedings conducted by the court enforcement officer or in enforcement proceedings conducted by a private bailiff under special legislation. In such case, the court shall issue a single resolution on both petitions with separate operative parts that must be properly reasoned. The resolution must contain reasons even if the court's ruling concerns only one of the petitions. **Subsection 4 hereof stipulates that the operative part of a decision that orders the enforcement of a decision in enforcement proceedings conducted by the court enforcement officer or enforcement proceedings conducted by a private bailiff cannot become final earlier than the operative part that**

---

[81]   Act No. 97/1963 Coll., Act on Private International Law and Procedure. This Act was replaced by Act No. 91/2012 Coll., on Private International Law, as a result of the recodification of Czech civil law, with effect from 01 January 2014.
[82]   Act No. 97/1963 Coll., Act on Private International Law and Procedure. This Act was replaced by Act No. 91/2012 Coll., on Private International Law, as a result of the recodification of Czech civil law, with effect from 01 January 2014.

declares the decision enforceable. (4) Article 38(1) of the Brussels I Regulation stipulates that a judgment given in a Member State and enforceable in that State shall be enforced in another Member State when, on the application of any interested party, it has been declared enforceable there. **(5)** Article 41 of the Brussels I Regulation stipulates that the judgment shall be declared enforceable immediately upon completion of the formalities in Article 53 of the Brussels I Regulation without any review under Articles 34 and 35 of the Brussels I Regulation. The party against whom enforcement is sought shall not at this stage of the proceedings be entitled to make any submissions on the application. **(6)** Article 44 of the Brussels I Regulation stipulates that the judgment given on the appeal may only be contested by the appeal referred to in Annex IV of the Brussels I Regulation. **(7)** Article 45(1) of the Brussels I Regulation stipulates that the court with which an appeal is lodged under Article 43 or Article 44 of the Brussels I Regulation shall refuse or revoke a declaration of enforceability only on one of the grounds specified in Articles 34 and 35 of the Brussels I Regulation. Pursuant to Subsection 2 hereof, under no circumstances may the foreign judgment be reviewed as to its substance. **(8)** According to Annex IV of the Brussels I Regulation, the appeals that may be lodged pursuant to Article 44 are the following: [...] – in the Czech Republic, appellate review ("dovolání") and action for annulment ("žaloba pro zmatečnost"), [...] **(9)** In view of the fact that the court's decision on the declaration of enforceability is a decision on the meris, the admissibility of the cassation appeal (appellate review) lodged against the operative part of the appellate court's resolution upholding the resolution of the first-instance court, in which the enforceable instrument was declared enforceable in the territory of the Czech Republic, can only be assessed from the perspective of Section 238(1)(c) of the Code of Civil Procedure in conjunction with Section 238(3) of the Code of Civil Procedure.[83] **(10)** If the enforceable instrument

---

[83] Section 238(1)(c) of the Code of Civil Procedure (cit., approximate translation): "*(1) A cassation appeal pursuant to Section 237 is not allowed (a) in matters set forth in Part Two of the Civil Code if the proceedings concerning such matters are conducted pursuant to this Act and if the case concerns matters other than marital property law, (b) in matters set forth in the Registered Partnership Act if the proceedings concerning such matters are conducted pursuant to this Act, (c) against judgments and resolutions issued in proceedings the subject matter of which was, at the time when the decision was made that contained the contested operative part, monetary performance not exceeding CZK 50,000, including enforcement proceedings, with the exception of relationships from consumer contracts and employment relationships; for this purpose, interest and other dues accruing to the claim shall be disregarded, (d) in matters concerning the postponement of enforcement proceedings, (e) against resolutions that can be challenged by an action for annulment pursuant to Section 229(4), (f) against resolutions on interim measures, measures against obstruction of justice, fees payable to expert witnesses or interpreters, (g) against resolutions on actions from disturbance of possession, (h) against the operative part of a decision that concerns the costs of proceedings, (i) against resolutions on petitions for an exemption from court fees or on the obligation to pay court fees, (j) against resolutions on a*

is enforceable in the country of origin and if the formalities were completed that are stipulated in Article 41 in conjunction with Article 55(1) of the Brussels I Regulation, the judgment must be declared enforceable in the territory of the Czech Republic. **(11)** The judgment debtor may challenge the enforceability of the decision in the court that made the underlying judgment, using the remedies afforded to the judgment debtor by the national law in the country of origin.[84] **(12)** The judgment debtor may make a petition in the course of the enforcement proceedings to deny recognition of the decision on the grounds specified in Articles 34 and 35 of the Brussels I Regulation. **(13)** If, in the given case, the appellate court ruled by a single resolution upholding the first-instance court's decision on the judgment debtor's appeal (i) against the resolution, whereby the enforceable instrument is declared enforceable in the territory of the Czech Republic, and (ii) against the writ of execution, the decisions became final on the same day. **(14)** If, in the said case, the appellate court ruled on the appeal against the first-instance court's writ of execution by the appellate court's resolution of 25 September 2009, the cassation appeal (appellate review) of the resolution is no longer admissible. This conclusion stands, despite the fact that the appellate court has erred in its instructions to the parties contained in the contested resolution, in which the appellate court advised the parties that a cassation appeal (appellate review) against the appellate court's decision is admissible subject to the conditions stipulated in Section 237(1)(c) of the Code of Civil Procedure. Such instructions do not establish the admissibility of the cassation appeal (appellate review).[85]

9.31. Resolution of the Supreme Court of the Czech Republic, Case No. 20 Cdo 776/2017 of 01 June 2017:[86] [enforcement

party's petition for the appointment of a representative, (k) against decisions whereby the appellate court set aside the first-instance court decision and the case reverted to the first-instance court for further proceedings, (l) against resolutions on a release from the obligation to deposit an advance payment or the withdrawal of the release from the obligation to deposit an advance payment pursuant to the Enforcement Code. (2) As concerns a repeated payment, the determination of whether or not a decision containing the operative part challenged by the cassation appeal was issued in proceedings the subject matter of which was, at the time when the decision was made, a monetary performance not exceeding CZK 50,000 [Subsection (1)(c)], depends on the sum total of all repeated payments; however, if the payment is to be made until a person dies, for an indefinite period of time or for a definite period of time exceeding 5 years, the relevant amount shall be merely five times the amount of the annual performance. (3) Decisions pursuant to Subsection (1)(c) shall also include decisions issued in proceedings for the determination of the existence or the amount of a claim not exceeding CZK 50,000."

[84] See also Resolution of the Supreme Court of the Czech Republic, Case No. 20 Cdo 5180/2008 of 24 March 2011.

[85] See also Resolution of the Supreme Court of the Czech Republic, Case No. 29 Odo 425/2002 of 27 June 2002, published under No. 51/2003 in Sbírka soudních rozhodnutí a stanovisek [Court Reports].

[86] Preceding decisions in the case: (i) Resolution of the Municipal Court in Prague [Czech Republic], Case No. 12 Co 156/2016-98 of 16 December 2016, (ii) Decision of the District Court in Floridsdorf [Austria], Case No. 12 E 1396/14g-2 of 14 November 2014, and (iii) Resolution of the District Court for Prague 4 [Czech Republic], Case No. 13 EXE 1004/2015-6 of 22 February 2016.

of a foreign court's decision; decision underlying the enforcement proceedings; territorial limitation of the effects of the declaration of enforceability; territorial effects of a decision; exequatur] **(1)** Article 38(1) of the Brussels I Regulation stipulates that a judgment given in a Member State and enforceable in that State shall be enforced in another Member State when, on the application of any interested party, it has been declared enforceable there. **(2)** A declaration of enforceability (exequatur) requires proceedings to be opened upon a motion, which may result in the declaration of the enforceability of the foreign decision or in the dismissal of the motion. If the decision is declared enforceable, it is possible to open enforcement proceedings conducted by a court or by a private bailiff. **(3)** At the same time, the declaration of enforceability is restricted to the State where it was issued. If the judgment creditor wishes to conduct enforcement proceedings in two or more EU Member States, the declaration of enforceability must be requested in each of the Member States separately. **(4)** The principle of the declaration of enforceability being restricted to the State where recognition is sought also means that any enforcement proceedings conducted subsequently may only be implemented within the territory of said State. The Brussels I Regulation does not allow enforcement proceedings opened by the court of an EU Member State to actually be implemented in the territory of another Member State, as such procedure would encroach upon the latter's sovereignty. This principle applies without question to enforcement by the sale of movable assets and real estate, but it applies just as unconditionally to attachment proceedings.[87] **(5)** However, recognition and the issuance of a writ of execution can only be considered in respect of those operative parts of the decision that constitute enforceable instruments for other, separate enforcement proceedings. In Czech law, this would include an operative part concerning the costs of the enforcement proceedings, provided that the judgment creditor's petition for enforcement did not include the enforcement of such costs as well. In such case, the resolution whereby the court opened the enforcement proceedings only awards the costs to the judgment creditor, and this operative part constitutes an enforceable instrument for separate enforcement proceedings. The operative part itself of the writ of execution is not subject to the Brussels I Regulation. Hence, no effects (not even substantive-law effects)

---

[87] VIKTOR VAŠKE, UZNÁNÍ A VÝKON CIZÍCH ROZHODNUTÍ V ČESKÉ REPUBLICE [title in translation – RECOGNITION AND ENFORCEMENT OF FOREIGN JUDGMENTS IN THE CZECH REPUBLIC], Prague: C. H. Beck (2007), et. 67.

can be recognised, for instance, of a decision whereby the court of an EU Member State ordered the judgment debtor's debtor established in the Czech Republic to pay the judgment debtor's claim (with the effects of a discharge of debt) directly to the judgment creditor, or of a decision whereby the court prohibited a bank established in the Czech Republic from paying out any funds to the judgment debtor. At the same time, a Czech resolution opening the attachment proceedings cannot be declared enforceable and subsequently enforced in any other EU Member State, because the resolution is not an enforceable instrument in terms of Article 32 of the Brussels I Regulation.[88] **(6)** If the judgment creditor wishes to conduct enforcement proceedings in two or more EU Member States, the declaration of enforceability of the enforceable instrument must be requested in each of the Member States separately. **(7)** Any subsequent enforcement proceedings can only be conducted in the territory of the State in which the writ of execution was issued. **(8)** If any enforcement proceedings were opened in a foreign State on the basis of a foreign decision, the operative part of the writ of execution cannot be declared enforceable in the territory of the Czech Republic. **(9)** Due to the fact that all operative parts of the decision presented for enforcement are acts whereby the enforcement itself is implemented and, as such, are not covered by the regime of the Brussels I Regulation under Article 32 of the Brussels I Regulation, it would be appropriate to dismiss the judgment creditor's petition for a declaration of enforceability, because the effects of the writ of execution in any EU Member State cannot be expanded to cover the territory of another EU Member State. **(10)** A judgment creditor who wishes to make sure that the judgment debtor's funds in accounts in the Czech Republic are seised in enforcement proceedings must bear in mind that such proceedings can only be opened by a Czech court on the basis of a foreign enforceable instrument that was declared enforceable in the Czech Republic.

9.32. **Resolution of the Supreme Court of the Czech Republic, Case No. 20 Cdo 1152/2020 of 16 June 2020:[89] [enforcement proceedings; recognition of foreign decisions; enforcement of a foreign court's decision; territorial limitation of the**

---

[88] In this regard, the Supreme Court invokes the opinions voiced in academic writings (see also VIKTOR VAŠKE, UZNÁNÍ A VÝKON CIZÍCH ROZHODNUTÍ V ČESKÉ REPUBLICE [title in translation – RECOGNITION AND ENFORCEMENT OF FOREIGN JUDGMENTS IN THE CZECH REPUBLIC], Prague: C. H. Beck (2007), et. 30-35 concerning Article 32 of the Brussels I Regulation).

[89] Preceding decisions in the case: (i) Resolution of the District Court for Prague 4, Case No. 13 EXE 1004/2015-250 of 18 April 2019, (ii) Decision of the District Court in Floridsdorf [Republic of Austria], Case No. 12 E 1396/14g-2 of 14 November 2014, and (iii) Resolution of the Municipal Court in Prague [Czech Republic], Case No. 12 Co 185/2019-305 of 29 November 2019.

Czech Yearbook of International Law®

effects of a declaration of enforceability; territorial effects of a judgment; exequatur; public policy; reciprocity; *acte clair*; preliminary reference; interpretation of EU law] **(1)** The operative part of a foreign writ of execution issued by a court of another EU Member State cannot be declared enforceable in the territory of the Czech Republic, because the effects of the opening of enforcement proceedings in an EU Member State cannot be expanded to the territory of another EU Member State.[90] **(2)** The operative part itself of the writ of execution does not fall within the scope of Article 32 of the Brussels I Regulation, because the latter can only apply to operative parts that serve as enforceable instruments for other, independent enforcement proceedings, such as an operative part concerning the costs of the enforcement proceedings, in which non-monetary (specific) performance is to be enforced where the judgment creditor did not propose that the enforcement proceedings also cover the enforcement of such claims. **(3)** If the judgment creditor wishes to conduct enforcement proceedings in two or more EU Member States, the declaration of enforceability of the enforceable instrument (exequatur) must be requested in each of the Member States separately, because the declaration of enforceability is limited to the State in which the declaration was made. Any subsequent enforcement proceedings can only be conducted in the territory of the State in which the writ of execution was issued. **(4)** A decision to seize the judgment debtor's funds in accounts in the Czech Republic in enforcement proceedings can only be made by a Czech court on the basis of a foreign enforceable instrument which was declared enforceable in the Czech Republic (exequatur). **(5)** The conclusion that it is not an enforceable instrument that could be enforced in the territory of the Czech Republic is clearly implied by the decision itself that the judgment creditor proposes to declare enforceable, because the operative part of the decision (in this case, a decision of an Austrian court) stipulates that the judgments of the Liechtenstein court were declared enforceable [only] "for enforcement proceedings in Austria", in other words, they were only declared enforceable for enforcement proceedings in the Republic of Austria. **(6)** Czech courts are entitled to refuse to declare a writ of execution enforceable if it was issued by a court of another EU Member State. **(7)** Article 38(1) of the Brussels I Regulation stipulates that a judgment given in a Member State

---

[90] See also Resolution of the Supreme Court of the Czech Republic, Case No. 20 Cdo 3689/2018-210 of 11 December 2018 (published under No. 108/2019 in Sbírka soudních rozhodnutí a stanovisek [Court Reports]), which was challenged by a constitutional complaint that was subsequently dismissed by the resolution of the Constitutional Court of the Czech Republic in Case No. IV. ÚS 902/19 of 20 March 2019.

and enforceable in that State shall be enforced in another Member State when, upon the application of any interested party, it has been declared enforceable there (exequatur), but Article 34(1) of the Brussels I Regulation stipulates that a judgment shall not be recognised if such recognition is manifestly contrary to public policy in the Member State in which recognition is sought. **(8)** The Court of Justice of the EU has consistently held that public policy may only be used in exceptional cases as a reason for not recognising a judgment when recognition of the effects of the foreign judgment were manifestly contrary to public policy of the State addressed.[91] **(9)** Protection of the fundamental rights of individuals belongs to the central principles of the Czech legal system and represents a key element thereof. Hence, the recognition of a decision that fails to comply with the principle of protection of fundamental rights would be **contrary to public policy** and, ultimately, the constitutional laws as such. It therefore constitutes the violation of a material legal principle that exhibits the features of a fundamental right.[92] **(10)** If the Austrian judgment were declared enforceable in the Czech Republic, the judgment debtor's right to a fair trial would be violated due to the reasons specified below. Indeed, if the Czech courts granted the judgment creditor's request and declared the Austrian writ of execution enforceable in the territory of the Czech Republic, and if enforcement proceedings were opened and a private bailiff appointed on the basis thereof, the actual enforceable instruments would be judgments of the Regional Court in Vaduz, but the Principality of Liechtenstein is not an EU Member State, the Czech Republic has not concluded any treaty with Liechtenstein that would provide for the recognition and enforcement of judgments, and there is no formal and material reciprocity between the two countries either. **(11)** Enforcement of a foreign decision that was issued in a State with which the Czech Republic has no binding international treaty on recognition and enforcement can only be ordered on the basis of a decision rendered by a Czech court and properly substantiated. As the appointment of the private bailiff does not meet the said criteria, it is necessary to conclude that it cannot serve as the basis for accepting the recognition of enforceability of the foreign decision in our territory.[93] **(12)** Enforcement of a

---

[91] See also Judgment of the European Court of Justice in Case 145/86 of 4 February 1988, *L., M. H.* v. *A.K.*
[92] See also Resolution of the Supreme Court of the Czech Republic, Case No. 20 Cdo 1877/2016 of 12 August 2016.
[93] Opinion of the Supreme Court of the Czech Republic articulated in the resolution in Case No. 20 Cdo 1349/2016 of 01 July 2016.

foreign decision that is subject to Sections 14 to 16 of the Private International Law Act[94] can only be implemented by enforcement proceedings conducted by the court enforcement officer. Enforcement proceedings pursuant to the Act on Private Bailiffs and Enforcement Proceedings[95] can in such case only be conducted on the basis of a foreign decision that was recognised on the basis of a special decision of a Czech court (exequatur) pursuant to Section 16(2) of the Private International Law Act,[96] i.e. by a judgment, which must contain reasons, whether the petition for the recognition of the foreign decision was granted or dismissed. **(13)** The person against whom the enforcement is targeted may invoke the impediments preventing recognition

---

[94] Sections 14 to 16 of Act No. 91/2012 Coll., on Private International Law (cit., approximate translation): "Section 14
Judgments of the courts of a foreign State and rulings of the authorities of a foreign State concerning any rights and obligations whose private-law nature would, in the Czech Republic, subject them to the jurisdiction of courts, as well as foreign judicial settlements and foreign notarial or other authentic instruments concerning these matters (hereafter referred to as 'foreign judgments') will have effects in the Czech Republic, provided that they have become final according to a confirmation issued by the competent foreign authority and have been recognised by Czech public authorities.
Section 15
(1) Unless the following provisions of this Act stipulate otherwise, a final foreign judgment cannot be recognised (a) if the matter falls within the exclusive jurisdiction of Czech courts or no authority of a foreign State would have had jurisdiction to conduct the proceedings if the provisions on the jurisdiction of Czech courts had been applied to the assessment of the foreign authority's jurisdiction, unless the party to the proceedings against whom the foreign judgment is made has voluntarily submitted to the jurisdiction of the foreign authority, (b) if any proceedings are pending in a Czech court concerning the same legal relationship and those proceedings had been opened earlier than the foreign proceedings in which the judgment was issued whose recognition is sought, (c) if a Czech court has already issued a final judgment regarding the same legal relationship or if a final judgment of a third State's authority has already been recognised in the Czech Republic, (d) if a party to the proceedings against whom the recognition of the judgment is sought was deprived of the opportunity to duly enter an appearance by the acts of the foreign authority, primarily if the party was not served with a summons or a petition to open the proceedings, (e) if the recognition were clearly contrary to public policy, or (f) if no reciprocity is guaranteed; reciprocity is not required if the foreign judgment is not directed against a citizen of the Czech Republic or a Czech legal entity.
Section 16
(1) Recognition of a foreign judgment in property matters is not pronounced by any special order. The foreign judgment is recognized by being taken into consideration by a Czech public authority as if it were a decision of a Czech public authority. If the public policy proviso or any other grounds for the refusal of recognition are invoked against the recognition that could not have been taken into account without further proceedings, the proceedings shall be suspended and a deadline shall be set for opening special proceedings pursuant to Subsection 4. The suspended proceedings shall continue after the special proceedings are closed with a final decision or after the said deadline expires without the special proceedings being opened. (2) Foreign judgments in other matters are recognised in special proceedings pursuant to Subsection (4), unless this Act stipulates that foreign judgments are recognised without any further proceedings. (3) If proposed by a party, a foreign judgment can also be recognised in the special proceedings pursuant to Subsection (4) even if the judgment is normally recognised without any further proceedings.(4) Recognition of the judgment awarded by the court in the special proceedings shall take the form of a judgment; no hearing needs to be summoned. The court with territorial jurisdiction to grant the recognition of the judgment is the district court of the party who seeks the recognition or, if not applicable, the district court in whose district the fact occurred or could occur that is material for the recognition, unless this Act or any other legislation indicates otherwise.(5) A foreign judgment in property matters that meets the criteria for recognition under this Act can serve as an enforceable instrument on the basis of which enforcement proceedings will be opened by a reasoned writ of execution issued by a Czech court."
[95] Act No. 120/2001 Coll., on Private Bailiffs and Enforcement Proceedings (Enforcement Code).
[96] Section 16(2) of Act No. 91/2012 Coll., on Private International Law (approximate translation cited above).

pursuant to Section 15 of the Private International Law Act;[97] for example, Section 15(1)(f) of the Private International Law Act[98] prohibits the recognition of a final foreign decision directed against a Czech legal entity if no **reciprocity** is guaranteed. **(14)** The declaration of the enforceability of an Austrian writ of execution would result in a situation in which a foreign decision, subject to the provisions of Section 14 to 16 of the Private International Law Act,[99] would be recognised without any special proceedings, and the person against whom the enforcement is directed would have no opportunity to invoke the impediments to recognition under Section 15 of the Private International Law Act,[100] the scope of which is broader than the scope of the impediments to recognition under Article 34 of the Brussels I Regulation, which would undermine the right of the judgment debtor to a fair trial and, consequently, be contrary to public policy of the Czech Republic; this constitutes grounds for the refusal to recognise the decision pursuant to Article 34(1) of the Brussels I Regulation. **(15)** The certificate pursuant to Article 54 of the Brussels I Regulation is the basis for the application of the principle of direct enforceability of a decision issued in Member States and, as such, it is an indispensable prerequisite for the free movement of decisions in the European judicial area; the issue of the certificate attests to the fact that the dispute falls within the scope of the Brussels I Regulation. **(16)** The court competent to issue the certificate is the court that rendered the decision in the case and, consequently, is best familiar with the dispute. Having said that, one cannot infer that the Court of Justice of the EU has held that after the certificate pursuant to Article 54 of the Brussels I Regulation is issued, the decision of a Member State will always and *eo ipso* be declared enforceable in another Member State; indeed, the Court of Justice of the EU has also emphasised the option open to the judgment debtor to raise objections to the recognition or enforcement of the decision pursuant to Article 34 of the Brussels I Regulation. **(17)** The material accuracy of the enforceable instrument, which cannot be reviewed by the appellate court, means accurate and complete factual findings underlying the enforceable instrument, as well as an accurate and comprehensive legal assessment of the established act, and

---

[97] Section 15 of Act No. 91/2012 Coll., on Private International Law (approximate translation cited above).
[98] Section 15(1)(f) of Act No. 91/2012 Coll., on Private International Law (approximate translation cited above).
[99] Sections 14 – 16 of Act No. 91/2012 Coll., on Private International Law (approximate translation cited above).
[100] Section 15 of Act No. 91/2012 Coll., on Private International Law (approximate translation cited above).

a reflection of the above in the operative part of the enforceable instrument.[101] **(18)** The fact that it is not for the courts in the country where the decision is enforced to challenge the enforceability of the underlying decision cannot be interpreted as meaning that a Czech court should ignore the fact that the recognition of the effects of a foreign decision would be manifestly contrary to the public policy of the Czech Republic. **(19)** The cassation court is not obliged to make a preliminary reference to the Court of Justice of the European Union if there are no doubts about the correctness of the interpretation of the contested issue, i.e. the case is an *acte clair* and the respective issue of interpretation of the EU law is clear. This conclusion does not conflict with the fact that the first-instance court and the appellate court each resolved the case in a different manner.[102] **(20)** From the practical perspective, the automatic obligation of the last-instance court to make a preliminary reference in the case of an inconsistent interpretation of EU law, at least within the framework of the same proceedings, is difficult to sustain, the criteria articulated in CILFIT cannot be perceived as absolute, and the degree of fulfilment of *acte clair* should be assessed in more material terms. The more effective approach is to directly remedy the error consisting in the unsustainable interpretation of the EU law by the lower court.[103] **(21)** In this regard, the existence itself of contradictory decisions issued by other national courts cannot be the decisive element for the imposition of the obligation stipulated in the third subparagraph of Article 267 of the Treaty on the Functioning of the European Union. Indeed, regardless of the interpretation presented by the lower courts with respect to any provision of EU law, the last-instance court may be convinced that the interpretation of the provision, proposed by the last-instance court and different from the interpretation of the lower courts, is beyond any reasonable doubt the only correct interpretation.[104] **(22)** If the courts of various Member States were each presented with and resolved a completely different matter, their decisions cannot be regarded as inconsistent. The Czech court would *de facto* adjudicate on the same matter as the Austrian court only if the

---

[101] See also (i) Resolution of the Supreme Court of the Czech Republic, Case No. 20 Cdo 5769/2017 of 10 July 2018, and Resolution of the Supreme Court of the Czech Republic, Case No. 20 Cdo 3031/2019 of 06 February 2019.

[102] A conclusion formulated in the resolution of the Supreme Court of the Czech Republic in Case No. 20 Cdo 3689/2018-210 of 11 December 2018.

[103] A conclusion formulated in the judgment of the Constitutional Court of the Czech Republic in Case No. II. ÚS 3432/17 of 11 September 2018.

[104] A conclusion formulated in the judgment of the Court of Justice of the EU in Case No. C-160/14 of 09 September 2015, *Ferreira da Silva*.

former were presented with a petition for the recognition of Liechtenstein judgments that would serve as enforceable instruments for enforcement proceedings conducted by a court or by a private bailiff; on the other hand, the Austrian court, in this particular case, issued a writ of execution for the enforcement of the foreign decision on the basis of a bilateral treaty between the Principality of Liechtenstein and the Republic of Austria on the recognition of judgments. In view of the fact that no analogous bilateral treaty between the Principality of Liechtenstein and the Czech Republic exists and the former is not an EU Member State, the Czech court would apply the Private International Law Act,[105] which could result in a decision different from the decision of the Austrian court, but not due to any inconsistent interpretation of EU law. **(23)** The operative part concerning the costs of the enforcement proceedings is enforceable within the framework of the opened enforcement proceedings and, consequently, does not constitute a new enforceable instrument, but a dependant order that merely relates to the permission of the Austrian court to conduct enforcement proceedings; hence, it cannot be declared enforceable in the territory of the Czech Republic.

9.33. **Resolution of the Supreme Court of the Czech Republic, Case No. 20 Cdo 1349/2016 of 01 July 2016:[106] [enforcement proceedings; enforcement of a foreign court's decision; recognition of foreign decisions] (1)** Section 2 of the Private International Law Act[107] stipulates that this Act shall be applied within the limits of the provisions incorporated in international treaties that are binding on the Czech Republic and of any directly applicable provisions of European Union law. **(2)** An enforceable instrument issued by the Florida District Court is a decision issued by a court of a foreign State, the recognition and enforcement of which must be governed by the Private International Law Act,[108] because no bilateral or multilateral international treaty on cooperation in the areas of the recognition and enforcement of judgments has been concluded by and between the United States (or Florida, as applicable) and the Czech Republic. At the same time, directly applicable provisions of EU law shall not apply either, because the decision has not been issued by a court of any EU Member State. **(3)** Section 16(3)

---

[105] Act No. 91/2012 Coll., on Private International Law.
[106] Preceding decisions in the case: (i) Resolution of the Regional Court in Brno [Czech Republic], Case No. 20 Co 537/2015-449 of 11 December 2015, (ii) Resolution of the District Court in Uherské Hradiště [Czech Republic], Case No. 3 EXE 259/2014-136 of 06 January 2015, and (iii) Judgment of the Brevard County and Circuit Court, 18th Judicial Circuit, Florida [U.S.], Case No. 05-2010 CA 049934 of 15 July 2013.
[107] Act No. 91/2012 Coll., on Private International Law.
[108] Act No. 91/2012 Coll., on Private International Law.

of the Private International Law Act,[109] which materially copies the previously applicable rule in Section 66 of Act No. 97/1963 Coll., on Private International Law and Procedure,[110] indicates that foreign decisions, the enforcement of which is sought in the Czech Republic, are not subject to any intermediate step, such as any special proceedings for recognition (exequatur) or proceedings for the declaration of enforceability, which applies within the regime established by certain EU laws and international treaties. (4) One may directly petition for the enforcement of the decision, specifically enforcement by court. The court will assess, as a preliminary issue, whether the foreign decision meets the criteria for recognition and, if so, issues a writ of execution. The writ of execution must always contain reasons. The reasons substantiating the writ of execution are necessary, because it must be clearly discernible that the court assessed the prerequisites for ordering enforcement by the court, and because the parties must have the right to invoke any potentially erroneous assessment of the criteria for enforcement in a remedial measure available to the party.[111] (5) The court shall depart from the procedure incorporated in Section 16(3) of the Private International Law Act[112] in the case of a foreign decision that was recognised in advance in special proceedings. Such decisions must be treated like national enforceable instruments. In other words, the criteria for recognition are not subject to a repeated review. Such cases retain the possibility of twofold enforcement. Hence, the party may petition for both enforcement proceedings conducted by the court enforcement officer and for enforcement proceedings conducted by a private bailiff. Consequently, foreign decisions may only be enforced in enforcement proceedings conducted by the court enforcement officer, not in enforcement proceedings conducted by a private bailiff, with the exception of (a) foreign decisions on maintenance for minors, (b) foreign decisions with respect to which a declaration of enforceability was issued pursuant to a directly applicable EU law or an international treaty, and (c)

---

[109] Section 16(3) of Act No. 91/2012 Coll., on Private International Law (cit., approximate translation): *"(3) If proposed by a party, a foreign judgment can also be recognised in the special proceedings pursuant to Subsection (4) even if the judgment is normally recognised without any further proceedings."*

[110] Section 66 of Act No. 97/1963 Coll., on Private International Law and Procedure (cit., approximate translation): *"Subject to the requirements stipulated in Sections 63 and 64, a foreign judgment on property rights can be enforced in the Czechoslovak Socialist Republic if the writ of execution is issued by a Czechoslovak court; the writ of execution must always be reasoned."* This Act was replaced by Act No. 91/2012 Coll., on Private International Law, with effect from 01 January 2014.

[111] See Opinion of the Supreme Court of the Czechoslovak Socialist Republic, Case No. Cpjf 27/86 of 27 August 1987.

[112] Section 16(3) of Act No. 91/2012 Coll., on Private International Law (approximate translation cited above).

foreign decisions that were recognised in separate proceedings for recognition pursuant to the Act.[113] **(6)** Section 130(1) of the Enforcement Code[114] targets decisions issued in enforcement proceedings and the methods of implementing enforcement, not the commencement of the enforcement proceedings, because – as opposed to the opening of enforcement proceedings conducted by the court enforcement officer – the appointment of the private bailiff to conduct the enforcement proceedings is not a judgment, contains no reasons and cannot be appealed. **(7)** The enforcement of a foreign judgment that was issued in a State with which the Czech Republic has no binding international treaty on recognition and enforcement can only be ordered on the basis of a decision rendered by a Czech court that is properly substantiated. As the appointment of the private bailiff does not meet the said criteria, it is necessary to conclude that it cannot serve as the basis for accepting the recognition of the enforceability of the foreign judgment in the territory of the Czech Republic. **(8)** The enforcement of a foreign judgment that is subject to Sections 14 to 16 of the Private International Law Act[115] can only be implemented by enforcement proceedings conducted by the court enforcement officer. Enforcement proceedings pursuant to the Enforcement Code can in such case only be conducted on the basis of a foreign decision that was recognised on the basis of a special decision of a Czech court pursuant to Section 16(2) of the Private International Law Act,[116] i.e. by a judgment, which must contain reasons, whether the petition for the recognition of the foreign decision was granted or dismissed.

9.34. Resolution of the Supreme Court of the Czech Republic, Case No. 20 Cdo 1702/2017 of 07 May 2018:[117] [enforcement proceedings, enforcement of a foreign court's decision; CMR

---

[113] PETR BŘÍZA, TOMÁŠ BŘICHÁČEK, ZUZANA FIŠEROVÁ, PAVEL HORÁK, LUBOMÍR PTÁČEK, JIŘÍ SVOBODA, ZÁKON O MEZINÁRODNÍM PRÁVU SOUKROMÉM. KOMENTÁŘ [title in translation – PRIVATE INTERNATIONAL LAW ACT. A COMMENTARY], Prague: C. H. Beck (2014), et. 115–116.

[114] Section 130(1) of Act No. 120/2001 Coll., on Private Bailiffs and Enforcement Proceedings (cit., approximate translation): *"(1) Any reference in special legislation to court enforcement of judgments or enforcement proceedings shall also include enforcement proceedings conducted by a private bailiff under this Act. Any reference in special legislation to a writ of execution shall also include the conduct of enforcement proceedings pursuant to this Act."*

[115] Sections 14 – 16 of Act No. 91/2012 Coll., on Private International Law (approximate translation cited above).

[116] Section 16(2) of Act No. 91/2012 Coll., on Private International Law (cit., approximate translation): *"(2) Foreign judgments in other matters are recognised in special proceedings pursuant to Subsection (4), unless this Act stipulates that foreign judgments are recognised without any further proceedings."*

[117] Preceding decisions in the case: (i) Resolution of the Regional Court in Pilsen [Czech Republic], Case No. 61 Co276/2016-187 of 14 December 2016, (ii) Resolution of the District Court in Karlovy Vary [Czech Republic], Case No. 27 EXE 2732/2015-51 of 12 October 2015, (iii) Resolution of the Strasbourg Court of First Instance for commercial matters [France], Case 03/01008 of 18 December 2009, and (iv) Decision of the Appellate Court in Colmar [France], Case 1 A 10/04260 of 14 November 2012.

Convention; contract of carriage; carriage; limitation of actions; applicability of the CMR Convention] **(1)** The CMR Convention[118] is an international treaty pursuant to Article 10 of the Czech Constitution; as such, it enjoys priority application over national laws, in this particular case the Commercial Code.[119] Besides, Article 41(1) of the Czech Constitution leads to the same conclusion, meaning that the period of limitation in the CMR Convention[120] applies to all claims relating to the contract of carriage, as well as any claims materially related to the parties to the contract of carriage or the international carriage of goods.[121] **(2)** Hence, the decisive criterion for the assessment of the duration and running of the period of limitation, the lapse of which means that a claim from carriage is barred, is whether or not the carriage falls within the scope of the CMR Convention.[122/123] **(3)** Consequently, the court must in each individual case address the issue of whether the claim – albeit not explicitly provided for in the CMR Convention[124] – is materially related to international carriage or the parties thereto. If the answer is yes, the court shall apply the special rules on limitation in the CMR Convention,[125] regardless of whether or not the requested claim is also provided for in the relevant national law (in the laws of national origin). **(4)** But the rules on limitation incorporated in the CMR Convention[126] are not applicable to any and all claims from international contracts of carriage.[127] **(5)** If the rules clearly provide for the standard application of the limitation of actions, restricted to the proceedings for a declaratory judgment, this is again reflected in the consequences of a party's failure to exercise their right by the stipulated deadline, consisting in the impairment of the right,

---

[118] Decree of the Ministry of Foreign Affairs No. 11/1975 Coll. on the Convention on the Contract for the International Carriage of Goods by Road (CMR).

[119] Act No. 513/1991 Coll., the Commercial Code.

[120] Decree of the Ministry of Foreign Affairs No. 11/1975 Coll. on the Convention on the Contract for the International Carriage of Goods by Road (CMR).

[121] See PAVEL SEDLÁČEK, ÚMLUVA CMR: (komentář): MEZINÁRODNÍ SILNIČNÍ NÁKLADNÍ DOPRAVA – SOUDNÍ ROZHODNUTÍ – VÝKLAD JEDNOTLIVÝCH USTANOVENÍ [title in translation – CMR CONVENTION: (A COMMENTARY): INTERNATIONAL CARRIAGE OF GOODS BY ROAD – COURT DECISIONS – INTERPRETATION OF THE INDIVIDUAL PROVISIONS], Prague: Vox (2009), et. 530 et seq.

[122] Decree of the Ministry of Foreign Affairs No. 11/1975 Coll. on the Convention on the Contract for the International Carriage of Goods by Road (CMR).

[123] See also Judgment of the Supreme Court of the Czech Republic, Case No. 32 Odo 53/2002 of 23 January 2003.

[124] Decree of the Ministry of Foreign Affairs No. 11/1975 Coll. on the Convention on the Contract for the International Carriage of Goods by Road (CMR).

[125] Decree of the Ministry of Foreign Affairs No. 11/1975 Coll. on the Convention on the Contract for the International Carriage of Goods by Road (CMR).

[126] Decree of the Ministry of Foreign Affairs No. 11/1975 Coll. on the Convention on the Contract for the International Carriage of Goods by Road (CMR).

[127] Cf. also Judgment of the Supreme Court, Case No. 32 Odo 805/2002 of 28 January 2004.

i.e. the fact that the claim made in court will not be awarded by the court in these proceedings (provided that the intervenor raises the relevant objection). **(6)** The CMR Convention[128] does not address the issue of the time limit within which the right – not subject to such impairment – can be presented in court for enforcement if the right had already been awarded in the proceedings for a declaratory judgment. **(7)** If instruments such as the "suspension of the period of limitation or interruption of limitation of actions" should (could) be available in such cases, it should be noted that Article 32(3) of the CMR Convention[129] refers to the "law of the court or tribunal seised of the case". **(8)** The connecting factor is a particular fact material for the given type of legal relationships or issues identified in the scope of the conflict-of-laws rule that is determinative of the subsequent choice of law that should be applied to the legal relationship. At the same time, Section 10(1) of the Private International Law Act[130] is clearly a general provision, while Section 10(2)(c) is a special provision. In other words, Section 10(2)(c) of the Private International Law Act[131] represents a special connecting factor that provides the contents of the connecting factor pursuant to Section 10(1) of the Private International Law Act for certain types of legal relationships.[132] If a fact is found that can be applied to establish the factor, the special factor is used instead of the default one, the former thus supplementing and particularising the latter. The accomplished aim is the application of the law with a closer connection to the legal relationships falling within the scope of the said conflict-of-laws rule, because the special conflict-of-laws rule has a more restrictive scope extracted from the scope of the default conflict-of-laws rule.[133] **(9)** The choice of the "appropriate" law in view of the facts of any individual case depends on the reasoned consideration of the court, respectful of the will of the legislature (explicitly

---

[128] Decree of the Ministry of Foreign Affairs No. 11/1975 Coll. on the Convention on the Contract for the International Carriage of Goods by Road (CMR).
[129] Decree of the Ministry of Foreign Affairs No. 11/1975 Coll. on the Convention on the Contract for the International Carriage of Goods by Road (CMR).
[130] Section 10(1) of Act No. 97/1963 Coll., on Private International Law and Procedure (cit., approximate translation): *"(1) In the absence of the parties' choice of the applicable law, their relationships shall be governed by the law the application of which conforms with a reasonable arrangement of the relationship."* This Act was replaced by Act No. 91/2012 Coll., on Private International Law, with effect from 01 January 2014.
[131] Section 10(2)(c) of Act No. 97/1963 Coll., on Private International Law and Procedure (cit., approximate translation): *"(2) In view of the above: (c) transportation contracts (contracts of carriage, shipping contracts, etc.) are usually governed by the law of the place where the carrier or forwarder has their registered office or residence when the contract is being entered into"*
[132] Section 10(1) of Act No. 97/1963 Coll., on Private International Law and Procedure (approximate translation cited above). This Act was replaced by Act No. 91/2012 Coll., on Private International Law, with effect from 01 January 2014.
[133] See ZDENĚK KUČERA, MEZINÁRODNÍ PRÁVO SOUKROMÉ [title in translation – PRIVATE INTERNATIONAL LAW], Brno: Doplněk (7th ed. 2009), et. 128.

incorporated in the wording of Section 10(1) and (2) of the Private International Law Act[134]), and the applied linguistic and systematic interpretation method. **(10)** If the courts of general jurisdiction chose Czech law as the applicable law by reference to Section 10(2)(c) of the Private International Law Act,[135] arguing that the judgment debtor had its registered office in the territory of the Czech Republic at the time at which the contract was entered into (and throughout the duration thereof) and at the time of the court proceedings, and simultaneously found no circumstances justifying the application of the general connecting factor in Section 10(1), the courts' opinion complies with the above considerations. **(11)** Having said that, the enforcement of the foreign decision is unquestionably subject to the same requirements as the enforcement of a domestic decision. The key point is that such proceedings are governed by the law of the state where the enforcement is conducted. Such proceedings are governed exclusively by the domestic laws on enforcement proceedings conducted by the court enforcement officer and enforcement proceedings conducted by a private bailiff (*lex fori* principle). **(12)** Naturally, this must also apply to the domestic provision of Section 268(1) of the Code of Civil Procedure,[136] which provides for the discontinuation of the enforcement proceedings, including Section 268(1)(h) of the Code of Civil Procedure,[137] which requires the discontinuation of the enforcement proceedings if enforcement is prohibited due to any other grounds preventing the enforcement of the decision. According to the consistent (domestic) case-law, such "other grounds" include the situation in which the right, the enforcement of which is sought, is barred due to the limitation

---

[134] Section 10(1) and (2) of Act No. 97/1963 Coll., on Private International Law and Procedure (approximate translation cited above). This Act was replaced by Act No. 91/2012 Coll., on Private International Law, with effect from 01 January 2014.

[135] Section 10(2)(c) of Act No. 97/1963 Coll., on Private International Law and Procedure (approximate translation cited above).

[136] Section 268(1) of Act No. 99/1963 Coll., Code of Civil Procedure (cit., approximate translation): *"(1) Enforcement proceedings shall be discontinued if (a) the writ of execution was issued despite the fact that the underlying decision has not yet become enforceable; (b) the enforceable instrument has been vacated or has become ineffective after the writ of execution was issued; (c) the discontinuation of the enforcement proceedings was proposed by the party that had lodged the petition for enforcement; (d) the enforcement proceedings affect property that is excluded from enforcement under Sections 321 and 322 or property from which the claim to be enforced cannot be satisfied; (e) the progress of the enforcement proceedings indicates that the proceeds to be generated by the enforcement will not even suffice to cover the costs thereof; (f) a final decision has been issued to the extent that the enforcement proceedings affect property to which a person has rights that prohibit enforcement (Section 267); (g) after the decision was rendered, the right awarded thereunder has been extinguished, unless the enforcement has already been completed; if the right was awarded by a default judgment, the enforcement proceedings will be discontinued even if the right had been extinguished before the judgment was rendered; (h) the enforcement is inadmissible for any other grounds prohibiting enforcement of the decision."*

[137] Section 268(1)(h) of Act No. 99/1963 Coll., Code of Civil Procedure (approximate translation cited above).

of actions and the respondent's corresponding objection. **(13)** The discontinuation of the enforcement proceedings pursuant to Section 268(1)(h) of the Code of Civil Procedure[138] as a result of the respondent invoking the limitation requires that the argument be similarly grounded in the law of the state of the enforcement court (*lex fori*). **(14)** Parties to international legal relationships must inherently count on the fact that the law applied to their particular case will not be "their" law, but the law of the foreign person or entity with whom they formed the respective legal relationship, even if the latter appeared "unusual" from the perspective of "domestic" law.

9.35. **Resolution of the Supreme Court of the Czech Republic, Case No. 20 Cdo 1722/2010 of 27 October 2011:[139] [payment order; enforcement proceedings; remedies against an enforceable decision] (1)** If a judgment issued by the Regional Court in Munich I [Germany] is enforceable in the country of origin and if the formalities stipulated in Article 41 of the Brussels I Regulation were completed, the judgment must be declared enforceable in the territory of the Czech Republic. **(2)** The judgment debtor may challenge the enforceability of the decision in the court that made the underlying judgment, using the remedies afforded to the judgment debtor by the national law in the country of origin.[140] **(3)** Section 254(5) of the Code of Civil Procedure[141] further stipulates that appeals against decisions issued in enforcement proceedings are not subject to the restriction on new facts and evidence. However, the appellate court will only have regard to new facts and evidence in such cases if they were invoked by a party in the appellate proceedings.[142] **(4)** Despite the fact that the judgment debtor argued in their appeal that the application for a

---

[138] Section 268(1)(h) of Act No. 99/1963 Coll., Code of Civil Procedure (approximate translation cited above).

[139] Preceding decisions in the case: (i) Resolution of the Municipal Court in Prague [Czech Republic], Case No. 18 Co 477/2009 – 98 of 12 November 2009, (ii) Resolution of the District Court for Prague 3 [Czech Republic], Case No. 34 E 1464/2008 – 20 of 09 March 2009, (iii) Default Judgment of the Regional Court of Munich I [Germany], Case No. 15 O 8488/07 of 02 January 2008, and (iv) Resolution on the determination of the costs of the Regional Court of Munich I [Germany], Case No. 15 O 8488/07 of 08 February 2008.

[140] See the reasoning in the resolution of the Supreme Court of the Czech Republic in Case No. 5180/2008 of 24 March 2011, and Case No. 20 Cdo 4154/2008 of 07 February 2011, in which the court has held that this procedure, as the recitals to the Brussels I Regulation suggest, is based on the principle of mutual trust in the administration of justice in the Community (the court in the country where enforcement is sought trusts the accuracy of the information concerning the enforceability of the decision that the court in the country of origin of the decision filled out in the certificate of enforceability).

[141] Section 254(5) of Act No. 99/1963 Coll., Code of Civil Procedure (cit., approximate translation): (5) "*It is permitted to include new facts and evidence in the appeal. The facts invoked against the writ of execution may only include those that are relevant for the opening of the enforcement proceedings; any other facts shall be disregarded by the court and any appeal that contains only such facts will be dismissed.*"

[142] See also Resolution of the Supreme Court of the Czech Republic, Case No. 20 Cdo 2207/2004 of 30 June 2005, published in: Soudní judikatura, Prague: C. H. Beck, 2005, No. 10, Case No. 166, or in the reasoning in the resolution of the Supreme Court of the Czech Republic in Case No. 20 Cdo 3384/2008 of 17 August 2010.

payment order and "other materials concerning the dispute" were being **delivered** to the debtor to a non-existing address or, as applicable, that they were being delivered belatedly and, in consequence thereof, the debtor could not make a proper defence, but at the same time the debtor failed to argue in the appellate proceedings that the debtor had employed a remedy to eliminate this alleged procedural flaw, the appellate court could not assess whether or not the grounds exist for a refusal to recognise the underlying default judgment. Having said that, the appellate court was not obliged, as corroborated by Section 254(5)[143] and Section 212a(3) of the Code of Civil Procedure,[144] to examine the fact (decisive for an assessment of the case from the perspective of Article 34(2) of the Brussels I Regulation) of its own motion, but indeed, only upon an objection raised by the judgment debtor in the appeal.[145] **(5)** The cassation appeal is also not rendered admissible under Section 238(1)(c) of the Code of Civil Procedure[146] by an objection that the underlying judgment is not enforceable in the Member State of origin because the judgment debtor had fulfilled their commitment before the payment order was issued; the reason is that Article 45(1) of the Brussels I Regulation stipulates that a foreign judgment may under no circumstances be reviewed as to its substance.

9.36. **Resolution of the Supreme Court of the Czech Republic, Case No. 20 Cdo 3282/2020 of 11 May 2021:[147] [discontinuation of the enforcement proceedings, enforcement of a foreign court's decision; arbitral award; application of international treaties; court jurisdiction] (1)** The Treaty between the

---

[143] Section 254(5) of Act No. 99/1963 Coll., Code of Civil Procedure (approximate translation cited above).

[144] Section 212a(3) of Act No. 99/1963 Coll., Code of Civil Procedure (cit., approximate translation): *"(3) The appellate court may only have regard to new facts or evidence (Sections 205a and 211a) if they were claimed."*

[145] Concerning this issue, cf. Judgment of the Constitutional Court of the Czech Republic, Case No. I. ÚS 709/05 of 25 April 2006, already invoked by the appellate court, in which the following conclusion was articulated – *inter alia* (cit., approximate translation): *"The appellate court hearing the appeal against the decision on the declaration of enforceability of a decision is obliged to ascertain whether there exist any grounds for the refusal of the recognition of the foreign court judgment. However, this obligation of the court is not an ex officio obligation, because the court is only obliged to perform such examination if any of the parties to the proceedings raises the appropriate objections; the litigant's first opportunity to raise such objections was in the appeal."*

[146] Section 238(1)(c) of Act No. 99/1963 Coll., Code of Civil Procedure (cit., approximate translation): *"(1) A cassation appeal pursuant to Section 237 is not allowed (c) against judgments and resolutions issued in proceedings the subject matter of which was, at the time when the decision was made that contained the contested operative part, monetary performance not exceeding CZK 50,000, including enforcement proceedings, with the exception of relationships from consumer contracts and employment relationships; for this purpose, interest and other dues accruing to the claim shall be disregarded [...]."*

[147] Preceding decisions in the case: (i) Resolution of the Regional Court in Pilsen [Czech Republic], Case No. 11 Co 163/2019-493 of 17 January 2020, (ii) Resolution of the District Court in Karlovy Vary [Czech Republic], Case No. 27 EXE 158/2017-412 of 08 April 2019, (iii) Judgment of the Central District Court in Voronezh [Russian Federation], Case No. 2-4667/2010 of 23 December 2010, and (iv) Resolution of the Voronezh District Court [Russian Federation], Case 33-2749 of 19 May 2011.

Slovak Republic and the Czech Republic on Legal Assistance provided by Judicial Authorities[148] does not offer any alternative that would render a foreign arbitral award enforceable in enforcement proceedings conducted by a private bailiff on the basis of priority in application; on the contrary, the wording of the Treaty only envisages enforcement through enforcement proceedings conducted by the court enforcement officer, which clearly follows from the linguistic interpretation of Article 24 of the Treaty, stipulating that a petition for the recognition and enforcement of a decision shall be submitted directly to the competent court of the Contracting Party in the territory of which the decision is to be recognised and enforced. **(2)** While Subsection (3) of the same Article of the Treaty stipulates that the court shall limit its review to the fulfilment of the requirements listed in Articles 22 and 23 of the Treaty and if the court ascertains that the requirements are fulfilled, the court recognizes the decision or issues a writ of execution thereof, the provision – again – explicitly refers to the court, and the court alone, as the public authority eligible for hearing the case and enforcing the foreign decision. **(3)** The court has no reason to depart from this conclusion if Article 24(1) of the Treaty between the Czech Republic and the Slovak Republic on Legal Assistance provided by Judicial Authorities[149] is identical to Article 54(1) of the Treaty between the Czechoslovak Socialist Republic and the Union of Soviet Socialist Republics on Legal Assistance,[150] in that the petition for recognition and enforcement shall be lodged with a court (the district court accepted the filing of the petition directly with the Czech court); and the wording of Article 24(3) of the Treaty between the Czech Republic and the Slovak Republic is identical to Article 56(2) of the Treaty between the Czechoslovak Socialist Republic and the Union of Soviet Socialist Republics on Legal Assistance,[151] in that the court that rules on the recognition of the decision and issues the writ of execution shall only ascertain whether the requirements contained in Articles 22 and 23 of the Treaty between the Czech

---

[148] Treaty between the Czech Republic and the Slovak Republic on Mutual Legal Assistance Provided by Judicial Authorities and the Regulation of Certain Legal Relations in Civil and Criminal Matters, promulgated in the Czech Republic under No. 209/1993 Coll.

[149] Treaty between the Czech Republic and the Slovak Republic on Mutual Legal Assistance Provided by Judicial Authorities and the Regulation of Certain Legal Relations in Civil and Criminal Matters, promulgated in the Czech Republic under No. 209/1993 Coll.

[150] Treaty between the Czechoslovak Socialist Republic and the Union of Soviet Socialist Republics on Legal Assistance and Legal Relations in Civil, Family and Criminal Matters of 12 August 1982, promulgated in Decree of the Ministry of Foreign Affairs No. 95/1983 Coll.

[151] Treaty between the Czechoslovak Socialist Republic and the Union of Soviet Socialist Republics on Legal Assistance and Legal Relations in Civil, Family and Criminal Matters of 12 August 1982, promulgated in Decree of the Ministry of Foreign Affairs No. 95/1983 Coll.

Republic and the Slovak Republic are fulfilled, and if the court ascertains that the requirements are fulfilled, the court issues the writ of execution. Finally, both Treaties also share the same wording of Article 1 concerning the equal protection of the rights of citizens of both Contracting Parties.

9.37. **Resolution of the Supreme Court of the Czech Republic, Case No. 20 Cdo 1165/2016 of 03 November 2016:**[152] **[enforcement proceedings, recognition of foreign decisions]** **(1)** The legal assessment of a case is generally incorrect if the appellate court assessed the case pursuant to a legal rule that does not apply to the facts of the case ascertained by the court, or if the court correctly identified the applicable legal rule, but did not interpret it correctly or did not apply it correctly to the facts of the case. **(2)** Decree No. 74/1959 of the Ministry of Foreign Affairs of 06 November 1959 (in conjunction with Article I of the Constitutional Act No. 4/1993 Coll., on Measures Relating to the Dissolution of the Czech and Slovak Federal Republic) has incorporated the Convention on the Recognition and Enforcement of Foreign Arbitral Awards, signed on 10 June 1958 in New York, in the law of the Czech Republic. **(3)** Article III of the Convention[153] stipulates that each Contracting State shall recognize arbitral awards as binding and shall enforce them in accordance with the rules of procedure of the territory where the award is relied upon, under the conditions laid down in the following articles (Articles IV and V). In the Czech Republic, such rules of procedure include the Code of Civil Procedure[154] and the Enforcement Code.[155] **(iv)** The Convention on the Recognition and Enforcement of Foreign Arbitral Awards[156] belongs to directly applicable international treaties; arbitral awards that fall within the scope of the Convention are consequently recognised as instruments enforceable in courts without any special proceedings. This fact alone does not mean that they could also be an eligible instrument as an *instrument enforceable in enforcement proceedings conducted by a private bailiff*. The answer to this question requires an analysis of Section 37(2) of the Enforcement Code,[157] which

---

[152] Preceding decisions in the case: (i) Resolution of the Regional Court in Brno [Czech Republic], Case No. 20 Co 281/2015-225 of 19 October 2015, (ii) Resolution of the District Court in Vyškov [Czech Republic], Case No. 10 EXE 1107/2013-117 of 10 April 2014, and (iii) Arbitral Awards of the Refined Sugar Association in London, Case 2274, 2275 and 2276 of 13 November 2012.

[153] Convention on the Recognition and Enforcement of Foreign Arbitral Awards, signed on 10 June 1958 in New York, promulgated in Decree of the Minister of Foreign Affairs No. 74/1959 Coll.

[154] Act No. 99/1963 Coll., Code of Civil Procedure.

[155] Act No. 120/2001 Coll., on Private Bailiffs and Enforcement Proceedings (Enforcement Code).

[156] Convention on the Recognition and Enforcement of Foreign Arbitral Awards, signed on 10 June 1958 in New York, promulgated in Decree of the Minister of Foreign Affairs No. 74/1959 Coll.

[157] Section 37(2) of Act No. 120/2001 Coll., on Private Bailiffs and Enforcement Proceedings (Enforcement

clearly stipulates that this would only be possible if a decision "on recognition" existed. **(5)** The logic of the preceding points is that, contrary to the order opening *court enforcement* of a foreign decision and the associated mandatory requirement of providing reasons for the decision, here – in "enforcement proceedings conducted by a private bailiff" – the fulfilment of this requirement is impossible.[158]

9.38. Resolution of the Supreme Court of the Czech Republic, Case No. 20 Cdo 5882/2016 of 16 August 2017:[159] **[enforcement proceedings conducted by a private bailiff; application of the New York Convention (1958); relation between the New York Convention (1958) and a bilateral legal assistance treaty] (1)** Whereas the New York Convention[160] regulates a specific subject matter, the Treaty between the Czech Republic and the Slovak Republic on Legal Assistance provided by Judicial Authorities[161] covers a whole range of issues (including the recognition of arbitral awards). Hence, the subject matter is not identical, as the contents of the rules only partially overlap. In such case, it is necessary to apply the *lex specialis derogat legi generali* rule, which requires the application of the New York Convention (1958).[162] **(2)** At the same time, however, it is necessary to keep in mind Article VII of the New York Convention (1958),[163] which in Paragraph 1 stipulates that the provisions of the present Convention shall not affect the validity of multilateral or bilateral agreements concerning the recognition and enforcement of arbitral awards entered into by the Contracting States, nor deprive any interested party of any right that they may have to avail themself of an arbitral award in the manner and to the extent allowed by the law or the treaties of the country where such award is sought to be relied upon. **(3)**

Code) (cit., approximate translation): *"(2) The judgment creditor may petition for enforcement pursuant to this Act if the judgment debtor fails to voluntarily fulfil the obligation stipulated by the enforceable instrument under this Act."*

[158] See Resolution of the Supreme Court of the Czech Republic, Case No. 20 Cdo 4663/2015 of 18 October 2016, and especially (ii) Resolution of the Supreme Court of the Czech Republic, Case No. 20 Cdo 1349/2016 of 01 July 2016.

[159] Preceding decisions in the case: (i) Resolution of the Regional Court in Brno [Czech Republic], Case No. 20 Co 559/2015 of 26 September 2016, (ii) Resolution of the private bailiff, Case No. 067 EX 14954/15-15 of 15 June 2015, and (iii) Arbitral Award of the Royal Development Arbitral Tribunal, Case No. RD/43/2015.

[160] Convention on the Recognition and Enforcement of Foreign Arbitral Awards, signed on 10 June 1958 in New York, promulgated in Decree of the Minister of Foreign Affairs No. 74/1959 Coll.

[161] Treaty between the Czech Republic and the Slovak Republic on Mutual Legal Assistance Provided by Judicial Authorities and the Regulation of Certain Legal Relations in Civil and Criminal Matters, promulgated under No. 209/1993 Coll.

[162] See NADĚŽDA ROZEHNALOVÁ, ROZHODČÍ ŘÍZENÍ V MEZINÁRODNÍM A VNITROSTÁTNÍM OBCHODNÍM STYKU [title in translation – RBITRATION IN INTERNATIONAL AND NATIONAL COMMERCE], Prague: ASPI (2nd ed. 2008), et. 94–97.

[163] Convention on the Recognition and Enforcement of Foreign Arbitral Awards, signed on 10 June 1958 in New York (Decree of the Minister of Foreign Affairs No. 74/1959 Coll.).

Article VII of the New York Convention (1958)[164] hereby incorporates the most favourable treatment principle, which allows the application of another contractual instrument or national law, in this particular case the Treaty between the Czech Republic and the Slovak Republic on Legal Assistance provided by Judicial Authorities,[165] if the latter is more liberal with respect to the recognition of the arbitral award, i.e. if it leads to the easier recognition and enforcement of a foreign arbitral award. Consequently, the legal assistance treaty can be applied, but only if the above requirements are fulfilled. **(4)** If the arbitral award was issued by an arbitral tribunal in the Slovak Republic established pursuant to Section 12 of Act No. 244/2002 Coll. [Act of the Slovak Republic], the enforcement of the arbitral award cannot be denied as being contrary to public policy merely based on the fact that the tribunal is not a permanent arbitral institution in terms of Section 13 of the Arbitration Act[166] (*Note*: (a) means Act No. 216/1994 Coll. and (b) which meets the requirement of a "transparent" choice of arbitrators).[167] **(5)** An arbitral award that the Contracting State enforces in accordance with the rules of procedure applicable in its territory (Article III of the New York Convention (1958)[168]) cannot be enforced in enforcement proceedings conducted by a private bailiff, unless a decision on recognition of the award was issued in terms of Section 37(2) of the Enforcement Code,[169] as

---

[164] Convention on the Recognition and Enforcement of Foreign Arbitral Awards, signed on 10 June 1958 in New York (Decree of the Minister of Foreign Affairs No. 74/1959 Coll.).

[165] Treaty between the Czech Republic and the Slovak Republic on Mutual Legal Assistance Provided by Judicial Authorities and the Regulation of Certain Legal Relations in Civil and Criminal Matters, promulgated under No. 209/1993 Coll.

[166] Section 13 of Act No. 216/1994 Coll., on Arbitration and Enforcement of Arbitral Awards (cit., approximate translation):*"(1) Permanent arbitral institutions may only be established by another law or only if another law expressly allows their establishment. (2) Permanent arbitral institutions can issue their own statutes and rules, which must be published in the Business Journal;[3] these statutes and rules may determine the method of appointment and the number of arbitrators and may stipulate that the arbitrators shall be selected from a list administered by the permanent arbitral institution. The statutes and rules may also determine how the arbitrators shall conduct the proceedings and render their decisions, as well as resolve other issues connected with the activities of the permanent arbitral institution and the arbitrators, including rules regulating the costs of proceedings and fees for the arbitrators. (3) If the parties agreed on the jurisdiction of a particular permanent arbitral institution and failed to agree otherwise in the arbitration agreement, they shall be deemed to have submitted to the regulations specified in Subsection (2), as applicable on the day of commencement of the proceedings before the permanent arbitral institution. (4) No entity may carry out its activities using a name that evokes a misleading impression that the entity is a permanent arbitral institution under this law, unless a different law or regulation or an international agreement integrated in the legal system authorizes the entity to use the name."*

[167] A conclusion formulated in the resolution of the Supreme Court of the Czech Republic in Case No. 20 Cdo 676/2016 of 13 December 2016.

[168] Convention on the Recognition and Enforcement of Foreign Arbitral Awards, signed on 10 June 1958 in New York (Decree of the Minister of Foreign Affairs No. 74/1959 Coll.).

[169] Section 37(2) of Act No. 120/2001 Coll., on Private Bailiffs and Enforcement Proceedings (Enforcement Code) (cit., approximate translation): *"(2) The judgment creditor may petition for enforcement pursuant to this Act if the judgment debtor fails to voluntarily fulfil the obligation stipulated by the enforceable instrument under this Act."*

applicable until 31 December 2013.[170] **(6)** If Article III of the New York Convention (1958)[171] stipulates that each Contracting State shall recognize arbitral awards as binding and enforce them in accordance with the rules of procedure of the territory where the award is relied upon, under the conditions laid down in Article IV and V of the New York Convention (1958), it is necessary to consider the rules of the Code of Civil Procedure[172] and of the Enforcement Code.[173] **(7)** The fact alone that the New York Convention (1958)[174] belongs to directly applicable international treaties and that the arbitral awards that fall within its scope are recognised as enforceable instruments *ipso facto* does not mean that they could also constitute *any* eligible instruments, in this particular case *instruments enforceable in enforcement proceedings conducted by a private bailiff*; an answer to this question requires another reference to Section 37(2) of the Enforcement Code,[175] which stipulates that this would be possible – for enforcement proceedings conducted by a private bailiff – only if a decision "on recognition" existed. **(8)** But the most relevant factor is that enforcement proceedings conducted by a private bailiff are not opened by a writ of execution, because the appointment of the private bailiff to conduct the enforcement proceedings is not a decision, contains no reasons and cannot be challenged.[176] **(9)** Act No. 91/2012 Coll., on Private International Law,[177] does not apply if any international treaties exist that provide for the recognition and enforcement of the arbitral award and which are binding on both States;[178] *however, this does not mean "never"* – the Act does not apply only if an international treaty provides otherwise.[179] **(10)** If an international treaty contains a reference to national laws, it is not out of the question that even Act No. 91/2012 Coll., on Private International Law,[180] could be "back in the game", at least as an interpretation tool for other national

---

[170] A conclusion formulated in the resolution of the Supreme Court of the Czech Republic in Case No. 20 Cdo 1165/16 of 03 November 2016.

[171] Convention on the Recognition and Enforcement of Foreign Arbitral Awards, signed on 10 June 1958 in New York (Decree of the Minister of Foreign Affairs No. 74/1959 Coll.).

[172] Act No. 99/1963 Coll., the Code of Civil Procedure.

[173] Act No. 120/2001 Coll., on Private Bailiffs and Enforcement Proceedings (Enforcement Code).

[174] Convention on the Recognition and Enforcement of Foreign Arbitral Awards, signed on 10 June 1958 in New York (Decree of the Minister of Foreign Affairs No. 74/1959 Coll.).

[175] Section 37(2) of Act No. 120/2001 Coll., on Private Bailiffs and Enforcement Proceedings (Enforcement Code) (approximate translation cited above).

[176] See Resolution of the Supreme Court of the Czech Republic, Case No. 20 Cdo 1349/2016 of 01 July 2016.

[177] Act No. 91/2012 Coll., on Private International Law.

[178] See Resolution of the Supreme Court of the Czech Republic, Case No. 26 Cdo 2983/2015 of 07 October 2015.

[179] See Resolution of the Supreme Court of the Czech Republic, Case No. 20 Cdo 2214/2009 of 20 December 2011.

[180] Act No. 91/2012 Coll., on Private International Law.

laws. **(11)** Indeed, one may even advocate a more weighty argument that there are no reasons why Section 122(2) of the Private International Law Act[181] could not stand (if its Subsection (1) stands), both under the New York Convention (1958)[182] and under the Treaty between the Czech Republic and the Slovak Republic on Legal Assistance provided by Judicial Authorities.[183] **(12)** The appointment of the private bailiff pursuant to the Enforcement Code could not constitute the recognition of the foreign decision, because the appointment does not concern the relevant requirements for the recognition and enforcement of foreign instruments and, as noted on multiple occasions, it is not a "writ of execution", i.e. a "decision" whereby the enforcement is ordered – albeit only by "being taken into consideration".[184] **(13)** It is specifically worth highlighting that *this is the reason why* "appointment of the private bailiff" is an instrument that inherently cannot constitute an authorisation to implement the procedures envisaged both in Article V of the New York Convention (1958)[185] and in Article 23 of the Treaty between the Czech Republic and the Slovak Republic on Legal Assistance provided by Judicial Authorities,[186] the framework of which allows the enforcement of the arbitral award to be denied, subject to the requirements stipulated therein. The court

---

[181] Section 122(2) of Act No. 91/2012 Coll., on Private International Law (cit., approximate translation): *"(2) Foreign arbitral awards can be recognised by a special decision issued upon a motion. The court with territorial jurisdiction to grant the recognition of the judgment is the district court of the party who seeks the recognition or, if not applicable, the district court in whose district the fact occurred or could occur that is material for the recognition, unless this Act or any other legislation indicates otherwise. Recognition of the award pronounced by the court shall take the form of a judgment; no hearing needs to be summoned."*

[182] Convention on the Recognition and Enforcement of Foreign Arbitral Awards, signed on 10 June 1958 in New York (Decree of the Minister of Foreign Affairs No. 74/1959 Coll.).

[183] Treaty between the Czech Republic and the Slovak Republic on Mutual Legal Assistance Provided by Judicial Authorities and the Regulation of Certain Legal Relations in Civil and Criminal Matters, promulgated under No. 209/1993 Coll.

[184] Resolution of the Supreme Court of the Czech Republic, Case No. 20 Cdo 1349/2016 of 01 July 2016.

[185] Convention on the Recognition and Enforcement of Foreign Arbitral Awards, signed on 10 June 1958 in New York (Decree of the Minister of Foreign Affairs No. 74/1959 Coll.).

[186] Article 23 of the Treaty between the Czech Republic and the Slovak Republic on Mutual Legal Assistance Provided by Judicial Authorities and the Regulation of Certain Legal Relations in Civil and Criminal Matters, promulgated in the Czech Republic under No. 209/1993 Coll. (cit., approximate translation): *"Decisions specified in Article 22 of this Treaty shall be recognised and enforced if: (a) the decision is final and enforceable according to a confirmation issued by the authority that rendered the decision; provisionally enforceable decisions and enforceable interim measures can be recognised and enforced in the territory of the requested Contracting Party whether or not they can be challenged by a regular remedy, (b) the judicial authorities of the other Contracting Party did not render any decision that had become final earlier or did not recognise and enforce any decision of a third country in the same matter and between the same parties, (c) the party had the opportunity to duly enter an appearance, i.e. the party especially (without limitation) received a due and timely summons to a hearing in compliance with the law of the Contracting Party where the proceedings were held and the decision was duly served on the party with instructions about the possibility of appeal and, if the party suffered from any procedural incapacity, the party was duly represented, (d) the proceedings did not fall within the exclusive jurisdiction of the authorities of the Contracting Party in whose territory recognition is sought, (e) the Contracting Party, in the territory of which recognition or enforcement is sought, is convinced that the recognition or enforcement will not jeopardise its sovereignty or security and will not be contrary to its public policy."*

intervention provided for in Section 43a(3) and (6) of the Enforcement Code[187] has no effect on this conclusion. **(14)** It does not conflict with the New York Convention (1958)[188] or with the Treaty between the Czech Republic and the Slovak Republic on Legal Assistance provided by Judicial Authorities,[189] because the principles enshrined in both international agreements do not apply (in their entirety) in Czech law only with respect to one of the two regimes provided for the enforcement of arbitral awards, namely enforcement proceedings conducted by a private bailiff. The principles remain applicable with respect to the other regime, i.e. enforcement proceedings conducted by the court enforcement officer. **(15)** If the enforcement of a foreign decision is governed by Sections 14 to 16 of Act No. 91/2012 Coll., on Private International Law,[190] it can only be implemented in enforcement proceedings conducted by the court enforcement officer. Conversely, enforcement proceedings conducted by a private bailiff under the Enforcement Code[191] may in such case only be implemented on the basis of a foreign decision that was recognised on the basis of a special decision of a Czech court pursuant to Section 16(2) of the Private International Law Act,[192] i.e. a judgment, which must contain reasons.[193] **(16)** The Treaty between the Czech Republic and the Slovak Republic on Legal Assistance provided by Judicial Authorities[194] does not offer any alternative that would render a foreign arbitral award enforceable in the enforcement proceedings conducted by a private bailiff

---

[187] Section 43a(3) and (6) of Act No. 120/2001 Coll., on Private Bailiffs and Enforcement Proceedings (Enforcement Code) (cit., approximate translation): *"(3) The court shall grant the authorisation within 15 days if all requirements stipulated by the Act are satisfied. If the court received the petition for authorisation together with a motion for declaration of enforceability or recognition, the court shall grant the authorisation after the court had ruled on the motion for declaration of enforceability or for recognition. The decision on declaration of enforceability or on recognition shall be made by the enforcement court without a hearing. The resolution or judgment on the declaration of enforceability or on recognition must contain reasons. (6) Unless all requirements are met that are stipulated by law for the conduct of the enforcement proceedings, the court instructs the private bailiff to reject or dismiss the petition for enforcement in whole or in part, or to discontinue the enforcement proceedings. The private bailiff is bound by the instruction."*

[188] Convention on the Recognition and Enforcement of Foreign Arbitral Awards, signed on 10 June 1958 in New York (Decree of the Minister of Foreign Affairs No. 74/1959 Coll.).

[189] Treaty between the Czech Republic and the Slovak Republic on Mutual Legal Assistance Provided by Judicial Authorities and the Regulation of Certain Legal Relations in Civil and Criminal Matters, promulgated under No. 209/1993 Coll.

[190] Sections 14 – 16 of Act No. 91/2012 Coll., on Private International Law (approximate translation cited above).

[191] Act No. 120/2001 Coll., on Private Bailiffs and Enforcement Proceedings (Enforcement Code).

[192] Section 16(2) of Act No. 91/2012 Coll., on Private International Law (approximate translation cited above).

[193] This line of reasoning in the case-law was supported by the resolution of the Supreme Court of the Czech Republic in Case No. 20 Cdo 1349/2016 of 01 July 2016.

[194] Treaty between the Czech Republic and the Slovak Republic on Mutual Legal Assistance Provided by Judicial Authorities and the Regulation of Certain Legal Relations in Civil and Criminal Matters, promulgated under No. 209/1993 Coll.

on the basis of priority in application. On the contrary, the wording of the Treaty only envisages enforcement through enforcement proceedings conducted by a court enforcement officer, which clearly follows from the linguistic interpretation of Article 24 of the Treaty, stipulating that a petition for the recognition and enforcement of a decision shall be submitted directly to the competent court of the Contracting Party in the territory in which the decision is to be recognised and enforced. While Subsection (3) of the same Article of the Treaty stipulates that the court shall limit its review to the fulfilment of the requirements listed in Articles 22 and 23 of this Legal Assistance Treaty, and if the court ascertains that the requirements are fulfilled, the court *recognizes the decision or issues a writ of execution thereof*, the provision – again – explicitly refers to the *court, and the court alone*, as the public authority eligible to hear the case and enforce the foreign decision. **(17)** Conclusions analogous to those in the preceding paragraph can also be inferred from Articles III and IV of the New York Convention (1958).[195]

9.39. **Resolution of the Supreme Court of the Czech Republic, Case No. 20 Cdo 4732/2015 of 01 March 2016:**[196] **[enforcement proceedings; enforceable instrument; enforcement of foreign courts' decisions; penalty for default; interest accrued to an awarded claim; separate determination of the penalty; enforcement of a substitute obligation] (1)** Article 49 of the Brussels I Regulation concerns decisions imposing an obligation to provide non-monetary performance. According to the laws of certain Member States (France and the Benelux countries), the decision then also determines the amount that the judgment debtor must pay to the judgment creditor if the debtor fails to perform under the judgment. **(2)** The penalty can only be enforced in other Member States if the total amount of the penalty was determined by the courts of the Member State of origin. Consequently, these requirements are not fulfilled if, for instance, the decision indicates the amount of the penalty for each individual default on the obligation to provide non-monetary performance, or for each day of default on such performance, and the number of the individual defaults or the duration of the default is only indicated by the judgment creditor

---

[195] Convention on the Recognition and Enforcement of Foreign Arbitral Awards, signed on 10 June 1958 in New York (see Decree of the Minister of Foreign Affairs No. 74/1959 Coll.).

[196] Preceding decisions in the case: (i) Resolution of the Municipal Court in Prague [Czech Republic], Case No. 19 Co 17/2015-61 of 28 August 2015, (ii) Resolution of the District Court for Prague 1 [Czech Republic], Case No. 48 EXE 5502/2014-32 of 06 November 2014, and (iii) Judgment of the Labour Court in Moulins [France], Case No. F 08/00084 of 09 March 2010.

in the petition for the declaration of enforceability. **(3)** Hence, in those Member States that are familiar with the concept of *"astreinte"*, the default on the non-monetary obligation must be followed by a separate decision stipulating the final total amount of the penalty; depending on the circumstances, the amount may be even lower than the amount of the penalty calculated according to the original decision, because the latter commonly contains an exaggerated amount of the penalty or merely a threat of penalty.[197] **(4)** The decision on enforceability of the enforceable instrument cannot precede the decision of the court of the Member State of origin on the final total amount of the penalty for failure to meet the non-monetary obligation stipulated by the enforceable instrument. [*From the factual and legal findings*]: The appellate court making the decision on the declaration of enforceability of a foreign enforceable instrument limited its decision in the given case to the assessment of the formal requirements of the enforceable instrument and an examination of the existence of the grounds for refusing enforceability pursuant to Articles 34 and 35 of the Brussels I Regulation. But the court failed to notice that the operative part of the enforceable instrument contains (*inter alia*) an order to the judgment debtor to provide non-monetary performance and, should the judgment debtor fail to perform the obligation, a secondary obligation to pay to the judgment creditor a penalty for each day of delay with the performance. In view of the fact that the enforceable instrument in the given case only determined the daily rate of the penalty for a default on the stipulated non-monetary obligation, the appellate court should have first requested the judgment creditor to present a decision of the court of the Member State of origin of the original decision, i.e. the State in which the enforceable instrument was issued, in which the final total amount of the penalty was determined, and only then make a decision on the (non)enforceability of the individual operative parts of the enforceable instrument.

9.40. **Resolution of the Supreme Court of the Czech Republic, Case No. 30 Cdo 2361/2011 of 30 September 2014:[198] [enforcement of foreign courts' decisions; document that instituted the proceedings; service of documents; remedy]**
(1) The concept of a document that instituted the proceedings

197 VIKTOR VAŠKE, UZNÁNÍ A VÝKON CIZÍCH ROZHODNUTÍ V ČESKÉ REPUBLICE [title in translation – RECOGNITION AND ENFORCEMENT OF FOREIGN JUDGMENTS IN THE CZECH REPUBLIC], Prague: C. H. Beck (2007), et. 72.
198 Preceding decisions in the case: (i) Resolution of the Regional Court in Brno, Case No. 20 Co 335/2007-44 of 18 January 2008, (ii) Resolution of the Municipal Court in Brno, Case No. 69 Nc 4064/2006-4 of 01 September 2006, and (iii) Default Judgment issued by the Regional Court in Linz, Case No. 5Cg 194/04 f-36 of 20 March 2006.

or an *equivalent document* employed in Article 34(2) of the Brussels I Regulation generally refers to a document(s) that, if served on the respondent in a proper and timely fashion, enables the exercise of rights before an enforceable judgment is issued in the State of dispatch.[199] **(2)** The written materials must contain a document or documents (if they are interconnected in essence) that will enable the respondent to understand the subject matter and the grounds of the action and the fact that court proceedings are pending in which the respondent may exercise their rights either by raising a defence in such proceedings or by challenging the decision issued on the basis of the action by a remedy.[200] **(3)** A document enabling the respondent to exercise their rights by raising a defence in the pending proceedings includes a summons to a hearing; a document enabling the respondent to exercise their rights by filing a remedy is a decision – in this case, a judgment for default issued by the foreign court.

9.41. **Resolution of the Supreme Court of the Czech Republic, Case No. 31 Cdo 2325/2008 of 14 July 2010:**[201] **[enforcement proceedings; enforceable instrument; EU law; enforcement of a foreign court's decision; impediments to recognition and enforcement] (1)** In view of the fact that no bilateral international treaty has been entered into between the Czech Republic and the Federal Republic of Germany, the conditions for the recognition and enforcement of an enforceable instrument must be assessed pursuant to Section 63 of the Private International Law Act.[202] **(2)** Section 48 of the Private International Law Act[203] requires the application of Czech law, specifically the Enforcement Code.[204]

---

[199] Judgment of the European Court of Justice, Case C-474/93, *Hengst Import BV* v. *Anna Maria Campese*.

[200] Judgment of the European Court of Justice, Case C-14/07, *Ingenieurbüro Michael Weiss und Partner GbR* v. *Industrie- und Handelskammer Berlin*, joined party: *Nicholas Grimshaw and Partners Ltd*. See L'UBOMÍR DRÁPAL, JAROSLAV BUREŠ, OBČANSKÝ SOUDNÍ ŘÁD II., § 201-376. KOMENTÁŘ [title in translation – CODE OF CIVIL PROCEDURE II. SECTIONS 201-376. A COMMENTARY], Prague: C.H.Beck (2009), et. 2999.

[201] Preceding decisions in the case: (i) Resolution of the Regional Court in Ostrava, Case No. 9 Co 892/2007 – 139 of 19 November 2007, (ii) Resolution of the District Court in Vsetín – Valašské Meziříčí Office [Czech Republic], Case No. 2 Nc 4459/2005 – 90 of 17 July 2007, (iii) Decision of the District Court in Stuttgart "Vollstreckungsbescheid", Case No. B 594/95 LM of 11 July 1995, and (iv) Judgment of the Regional Court in Heilbronn, Case No. 2 O 2400/96 I of 06 June 1997.

[202] Section 63 of Act No. 97/1963 Coll., on Private International Law and Procedure (cit., approximate translation): *"Decisions of the judicial authorities of a foreign State in matters specified in Section 1, as well as foreign judicial settlements and foreign notarial instruments in such matters (hereafter referred to as 'foreign judgments') have effects in the Czechoslovak Socialist Republic if they have become final pursuant to a confirmation issued by the competent foreign authority and if they have been recognised by Czechoslovak authorities."* This Act was replaced by Act No. 91/2012 Coll., on Private International Law, with effect from 01 January 2014.

[203] Act No. 97/1963 Coll., on Private International Law and Procedure. Czechoslovak courts apply Czechoslovak procedural laws in the proceedings and all parties have equal standing in the exercise of their rights. This Act was replaced by Act No. 91/2012 Coll., on Private International Law, with effect from 01 January 2014.

[204] Act No. 120/2001 Coll., on Private Bailiffs and Enforcement Proceedings and Amending Other Laws (Enforcement Code).

(3) If the effects of a foreign court's decision can be perceived as consistent with Czech laws, and there are no impediments preventing the enforcement thereof stipulated in Section 64 of the Private International Law Act,[205] and if, at the same time, there is reciprocity in the recognition and enforcement of judgments in civil and commercial matters with the respective State, the requirements for ordering enforcement pursuant to Section 44(2) of the Enforcement Code[206] were fulfilled.

| | |

Bibliography:

PETR BŘÍZA, TOMÁŠ BŘICHÁČEK, ZUZANA FIŠEROVÁ, PAVEL HORÁK, LUBOMÍR PTÁČEK, JIŘÍ SVOBODA, ZÁKON O MEZINÁRODNÍM PRÁVU SOUKROMÉM. KOMENTÁŘ [title in translation – PRIVATE INTERNATIONAL LAW ACT. A COMMENTARY], Prague: C. H. Beck (2014).

L'UBOMÍR DRÁPAL, JAROSLAV BUREŠ, OBČANSKÝ SOUDNÍ ŘÁD II., § 201-376. KOMENTÁŘ [title in translation – CODE OF CIVIL PROCEDURE II. SECTIONS 201-376. A COMMENTARY], Prague: C.H.Beck (2009).

Helmut Koziol, Vanessa Wilcox, *Punitive Damages: Common Law and Civil Law Perspectives. Tort and Insurance Law*, 25 SPRINGER 198–199 (2009).

ZDENĚK KUČERA, MEZINÁRODNÍ PRÁVO SOUKROMÉ [title in translation – PRIVATE INTERNATIONAL LAW], Brno: Doplněk (7th ed. 2009).

ZDENĚK KUČERA, LUBOŠ TICHÝ, ZÁKON O MEZINÁRODNÍM PRÁVU SOUKROMÉM A PROCESNÍM. KOMENTÁŘ [title in translation – ACT ON PRIVATE INTERNATIONAL LAW AND PROCEDURE. A COMMENTARY], Prague: Panorama (1989).

---

[205] Section 64 of Act No. 97/1963 Coll., on Private International Law and Procedure (cit., approximate translation): *"Foreign judgments cannot be recognised or enforced if (a) the judgment cannot be recognised due to the exclusive jurisdiction of Czechoslovak authorities or if no authority of a foreign State could conduct the proceedings if the provisions on the jurisdiction of Czechoslovak courts had been applied to the assessment of the foreign authority's jurisdiction; (b) a Czechoslovak authority has already issued a final judgment regarding the same legal relationship or if a final judgment of a third State's authority has already been recognised in the Czechoslovak Socialist Republic, (c) a party to the proceedings against whom the recognition of the judgment is sought was deprived by the acts of the foreign authority of the opportunity to duly enter an appearance, primarily if the party was not personally served with a summons or a petition to open the proceedings, or if the respondent was not personally served with the petition to open the proceedings; (d) if the recognition were contrary to the Czechoslovak public policy; (e) no reciprocity is guaranteed; reciprocity is not required if the foreign judgment is not directed against a Czechoslovak citizen or legal entity."* This Act was replaced by Act No. 91/2012 Coll., on Private International Law, with effect from 01 January 2014.

[206] Section 44(2) of Act No. 120/2001 Coll., on Private Bailiffs and Enforcement Proceedings and Amending Other Laws (Enforcement Code) (cit., approximate translation): *"(2) The notice shall be served on the judgment debtor personally."*

Clarence Morris, *Punitive Damages in Tort Cases*, 44 HARVARD LAW REVIEW 1184 (1931).

Csongor István Nagy, *Recognition and enforcement of U.S. judgments involving punitive damages in continental Europe*, 30(1) NEDERLANDS INTERNATIONAAL PRIVAATRECHT 4–11 (2012).

NADĚŽDA ROZEHNALOVÁ, ROZHODČÍ ŘÍZENÍ V MEZINÁROD-NÍM A VNITROSTÁTNÍM OBCHODNÍM STYKU [title in translation – ARBITRATION IN INTERNATIONAL AND NATIONAL COMMERCE], Prague: ASPI (2nd ed. 2008).

Anthony Sebok, *Punitive Damages in the United States*, in HELMUT KOZIOL, VANESSA WILCOX, PUNITIVE DAMAGES: COMMON LAW AND CIVIL LAW PERSPECTIVES, Springer: Vienna (2009).

PAVEL SEDLÁČEK, ÚMLUVA CMR: (komentář): MEZINÁRODNÍ SILNIČNÍ NÁKLADNÍ DOPRAVA – SOUDNÍ ROZHODNUTÍ – VÝKLAD JEDNOTLIVÝCH USTANOVENÍ [title in translation – CMR CONVENTION: (A COMMENTARY): INTERNATIONAL CARRIAGE OF GOODS BY ROAD – COURT DECISIONS – INTERPRETATION OF THE INDIVIDUAL PROVISIONS], Prague: Vox (2009).

Soudní judikatura, Prague: C. H. Beck, 2005, No. 10, Case No. 166.

Soudní judikatura z oblasti občanského, obchodního a pracovního práva [title in translation - Court Case-Law Concerning Civil, Commercial and Labour Law], 5th edition (volume), 2020, p. 321. Published under Reg. No. 47/2020.

Soudní judikatura z oblasti občanského, obchodního a pracovního práva [Court Case-Law Concerning Civil, Commercial and Labour Law], 1st edition (volume), 2017, p. 15. Published under Reg. No. 4/2017.

VIKTOR VAŠKE, UZNÁNÍ A VÝKON CIZÍCH ROZHODNUTÍ V ČESKÉ REPUBLICE [title in translation – RECOGNITION AND ENFORCEMENT OF FOREIGN JUDGMENTS IN THE CZECH REPUBLIC], Prague: C. H. Beck (2007).

Bibliography, Current Events, Important Web Sites

Alexander J. Bělohlávek

I. SELECTED BIBLIOGRAPHY FOR 2021[1]

Opening Remarks:

This overview lists only works published in 2021. The individual chapters into which this overview is divided always cover both substantive and procedural issues.

Titles in translations are indicative.

I.1. (Public) international law, including constitutional issues and other public-law areas with transnational dimensions and including the legal issues of international business relations, international relationships.

I.1.1. [CZE] – [CZECH REPUBLIC] – Titles published within the Czech Republic

<u>Monographs and Collections</u>

ŠÁRKA DUŠKOVÁ; ANNA HOFSCHNEIDEROVÁ; KAMILA KOUŘILOVÁ, ÚMLUVA O PRÁVECH DÍTĚTE. KOMENTÁŘ, [title in translation – CONVENTION ON THE RIGHTS OF THE CHILD. A COMMENTARY], Prague: Wolters Kluwer (2021), ISBN: 978-80-7598-683-2.

MAGDALENA PFEIFFER; JAN BRODEC; PETR BŘÍZA; MARTA ZAVADILOVÁ, LIBER AMICORUM MONIKA PAUKNEROVÁ, Praha: Wolters Kluwer ČR (2021), ISBN: 978-80-7676-186-5 (paperback); ISBN: 978-80-7676-187-2 (e-Publication).

- Alexander J. Bělohlávek, *Conflicting Interpretations of International Treaties*, p. 37-46.

- Hans Ulrich Jessurun d´Oliveira, *„Latent" Citizens. What Do They Tell Us about the Concept of Citizenship?*, p. 297-308.

- Pavel Svoboda, *Trnitá cesta ke kodexu unijního správního práva procesního* [title in translation – *The Thorny Path to the European Administrative Procedure Code*], p. 463-470.

- Pavel Šturma, *Pojem due diligence v mezinárodním investičním právu* [title in translation – *The Concept of Due Diligence in International Investment Law*], p. 471-480.

---

[1] Collected by: Alexander J. BĚLOHLÁVEK, Prague (Czech Republic).
Translations of titles to English are for easy reference only. In certain cases (exceptionally), the translation is not a *literal* translation, but an adapted translation of the title intended to best express the actual contents of the publication in English.

NADĚŽDA ŠIŠKOVÁ, LIDSKOPRÁVNÍ MECHANISMY NA ÚROVNI EU A OTÁZKY SOUVISEJÍCÍ [title in translation – HUMAN RIGHTS MECHANISMUS AT THE EU LEVEL AND RELATED ISSUES], Prague: Wolters Kluwer (2021), ISBN: 978-80-7598-623-8.

Mezinárodní vztahy [*International Relations*], Prague: Institute of International Relations Prague, 2021, Vol. LVI[2]

Maria Avanesova, *The Russian Orthodox Church and the Protection of Christians as a Direction of Russia´s Foreign Policy*, No. 3, p. 7-38.

Hrvoje Butković, *The Impacts of Executive Responses on Democracy During the Coronavirus Crisis in Croatia, Slovenia and Austria*, No. 2, p. 7-34.

Michaela Grančayová, *Plagues of Egypt – the COVID-19 crisis and the role of securitization dilemmas in the authoritarian regime survival strategies in Egypt and Turkey*, No. 1, p. 69-97.

Petra Guasti, *Democratic Erosion and Democratic resilience in Central Europe during COVID-19*, No. 4, p. 91-104.

Pavol Hardoš; Zuzana Maďarová, *On the Forms of Vulnerability and Ungrievability in the Pandemic*, No. 4, p. 119-130.

Aliaksei Kazharski; Andrey Makarychev, *Russia´s Vaccine Diplomacy in Central Europe: Between a Policital Campaign and a Business Project*, No. 4, p. 131-146.

Suneel Kumar, *China´s Revisionism and Cessation of the Doklam Impasse*, No. 2, p. 65-88.

Ahmed Maati; Žilvinas Švedkauskas, *Long-term Prescription? Digital Surveillance is Here to Stay*, No. 4, p. 105-118.

Branislav Mičko, *NATO between Exclusivity and Inclusivity: Measuring NATO´s Partnerships*, No. 4, p. 7-40.

Dagmar Rychnovská, *Rethinking the Infodemic: Global Health Security and Information Disorder*, No. 4, p. 77-90.

Erica Simone Almeida Resende, *Pandemics as Crisis Performance: How Populists Tried to Take Ownership of the Covid-19 Pandemic*, No. 4, p. 147-157.

Jana Stehlíková, *The corona crisis, data protection and tracking apps in the EU: the Czech and Austrian COVID-19 mobile phone apps in the battle against the virus*, No. 1, p. 35-67.

Daniel Svoboda, *Spreading of Salafism in Africa: Mechanisms, Strategies,*

---

[2] Majority of papers published in Czech, summary in English.

Czech Yearbook of International Law®

and Tools of Saudi Arabia´s Foreign Policy, No. 3, p. 39-71.

Tomáš Šmíd; Alexandra Šmídová, *Anti-government Non-state Armed Actors in the Conflict in Eastern Ukraine*, No. 2, p. 35-64.

Lucie Tungul, *Framing as a Social Movement´s Transnational Strategy: The Gülen Movement´s EU-Turkey Discourses in the Post-2016 Online Media*, No. 4, p. 41-71.

Václav Vlček, *How Many and Why? Size Variation of National Delegations to Plenary Meetings of International Organizations*, No. 1, p. 7-33.

Právní rozhledy [*Law Review*], Prague: C. H. Beck, 2021, Vol. 29, ISSN: 1210-6410[3]

Kateřina Burečová, *Strategie proti diskriminaci LGBTIQ lidí* [title in translation – *Strategies to Combat Discrimination of LGBTIQ People*], No. 1, p. 17-22.

Jan Kupčík, *Kontrola zahraničních investic* [title in translation – *Foreign Investment Control*], No. 8, p. 283-287.

Dalibor Nový, *Ukončení pobytu cizince ohrožujícího bezpečnost. Zrychlení, nebo zpomalení?!* [title in translation – *Terminating the Residence of a Foreigner Who Poses a Safety Risk. Acceleration or Deceleration?!*], No. 1, p. 7-12.

Ondřej Svoboda, *Dohoda o ukončení platnosti dohod o ochraně investic v EU: Problém konečně vyřešen?* [title in translation – *Agreement for the Termination of Bilateral Investment Treaties between the Member States of the European Union: Problem Finally Solved?*], No. 1, p. 12-17.

Právnické listy [Title in translation – *Legal Papers*], Prague: Wolters Kluwer a.s. / Faculty of Law West Bohemia University, 2021, ISSN: 2533-736X[4]

Jiří Zemánek, *Konstitucionalizace práva Evropské unie* [title in translation – *Constitutionalisation of EU Law*], No. 1, p. 32-38.

Právník [Title in translation - *The Lawyer*], Prague: Ústav státu a práva Akademie věd České republiky [*Institute of State and Law of the Academy of Sciences of the Czech Republic*], 2021, Vol. 160, ISSN: 0231-6625[5]

Pavel Caban, *Význam stanovisek lidskoprávních výborů a jiných expertních smluvních orgánů pro výklad mezinárodních smluv* [title

---

[3]   Papers published in Czech.
[4]   Papers published in Czech.
[5]   Papers published in Czech with abstracts in a foreign language. The abstract is most often in English (exceptionally in German or French).

Czech Yearbook of International Law®

in translation – *The Relevance of Pronouncemens of Human Rights Committees and other Expertt Treaty Bodies for the Interpreation of Treaties*], No. 10, p. 822-842.

Eva Procházková, *Podoba základních lidských práv a svobod na pozadí myšlenkového relativismu* [title in transation – *Form of Fundamenal Human Rights and Feedoms against he Background of Relativism*], No. 5, p. 374-378.

Pavel Šturma, *"Náležitá péče" v mezinárodním právu: obecný pojem s variabilním obsahem* [title in translation – *"Due Diligence" in International Law: a General Concept with Variable Content*], No. 6, p. 401-415.

Marek Zukal, *Problémy spojené s aplikací mezinárodního práva na vnitrostátní úrovni* [title in translation – *Difficulties Associated with Application of International Law at the National Level*], No. 5, p. 350-373.

The Lawyer Quarterly, Prague: Ústav státu a práva Akademie věd České republiky [*Institute of State and Law of the Academy of Sciences of the Czech Republic*], 2021, Vol. XI, ISSN: 0231-6625[6]

Jakub Handrlica, *A treatise for international administrative law*, No. 1, p. 178-191.

Oleksiy Kresin; Iryna Kresina, *Crisis management instead of peacekeeping: EU security law transofrmation in the context of Russian armed aggression in Ukraine*, No. 1, p. 29-49.

I.1.2. [CZE] – [CZECH REPUBLIC] – Selected titles of Czech authors published outside the Czech Republic

David Sehnálek, *Interpretation of Fundamental Rights in the Czech Republic*, in ZOLTÁN J. TÓTH, CONSTITUTIONAL REASONING AND CONSTITUTIONAL INTERPRETATION: ANALYSIS ON CERTAIN CENTRAL EUROPEAN COUNTRIES, Miskolc: Ferenc Mádl Institute of Comparative Law & Central European Academic Publishing (2021), p. 245-300, ISBN: 978-615-01-3003-3.

David Sehnálek, *The Interpretation and Application of Fundamental Rights in Civil Cases in the Czech Republic*, 4 JOGELMÉLETI SZEMLE

---

[6] A subsidiary title to the monthly periodical Právník [in translation – *The Lawyer*] which will be published by the Institute of State and Law of the Academy of Science of the Czech Republic in Czech. Papers published in *The Lawyer Quarterly* are primarily in English, exceptionally in other languages (such as German); abstracts are in English. For papers published in the periodical *"Pravnik"* [in translation – *The Lawyer*], issued monthly, see the separate excerpt from papers listed under the heading of the respective periodical.

[JOURNAL OF LEGAL THEORY] (2021), p. 142-151, ISSN: 1588-080X.

I.1.3. [SVK] – [SLOVAK REPUBLIC] – Selected titles published within the Slovak Republic

Bulletin slovenskej advokacie [*Bulletin of the Slovak Bar*]**, Bratislava: Slovenská advokátska komora** [*Slovak Bar Association*]**, 2021, Vol. 27, ISSN: 1335-1079**[7]

Marica Pirošíková, *Podmienky väzby a výkonu trestu odňatia slobody z pohľadu medzinárodných a európskych štandardov* [title in translation – *Custody and Imprisonment Conditions from the Perspective of International and EU Standards*], No. 4, p. 10-19.

František Sedlačko, *Hranice ochrany „whistleblowingu" podľa ESĽP (prípad Gawlik)* [title in translation – *Limits to the Protection of 'Whistleblowing' under the ECHR (Gawlik Case)*], No. 5, p. 4-5.

Marián Šuška, *Komu vrátiť historické poklady? Kauza tzv. Krymských pokladov* [title in translation – *Who Should Historical Treasures Be Returned To? Crimea Treasures Case*], No. 6, p. 10-15.

Právny obzor: časopis Ústavu štátu a práva Slovenskej akadémie vied, [*Legal Horizon: The Review of the Institute of State and Law of the Slovak Academy of Science*] **Bratislava, 2021, Vol. 104, ISSN: 0032-6984**

Lukáš Marešek, *O súdnom dvore Eurázijskej hospodárskej únie: postavenie, konanie a prínos* [title in translation – *On the court of the Eurasian Economic Union: its status, proceedings and contribution*], No. 3, p. 247-264.

Justičná revue [*Judicial Revue*]**, Bratislava: Ministry of Justice Slovak Republic, 2021, Vol. 73, ISSN: 1335-6461**[8]

Alexandra Kapišovská; Ján Králik, *Trestná zodpovednosť právnických osôb v Slovenskej republike z pohľadu OECD* [title in translation – *Criminal Responsibility of Legal Entities in the Slovak Republic from the OECD Perspective*], No. 4, p. 530-549.

Peter Matuška, *Post Achmea: súboj o investičné arbitráže medzi právom EÚ a medzinárodným právom* [title in translation – *Post Achmea: Conflict between EU Law and International Law over Investment Arbitration*], No. 5, p. 597-616.

Jozef Záhora, *Znásilnenie v judikatúre Európskeho súdu pre ľudské práva* [title in translation – *Rape in the Case-Law of the European Court*

---

[7] Papers published in Slovak with abstracts in a foreign language. Abstracts in English and in German.
[8] Papers published in Czech. Abstracts in English.

of Human Rights], No. 5, p. 677-691.

I.2. (Private) international law, European private international law and legal relations in foreign trade relations, including international arbitration and other private-law areas with transnational dimensions

I.2.1. [CZE] – [CZECH REPUBLIC] – Titles published within the Czech Republic

Monographs, Collections and Conference Proceedings published in the Czech Republic

ZUZANA FIŠEROVÁ; KATEŘINA PUTNOVÁ; JANA HOFMANNOVÁ; MARTA ZAVADILOVÁ; MAGDALENA PFEIFFER, SBÍRKA PRÁVNÍCH PŘEDPISŮ PRO OBLAST PŘESHRANIČNÍ JUSTIČNÍ SPOLUPRÁCE V OBČANSKÝCH A OBCHODNÍCH VĚCECH [title in translation – COLLECTION OF LAWS CONCERNING CROSS-BORDER JUDICIAL COOPERATION IN CIVIL AND COMMERCIAL MATTERS], Prague: Leges (2020), p. 1147, ISBN: 978-80-7502-473-2.

TOMÁŠ MORAVEC, EVROPSKÉ INSOLVENČNÍ PRÁVO [title in translation – EUROPEAN INSOLVENCY LAW], Prague: C.H.BECK (2021), p. 284, ISBN: 978-80-7400-832-0.[9]

MAGDALENA PFEIFFER; JAN BRODEC; PETR BŘÍZA; MARTA ZAVADILOVÁ, LIBER AMICORUM MONIKA PAUKNEROVÁ, Praha: Wolters Kluwer ČR (2021), ISBN: 978-80-7676-186-5 (paperback); ISBN: 978-80-7676-187-2 (e-Publication).

- Nadia de Araujo; Marcelo De Nardi, *International Jurisdiction in Civil or Commercial Matters: HCCH´s New Challenge*, p. 1-10.

- Jürgen Basedow, *International Transport Conventions and the European Union*, p. 11-26.

- Paul Beaumont; Jayne Holliday, *Habitual Residence in Child Abduction Cases: The Hybrid Approach Is Now the Norm but How Much Weight Should Be Given to Parental Intention?*, p. 27-36.

- Alexander J. Bělohlávek, *Conflicting Interpretations of International Treaties*, p. 37-46.

[9]   Title published in Czech.

- Karel Beran, Čím se liší „právní entita" od právnické osoby (úvaha nad „jinou než fyzickou osobou" podle § 30 odst. 1 z. m. p. s. /zákona o mezinárodním právu soukromém/ [title in translation – *What Distinguishes a "Legal Entity" from a Juristic Person (Consideration of "non-natural persons" according to Section 30 (1) of the Czech Private International Law Act)*], p. 47-56.

- Michael Bogdan, *Article 36 of the EU Insolvency Regulation and the Treatment of General Priority Rights*, p. 57-64.

- Jan Brodec, *Vliv lex loci arbitri na průběh mezinárodní obchodní arbitráže* [title in translation – *The Impact of Lex Loci Arbitri on International Commercial Arbitration*], p. 65-74.

- Petr Bříza, *Determination of the Law Applicable to a Share Transfer Agreement: Are All Doubts Dispelled after the TVP Case?*, p. 75-92.

- Giuditta Cordero-Moss, *Private International Law in Arbitration*, p. 93-102.

- Elizabeth B. Crawford; Janeen M. Carruthers, *The Incurious Curia*, p. 103-112.

- Richard Fentiman, *Foreign Law as Local Law: a Case of Mistaken Identity?*, p. 143-152.

- Zuzana Fišerová, *Zamyšlení nad kolizní úpravou pro rozvod manželství s mezinárodním prvkem aneb nastal čas, aby ČR přistoupila k nařízení Řím III?*, p. 153-168.

- Cristina González Beilfuss, *Prorogation of Jurisdiction in Parental Responsibility Matters under Regulation (EU) No. 2019/1111*, p. 169-176.

- Trevor Hartley, *The Concept of a Consumer under Brussels I: the Petruchová Case*, p. 177-186.

- Elena Júdová, Špeciálne režimy v európskom medzinárodnom práve súkromnom [title in translation – *Special Regimes in European Private International Law*], p. 187-203.

- Zdeněk Kapitán, *Mezinárodní pravomoc českých soudů ve věcech péče o děti založená na státním občanství* [title in translation – *International Jurisdiction of Czech Courts in Child Care Matters Based on Citizenship*], p. 203-222.

- Catherine Kessedjian, *Mediation for Disputes in Investment Matters*, p. 223-230.

- Ivana Kunda, *Overriding Mandatory Provisions before the CJEU: Takeways or Gataways?*, p. 241-258.

- Tuula Linna, *Sustainability and Insolvency Proceedings*, p. 259-270.

- Peter Mankowski, *Presumptions, Escape Clauses and Protective Regimes under the Rome I Regulation*, p. 277-286.

- Milan Müller, *Mezinárodní postoupení pohledávek a jeho účinky na třetí strany ve světle připravované nové evropské právní úpravy* [title in translation – *International Assignment of Claims and its Effects on Third Parties in the Light of the Forthcoming New European Legislation*], p. 287-297.

- Hans Ulrich Jessurun d´Oliveira, *„Latent" Citizens. What Do They Tell Us about the Concept of Citizenship?*, p. 297-308.

- Jan Ondřej, *Smlouvy o mezinárodní přepravě se zaměřením na Úmluvu o přepravní smlouvě v mezinárodní silniční nákladní dopravě a její provádění v právu ČR* [title in translation – *Contracts about International Transport with the Focus on the Convention on the Contract for the International Carriage of Goods by Road and its Incorporation into the Law of the Czech Republic (Jurisdiction of the Courts of Law of the CR]*, p. 309-318.

- Marta Pertegás Sender, *Cross-Border Liability Cases in the European Union: No Good Match with the Special Jurisdiction Rules of the Brussels I Regulation?*, p. 325-334.

- Magdalena Pfeiffer, *The Cinderella Treatment of Foreign Arbitral Awards in the Czech Enforcement Procedure*, p. 335-344.

- Fausto Pocar, *Brief Remarks on the Relationship between the Hague Judgments and Choice of Court Conventions*, p. 345-352.

- Ilaria Pretelli, *Three Patterns, One Law: Plea for a Reinterpretation of The Hague Child Abduction Convention To Protect Children from Exposure to Sexism, Misogyny and Violence Against Women*, p. 363-394.

- Elena Rodrígues Pineau, *Parallel Litigation in Proceedings Relating to Data Protection*, p. 395-404.

- Naděžda Rozehnalová, *Cesta k současnému uchopení imperativních předpisů* [title in translation – *The Path to the Current Understanding of Overriding Mandatory Rules*], p. 405-412.

- Květoslav Růžička, *Náklady stran v rozhodčím řízení* [title in translation – *Party Costs in Arbitration Proceedings*], p. 413-420.

- Pavel Simon, *Potíže spojené s určením místně příslušného soudu ve sporech s mezinárodním prvkem aneb o zbytečnosti § 11 odst. 3 o. s. ř. /občanského soudního řádu/* [title in translation - *Troubles with the Determination of the Court with Territorial Jurisdiction in Disputes with an International Dimension, or the Uselessness of Section 11(3) of the CCP /Code of Civil Procedure/*].

- Pavel Svoboda, *Trnitá cesta ke kodexu unijního správního práva procesního* [title in translation – *The Thorny Path to the European Administrative Procedure Code*], p. 463-470.

- Pavel Šturma, *Pojem due diligence v mezinárodním investičním právu* [title in translation – *The Concept of Due Diligence in International Investment Law*], p. 471-480.

- Zbyněk Švarc, *Odpovědnost dopravce za škodu v mezinárodní silniční přepravě zboží* [title in translation – *Carrier Liability for Damage in International Road Freight Transport*], p. 481-494.

- Marta Zavadilová, *Kulhající manželství osob stejného pohlaví* [title in translation – *Matrimonium Claudicans of the Same-Sex Marriages*], p. 525-537.

NADĚŽDA ROZEHNALOVÁ; JIŘÍ VALDHANS; TEREZA KYSELOVSKÁ, PRÁVO MEZINÁRODNÍHO OBCHODU. VČETNĚ PROBLEMATIKY MEZINÁRODNÍHO ROZHODČÍHO ŘÍZENÍ [title in translation – LAW OF INTERNAIONAL COMMERCE. INCLUDING INTERNATIONAL ARBITRATION ISSUES], Prague: Wolters Kluwer (4th ed. 2021), p. 524, ISBN: 978-80-7676-046-2.

NADĚŽDA ROZEHNALOVÁ; JIŘÍ VALDHANS; RADOVAN MALACHTA, E-KNIHA: VYBRANÉ KAPITOLY Z MEZINÁRODNÍHO PRÁVA SOUKROMÉHO [title in translation – E-BOOK: SELECTED CHAPTERS FROM PRIVATE INTERNATIONAL LAW], Brno: Masaryk University (3rd ed. 2021), p. 128, ISBN: 978-80-210-9895-4.

Obchodní právo [*Commercial Law*], Prague: Wolters Kluwer ČR, a.s., 2021, Vol. XXX, ISSN: 1210-8278, Reg.No Ministry of Cultural Affairs Czech Republic E 6020 MIČ 46032[10]

Anna Dufková, *Účtování podnákladových cen jako možný způsob zneužití dominantního postavení - případ Falcon* [title in translation – *Predatory Pricing as a Potential Abuse of Dominant Position – Falcon Case*], No. 5, p. 18-26.

---

[10]   Papers published in Czech. Summary in English.

Anežka Janoušková, *Směrnice o zástupných žalobách na ochranu kolektivních zájmů spotřebitelů* [title in translation – *Directive on Representative Actions for the Protection of the Collective Interests of Consumers*], No. 2, p. 2-16.

Právnické listy [Title in translation – *Legal Papers*], Prague: Wolters Kluwer a.s. / Faculty of Law West Bohemia University, 2021, ISSN: 2533-736X[11]

Adam Köszeghy, *Nadobudnutie vlastníckeho práva podľa zákoníku medzinárodného obchodu v medzinárodnom obchodnom styku* [title in translation – *Acquisition of (Ownership) Title under the Code of International Commerce in International Commercial Transactions*], No. 1, p. 18-26.

Právní rozhledy [*Law Review*], Prague: C. H. Beck, 2021, Vol. 29, ISSN: 1210-6410, Reg.No Ministry of Cultural Affairs Czech Republic] E 18487[12]

Anna Dufková, *Určení mezinárodní pravomoci soudu v rámci nekalosoutěžního jednání v prostředí internetu evropských zemí* [title in translation – *Determination of International Jurisdiction of Courts in Cases Involving Unfair Competition on Internet in the Countries of Europe*], No. 1, p. 26-30.

Jan Kupčík, *Kontrola zahraničních investic* [title in translation – *Foreign Investment Control*], No. 8, p. 283-287.

Právník [Title in translation - *The Lawyer*], Prague: Ústav státu a práva Akademie věd České republiky [*Institute of State and Law of the Academy of Sciences of the Czech Republic*], 2021, Vol. 160, ISSN: 0231-6625[13]

Klára Drličková, *Význam a pojetí obvyklého pobytu (nejen) v evropském mezinárodním právu soukroméma procesním* [title in translation – *The Importance and Conception of Habitual Residence (Not Only) in European Private International Law*], No. 6, p. 466-476.

Monika Pauknerová, *Imperativní normy a mezinárodní právo soukromé – klasické téma v současnosti* [title in translation – *Overriding Mandatory Rules and Private International Law – Classical Topic at the Present Time*], No. 1, p. 1-20.

Právo v přepravě a zasilatelství [Title in translation – *Law in Transport and Carriage*], Prague: Wolters Kluwer, 2021, ISSN:

---

[11]   Papers published in Czech.
[12]   Papers published in Czech.
[13]   Papers published in Czech with abstracts in a foreign language. The abstract is most often in English (exceptionally in German or French).

Czech Yearbook of International Law®

2694-5095[14]

Iveta Ille Hofmannová, *Dopady Brexitu pro tuzemské dopravní a spediční firmy* [title in translation – *Impact of Brexit on Domestic Carriers and Freight Forwarders*], No. 1, p. 2-3.

Jan Pravda, *Odpovědnost dopravce v multimodální mezinárodní přepravě zboží* [title in translation – *Liability of the Carrier in International Multimodal Carriage of Goods*], No. 2, p. 20-27.

Petr Rožek, *Abandoned goods – opuštěné zboží jako rostoucí obtíž pro zasílatele v mezinárodní přepravě zboží* [title in translation – *Abandoned goods – Increasingly Onerous Burden on the Freight Forwarder in International Carriage of Goods*], No. 1, p. 4-7.

Petr Rožek, *Aplikace vybraných úprav a novinek pravidel Incoterms 2020 v budoucí praxi – závěr. Problém s pravidly EXW a DDP vs. Brexit* [title in translation – *Application of Selected and New Incoterms 2020 in Future Practice – Conclusion. Trouble with EXW and DDP v. Brexit*], No. 3, p. 16-21.

Petr Rožek, *Aplikace vybraných úprav a novinek pravidel Incoterms 2020 v budoucí praxi* [title in translation – *Application of Selected and New Incoterms 2020 in Future Practice*], No. 2, p. 2-5.

Tomáš Tyll, *Pravomoci UPDI a prohlášení o dráze z hlediska hospodářské soutěže* [title in translation – *Powers of the Transport Infrastructure Access Authority and the Network Statement from the Perspective of Competition*], No. 2, p. 16-20.

Soukromé právo [Title in translation – *Private Law*], Prague: Wolers Kluwer ČR, a.s., 2021, Vol. IX, ISSN: 2533-4239[15]

Alexander J. Bělohlávek, *Rozsah, účel a charakter speciální úpravy o doručování v zákoně o rozhodčím řízení. Část I* [title in translation – *Extent, Purpose and Nature of Special Rules on Service in the Arbitration Act. Part I*], No. 5, p. 2-9.

Alexander J. Bělohlávek, *Rozsah, účel a charakter speciální úpravy o doručování v zákoně o rozhodčím řízení. Část II* [title in translation – *Extent, Purpose and Nature of Special Rules on Service in the Arbitration Act. Part II*], No. 6, p. 2-9.

The Lawyer Quarterly, Prague: Ústav státu a práva Akademie věd České republiky [*Institute of State and Law of the Academy of Sciences of the Czech Republic*], 2021, Vol. XI, ISSN: 0231-6625[16]

---

[14] Papers published in Czech.
[15] Papers published in Czech.
[16] A subsidiary title to the monthly periodical Právník [in translation – *The Lawyer*] which will be published by the Institute of State and Law of the Academy of Science of the Czech Republic in Czech.

Lukáš Grodl, *England To Become The Prime Jurisdiction For International Commercial Disputes – Anti-Suit Injunction As A Tool For Assurance*, No. 2, p. 360-380.

Tariq Abdel Rahman Kameel; Ibrahim Khalid Abd Yahya; Firas Abdel-Mahdi Massadeh; Ramzi Madi, *The Impact Of The Doctrine Of Forum Non Conveniens On Nationality Criterion In The Light of Palestinian Civil and Commercial Procedures Law: The Case Of Palestinians With Residency In Israel*, No. 2, p. 252-270.

Other publications

Bára Bečvářová, *Vliv změny okolností na povinnosti stran kupní smlouvy podle českého práva a Vídeňské úmluvy* [title in translation – *Impact of a Change in Circumstances on the Obligations of Parties to a Purchase Contract under Czech Law and under the Vienna Convention*], in MIROSLAV SEDLÁČEK; TOMÁŠ STŘELEČEK, POVINNOST A ODPOVĚDNOST V CIVILNÍM PRÁVU HMOTNÉM A PROCESNÍM [title in translation – OBLIGATION AND LIABILITY IN SUBSTANTIVE AND PROCEDURAL CIVIL LAW], Prague: Wolters Kluwer ČR (2021).

Bára Bečvářová, *Virtual arbitration hearings in times of Covid-19 (and beyond)*, in RADOVAN MALACHTA; PATRIK PROVAZNÍK, COFOLA INTERNATIONAL 2021. INTERNATIONAL AND NATIONAL ARBITRATION – CHALLENGES AND TRENDS OF THE PRESENT AND FUTURE, Brno: Masaryk University Press (2021).

Petr Bříza, *Převod podílu a akcie s cizím prvkem* [title in translation – *Transfer of Shares and Stock with a Foreign Dimension*], in KRISTIÁN CSACH; BOHUMIL HAVEL, ZMLUVY O PREVODE OBCHODNÝCH PODIELOV A AKCII [title in translation – SHARES AND STOCK TRANSFER AGREEMENTS], Prague: Wolters Kluwer (2021).

Anna Dufková, *Určení mezinárodního fóra při souběhu porušení práv na označení a nekalosoutěžního jednání* [title in translation – *Determination of International Forum in Cases Involving Simultaneous Infringement of the Right to Designation and Unfair Competition*], in RADOVAN MALACHTA; PATRIK PROVAZNÍK, COFOLA INTERNATIONAL 2021. INTERNATIONAL AND NATIONAL ARBITRATION – CHALLENGES AND TRENDS OF THE PRESENT AND FUTURE, Brno: Masaryk University Press (2021), p. 592-610.

Papers published in *The Lawyer Quarterly* are primarily in English, exceptionally in other languages (such as German); abstracts are in English. For papers published in the periodical *"Pravnik"* [in translation – *The Lawyer*], issued monthly, see the separate excerpt from papers listed under the heading of the respective periodical.

300 |

I.2.2. [CZE] – [CZECH REPUBLIC] – Selected titles of Czech authors published outside the Czech Republic

Zuzana Fišerová; Tijana Kokić, *Application of EU Instruments in Civil Justice*, CEELI INSTITUTE (2021).

Pavel Koukal; Tereza Kyselovská; Zuzana Vlachová, *Employment Contracts and the Law Applicable to the Right to a Patent: Czech Considerations*, in BALKAN YEARBOOK OF EUROPEAN AND INTERNATIONAL LAW, Cham: Springer (2021), p. 177-198, ISBN: 978-3-030-65294-4.

Monika Pauknerová; Magdalena Pfeiffer, *National Report – Czech Republic. National Report – Slovakia*, in EVA LEIN, STUDY ON THE ROME II REGULATION (EC) 864/2007 ON THE LAW APPLICABLE TO NON-CONTRACTUAL OBLIGATIONS, European Union (2021), ISBN: 978-92-76-41525-1.

Monika Pauknerová; Magdalena Pfeiffer, *UNIDROIT Principles as Reference to Uniform Interpretation of National Laws: Czech Republic*, in ALEJANDRO GARRO; JOSE ANTONIO MORENO RODRIGUEZ, USE OF THE UNIDROIT PRINCIPLES TO INTERPRET AND SUPPLEMENT DOMESTIC CONTRACT LAW, Cham: Springer Nature Switzerland (2021), p. 101-124, ISBN: 978-3-030-54321-1.

Luboš Tichý, *Lis Pendens in the Brussels Ia Regulation with Regard to Third Countries*, in ALEXANDER TRUNK; NIKITAS HATZIMIHAIL, EU CIVIL PROCEDURE LAW AND THIRD COUNTRIES: WHICH WAY FORWARD?, London: Bloomsbury Publishing (2021), p. 95-126, ISBN: 978-1509948765.

I.3.   EU Law (general, not classified under Chapter I.1. or I.2. above)

I.3.1. [CZE] – [CZECH REPUBLIC] – Titles published within the Czech Republic

Monographs, Collections and Conference Proceedings

MAGDALENA PFEIFFER; JAN BRODEC; PETR BŘÍZA; MARTA ZAVADILOVÁ, LIBER AMICORUM MONIKA PAUKNEROVÁ, Praha: Wolters Kluwer ČR (2021), ISBN: 978-80-7676-186-5 (paperback); ISBN: 978-80-7676-187-2 (e-Publication).

- Jürgen Basedow, *International Transport Conventions and the European Union*, p. 11-26.

Czech Yearbook of International Law®

- Alexander J. Bělohlávek, *Conflicting Interpretations of International Treaties*, p. 37-46.

- Michael Bogdan, *Article 36 of the EU Insolvency Regulation and the Treatment of General Priority Rights*, p. 57-64.

- Petr Bříza, *Determination of the Law Applicable to a Share Transfer Agreement: Are All Doubts Dispelled after the TVP Case?*, p. 75-92.

- Zuzana Fišerová, *Zamyšlení nad kolizní úpravou pro rozvod manželství s mezinárodním prvkem aneb nastal čas, aby ČR přistoupila k nařízení Řím III?*, p. 153-168.

- Cristina González Beilfuss, *Prorogation of Jurisdiction in Parental Responsibility Matters under Regulation (EU) No. 2019/1111*, p. 169-176.

- Trevor Hartley, *The Concept of a Consumer under Brussels I: the Petruchová Case*, p. 177-186.

- Ivana Kunda, *Overriding Mandatory Provisions before the CJEU: Takeways or Gataways?*, p. 241-258.

- Tuula Linna, *Sustainability and Insolvency Proceedings*, p. 259-270.

- Peter Mankowski, *Presumptions, Escape Clauses and Protective Regimes under the Rome I Regulation*, p. 277-286.

- Milan Müller, *Mezinárodní postoupení pohledávek a jeho účinky na třetí strany ve světle připravované nové evropské právní úpravy* [title in translation – *International Assignment of Claims and its Effects on Third Parties in the Light of the Forthcoming New European Legislation*], p. 287-297.

- Marta Pertegás Sender, *Cross-Border Liability Cases in the European Union: No Good Match with the Special Jurisdiction Rules of the Brussels I Regulation?*, p. 325-334.

- Naděžda Rozehnalová, *Cesta k současnému uchopení imperativních předpisů* [title in translation – *The Path to the Current Understanding of Overriding Mandatory Rules*], p. 405-412.

- Pavel Svoboda, *Trnitá cesta ke kodexu unijního správního práva procesního* [title in translation – *The Thorny Path to the European Administrative Procedure Code*], p. 463-470.

MILOŠ KOCÍ, PROGRAMY SHOVÍVAVOSTI A SOUKROMOPRÁVNÍ VYMÁHÁNÍ KARTELOVÉHO PRÁVA [title in translation –

LENIENCY PROGRAMMES AND ENFORCEMENT OF CARTEL LAW UNDER PRIVATE LAW] Prague: Wolters Kluwer (2021), ISBN: 978-80-7676-149-0.

TEREZA KYSELOVSKÁ, NAŘÍZENÍ ŘÍM I, NAŘÍZENÍ ŘÍM II: KOMENTÁŘ [title in translation – ROME I REGULATION, ROME II REGULATION: COMMENTARY], Prague: Wolters Kluwer (2021), ISBN: 978-80-7598-971-0.

DAVID SEHNÁLEK; IVETA ROHOVÁ, KOMENTÁŘ K VYBRANÉ JUDIKATUŘE SOUDNÍHO DVORA EU [title in translation – A COMMENTARY ON SELECTED CASE-LAW OF THE COURT OF JUSTICE OF THE EU], Brno: Masaryk University Press (2nd ed. 2021), p. 250, ISBN: 978-80-210-9789-6.

NADĚŽDA ŠIŠKOVÁ, LIDSKOPRÁVNÍ MECHANISMY NA ÚROVNI EU A OTÁZKY SOUVISEJÍCÍ [title in translation – HUMAN RIGHTS MECHANISMUS AT THE EU LEVEL AND RELATED ISSUES], Prague: Wolters Kluwer (2021), ISBN: 978-80-7598-623-8.

MICHAL TOMÁŠEK; VLADIMÍR TÝČ; JIŘÍ MAENOVSKÝ; IRENA PELIKÁNOVÁ; DAVID PETRLÍK; FILIP KŘEPELKA; LENKA PÍTROVÁ; VÁCLAV ŠMEJKAL; DAVID SEHNÁLEK; ANETA VONDRÁČKOVÁ; MAGDALENA SVOBODOVÁ; MARTIN SMOLEK; JAN EXNER; NADĚŽDA ROZEHNALOVÁ, PRÁVO EVROPSKÉ UNIE [title in translation – EU LAW], Prague: Leges (2021), p. 512, ISBN: 978-80-7502-491-6.

LUCIE ZAVADILOVÁ, MAJETKOVÉ POMĚRY MANŽELŮ – UNIFIKACE KOLIZNÍHO PRÁVA V RÁMCI EVROPSKÉ UNIE [title in translation – MARITAL PROPERTY – UNIFICATION OF CONFLICT-OF-LAWS RULES IN THE EUROPEAN UNION], Brno: Masaryk University Press (2021), p. 233.

The Lawyer Quarterly, Prague: Ústav státu a práva Akademie věd České republiky [*Institute of State and Law of the Academy of Sciences of the Czech Republic*], 2021, Vol. XI, ISSN: 0231-6625[17]

František Kasl, *The US lessons for the EU personal data breach notification*, No. 1, p. 192-205.

Oleksiy Kresin; Iryna Kresina, *Crisis management instead of peacekeeping: EU security law 12ransformation in the context of Russian armed aggression in Ukraine*, No. 1, p. 29-49.

---

[17] A subsidiary title to the monthly periodical Právník [in translation – *The Lawyer*] which will be published by the Institute of State and Law of the Academy of Science of the Czech Republic in Czech. Papers published in *The Lawyer Quarterly* are primarily in English, exceptionally in other languages (such as German); abstracts are in English. For papers published in the periodical "*Pravnik*" [in translation – *The Lawyer*], issued monthly, see the separate excerpt from papers listed under the heading of the respective periodical.

Obchodní právo [*Commercial Law*], Prague: Wolters Kluwer ČR, a.s., 2021, Vol. XXX, ISSN: 1210-8278, Reg.No Ministry of Cultural Affairs Czech Republic E 6020 MIČ 46032[18]

Anežka Janoušková, *Směrnice o zástupných žalobách na ochranu kolektivních zájmů spotřebitelů* [title in translation – *Directive on Representative Actions for the Protection of the Collective Interests of Consumers*], No. 2, p. 2-16.

Irena Pelikánová, *Studie o soukromém a veřejném právu EU – uzavření* [title in translation – *Essay About European Private And Public Law – Conclusion*], No 5, p. 2- 12.

Právník [Title in translation – *The Lawyer*], Prague: Ústav státu a práva Akademie věd České republiky [*Institute of State and Law of the Academy of Sciences of the Czech Republic*], 2021, Vol. 160, ISSN: 0231-6625[19]

Jaroslav Denemark, *Kam jsme se posunuli od zrušení směrnice o uchovávání údajů* [title in translation – *Where have we shifted since Declaring Data Retention Directive Invalid*], No. 12, p. 1054-1070.

Klára Drličková, *Význam a pojetí obvyklého pobytu (nejen) v evropském mezinárodním právu soukroméma procesním* [title in translation – *The Importance and Conception of Habitual Residence (Not Only) in European Private International Law*], No. 6, p. 466-476.

Jan Malíř, *Konsorcia ERIC a jejich místo v systému práva EU* [title in translation – *Consortia ERIC and their Place in the System of EU Law*], No. 2, p. 81-104.

Ľuboslav Sisák, *Európske osvedčenie o dedičstve a prepis vlastníctva zdedenej nehnuteľnosti* [title in translation – *European Certiicatte o Succession and the ranscription of Ownership to an Inherited Immovable*], No. 10, p. 854-870.

Právní rozhledy [Title in translation – *Law Review*], Prague: C. H. Beck, 2021, Vol. 29, ISSN: 1210-6410[20]

Anna Dufková, *Účtování podnákladových cen jako možný způsob zneužití dominantního postavení – případ Falcon* [title in translation – *Predatory Pricing as a Potential Abuse of Dominant Position – Falcon Case*], No. 5, p. 18-26.

Kateřina Burečová, *Strategie proti diskriminaci LGBTIQ lidí* [title in translation – *Strategies to Combat Discrimination of LGBTIQ People*],

---

[18] Papers published in Czech. Summary in English.
[19] Papers published in Czech with abstracts in a foreign language. The abstract is most often in English (exceptionally in German or French).
[20] Papers published in Czech.

No. 1, p. 17-22.

Olga Pouperová, *Veřejné financování vysílání veřejné služby v kontextu práva EU o státních podporách* [title in translation – *Financing Public Service Broadcasting from Public Funds in the Context of EU State Aid Rules*], No. 3, p. 204-213.

Daniella Sarah Sotolářová, *Finanční zájmy EU a jejich trestněprávní ochrana v České republice* [title in translation – *EU Financial Interests and Their Protection under Czech Criminal Law*], No. 18, p. 618-628.

Ondřej Svoboda, *Dohoda o ukončení platnosti dohod o ochraně investic v EU: Problém konečně vyřešen?* [title in translation – *Agreement for the Termination of Bilateral Investment Treaties between the Member States of the European Union: Problem Finally Solved?*], No 18.

Pavel Svoboda, *Nový vývoj v prosazování vlády práva v EU* [title in translation – *New Developments in Asserting the Rule of Law in the EU*], No. 4, p. 134-136.

Právo v přepravě a zasilatelství [Title in translation – *Law in Transport and Carriage*], Prague: Wolters Kluwer, 2021, ISSN: 2694-5095[21]

Iveta Ille Hofmannová, *Dopady Brexitu pro tuzemské dopravní a spediční firmy* [title in translation – *Impact of Brexit on Domestic Carriers and Freight Forwarders*], No. 1, p. 2-3.

Petr Rožek, *Aplikace vybraných úprav a novinek pravidel Incoterms 2020 v budoucí praxi – závěr. Problém s pravidly EXW a DDP vs. Brexit* [title in translation – *Application of Selected and New Incoterms 2020 in Future Practice – Conclusion. Trouble with EXW and DDP v. Brexit*], No. 3, p. 16-21.

Tomáš Tyll, *Pravomoci UPDI a prohlášení o dráze z hlediska hospodářské soutěže* [title in translation – *Powers of the Transport Infrastructure Access Authority and the Network Statement from the Perspective of Competition*], No. 2, p. 16-20.

Jana Zárybnická, *Odpovědnost českých silničních nákladních dopravců při provádění kabotážní přepravy v zemích Evropské unie a pojištění* [title in translation – *Liability of Czech Road Cargo Carriers Arising from Cabotage in EU Member States and Insurance*], No. 3, p. 16-21.

The Lawyer Quarterly, Prague: Ústav státu a práva Akademie věd České republiky [*Institute of State and Law of the Academy of Sciences of the Czech Republic*],

---

[21] Papers published in Czech.

Supplement to Journal Právník [Title in translation – *The Lawyer*], 2021, Vol. 11, ISSN: 0231-6625[22]

Justyna Bazylińska-Nagler, *Harmonization of Automobile Emission Standards Under EU Law*, No. 4, p. 585-594.

Valéria Růžičková, *Judicial Review of the Acts of the European Public Prosecutor´s Office Possible Shortcomming and Several Considerations in Relation to the Slovak Republic and its Legislation*, No. 4, p. 665-681.

Roman Zapletal, *Work-Life Balance in the Light of the Directive (EU) 2019/1158 on the Example of Job-Sharing in Accordance with the Czech Labour Code*, No. 4, p. 641-650.

Právnické listy [Title in translation – *Legal Papers*], Prague: Wolters Kluwer a.s. / Faculty of Law West Bohemia University, 2021, ISSN: 2533-736X[23]

Darina Králiková, *Komparácia poskytovania reverzných hypoték vo vybraných štátoch Európskej únie* [title in translation – *Comparative Analysis of Reverse Mortgages in Selected EU Member States*], No. 1, p. 27-31.

Jiří Zemánek, *Konstitucionalizace práva Evropské unie* [title in translation – *Constitutionalisation of EU Law*], No. 1, p. 32-38.

Soudce [Title in translation – *The Judge*], Prague: Wolters Kluwer a.s. / Soudcovská unie [Union of Judges], 2021, Vol. XXIII[24]

Petr Navrátil, *Náhrada újmy způsobené porušením požadavku na projednání věci v přiměřené lhůtě v soutěžně-právní judikatuře Soudního dvora EU: nemo iudex in causa sua?* [title in translation – *Compensation for Damage and Losses Resulting from a Breach of the Requirement of Hearing a Case within a Reasonable Time in Competition Case-Law of the Court of Justice of the EU: Nemo Judex in Causa Sua?*], No. 9, p. 12-28.

Other publications

Lukáš Grodl; Ondřej Dlouhý, *Covid-19 Influences on Insolvency Proceeding Openings – threat to Legitimate Expectation of International Jurisdiction?*, in JAN ŠKRABKA; LUKÁŠ VACUŠKA, PRÁVO V PODNIKÁNÍ VYBRANÝCH ŠLENSKÝCH STÁTŮ EVROPSKÉ UNIE. SBORNÍK PŘÍSPĚVKŮ K XII. ROČNÍKU MEZINÁRODNÍ VĚDECKÉ KONFERENCE [title in translation – LAW IN BUSINESS OF SELECTED EU MEMBER STATES. COLLECTION OF PAPERS FROM THE 12TH ANNUAL INTERNATIONAL SCIENCE CONFERENCE],

---

[22] Papers published in English.
[23] Papers published in Czech.
[24] Papers published in Czech.

Prague: TROAS, s.r.o. (2021), p. 332-341, ISBN: 978-80-88055-10-5.

I.3.2. Papers and Writings of Czech Authors published out of the Czech Republic

Luboš Tichý, *Lis Pendens in the Brussels Ia Regulation with Regard to Third Countries,* in ALEXANDER TRUNK; NIKITAS HATZIMIHAIL, EU CIVIL PROCEDURE LAW AND THIRD COUNTRIES: WHICH WAY FORWARD?, London: Bloomsbury Publishing (2021), p. 95-126, ISBN: 978-1509948765.

Radim Charvát, *Protection of Appellations of Origin Registered under the Lisbon Agreement in the Context of the Exhaustive Nature of the EU Protection of Geographical Indications and Designations of Origin,* 43(10) EUROPEAN INTELLECTUAL PROPERTY REVIEW. SWEET&MAXWELL (2021), p. 653-664, ISSN: 0142-0461.

I.3.3. [SVK] – [SLOVAK REPUBLIC]

Monographs, Collections and Conference Proceedings

JOZEF MILUČKÝ; SAMUEL MILUŠKÝ, SPRÁVNE TRESTANIE NA SLOVENSKU A V EURÓPSKOM PRIESTORE: JUDIKATURA, Žilina: Eurokódex, s.r.o. (2021).

Bulletin slovenskej advokacie [*Bulletin of the Slovak Bar*], Bratislava: Slovenská advokátska komora [*Slovak Bar Association*], 2016, Vol. 22, ISSN: 1335-1079[25]

Matej Michalec, *Medzinárodní súdna právomoc pro porušení práv k ochrannej známke EÚ v online prostredí* [title in translation – *International Court Jurisdiction over EU Trademark Online Infringement*], No. 1-2.

Marica Pirošíková, *Podmienky väzby a výkonu trestu odňatia slobody z pohľadu medzinárodných a európskych štandardov* [title in translation – *Custody and Imprisonment Conditions from the Perspective of International and EU Standards*], No. 4, p. 10-19.

Justičná revue [*Judicial Revue*], Bratislava: Ministry of Justice Slovak Republic, 2021, Vol. 73, ISSN: 1335-6461[26]

Dana Jelinková Dudzíková, *Cezhraničné premiestnenie sídla právnických osôb v Európskej únii* [title in translation – *Cross-Border Relocation of the Registered Office of Legal Entities in the European Union*], No. 2, p. 208-217.

---

[25] Papers published in Slovak with abstracts in a foreign language. Abstracts in English and in German.
[26] Papers published in Czech. Abstracts in English.

Peter Matuška. *Post Achmea: súboj o investičné arbitráže medzi právom EÚ a medzinárodným právom* [title in translation – *Post Achmea: Conflict between EU Law and International Law over Investment Arbitration*], No. 5, p. 597-616.

Matúš Mesarčík, *Cezhraničné prenosy osobných údajov do Spojeného kráľovstva po Brexite: minulosť, prítomnosť, budúcnosť* [title in translation – *Cross-Border Transfers of Personal Data to the United Kingdom after Brexit: Past, Present, Future*], No. 4, p. 476-491.

Martin Mihók, *Dokazovanie v konaní o európskom zatýkacom rozkaze a videokonferečný výsluch osoby na základe európskeho vyšetrovacieho príkazu* [title in translation – *Taking of Evidence in the European Arrest Warrant Proceedings and Video Conference Interrogation of Individuals on the Basis of the European Investigation Order*], No. 8-9, p. 986-1001.

Michael Siman; Milan Jančo, *Priamy účinok medzinárodných dohôd zaväzujúcich Európsku úniu a jej členské štáty* [title in translation – *Direct Effect of International Agreements Binding on the European Union and on the EU Member States*], No. 8-9, p. 929-947.

Jana Žuľová, *Používanie umelej inteligencie pri výbere zamestnancov z perspektívy GDPR* [title in translation – *Using Artificial Intelligence in Employee Recruitment from the GDPR Perspective*], No. 1, p. 30-39.

Právny obzor: časopis Ústavu štátu a práva Slovenskej akadémie vied, [*Legal Horizon: The Review of the Institute of State and Law of the Slovak Academy of Science*] Bratislava, 2021, Vol. 104, ISSN: 0032-6984

Ľubomír Zlocha, *Uplatňovanie práva na náhradu škody v dôsledku zneužitia súťažného práva EÚ (základné východiska)* [title in translation – *Exercise of the right to compensation for damage due to abuse of EU competition law (basic principles)*], No. 6, p. 443-457.

II.   CURRENT EVENTS

We sincerely apologize to our readers for omitting this traditional section from this CYIL edition due to the exceptional circumstances attending the COVID-19 pandemic in 2021 that have resulted in the cancellation of principally all conferences and similar events (at least those where personal attendance is anticipated) since March 2020. CYIL editors have concluded that it would be difficult to keep account of virtual events, both due to the lack of any clear details concerning these events and due to the absence of references and response. We firmly believe, though, that this section will be renewed and presented to our readers in the next CYIL edition.

III.   IMPORTANT WEB SITES

http://www.czechyearbook.org; http://www.lexlata.pro

Czech Yearbook of International Law® and Czech (& Central European) Yearbook of Arbitration®

The website is currently available in sixteen languages: English, Bulgarian, Czech, Chinese, Japanese, Korean, Hungarian, German, Polish, Romanian, Russian, Portuguese, Slovenian, Spanish, Ukrainian, Vietnamese. This website allows access to the annotations of all core articles and to information about the authors of these articles as well as to the entire remaining contents (except core articles) of both yearbooks (CYIL and CYArb®).

III.1.   [CZE] – [CZECH REPUBLIC]

- http://www.cnb.cz. Česká národní banka (Czech National Bank as the Central bank of the Czech Republic).[1]
- http://www.compet.cz. Office for the protection of competition.[2]
- http://www.concourt.cz. The Constitutional Court of the Czech Republic.[3]
- http://www.csesp.cz. Czech Society for European and Comparative Law.[4]
- http://www.csmp-csil.org. The Czech Society Of International Law.[5]
- http://www.czech.cz. Portal „Hello Czech Republic". Basic information about the Czech Republic and news interesting for foreigners. Rather a promotional portal.[6]
- http://www.czso.cz. Czech Statistical Office.[7]
- http://dtjvcnsp.org. Česko-německý spolek právníků. [Czech-German Lawyers Association]. Deutsch-Tschechische Juristenvereinigung e.V.[8]
- http://ekf.vsb.cz. Faculty of Economics, VŠB Technical University of Ostrava.[9]

---

[1]   Website available in English and Czech.
[2]   Website available in English and Czech. Basic laws and regulations on the protection of competition in the Czech Republic are also available at the website, both in Czech and in English (unofficial translation).
[3]   Website available in English and Czech. Part of the (significant) case law also available in English.
[4]   Website available in English and Czech.
[5]   Website available in Czech. In English only a brief summary of the webpages.
[6]   Website available in English, Czech, French, German, Russian and Spanish.
[7]   Website available in English and Czech.
[8]   Website available in German.
[9]   Website available in English and Czech. Some information (regarding post-graduate studies) also available in German. Department of Law see http://en.ekf.vsb.cz/information-about/departments/structure/departments/dept-119 (in English).

- http://www.hrad.cz.[10] Website of the Office of the President of the Czech Republic.
- http://www.icc-cr.cz. ICC National Committee Czech Republic.
- http://www.iir.cz. Institute Of International Relations Prague.[11]
- http://www.ilaw.cas.cz. Ústav státu a práva Akademie věd ČR, v.v.i. [Institute of State and Law of the Academy of Sciences of the Czech Republic].[12]
- http://www.jednotaceskychpravniku.cz. Jednota českých právníků [Czech Lawyers Union].
- http://justice.cz. Czech justice portal including both courts and the Ministry of Justice, prosecution departments, Judicial Academy, Institute of Criminology and Social Prevention, as well as the Probation and Mediation Service and the Prison Service.[13]
- http://www.law.muni.cz. Faculty of Law, Masaryk University, Brno.[14]
- http://www.mzv.cz. Ministry of Foreign Affairs of the Czech Republic.[15]
- http://www.nsoud.cz. The Supreme Court of the Czech Republic.[16]
- http://www.nssoud.cz. The Supreme Administrative Court of the Czech Republic.[17]
- http://www.ochrance.cz. Public Defender of Rights (Ombudsman).[18]
- http://www.ok.cz/iksp/en/aboutus.html. Institute of Criminology and Social Prevention.[19]
- http://portal.gov.cz. Portal of the Public Administration.[20] This website allows access to the websites of most supreme public administration authorities (including ministries).
- http://www.prf.cuni.cz. Faculty of Law, Charles University in Prague.[21]
- http://www.psp.cz. Parliament of the Czech Republic. Chamber

---

[10] Website available in English and Czech. This website also allows access to the personal webpage of the President of the Czech Republic.
[11] Website available in English and Czech. This Institute was founded by the Ministry of Foreign Affairs of the Czech Republic.
[12] Website available in English and Czech.
[13] Website available in Czech. The individual websites of the institutions covered by this portal also contain pages or summary information in English.
[14] Website available in English and Czech.
[15] Website available in English and Czech. Important information from this portal also available in English.
[16] Website available in Czech. Some basic information also in English and French.
[17] Website available in English and Czech.
[18] Website available in English and Czech.
[19] Website available in English and Czech.
[20] Website available in English and Czech.
[21] Website available in Czech. Basic information available in English.

of Deputies.[22]
- http://www.senat.cz. Parliament of the Czech Republic. Senate.[23]
- http://www.society.cz/wordpress/#awp. Common Law Society.[24]
- http://www.soud.cz. Arbitration Court attached to the Economic Chamber of the Czech Republic and Agricultural Chamber of the Czech Republic.[25]
- http://www.umpod.cz. Office for International Legal Protection of Children.[26]
- http://www.upol.cz/fakulty/pf/. Faculty of Law. Palacký University, Olomouc.
- http://www.vse.cz. The University of Economics, Prague.[27]
- http://www.zcu.cz/fpr/. Faculty of Law, Western Bohemia University in Pilsen.[28]

III.2. [SVK] – [SLOVAK REPUBLIC]

- http://www.concourt.sk. Constitutional Court of the Slovak Republic.[29]
- http://www.flaw.uniba.sk. Faculty of Law, Comenius University in Bratislava (SVK).[30]
- http://iuridica.truni.sk. Faculty of Law. Trnava University in Trnava (SVK).[31]
- http://www.justice.gov.sk. Ministry of Justice of the Slovak Republic.[32]
- http://www.nbs.sk. Národná banka Slovenska (National Bank of Slovakia as the Central bank of Slovak Republic).[33]
- http://www.nrsr.sk. National Council of the Slovak Republic (*Slovak Parliament*).[34]
- http://www.prf.umb.sk. Faculty of Law. Matej Bel University, Banská Bystrica (SVK).
- http://www.prezident.sk. President of the Slovak Republic and

---

[22]   Website available in English and Czech.
[23]   Website available in English and Czech.
[24]   Website available in Czech.
[25]   Website available in English, Czech, German and Russian.
[26]   The Office is the Central authority responsible for protection of children in civil matters having cross-border implications. Website available in English and Czech.
[27]   Website available in English and Czech.
[28]   Website available in Czech.
[29]   Website available in English and Slovak.
[30]   Website available in English and Slovak.
[31]   Website available in English and Slovak.
[32]   Website available in English and Slovak. This website also allows access to the following portals: Courts, Slovak Agent before the European Court for Human Rights, Slovak Agent before the Court of Justice of the European Union, The Judicial Academy.
[33]   Website available in English and Slovak.
[34]   Website available in English, French, German and Slovak.

Office of the President (SVK).[35]

- http://www.uninova.sk/pf_bvsp/src_angl/index.php. Faculty of Law, Pan European University (SVK).[36]
- http://www.upjs.sk/pravnicka-fakulta. Faculty of Law, Pavol Jozef Šafárik University in Košice (SVK).[37]
- http://www.usap.sav.sk. Institute of State and Law, Slovak Academy of Science.[38]

Czech Yearbook of International Law®

---

[35]   Website available in English and Slovak.
[36]   Website available in English, German and Slovak.
[37]   Website available in English and Slovak.
[38]   Website available in Slovak.

Index

A

accident
- traffic - *see traffic accident*

acte clair **3**/19, 25; **9**/1, 5, 32

action against executive officer **9**/13, 30, 34, 38

admissibility
1/11, 18; **2**/32, 74; **6**/34, 51, 74, 75; **9**/2, 3, 30, 35
- of a cassation appeal **9**/3, 30, 35

agency
- commercial - *see commercial agency*

agreement
- framework - *see framework agreement*
- of the parties
1/8, 14, 15, 25; **2**/1, 12, 22, 23, 24, 25, 26, 27, 28, 29, 38, 47, 53, 67, 68, 69, 71, 74; **5**/10; **6**/9, 11, 12, 22, 24, 33, 38, 47, 48, 54, 56, 65, 75, 80, 84, 102, 104, 105; **7**/19, 41; **8**/4, 5, 6, 7, 10, 11, 14, 23, 31, 33, 34, 38; **9**/4, 11, 22, 23, 24, 25, 38

Al Bosco **4**/17, 46

applicability

- applicability of the CMR Convention - *see CMR Convention; applicability*

application
- of EU law - *see EU law; application*
- of international treaties
1/9, 11, 17, 18, 19, 24, 25, 27; **2**/1, 2, 3, 4, 5, 6, 9, 10, 12, 13, 16, 17, 20, 28, 29, 30, 31, 40, 43, 45, 46, 47, 48, 56, 60, 61, 62, 65, 67, 68, 71, 79; **5**/9; **6**/24, 59, 60, 85; **7**/20, 27; **8**/11, 29; **9**/20, 29, 30, 32, 33, 34, 36, 37, 38, 41
- of rules on consumer contract **7**/11; **9**/17, 30
- of New York Convention - *see New York Convention; application*

arbitral award
1/1, 2, 5, 6, 7, 9, 11, 16, 25; **2**/3, 10, 32, 43, 47, 70, 71, 72, 73, 74; **6**/1, 7, 15, 20, 24, 27, 29, 37, 43, 46, 51, 59, 60, 66, 76; **7**/27; **9**/36, 37, 38

arbitration **1**/1, 2, 3, 5, 6, 7, 8, 9, 10, 11, 12, 13, 14, 15, 16, 17, 18, 19, 20, 21, 22, 23, 24, 25, 26, 27; **2**/3, 6, 9, 10, 16, 20, 32, 35,

I

CALL FOR PAPERS FOR VOLUMES 2023/2024

Did you find the articles in the thirteenth
volume of CYIL interesting?

Would you like to react to a current article
or contribute to future volumes?

We are seeking authors for both
the Czech Yearbook on International Law® and the
Czech (& Central European) Yearbook of Arbitration®.

The general topics for the 2023/2024 volumes are following:

CYIL 2023
*Limits to Enforcement
of National Interests*

CYArb® 2023
*Public Interest
in Arbitration*

CYIL 2024
*Force Majeure, Restrictions
and Sanctions*

CYArb® 2024
Abuse of Arbitration

More general and contact information available at:

www.czechyearbook.org
www.lexlata.pro

CYIL – Czech Yearbook of International Law®, 2023
Limits to Enforcement of National Interests

The increasing tendencies of nations to promote their country's own interests may be the reverse side of and a form of defence against globalisation, and in many regards such tendencies naturally also manifest themselves in law. This phenomenon represents a very broad category that includes, for instance, security issues, protection of a nation's own territory or territorial interests, etc. National tendencies in private law include, inter alia, the advancement of a country's own law (national law / law of national origin) as the properly determined applicable law, the application of the public policy exception, or the application of overriding mandatory provisions. Procedural aspects also represent a specific and, naturally, a most welcome topic for our yearbook, with such aspects typically including the jurisdiction of national judicial authorities, as well as the promotion of national interests in supranational judicial authorities, the recognition and enforcement of or, conversely, the refusal to recognise and enforce foreign decisions. We will especially welcome any articles dealing with specific cross-border manifestations of the effort to promote national interests and with their (non)compliance with international law and private international law, and the rules and principles thereof.

CYArb® – Czech (& Central European) Yearbook of Arbitration®, 2023
Public Interest in Arbitration

Various forms of public-law elements and public interest have been increasingly encroaching upon arbitration, whether this involves the status of the parties, factoring in acts that could be prosecuted as anti-money laundering, corruption and many other violations, or the result of the nature of the disputes submitted to arbitration. This corroborates the fact that arbitration has become a widely-used and universal instrument for resolving both domestic and cross-border disputes, even including truly supranational and global disputes. Increasingly rigorous transparency requirements being measured against the traditional privacy and confidentiality of arbitration, the inalienable right of the parties to choose and to appoint the arbitrator being in conflict with the requirements of the maximum independence and impartiality of arbitrators that sometimes restrict the parties' right, and many other intensely discussed issues reveal the fact that arbitration has long ceased to be the exclusive domain of the individual relationship between the parties to the dispute, and that the autonomy of the parties, and indeed of the arbitrators themselves, is gradually being restricted, if not in fact in law. At the same time, however, arbitration is a process that has been measured more and more frequently against civil proceedings in courts, and has gradually become a full-fledged alternative to litigation.

It appears as though, unless in entirely exceptional cases, the theory of the anational and autonomous supranational nature of arbitration has given way to the domiciliation of arbitration in a given national environment, determined according to the place (seat) of arbitration in particular states, and to the importance of this place. That said, the influence of specific national procedural standards on arbitration is currently an indisputable fact. This also entails increasing demands for the application of fundamental national procedural rules and their principles in arbitration. This and many other related topics will represent the key subject of the XIIIth edition of CYArb® scheduled for 2023.

CYIL – Czech Yearbook of International Law®, 2024
Force Majeure, Restrictions and Sanctions

Looking at modern history, it is probably impossible to find a time period in which one of these three terms and institutions, *force majeure*, *restrictions* and *sanctions,* would not be applied and discussed by the legal community. Especially recently, we are more often confronted with specific restrictions, or rather with situations in which it is not easy to determine which of the particular institutions and mechanisms we are really dealing with, and which consequences they carry.

The topic aims to focus on these three concepts in order to qualify them as legal institutes and to analyse the manifestations and common signs thereof, as well as to identify their differences, their application and the settlement of disputes arising out of situations brought by force majeure and the application of restrictions and/or sanctions.

CYArb® – Czech (& Central European) Yearbook of Arbitration®, 2024
Abuse of Arbitration

The popularity of arbitration is on the rise in the modern world. Although there is an effort to expand the practicability and reach thereof, it is necessary to keep in mind that it has certain limits. However, due to the latency of the "boundaries" limiting the scope of arbitration, there is a growing effort to abuse arbitration so as to exploit it, or at least use it in such a way and in such situations for which arbitration was not intended. In the same way, however, certain elements of arbitral proceedings are being abused as well, where it is not just a question of pushing these "imaginary boundaries", but rather the abuse of arbitration itself.

In order to ensure and define basic rules (including ethical rules) to prevent the above-mentioned practices, the aim of the chosen topic is to focus on possible cases of abuse of arbitration, both at the substantive and procedural level, in order to identify and clarify them.